Memory Studies in the Digital Age

This interdisciplinary volume attempts to gauge the individual and social issues related to memory, with an understanding of memory studies as an independent body of scholarship. It draws on multiple fields of knowledge, like popular culture, history, literature, oral cultures, and storytelling, which facilitates a panoramic view of memory studies.

This book investigates the intersection between memory studies, partition, oral literature, and digital technology. It is also informed by the consciousness of memory in the digital age, which plays an integral role in what is remembered/forgotten, the form in which such memories are stored, and how they might be retrieved in future.

This book will be an invaluable resource for those involved in research from undergraduate to post-doctoral level. This includes sociologists, psychologists, historians, artists, academicians, as well as research scholars from other disciplines.

D. Sudha Rani is an Associate Professor of English with over 30 years of extensive teaching/research experience in English language, literature, and memory studies. She is an active scholar and has presented and published a lot of research work along with nine books that are prescribed in different universities and colleges. Since her research area is Memory Studies, she established the Centre for Memory Studies and Storytelling at VNR Vignana Jyothi Institute of Engineering and Technology (Autonomous), Hyderabad.

Rachel Irdaya Raj is an Assistant Professor in English and has two decades of teaching/research experience in English language, literature, soft skills, memory studies, gender studies, research methodology, and English for academic writing. She has contributed towards content development for listening skills tests for Osmania University and co-authored textbooks for undergraduates at Osmania University, Mahatma Gandhi University, and Dr. B. R. Ambedkar Open University. She is involved in establishing the Centre for Memory Studies and Storytelling at VNR Vignana Jyothi Institute of Engineering and Technology (Autonomous), Hyderabad.

Memory Studies in the Digital Age

An Interdisciplinary Perspective

Edited by D. Sudha Rani
and Rachel Irdaya Raj

Routledge
Taylor & Francis Group
LONDON AND NEW YORK

First published 2025
by Routledge
4 Park Square, Milton Park, Abingdon, Oxon OX14 4RN

and by Routledge
605 Third Avenue, New York, NY 10158

Routledge is an imprint of the Taylor & Francis Group, an informa business

British Library Cataloguing-in-Publication Data
A catalogue record for this book is available from the British Library

ISBN: 978-1-032-76049-0 (hbk)
ISBN: 978-1-032-83268-5 (pbk)
ISBN: 978-1-003-50856-4 (ebk)

DOI: 10.4324/9781003508564

Typeset in Sabon
by Deanta Global Publishing Services, Chennai, India

Contents

Tables

Contributors

Aiswarya S. Babu is an Associate Professor at the Department of English, Pondicherry University. She is interested in Cultural Studies, Gender Studies, Memory Studies, Nationalism Studies, and Translation Studies. She is passionate about translation and has several academic and literary translations to her credit. She has been associating with people's collectives for more than a decade and is committed to contribute towards a knowledge society.

Isha Banerjee is a literature enthusiast. Her doctoral thesis focused on the aspects of cultural diversity in select Caribbean novels. She aspires to create impactful literary works, hoping to live up to the self-claimed sobriquet of 'worder'. Dr. Banerjee currently lives in Boston where she briefly worked with the Early Caribbean Digital Archive.

Mahuya Bhaumik is Associate Professor and Head, Department of English, Derozio Memorial College, Kolkata. She is Guest Faculty in the Department of English, West Bengal State University. Her doctoral thesis was on "Modernism and T.S. Eliot". Her present areas of interest include Culture Studies, Dalit Literature, Partition Literature, and Gender Studies. She has published articles in various international journals. She is also a Content Writer for UGC e-pathshala.

Geetha Bhasker is a Senior Professor at the Department of English, Bangalore University, specializing in English Language and Linguistics. Prof. Bhasker's academic credentials are extensive, holding a doctorate in English from Bangalore University and a Postgraduate Diploma in Teaching of English (PGDTE) from the English and Foreign Languages University, Hyderabad. Additionally, she has earned a Diplome Superieure in French and a certificate in German, showcasing her proficiency in multiple languages. Prof. Bhasker's excellence in academia and research has been recognized with six prestigious National Awards, affirming her significant contributions to the field of English Studies and her dedication to educational excellence.

Rafid C. is a PhD scholar in the Department of Comparative Literature at the English and Foreign Languages University in India. His research explores the nature of 'literary reading' as a relational 'event' between a reader and a text. He is also interested in the recent trends in interdisciplinary research including the emergence of memory studies.

Hindol Chakraborty is the pioneer of Crick-God Theory. He teaches English Literature at Shri Ramasamy Memorial University Sikkim, Gangtok. Chakraborty is the author of On the Sublime: Criticism, Longinus, The Beautiful. He has edited Tagore and More: Selected Stories and Palli Samaj, the Homecoming and is the translator of Rantidev Sengupta's historical fiction Ishqnama. Hindol specializes in Art and the Sublime, Translation Studies, and the Theory of Mimesis.

Soutik Chakraborty is a PhD Research scholar at Coochbehar Panchanan Barma University, West Bengal, India and a faculty of the Department of English, Balurghat College under University of Gour Banga. His research focuses on the historic development of regional scroll paintings of India. He has worked as an intern researcher at Indian Knowledge System Division (Ministry of Education, Govt. of India) on preservation of scroll painting traditions in modern times.

Puja Ghosh is a Junior Research Fellow at the Department of Humanities and Social Sciences in Indian Institute of Engineering Science and Technology (IIEST), Shibpur, West Bengal. Her research interests include Postcolonialism, Feminism, South Asian Diaspora, and Indian English Literature. Her poems have been published in journals like Indian Literature (Sahitya Akademi), Muse India, and in the anthology Between Senses and Silences.

Haritha Guduru teaches General English, Communication Skills, Business Communication, Theatre, and Films at Institute of Management, Nirma University. She is a passionate teacher with one year of industry experience and twelve years of teaching experience in undergraduate and postgraduate courses in English Language and Literature. She has hands-on experience in English Language Teaching, Indian Writing in English, and contemporary English teaching.

Vishesh Pratap Gurjar is an Ethnographer and Political Sociologist and is an Assistant Professor at the Institute of Management, Nirma University, Ahmedabad. His work that explores the questions of 'belonging' and 'becoming' among the young men of dominant caste delves into the complexities of social identity, particularly focusing on caste dynamics and youth culture in urban landscapes.

Kavya R. K. is a Research Scholar in the Department of Indian and World Literatures at The English and Foreign Languages University, Hyderabad. Her research interests include Affect Theory, Human Experience, Trauma, and Memory Studies. Her work explores the everyday as well as traumatic life situations through the dynamics of affect and bodily experience.

Athira Manoharan is pursuing her PhD in Literary and Cultural Studies from BITS Pilani. She received her MPhil in English Language and Literature from Sankaracharya University, Kalady. She is also involved in creative production pertaining to the field of visual arts, performing arts, and writing and has collaborated with Kochi-Muziris Biennale, 2022. Her research interests pertain to the field of cultural studies with a special emphasis on urban studies and architectural performances.

Averi Mukhopadhyay is an Assistant Professor of English at the Department of Humanities and Social Sciences, IIEST, Shibpur. Previously, she was a faculty in the P.G. Department of English, Magadh University, Bodh-Gaya. She had done her PhD from IIT, Roorkee, and her MPhil from IIT (ISM), Dhanbad.

Sreya Mukherjee is a PhD Researcher at the Department of Indian and World Literatures in The English and Foreign Languages University, Hyderabad, India. She has been awarded Junior Research Fellow by University Grants Commission of India. She is working on the representation of motherhoods in the Indian epics for her doctoral research. Her areas of interest are Mythology, Women's Writing, Translation Studies, and Postcolonial Literature.

Rashmi Naik, a UGC-JRF holder and master's graduate from Jyoti Nivas College, Autonomous, Bengaluru, is pursuing her doctoral studies at Bangalore University. Her research is a deep dive into the narrative structures of South Korean TV dramas, analysing their construction and reception by global audiences. This study hopes to contribute to a broader comprehension of how Korean dramas act as vehicles for cultural exchange in the digital era, emphasizing the interaction between narratives and the audience. She is also a faculty member at Bengaluru City University, actively engaging in teaching and academic discourse and holds a certificate in Korean language.

Shashibhusan Nayak teaches English at GP Nayagarh, Odisha. His works have appeared in Rock Pebbles, Media Watch, iEnglish, Auto/Fiction, R.J.L.C.S. He is the Founder of the Centre for Autofiction Studies, Convener of Autofiction Studies Network, Editor of Auto/Fiction (M.L.A.), Review Editor of Media Watch (SAGE), Reviews Editor of Publishing History (Proquest/Clarivate)and an M.L.A. international bibliography field bibliographer (M.L.A., U.S.A.).

Vishnu Priya T. P. is a PhD scholar at the University of Hyderabad, specializing in the intersection of gender, power, and transnational literary systems in South Indian missionary narratives. Her research explores Victorian ideologies of domesticity, missionary literature, and the reform of gender roles in colonial contexts. With a strong foundation in Victorian literature, postcolonial thought, and memory studies, she also engages in English-Malayalam translation. Vishnu Priya has taught at reputed colleges in

Hyderabad, published research in UGC-approved and popular journals, and delivered invited lectures on Gender Studies at esteemed institutions.

Ananya Parida is an Assistant Professor of English at Government Autonomous College, Phulbani, Odisha. Additionally, she is a UGC-IUC Associate at IIAS, Shimla, and OURIIP Fellow at OSHEC, Odisha. Her research interests include Postcolonial literature, Indian Writing in English, Intellectual History and Archival studies.

Joly Puthussery is a Professor and Head of CFCS, School of Social Sciences, University of Hyderabad. His academic areas of interest include: Performance Studies; Folk Theatre in India; Public Performance and Discourse; Religion and Theatrical Practices. Having twenty-seven years of teaching and research experience, he has published widely. He has accomplished Fulbright Fellowship in Theatre Education at Illinois State University, U.S.A.(2004–2005) funded by IIE and USEFI, Junior Research Fellowship, Dept. of Culture, HRD Ministry, Govt. of India (2000–2002), and Sax I Fund post-doc Fellowship 1999–2000, Warburg Institute, University of London.

D. Sudha Rani is an Associate Professor of English with over 30 years of extensive teaching/research experience in English Language, Literature, and Memory Studies. She is an active scholar and has presented and published a lot of research work along with nine books that are prescribed in different universities and colleges. Since her research area is Memory Studies, she established the Centre for Memory Studies and Storytelling at VNR Vignana Jyothi Institute of Engineering and Technology (Autonomous), Hyderabad.

Rachel Irdaya Raj is an Assistant Professor in English and has two decades of teaching/research experience in English language, literature, soft skills, memory studies, gender studies, research methodology, and English for academic writing. She has contributed towards content development for listening skills tests for Osmania University and co-authored textbooks for undergraduates at Osmania University, Mahatma Gandhi University, and Dr. B. R. Ambedkar Open University. She is involved in establishing The Centre for Memory Studies and Storytelling at VNR Vignana Jyothi Institute of Engineering and Technology (Autonomous), Hyderabad.

Divyasree J. S. is an Assistant Professor at the Department of English, Sree Ayyappa College for Women, Nagercoil, Kanyakumari District, Tamil Nadu. She is currently pursuing her doctoral research (part-time) at the Department of English and Research Centre, Sree Ayyappa College for Women affiliated to Manonmaniam Sundaranar University, Tirunelveli. Her areas of interest are Travel Literature, Linguistics, Communicative English, and ELT.

Santhwana Santhosh is a Senior Research Fellow in CFCS, School of Social Sciences, University of Hyderabad. Her work is based on select oral narratives and its intersections with narratology, memory, performance, and storytelling. She has presented and published in national and international conferences and journals.

B. Sajeetha is an Assistant Professor and Research Supervisor at the Department of English, Sree Ayyappa College for Women, Nagercoil, Kanyakumari District, Tamil Nadu. She has more than fifteen years of teaching experience. Her areas of interest are Canadian Literature, Literary Theory, and Indian Literature in English.

Urmi Sengupta is Assistant Professor of English at The ICFAI University, Tripura. She has been a former Faculty of Communicative English at The British Institutes, Kolkata. She holds a PhD in Comparative Literature from Jadavpur University, Kolkata. Her research interests include Canadian Studies, Ecocriticism, Diasporic Studies, Gender and Indigenous Studies. She has contributed book chapters in peer-reviewed volumes on Ecocriticism and Environment (Primus, 2018) and Nation-building, Education and Culture in India and Canada (Springer, 2019).

Ashma Shamail is an Interdisciplinary Researcher, currently serving as Assistant Professor at Imam Abdulrahman Bin Faisal University, Saudi Arabia. She has published articles in international journals, books, and anthologies on cultural studies, migration and diaspora studies, memory, gender, and critical race studies. Dr. Shamail specializes in African American, Anglophone Caribbean, and South Asian Literature, especially fiction by women, in addition to English Language education.

Maithry Shinde is an Associate Professor in English, and she co-authored undergraduate textbooks in General English and Literature for Osmania University and Dr. B. R. Ambedkar Open University. She has been freelancing on projects by Cambridge University Press and has been engaged in 'Train the Trainers' on Soft Skills and Language. She has authored a book titled Ethnicity in Afghanistan Literature and has been the lead author for the book titled Life Skills and Personality Development published by Cambridge University Press. She has been a resource person at the Telangana Judicial Academy for ten years.

M. Subhasree is the Manager of Content and Communications at Human Factors International and an independent researcher. She earned her master's in English Literature from Stella Maris College, Chennai. She served in the field of academia as an Assistant Professor in reputed Chennai-based institutions including D.G. Vaishnav College and Stella Maris College, teaching courses ranging from Writing for the Media, Linguistics, World Classics and Indian Literatures. Her creative works, including "Chalking My Love," "Subhadra," and "Memoirs," feature in the Indian English

Poetry Anthology by Young Minds, with "Chalking My Love" winning the Best Poem award.

Chaithanya V. is an Assistant Professor at the Department of Communicative English, St. Teresa's College, Ernakulam. Her interests lie in Linguistics, Mystical Studies, and Partition Studies. Her efforts have been recognized through awards and recognition at college and inter-collegiate levels.

Acknowledgements

At the outset, we would like to thank God Almighty for being our rock of refugee in this enterprising journey. This book is a testament of his unfailing love and kindness. Every time we faced obstacles, our faith in Him helped us overcome those challenges. This journey has taught us patience, perseverance and above all helped us to evolve as better humans.

Our heartfelt thanks to our college – VNR Vignana Jyothi Institute of Engineering and Technology – for encouraging us to conduct the International Conference on "Interdisciplinary Perspectives on Memory Studies: Storytelling and the Impact of Digital Technologies" in 2022 which ignited our zeal to publish a book. We also thank the college leadership for providing access to the necessary resources. Thier support was crucial in bringing this project to fruition. We are also grateful to our peers and colleagues for their support in this endeavour.

We like to express our deepest gratitude to all the authors, for their unwavering support. Their contribution has greatly enriched this work.

We are thankful to our reviewers, whose feedback was instrumental in shaping this book and pushing it to greater heights.

A special thank you to our families who have been a source of strength throughout this journey.

We would like to acknowledge the support of Routledge publishers, especially, Mr.Amit Kumar and Srimoyee Chakraborty whose contributions, whether direct or indirect, have played a role in the evolution of this book.

Thank you all for being a part of this journey.

Introduction
Prominence of Memory and Its Transmission

Memory assumes greater significance as everything, everyone, and every living object on the surface of the earth is a memory. A keen observation of human societies reveals that we form, sustain, and function only because human beings are gifted with that intelligence to recreate things. The process of recreation of a community that includes the traditions and culture is an interesting phenomena to study. Human societies found innovative ways to remember, recollect, and resonate their knowledge from one generation to another generation. They include both lithic and alithic means. As we all know, lithic memories are nothing but those technics which prefer inscribing articulated memories in external available retentional systems like a stone, clay tablet, metal surface, quill, palm leaf, wax, paper, a silicon chip, etc. This technic also requires a system of recording and storing like a bookshelf, library, a museum, a temple, a datalink, etc. It is quite clear; this technic requires a certain amount of effort from the individual/community. And these individuals or communities can be selective/ biased/prejudiced in nature while recording or preserving. In contrast to the lithic memory, the alithic memories are perennial in nurture and retain memory in the complex apparatus of the body in which they emerge. Although the alithic mode too externalizes memory through certain technics – speech and gesture/performance – it prefers to kindle, succor, enhance, and disseminate its articulations only through the organic body. Alithic modes embody and enact memories through acoustic and gestural performative technics (Venkat: 2014). In conclusion, they don't use surrogate bodies of memory and their inscriptional paraphernalia, thus decreasing the scope of being selective or prejudiced. India along with some more ancient civilizations practiced this strategy for transferring the memory for a long time in the history. Dr. Venkat Rao observes that the so-called expression of memory through sculptures, paintings, etc., was thought after much later. The difference between the East and the West interms of memory is rightly identified by Diana Taylor, "The unidirectionality of meaning making and communication also stemmed from and reflected the centuries-old privileging of written over embodied knowledge. Moreover, little thought was given to the many ways in which contact with the "non-Western" had, for centuries, shaped the very notion of "Western" identity" (Taylor, Diana , 07). But globally the memory making took a radical spin once globalization

DOI: 10.4324/9781003508564-1

took momentum. Therefore, the storage of memory over at least the past three millennia has evolved with great speed. The acceleration after internet and digital media entered is particularly noteworthy. A keen observation of these media indicates that they were never passive, and their dynamic nature affects the memory making and retrieval process complex. Such complexity increases the credibility of retrieval system and gives scope for selected retrieval. Therefore, "the relation of any culture to its past is proven to be politically relevant" (Pethes 2019, Oxford Scholars Publishing, UK).

Significance of Memory Studies

Therefore, memory studies holds greater importance for understanding an individual, a community, a nation's life that gets shaped profoundly by memory. It encompasses many things from our most personal and intimate recollections of the past, our sense of self and our ability to successfully execute daily routines, to the ways in which many things happen, like remembering communities, constructing the past through language, ceremonial and mundane practices, political policy, and physical structures. Various individual departments like cognitive science, history, ethnography, sociology, literature, and others were independently attempting to comprehend individual aspects of the above but it is essential to address the complex nexus of all these aspects to get a complete picture. Thus, the mobilization of memory studies, at first glance, has endless potential for interesting interactions and collaborations that reveal a larger piece of the puzzle called the human race yesterday, today, and thus guess tomorrow.

The question here is, should we give importance to the knowledge transmitted, or the strategies devised- to understand this we need to understand the evolution of memory studies. The evolution of memory studies as a branch of knowledge claims interdisciplinarity in nature involving, psychology, literature, history, anthropology, ethnography, cognitive sciences, sociology, neurology, media studies and some more to name. The identification and acknowledgment of the interdisciplinary interest in memory has been referred to as "memory studies."

Evolution of Memory Studies

Memory studies as a distinct field of study doesn't belong to any one specific country or part of the world; on the contrary, it is international in its approach and interdisciplinary in character. Its journey notably took a momentum when Maurice Halbwachs published his work, "On Collective Memory," in 1925. He proved that individual memory is important which creates collective memory of the community. According to him, the world in the mind of an individual and the world in which he lives are both equally important. He further discusses how minds work together in a society, how their operations are not simply mediated by social arrangements but are in fact structured by them: "It is in society that people normally acquire their memories. It is also in society that they recall, recognize, and localize their memories" (1992: 38). Moreover, for Halbwachs, memory is framed in the present as much as in the past, variable rather than constant. Studying memory, as a result, is a matter not of reflecting philosophically on inherent properties of the subjective mind but of identifying its shifting social frames. The social frameworks in which we are called on to recall, moreover, are inevitably tied up with what and how we recall. Groups provide us with the stimulus or opportunity to recall; they also shape the ways in which we do so, and often provide the materials. As Victor Turner pointed out, we are all members of many groups, formal or informal, from the family to the nation or some international religion or political institution (Turner Victor, 1980) Following this argument, the very distinction between the individual and social components of remembering ceases to make absolute sense: "There is no point," Halbwachs (1992: 38) argued,

> in seeking where ... [memories] are preserved in my brain or in some nook of my mind to which I alone have access: for they are recalled by me externally, and the groups of which I am a part at any given time give me the means to reconstruct them.

All individual remembering takes place with social materials, within social contexts, and in response to social cues. Even when we do it alone, we do so as social beings with reference to our social identities, and with languages and symbols that we may use in creative ways but certainly did not invent. His argument is rightly summarized by Astrid Erll,

> In other words, we have to differentiate between two levels on which culture and memory intersect: the individual and the collective or, more precisely, the level of the cognitive on the one hand, and the levels of the social and the medial on the other.(2010)
>
> (5)

The proposal of communicative, collective, and cultural memory theories by Jan Assmann (1995) and Aleida Assmann is another important milestone in trying to understand why we are what we are. Communicative memory focuses on day-to-day-based memories of an individual and as we know, their life is shorter. On the other hand, cultural memory is formed by symbolic heritage embodied in texts, rites, monuments, celebrations, objects, sacred scriptures, and other media that serve as mnemonic triggers to initiate meanings associated with what has happened. Also, it brings back the time of the mythical origins, crystallizes collective experiences of the past, and can last for millennia. According to this, a society's cultural memory is always a reflection of its present interests, needs, and current levels of experience (2011). In summary, a provisional definition of cultural memory is suggested as "the interplay of present and past in socio-cultural contexts."

This definition allows the inclusion of a wide range of possible research from everyday activities of individuals, to the most remembered or, for that matter, the most forgotten contexts of the society, to the striking and transnational activities, to the national memory of a nation-state. At the same time memory studies is not just about making sense of the activities of the past which are intentional and contribute to identity forming. While we discuss intentional remembering to identity formation of an individual or a community, it is also very essential for us to probe into unintentional and implicit ways of cultural remembering or of inherently non-narrative, for example visual or bodily, forms of memory (E. Cote James and G. Levine Charles 2002). Though Aby Warburg, a German historian wrote about social memory and the afterlife of pagan images in art, it is Astrid Erll who elaborated the idea of "travelling memory." Her theory of "travelling memory" between time periods, nations, generations, media, and branches of knowledge is noteworthy. Liedeke Plate and H. G. Els Rose (2013) proposed that rewriting of the texts as a helpful tool to see through presumed distinctions between these periods in which various texts are produced.

Therefore, memory studies has seen evolution where many scholars contributed for the development of this field as a robust, interdisciplinary, and significant field for the human race. But as Jeffrey Olick and Joyce Robbins (1998: 106) have observed, memory research is a "nonparadigmatic, transdisciplinary, centerless enterprise." Sincere efforts are underway to design a conceptual toolbox for memory studies which is currently "more practiced than theorized." As it is multidisciplinary in approach and must cross intellectual and linguistic boundaries, it can be successful only if it is based on cooperation among all the concerned fields of study. This cooperation, based on a dialogue at different levels like conceptual, methodological, and theoretical premise of these fields of research, would be much desirable to make memory studies more desirable for future scholars.

Nevertheless, on the analytical side, the memory boom has supposedly also given rise to varieties of inquiry, including science, scholarship, memoir writing, curatorial work, oral history projects, and the like. While babyboomers worry about the living death of Alzheimer's disease, neuroscientists search for its biological basis (Eichenbaum 2002; Pillemer 1998; Schacter 1997). While trauma victims seek to overcome their ongoing suffering from post-traumatic stress, psychologists develop frameworks for treatment (Leys 2000; Herman 1997; Caruth 1995). While past oppression has seemingly become the coin of identity, cultural theorists inquire into the origins of the politics of victimhood (Fassin and Rechtman 2009; Olick 2007; Bell 2006; Kaplan 2005; Edkins 2003; Antze and Lambek 1996). And while societies confront the legacies of their misdeeds, social and political scientists analyze the conditions for successful transition and salutary commemoration (Elster 2004; Vinitzky-Seroussi 2002; Teitel 2002; Minow 1999; McAdams 1997). All of these, and more, are constituents of what has come to be referred to as the new "memory studies," which has acquired its own journals, been elaborated in countless edited volumes, established research centers, received grants, and been the subject of university courses. '

The more we research, the more we get clarity regarding the myriad facets of this subject. So, it is quite appreciative to think and bring together many voices related to memory studies from different parts of the globe. The present book is one more such attempt to bring together a collection of research articles that discuss and deliberate various facets of memory studies. Humans beings are, at their core, a sum of memories related to their own experiences and the stories of those around them. The art of storytelling dates back to centuries when orality was the primary mode of communication and preservation of all knowledge base. Stories were told not just as a means of passing down memories, but with many more purposes, for example, to act as cautionary tales, to inspire, entertain, etc. According to Langer Neili, "Memories are not just a storehouse for facts but a creative blend of fact and fiction that helps people tell meaningful stories about their lives. Throughout history, the older members of our collective cultures have been civilization's best storytellers" (p 379). This storytelling formed the stronghold for what we now refer to as "Literature." A similar trait runs through the following chapters where the finer nuances of storytelling become the crux in various literary works. Chapter 1, "Storytelling as a Cultural Practice: Memory, Emancipation, and Survival as Sites of Resistance," explores the concepts of emancipation and survival as sites of resistance. In this chapter, Paule Marshall's second novel *The Chosen Place, the Timeless People* (1969) envisions the memory of a former slave hero's valiant past through the mode of storytelling. And the memory of this hero is celebrated annually in the Caribbean carnival. The memory of Cuffee Ned's heroic deeds is preserved through the re-enactment practices and re-narrated as a story. The Bourne Islanders' reverence to this memory and its cultural transmission to the next generation portrays the significant role of memory in this entire journey. A journey tends to bring about change and challenges one to introspect. As such, exploring the significance of cultural memory and cultural identity forms the crux of Chapter 2, "In Search of Fragments of Recollection: Cultural Memory and Identity in the Select Travel Narratives of Tahir Shah." The works *The Caliph's House* (2007) and *In Arabian Nights* (2009) portray how memory and storytelling are essential tools in the formation and conservation of one's identity. As an immigrant traveler in Morocco, the author tries to establish his cultural identity through his varied experiences. Consistent acts of remembering and recalling stories and events from the past enable in realizing one's own identity as well as one's cultural identity. An individual's identity is nurtured from a young age, by being a part of the family unit, wherein parents share their memories. Thus, bedtime stories formed the staple diet in every household; a parenting tool that is embedded in the cultural practice of every society. Chapter 3, "Contextualising Memory Studies in Bedtime Stories: Understanding the Praxis of Formative Literary Frameworks," takes it a notch higher by discussing how retelling of these stories has led to formative frameworks which are in "poiein" state of perpetual transformation. The story "Red Riding Hood" is taken to discuss how multiple retellings of the same story results in continuous (re)formations.

> Culture and individual memory are constantly produced through, and mediated by, the technologies of memory. The question of mediation is thus central to the way in which memory is conceived in the fields of study of visual culture, cultural studies and media studies.
>
> (Sturken 2008)

Thus, cultural memory has found a new means of storing its repository in the digital age. Films and TV series have a major role to play in contributing to this repository. Remembering, forgetting, and recalling are essentially what memory is all about. When this remediating happens, there are two possibilities – reality remains constant or there is variation with each mediation. This aspect of memory is deliberated in Chapter 4, "Remediating Karna: A Critique of the Canon and Caste." The portrayal of the mythical character Karna in the Tamil movie *Karnan* (2021) with reference to the same character as described in the text of the Mahabharata is analyzed. Remediated narratives become powerful sites of memory and an inspiration to the present generation. Chapter 5, "Ways of Remembering: A Study on the Use of Collective Memory in *Stranger Things* and *Miss Marvel*," examines how popular American science web series integrate cultural memory. Both web series explore how commemorative aspects are included in the construction and reconstruction of collective memory in their respective cultural settings. The pop culture references of the 1980s in terms of American food, fashion, and music showcased in *Stranger Things* are all examples of remediating memory. On the other end of the spectrum, the series *Miss Marvel* challenges the mistrust directed toward the Pakistani Muslim community and addresses the wounds of migration and division experienced by the third-generation Pakistani Americans. Regarding generations, in the last decade, Korean drama has evolved as the one of most popular series watched by people globally. Several of these series gave us the opportunity to learn about the Korean culture. Their dressing and food habits, their cultural practices, and so on leave an indelible impression on our minds. These series also form a rich source for studying how memory played an important role in preserving and shaping their culture. Chapter 6, "Memory Studies in Korean Drama: Exploring the Intersections of Memory through a Theoretical Interdisciplinary Lens," is one such example that dwells on how remembering and forgetting shapes the characters in the series. The series *Healer*, *Kill Me, Heal Me*, and *Shopping King Louie* explore the idea of identity and how it shapes the characters' social behavior and the environment around them through the sociological lens. It also uses memory in the form of amnesia, flashbacks, and other manifestations to shape the plots and heighten the drama. These series achieved a global reach through advancements in technology. When it comes to utilizing digital technology, even the people living in remote villages in India are not far behind. They have learnt how to use technology for various purposes including passing on their cultural memory to the next generation with the help of virtual platforms. Chapter 7, "Making the Village Alive in the City: Understanding Village-ness among Gurjars in Madanpur Khadar," presents the ethnographic narratives of young men of the Gurjar caste from an urban village in Delhi. These narratives are crucial in reconstructing the connections that members of the prevailing caste group have with their own caste and in recreating a sense of village identity inside Delhi's metropolitan area. As a result, the village continues to exist as an adjunct to the expanding metropolis and, in addition to caste, reappears as a type of "community" in the people's stories.

Autobiographical memory is a system unique to human beings, which weaves recollections of past events into an overarching life narrative. In an autobiography, memory goes beyond simply recalling past experiences, in order to construct a personal history. Instead, it integrates perspective, interpretation, and evaluation across the self, other, and time. In a nutshell, autobiographical memory is the recall of oneself interacting with others to further short- and long-term objectives that determine who we are and what we are here on Earth for (Robyn 2011). Chapter 8, "Memoirs Doubting Memory: An Exploration of Tara Westover's *Educated*," examines how the author's traumatic experiences as a child and her relationship with her family members impact her life as an adult. The research explores Tara Westover's memoir, *Educated*, from two angles, revealing two distinct ways to read the work: one traditional, covering genre, family, and self, and the other critical, focusing on the memoir's main idea of skeptical remembering. The chapter showcases how the memoir portrays personal tenacity and disproves common beliefs about memory, opening the door for innovative methods in the study of memoirs. Prison literature is another genre where people imprisoned pen down their thoughts and experiences. Many such freedom fighters who were imprisoned during India's struggle for independence have recorded their experiences in the form of their autobiographies. Chapter 9, "Memory in Question: Decoding the 'Self' in Select Indian Penal Autobiographies," investigates memory through historical, political, social, and cultural perspectives. Gopabandhu Das's *Biography of a Prisoner* (2017), Aurobindo Ghose's *Tales of Prison Life* (2008), and his brother Barindra Ghose's *The Tale of My Exile* (1922) focus on the journey of the three revolutionaries who began the freedom movement from in Bengal, Bihar, and Orissa. The concept of autobiography is taken a step further in Chapter 10, "Affect: Human Libraries as an Intersection of Memory and Affect Archiving," where one gets to listen to a person's life story sitting right in front of them. The idea behind the human library is to provide an unbiased environment where people may engage with one another without fear of judgment; it's a place where people feel comfortable sharing their vulnerabilities. The goal is to examine how being vulnerable becomes an essential starting point for comprehending the ways in which personal narratives progressively impact the dynamics of daily existence.The concept of flash bulb memory is another technique to investigate if people retain memories about significant public events that have occurred in the past. Chapter 11 "An Analysis of Emotional and Media Factors of the Flashbulb Memory on Recollection of YSR's Demise" analyses the events surroundings the sudden death of former Chief Minister Y. S. Rajashekar Reddy in a helicopter crash. In order to understand the emotional and media components of flashbulb memory through an event that occurred in 2009 and the current situation that brought back the flashbulb theory, the study takes into account the sociopolitical conditions and situations faced by the individuals chosen for the study from the states of Telangana and Andhra Pradesh. According to the results, Andhra Pradesh residents demonstrated greater levels of flashbulb memory characteristics than Telangana residents. The study reveals a novel finding about the Telangana groups' time-based memory deterioration.

15 August 1947 is etched in the memory of every Indian. It is a day that is celebrated across the nation with much fervor. Yet, there is a group of people who have been traumatized across the border because of Partition. "The process of partition with its seemingly unassailable demographic logic was... marked by unprecedented violence in which about one million people died, while an estimated twelve to fifteen million left the place of their birth and crossed the new international border" (Mookerjea 2017). Of the scores of people who migrated across India and Pakistan, many died. The survivors of this blood bath have horrifying tales to narrate on both sides of the border. Chapter 12, "Challenges of Using Memory as a Tool in Oral Historiography: An Analysis with Respect to Urvashi Butalia's *The Other Side of Silence*," studies the accounts of the oral narratives of the survivors. It aims to present the challenges faced by this oral account of history, narrated through the faculty of individual memories with all its fallacies. The chapter also analyzes how oral history highlights the gaps in recorded history and the difficulties that an oral historian faces in presenting these viewpoints. In continuation with the same theme, Chapter 13, "Reconstructing Memoryscapes: The Role of Imagined Homelands in Post-Partition Bengali Memoirs," explores the concept of home and homeland in the Bangla memoirs. It delves into the recesses of memory, where a narrative of resilience and creative reconstitution is unraveled. Texts such as *Romanthan* (1993) by Tapan Raychaudhuri, *Bishadbriksha* (2004) by Mihir Sengupta, *Oparer Chhelebela 1931–1947* (2005) by Jayantanuj Bandyopadhyay, and *Smritichitran* (1994) by Parimal Goswami highlight the ability of the human imagination to both retain and revitalize memories. Partition memories have been recorded in multiple ways including creating online platforms where archives of this tragic event are stored for posterity. Chapter 14, "Memories of 1947: A Journey from Oral to Digital," aims to examine the journey of memory and find out how the diverse forms of preservation have served as repositories of personal and collective trauma of Partition. This research seeks to identify the social impact

of this memory trip as the democratization of Partition history, ensuring the establishment of a borderless digital world that forges transnational identity and fosters a sense of togetherness through suffering. Partition memories have also been showcased in many movies through the last sixty years. These movies talk of tales of unsung heroes and their tragic closing chapters, thus refreshing our memories of the traumatic past. In a similar vein, Chapter 15, "Unravelling the Narratives of Partition: A Study of Individual and Historical Memories in Film," examines the text *The Other Side of Silence* by Urvashi Bhutalia and the movies *Gadar: Ek Prem Katha* and *Partition* and focuses on how oral narratives are depicted in the movies. It studies how in its attempt to construct and reconstruct individual and historical memories, films have mediated facts to make narratives impactful to evoke desired impulses. According to the study, these memoirs provide a distinctive lens through which one may comprehend the complex structure of memory and the ability of people to create strong, imaginative narratives even in the midst of severe loss and turbulence.

India is a country where people from diverse cultural backgrounds and varied cultural practices reside in harmony. The people are divided into sects based on their caste, region, religion, language, and so on. Each community has its unique set of traditions that includes their food habits, their dressing style, their religious beliefs, their manner of worship, their matrimonial customs, etc. Added to this, there have been invaders and settlers who have left their own impressions on the given cultural setup. For example, the influence of the Portuguese is still evident in Goa, the influence of the Nizams is strongly reflected in some parts of Telangana, and the colonial rule of the British has left a lasting impression in the education system and administration of India. Apart from this, there are several tribal communities residing in small pockets all over India. The study of the role of memory becomes interesting and humungous in the above scenario. The following chapters touch upon varied themes like films, folk art, and folk painting and examine them through the lens of memory studies. Chapter 16, "Memory of 1971 War in Indian Cinema: A *lieux de mémoire*" scrutinizes several Indian movies that depict the war of 1971. It aims to investigate the nationalism that these films try to inspire, as well as the historical reasons these memories were in transit for such a long period. The movies employ experiential, mythical, antagonistic, and reflexive strategies to develop nationalistic consciousness among Indian citizens, thus ensuring premediation, remediation, and plurimediation of the 1971 war. Folklore has been an integral part of Indian culture for a long time. Folk art has a rich cultural heritage that needs to be preserved and passed on to the next generation. Chapter 17, "Stor(y)ing Memory and *Totam*: Perspectives towards Oral Narratives," studies the intersections of memory, oral narratives, and storytelling in the ritual phenomenon of *Teyyam* and the oral narratives, *totam*, of North Malabar, Kerala. In *Teyyam* and *totam*, oral storytelling is used to communicate complicated narratives and memory becomes an essential tool to transfer this from generation to generation. Simultaneously storytelling is facilitating cultural transmission and fostering social togetherness in the community. The chapter draws on theoretical deliberations from the fields of narratology, cultural studies and memory studies in its pursuit. Among the many art forms prevalent in India, the art of picture storytelling in one such art. Chapter 18, titled "The Patua and Patachitra: Religiosity, Tradition and Memory in Scroll Paintings of Bengal," explores how memory is preserved in scroll paintings. This art form involves a display of painting and a narration of the illustrated story painted on a cloth canvas by the artists or the performer. The unique quality about these paintings is that the painter of the Hindu gods is a Muslim. But surprisingly this has not altered the art form in any way. Thus, the chapter scrutinizes religious memory, community memory, and the individual memory to understand and analyze the diverging ways of religiosity and art. In a land divided by religion and tradition, patriarchy has dictated how stories are told for centuries. Among the many male voices that talk about memory in the Indian discourse, there are a few female voices that are prominent as well. K. R. Meera is one such author whose novels record the female voices that have suffered subjection in a male-dominated society. Her Sahitya Akademi Award-winning novel, *Hangwoman*, talks about women's liberation and empowerment. Chapter 19, "Memories of Her-stories as Feminist Praxis in K. R. Meera's *Hangwoman*," explores how storytelling is used by the women so as to remain visible and audible in a patriarchal setup.

The concept of memory studies has become a global phenomenon, gaining significance in the last decade. Several texts from around the world are now being examined through the memory lens giving rise to new interpretations. This is evident in the following chapters that study texts of diaspora, racism, and the American dream in the light of memory. Chapter 20, "Exploration of Memory in Oonya Kempadoo's *All Decent Animals* and *Buxton Spice*," celebrates the vivacity of Caribbean life and cultural heritage. Even the most remote readers of the diaspora have found a sense of familiarity in the novels' microcosmic depictions of Caribbean multiculturalism. Kempadoo explores the strength and limitations of memory through a variety of storytelling devices, highlighting how it affects the lives of the individuals and how important it is in the Caribbean setting. The limitations of memory are further tested in Chapter 21, "Memory, Expectation, and Failure in the Theatre and Film Productions of Tennessee Williams's *The Glass Menagerie*: A Case Study." It demonstrates how memory becomes the most crucial instrument in portraying "the blurred" as reality – or rather, the truth as "the blurred" in the play *The Glass Menagerie*. In the play, memory serves as both a distorting and a clarifying prism for interpreting the events' actual circumstances. Memory and storytelling go hand in glove in knowledge preservation and dissemination in communities where written sources are absent. This is evident in Chapter 22, "Voices of Resonance: Cultural Decolonization through Collective Memory within Indigenous Literatures of Canada." The chapter explores how the indigenous tribes of Canada have used oral storytelling to pass down their traditional knowledge of survival from one generation to the next. This information has continued to be preserved in their collective community memory in the guise of ceremonial songs, tales of tricksters, ancestor stories, dream-vision narratives, and ritualistic recitals. The texts *Ravensong* (1993) and *Whispering in Shadows* (2001) are explored to study how collective cultural memory resisted the erosion of the Native-Canadians for centuries. Similar stories evolve in African American literature where the enslaved Africans keep their ethnicity alive through their songs and stories. Chapter 23, "Revisiting African Origins through Memory Codes: A Study of Alex Haley's *Roots*," showcases how memory and storytelling became essential instruments for transferring knowledge from one generation to the next. In *Roots*, his semi-autobiographical book, Alex Haley tries to go back six generations in his family tree. The chapter aims to explore the significant impact that memory codes have played in assisting the writer in discovering his ancestry.

Works Cited

Antze, Paul & Michael Lambek. (Eds.). (1996). *Tense Past: Cultural Essays in Trauma and Memory*. Routledge, London.

Assmann, Jan. (1995). "Collective Memory and Cultural Identity." *New German Critique*, 65: 125–133.

Assmann, Jan. (2011). *Cultural Memory and Early Civilization: Writing, Remembrance and Political Imagination*. Cambridge University Press, New York.

Bell, Duncan. (Ed.). (2006). *Memory, Trauma and World Politics: Reflections on the Relationship between Past and Present*. Palgrave Macmillan, London.

Caruth, Cathy. (1995). *Trauma: Explorations in Memory*. Johns Hopkins University Press, Baltimore.

Connerton, Paul. (1989). *How Societies Remember*. Cambridge University Press, Cambridge.

E. Cote, James & Levine, Charles G. (2002). *Identity, Formation, Agency, and Culture A Social Psychological Synthesis*. Psychology Press, New York.

Edkins, Jenny. (2003). *Trauma and the Memory of Politics*. Cambridge University Press, Cambridge.

Eichenbaum, Howard. (2002). *The Cognitive Neuroscience of Memory*. Oxford University Press, New York.

Erll, A., & Nu¨nning, A. (Eds.). (2010). *A Companion to Cultural Memory Studies*. De Gruyter, Berlin.

Elster, Jon. (2004). *Closing the Books: Transitional Justice in Historical Perspective*. Cambridge University Press, Cambridge.

Fassin, Didier & Richard Rechtman. (2009). *The Empire of Trauma: An Inquiry into the Condition of Victimhood*. Trans. Rachel Gomme. Princeton University Press, Princeton.

Fivush, Robyn. (2011). "The Development of Autobiographical Memory." *Annual Review of Psychology* 62.1: 559–582.

Halbwachs, M. (1992). *On Collective Memory*. University of Chicago Press, Chicago, p. 81.

Kaplan, E. Ann. (2005). *Trauma Culture: The Politics of Terror and Loss in Media and Literature*. Rutgers University Press, New Brunswick.

Koller, John M. Koller. (1972, April). *Dharma: An Expression of Universal Order Philosophy East and West.* Vol. 22, No. 2, On Dharma and Li (Apr., 1972), pp. 131–144 (14 pages) University of Hawai'i Press, Honalulu.
Langer, Nieli. (2016). "The Power of Storytelling and the Preservation of Memories…." *Educational Gerontology* 42.11: 739–739.
Leys, Ruth. (2000). *Trauma: A Genealogy.* University of Chicago Press, Chicago.
McAdams, A. James. (1997). *Transitional Justice and the Rule of Law in New Democracies.* University of Notre Dame Press, South Bend.
Minow, Martha. (1999). *Between Vengeance and Forgiveness: Facing History after Genocide and Mass Violence.* Beacon Press, Boston.
Mookerjea-Leonard, Debali. (2017). *Literature, Gender, and the Trauma of Partition: The Paradox of Independence.* Routledge, London.
Pillemer, David B. (1998). *Momentous Events, Vivid Memories.* Harvard University Press, Cambridge.
Olick, Jeffrey & Joyce Robbins. (1998). "Social Memory Studies: From "Collective Memory" to the Historical Sociology of Mnemonic Practices." *Annual Review of Sociology* 24.1: 105–140
Olick, Jeffrey K. (2007). *The Politics of Regret: On Collective Memory and Historical Responsibility.* Routledge, New York.
Pethes, Nicolas. (2019). *Cultural Memory Studies – An Introduction.* Cambridge Scholars Publishing, Newcastle.
Plate, Liedeke, & ElsRose, H. G. (2013). Rewriting, a Literary Concept for the Study of Cultural Memory: Towards a Transhistorical Approach to Cultural Remembrance. *Neophilologus: An International Journal of Modern and Mediaval Languages and Literature*, 97.4: 611–625.
Rao, Venkat D. (2014). *Cultures of Memory in South Asia, Orality, Literacy and the Problem of Inheritance.* Spinger Publications, New Delhi.
Schacter, Daniel L. (1997). *Searching for Memory: The Brain, the Mind, and the Past.* Basic Books, New York.
Sturken, Marita. (2008). "Memory, Consumerism and Media: Reflections on the Emergence of the Field." *Memory Studies* 1.1: 73–78.
Teitel, Ruti G. (2002). *Transitional Justice.* Oxford University Press, New York.
Taylor, Diana. (2003). *The Archive and the Repertoire Performing Cultural Memory in the Americas.* Duke University Press, Durham.
Turner, Victor. (1980). "Social Dramas and Stories about Them." *Critical Inquiry*, 7.1: 141–168, On Narrative, The University of Chicago Press.
Vinitzky-Seroussi, Vered. (2002). "Commemorating a Difficult Past: Yitzhak Rabin's Memorial." *American Sociological Review* 67.1: 30–51.

Part I

The Mnemonics of Storytelling and Memory Studies

1 Storytelling as a Cultural Practice

Memory, Emancipation, and Survival as Sites of Resistance

Ashma Shamail

Introduction

> ... story is latent in all things, whether object or abstract, material or imagination. All a story needs is a means of being told. And that is where narrative comes in ... narrative is also the container and the contents of tale and myth, chronicle and history, drama, anecdote and legend. Narrative is simultaneously the telling of the story (i.e., the methods and media involved in the telling) as well as the related events, emotions, and imagined cognitive constructs that are evoked in the mind of the audience as the story takes shape. In other words, storytelling is the practice of narrative, and the act of narration is the place and moment of story.
>
> (Heitkemper-Yates and Penjak vii)

Narrative has been existing "in all periods, all places, all societies" (Barthes 95). Narratives encapsulate a mystic world in which we visualize the existence of our ancestors, both living and dead. Both narratives and stories are a living form, a persistent world functioning on a level of consciousness, giving meaning to our experiences, thought-processes, values, and norms. Schachtner believes, if "narrative acts as a means with which to understand the world; storytelling acts as a means of conveying that understanding and as an instrument for configuring the world" (30). She further says, while narratives or narrations "combine various episodes, points in time, and places, linking them to each other ... [and] can change, subject to time and space ... storytelling includes emotions and moods as well as reflections and interpretations" (30). Stories embody a never-ending process of knowledge retrieved from memory. Rooted inherently in a re-examination of the past and directions for the future, stories define one's being or existence in this world. In essence, the act of storytelling involves dramatic depiction or narration of thoughts, notions, curiosities, beliefs, and norms fused with emotions. Storytelling as a lived experience is laden with our histories, pasts, cultures, and traditions.

Kraus perceives storytelling as the "essence of the social construction of reality" (4). A reality rooted in the past as well as the future. Providing

DOI: 10.4324/9781003508564-3

sustenance and strength, the past presents "evaluations, priorities, patterns of behaviour, and rationales which serve as templates and blueprints" (Meuter 143). And this knowledge of the past is essential to determine our sense of belonging in this world. Stories have a purpose, a place, and a goal set to reach out to future generations, which when gleaned retrospectively provide new meanings. Stories establish a base as powerful mediums for diverse modes of communication and expression. Stories open the doors of stored memories, exposing the actions and experiences of a collective community's past. Stories teach, preach, educate, and demand the partnership of future generations to carry forward the legacy of storytelling.

While stories embody loads of information about one's culture and ethnicity, African Americans and African Caribbeans are distinct communities whose transportation to the American soil and Caribbean islands is a story in itself. Because of their long line of storytelling lineages, these enslaved populations of African descent were able to preserve their accounts. In fact, their lived experiences provided the impetus for these stories, and one did not have to be taught to become a storyteller, but stories were born instantly. These formerly enslaved Africans, who were master storytellers back in their motherland, were not merely giving character to real incidents through their oral narratives but were reinforcing their indomitable spirit and displaying what they endured and how they survived. When slaves were prohibited from reading and writing, their oral tradition of storytelling proved to be the vehicle of connection and link to their future generations. With free speech being the only entity, oral narratives showcased testimonies of their own stored accounts. The traditional mode of storytelling, one of the prominent vestiges of African culture, encompasses proverbs, songs, dance, and other forms of oral traditions transferred from generation to generation. Researcher Opondo believes, "Oral traditions contribute to create an 'authentic' identity that people, in a context of little or recent diffusion of literacy, perceive as closer to them than a written tradition. The oral narrative in this sense, tells of a people's culture" (119). Preserved and passed on in the orature, the rich African culture has survived in orate communities. Hence, by adapting their ancestor's African tradition of storytelling legacy, these enslaved people tried to recuperate and deal with their situations and likewise document their lived experiences on the American soil and the Caribbean islands.

Centering on Paule Marshall's second novel *The Chosen Place, the Timeless People* (1969), this paper envisions the memory of a former slave hero's gallant past through the mode of storytelling. Transmitted from generation to generation, the story as a cultural practice is enacted annually in the carnival. Emancipation and survival as sites of resistance take an embellished form in this novel. Recalled through memories, this slave hero's story is remembered by actions of individuals in the present. And this mode of generational continuity helps assert narrative empowerment, sense of self, and becoming.

A novelist of dual heritage, Paule Marshall proudly establishes herself as an African American as well as an African-Caribbean writer. A United States citizen with African-Caribbean immigrant ancestry, Marshall's characters populate both the landscapes of Barbados (Caribbean) and Brooklyn (U.S.A.). Her protagonists reclaim their individual self and try to assert their place in society by harboring memories of the past, acknowledging history, and preserving their culture and communities.

Storytelling and the Bournehills Community

The Chosen Place, the Timeless People (1969) is a novel examining the importance of cultural roots, rituals, and re-enactment of memories of slavery through a cultural performance. In her novel, Marshall demonstrates a tiny island community's annual performance of a historical episode of struggle, survival, and liberation through a cultural ritual. Bourne Island or Bournehills, the fictitious landscape set in the Caribbean, seems to appear in a separate time zone:

> ... the island below had broken rank and stood off by itself to the right, almost out in the Atlantic. It might have been put there by the giants to mark the eastern boundary of the entire continent, to serve as its bourn ... it remained – alone amid an immensity of sea and sky, becalmed now that its turbulent history was past, facing east, the open sea, and across the sea, hidden beyond the horizon, the colossus of Africa.
>
> (Marshall, *The Chosen Place* 13)

Marshall presents the (dis)placement of Bourne Islanders stating that "it is difficult, for example, to say in what time and space the villagers actually exist. Indeed, they seem apart from the Western notion of time altogether and as much a part of the past as the present" (Marshall, *Shaping the World* 111). It appears as if the ordinary notions of time do not adhere to this specific island community, and they seem to have hovered elsewhere. She displays the Bourne Islanders as "the seemingly static forms of the men and women working in the fields under the overseeing eye of the sun ... they went about the work at the same slow, almost dreamlike pace" (Marshall, *The Chosen Place* 103). Marshall also portrays how despite acquiring liberation from the colonial rule, these poor, black, '*static*' islanders are subjected to exploitative labor and domination by the wealthy barons and English landowners. Regardless of many efforts by outside projects and research teams to promote development on this island, these citizens never yielded to submission or change. This markedly differentiated them from the rich (local) elite people of the Island. Bourne Island itself is "anthropomorphized as both the victim of the colonial giants who created it and as the resistant counteragent standing in both remembrance and defiance of those giants" (Slappey 95). In their refusal to transform or change, these backward and disorderly 'timeless' people view both the past and the present fused together, as Grant states,

> there is a constant overlapping of past and present that emphasizes the continuum of past injustices in the present time of Bournehill ... the "timeless people's" revolt against exploitation makes time cyclical, since it is a repetition of the same struggles to which they have been frequently confronted.
>
> (38–39)

These islanders belong to a type of 'timeless' condition. However, the novelist does not associate these Bourne Islanders' silence with powerlessness and voice with power. As De Lamotte ascribes:

> Transformation is not only a central theme of the novel; it is one of the central modes of superimposition by which Marshall's narrative proceeds. By means of it, her double images of dispossession and power, tragedy and hope, picture the triumphant self-possession of the dispossessed, their ability to make even the signs of their powerlessness signify their power. One of these signs is silence.
>
> (42)

Marshall affirms that if this is a story of Bourne Islanders' oppression and suppression, it is also a story of their refusal, assertion, and resistance. Most importantly, the story of these Bournehills inhabitants is embedded and tied up to their historical past, a past from where they gain sustenance, power, and freedom.

The historical legacy of the tradition of storytelling casts a dynamic influence on these citizens, who claim themselves as heirs to an oral culture. The story dates back to their legend Cuffee Ned. Cuffee, considered as the rebel hero of Bourne Island, is remembered for freeing the slave community through his fight and political revolt against the British on Pyre Hill. This particular incident is described as "the defining moment of Bournehills' history and the greatest hope for its future" (Slappey 113). The story as old as two hundred years is popular throughout the island, for Cuffee's act of bravery is a story retold through generations. Living with this legacy of a triumphant past, these islanders' existence in the present is similar to how "Bournehills, under Cuffee, had been a nation and its people a People, one could almost sense something of that same spirit moving in the district again" (Marshall, *The Chosen Place* 405). This state or condition is also very much evident in one of the local resident's words, who says, "Years back when Cuffee was alive, ... we did different, maybe because we knew that if we had lived selfish we couldn't live at all. Well, it's the same now" (Marshall, *The Chosen Place* 394). Cuffee's heroism, valor, and the act of sacrificing his life for the sake of his community are living examples for the entire Bournehills.

Marshall's emphasis on communal unity and survival of cultural memory of the Bourne Islanders is in a way different from the rest of the neighboring islands that surround Bourne. Bournehills reflects the community's collective oppression that can be envisaged through their everyday actions as well as through their rehearsal of history at the carnival. Despite centuries of slavery and racism, the people and the place have stood the test of time, which makes it distinct and recognizable. Their resistance to even technological tools like televisions and automobiles goes beyond the thinking of research teams set up for development. It is only at a later stage of the novel that the Jewish American anthropologist Saul Amron, assigned to bring economic progress, realizes that the failure of development programs on the island has got nothing to do with its inhabitants or the location, but lies in failing to understand the inhabitants' history and their roles in that history (Slappey 115–116). Understanding Bournehills culture and history is at the forefront. Hence, Marshall presents Bournehills community with a unified history, remembering Cuffee's heroic act through the space of cultural memory as an ongoing practice. In the words of Assmann, "Cultural memory is an institution ... [It] is disembodied. In order to function as memory, however, its symbolic forms must not only be preserved but also circulated and re-embodied in a society" (17). Certainly, for these timeless islanders, cultural memory is viewed as an institution of transmission, wisdom, and more specifically summoned and celebrated annually.

Storytelling for these Bourne Islanders acts as an emancipatory tool. By re-narrating Cuffee's vision to their young generations, they revive memories of their proud history through role-playing in the carnival. All through their marching parade in the carnival, these timeless Bourne Island actors or performers breathe life into the historically revolutionary characters fighting for freedom. Marshall denotes that not only Cuffee's or the community's status is glorified in the parade, but the live performance ends by showcasing Cuffee's demise as a "return" (Marshall, *The Chosen Place* 288). The annual repetition of this carnival parade documents not only sharing wisdom of a valiant past, but it also signals a 'second coming,' as stated by an islander "He's goin' come again I say—or he's goin' send somebody just like him" (Marshall, *The Chosen Place* 135). Cuffee, the slave hero, dwells on the collective consciousness and oneness of these people, signaling them to uphold their unity and consider themselves as a 'nation.' Therefore, Bournehills lives with a greater purpose than the remaining islands through the storytelling tradition.

Storytelling as a Cultural Practice: History Remembered

In African culture, the storyteller, also known as the 'griot,' has a decisive role to play in preserving and transmitting the community's oral history and traditions. Known as caretakers of cultural memory, these storytellers are identified by varied names, as Assmann states:

> Cultural memory always has its specialists. These carriers of memory are known under a rich assortment of names, such as shamans, bards, griots, priests, teachers, artists, clerks, scholars, mandarins, rabbis, and mullahs. In oral societies, the degree of their specialization depends on the magnitude of the demands on their memory. The highest rank is accorded verbatim transmission.
>
> (20)

An African community's participation in cultural memory largely involves the role of the griots. They do not merely function as concierges of culture, but also enable the people to remember and pass on the cultural practices and traditions and hand over the native rituals' knowledge to subsequent generations.

In any culture, stories function as a storehouse of knowledge. And the African-Caribbean historical past is undoubtedly laden with bounteous stories. Centuries ago, the cultural tradition of storytelling was predominant among the African slaves. Slavery stories emerged out of a troubled African enslavement history and slaves' dislocation from their motherland necessitated documentation of their cultural practices and traditions. The storying practices on the Caribbean islands enabled people to discover themselves. In the process of recounting stories, individuals or communities cemented bonds of group cohesion and solidarity. Marshall's rendering of the storytelling legacy as a cultural practice in *The Chosen Place* is akin to Henry Louis Gates Jr. who believes, "the stories that manage to resurface under different guises ... these are a culture's *canonical* tales, the tales that contain the cultural codes that are *assumed* or internalized by members of that culture" (17–18). The Bournehills inhabitants' remembrance and carrying forward of Cuffee's tale as a tradition each year in the carnival ritual contains elements of 'cultural codes,' the meanings of which can be deciphered and internalized by the community with the purpose of conveying those meanings to the outside world. This community's history is not just remembered but glorified and celebrated publicly.

Storytelling as a cultural practice comes so naturally to the islanders just as one breathes oxygen for survival. Through memories, the mode of storytelling sets the stage annually for re-playing the legendary slave hero's historical accomplishment in the carnival. In African-Caribbean communities, memory is a significant entity, for "the replication of memories ... links the black experience and provides a cultural continuity with those back home and in the diaspora" (Chamberlain 185).

Sharing stories not only connects and reconnects to one's ancestry, but also heals individuals and communities psychologically. Healing also "helps in reflecting, (re)-membering, and aiding in the formation of one's identity through recovered pasts connected to present realities" (Shamail, *(Re) Dressing the Cultural Wounds* 28). Indeed, through the workings of memory, the past is made experienceable in the present as is the case in this novel.

Storytelling practices evolved from the basket of memories act as a bridge connecting past and present, and this helps the community to overcome adversities and cope under appalling circumstances. Bournehills lives with a reality and the storyteller gives voice to that reality. Most importantly, "the survival of this ritual on the island is itself a form of resistance ... resistance against the history of slavery and violence, against assimilation, [and] against both the English and the Americans who shift roles of domination" (Shamail, *Ritualistic Carnival* 17). This novel advocates how a community nurtured a private but collective cultural practice of oral history, a history that is made visible by its inhabitants through collective memory and a storytelling legacy that permeates their community of origin.

Memory, Emancipation, and Survival as Sites of Resistance

> As a form of memory, ritual is based on repetition. Each performance must follow a fixed model as closely as possible in order to make the actual performance resemble the previous ones in every respect. The flow of time is brought into a pattern that combines the irreversible and the reversible, the passing time and the returning time. Human life and social institutions are thereby rescued from just passing away, decaying, and vanishing; they are integrated into the natural cycles of regeneration. Repetition is a form of preservation, of memory.
>
> (Assmann 23–24)

Remembering or the function of memory plays a vital role for any community's historical continuity and group identity. The repetition of the annual carnival ritual on Bourne Island is indeed a form of 'preservation, of memory,' signaling a community's collective identification with history. However, memory's relation to history continues to remain as one of the most engaging theoretical challenges (Kansteiner 184).

Memory as an illuminating power accentuates remembering. For the Bournehills community, this historical event, in addition to remembering, also informs other modes of survival and resistance against the dominant European forces and outside (U.S.) interventions in the present. Through collective oppression, they are also able to find meaning in their lives. Renewing memories helps them to stay connected to each other. Cuffee's story, by all means, is the story of emancipation and survival. Through the act of remembrance, this emancipatory spirit is re-kindled strengthening their endurance, "the story of Cuffee and the revolt ... the one thing to which they were willing to give themselves" (Marshall, *The Chosen Place* 281).

Furthermore, memory is also connected to places which play a significant role in the process of memorialization. Hence in this context, it is appropriate to draw upon the French historian Pierre Nora's "*lieux de mémoire*, sites of memory" (284). Nora states that these sites of memory evolved through the interaction between memory and history or to say it better, "*lieux de mémoire* would be indistinguishable from *lieux d'histoire*" (295). Nora addresses "*lieux*" in three senses—"material, symbolic, and functional," adding that they exist together, and gives an example through the notion of a historical generation, which "is material by its demographic content and supposedly functional—since memories are crystallized and transmitted from one generation to the next—but it is also symbolic, since it characterizes, by referring to events or experiences" (295). Undoubtedly, Bournehills history is suffused or interwoven with the memories of the island's landscape, events, stories, and rituals. Another interesting study by Edward Casey offers insights into the poignant link between places and memory where "places, instead of being merely settings or scenes, are active agents of commemoration" (277). The landscapes of Bournehills are sites of remembrances, resistances, and repressions. Bournehills when viewed from the plane resembles "a ruined amphitheater," and the "wrecked," "ravaged hills" stand "as a memorial" (Marshall, *The Chosen Place* 14,99, 402). Overtly, Bournehills acts as a site of memory even through its ruined landscape, where remembrance of painful memories operates as a form of resistance. Also, places like the Sugar's nightclub capture memories of slavery, where there is "never tiring talk of Cuffee Ned," with the Islanders' perpetual talk encapsulating Cuffee's story of resistance (Marshall, *The Chosen Place* 414). Further addressing the connection between places and memory, Casey highlights that place, not historical events, is the active agent, with the former actively remembering the latter (277). Certain historical places (also the community's source of sustenance) like the cane field, the old sugar mill, and Sugar's bar validate history and remembrance.

In addition, the Pyre Hill, the "blackened heap against the blue unclouded sky—an awesome sight, which held the eye even when you tried looking away," is a constant reminder of Cuffee and his rebels' act (Marshall, *The Chosen Place* 101). For this chosen diasporic community, the memory of "the blackened ruin of Pyre Hill" re-lights their spirit as well as purifies them (Marshall, *The Chosen Place* 410). As Professor Ferguson states, burning the pyre is a cleansing ritual, which constitutes a great purifying (49). This hill acts as an unofficial memorial to that single historical event the Bournehills takes pride in (Jörngården 157). Therefore, through ruined places, Marshall advocates the need for a revolutionary consciousness or inspiration, which can best be achieved by keeping alive the officially uncelebrated history of resistance (Jörngården 158). Subsequently, places in Bournehills act as memorial sites.

Similarly, it is not just the land but also the sea that carries memories. Memories of the saga of the African diaspora and the horrors of the Middle Passage, "all those, the nine million and more it is said ... This sea mourned them" (Marshall, *The Chosen Place* 106). The Bournehills' association and affinity with their enslaved African past through the image of the sea recasts them with a memory they have not lost. A memory of black resistance, endurance, emancipation, and the will to survive against all odds. In a way,

Bournehills population's "*lieux*" are not based on "a schematic outline of the objects of memory" (Nora 295) but are "active agents of commemoration" (Casey 277). As Rosca states, Marshall's novel engages in depicting memory in places as fundamental for the survival of the Bournehills community, even if remembrance is voice-less or silent, the past being materialized and persistent in the place that itself is significant (87).

Through memories, people embark on journeys toward freedom, reclamation, ritual purification, and celebrations, where they find voice to their existence across decades and centuries. Following Cuffee's path, this community's collective memory holds them against forgetting, and against assimilation. Group solidarity and kinship networks act as key factors for these chosen people in achieving emancipation. Marshall's novel showcases the history of resistance, of survival, of memories, with the islanders orienting themselves both in terms of the past and the present.

Memories are the backbone of any community's history. Significantly, the field of memory studies is vast and filled with unending investigations and additions. With the constant expansion of the memory field, the term 'collective memory' has been referred to in varied ways in terms of methodologies, concepts, techniques, and forms (Halbwachs; Confino; Kansteiner; Assmann; Hirst et al.). Jan Assmann's valuable and important contributions to the research field of cultural memory are remarkably notable. Jan Assmann, working on the well-known French philosopher and sociologist Maurice Halbwachs's concept of collective memory, or "la mémoire collective," preserves it, while breaking it down into "communicative memory" and "cultural memory," treating it as two different "modi memorandi," or "ways of remembering" (17). While communicative memory is noninstitutional and is formed by everyday interactions, communications, and socializations, cultural memory on the other hand, as a form of collective memory, is shaped by cultural frames or artifacts (Assmann 17–18). Assmann addresses Halbwachs's solitary focus on social frames, but goes a step further in speaking about human memory being embedded in "cultural frames," as well, which include the places or landscapes where people were raised, the feasts they participated in, the texts they learned, the churches or synagogues they visited, the music they listened to, the stories they heard and by and in which they live. All of these constitute as reminding objects (mnemonic institutions) and these cultural frames or carriers necessitate inclusion in the concept of memory (17–18).

Cultural memory, as perceived by Assmann, is externalized, situation-transcendent, stable, and may be transferred and transmitted from one situation to another, or from one generation to another. Whereas communicative memory, Assmann states, that involves direct interaction between members of a group, is not supported by transmission, or explanation, or by any organizations of learning, nor is it formalized or stabilized by any form of material symbols. Rather it exists for a limited period (17–18).

The Bourne Island community has carved a niche for itself based on shared collective cultural memories, cultural frames (places, stories), images (the Pyre

Hill and the sea as markers of resistance), events (rituals), and experiences. Researcher Confino's approach of collective memory is captivating in the way it questions the critical aspect of how past is received or rejected. As a shared identity, collective memory, Confino perceives, ought to encourage people, maneuver their emotions, inspire them to act, and influence socio-cultural mode of action (1390). This is exactly what the Bournehills residents employ in their everyday life. In the act of documenting the past and keeping it alive through collective memory, Cuffee's story encourages these Islanders to participate in rituals, inspires them to act by declining change or holding back progress, and influences them on remembering, but not forgetting, all of which function as forms of resistance. In essence, memory takes its symbolic meaning in articulating the connections between culture and society and that goes beyond generally perceiving it as a tool or equipment to understand the past.

Furthermore, in Wulf Kansteiner's opinion, collective memory can only be envisioned and accessed through its expression in individuals. Kansteiner's discussion necessitates the differentiation in types of memories ('social' and 'autobiographical' on one side and 'collective' on the other). And in failing to make such differentiation, Kansteiner believes, many investigations into collective memories commit serious methodological error: they recognize and conceptualize collective memory exclusively in terms of the psychological and emotional dynamics of individual remembering. In line with Kansteiner's views, collective memories have their own dynamics, and we have to search for appropriate methods of analysis (186). Eventually, collective memories have to be explored and understood from different perspectives, filtered in terms of their right places, positionings, and concepts under respective disciplines.

During their process of formulating collective memories, communities have been preserving their culture, knowledge, experiences, and past accounts since time immemorial. Still, collective memory studies continue to expand, undergo transitions and modulations, and are re-visited by scholars and researchers over time. Paule Marshall's small island community is one example which supports and governs the practice of storytelling, enhances survival and resistance, prevents forgetting, retains memory in places and rituals, with its inhabitants proclaiming both remembering and belonging.

Conclusion

Spanning over many decades, storytellers, as heirs to oral narratives, have provided significant meaning to stories. The role of a storyteller as an artist has evolved over the passage of time and the art of storytelling continues to thrive in the re-creation of individual and national identities. Storytellers in contemporary societies have shaped and ignited audiences' imagination, and showcased recognition to storytelling as a transformative art. Storytellers as intermediaries of memory play a significant role in discerning meaning of past practices, events, and experiences. Also, "in memory practices, people are often required to re-live, re-experience, or 're-enact' the important moments in the past and thereby make themselves vulnerable to the world of the memory" (qtd. in Kim 8). As such, memory is preserved through the re-enactment practices and re-narrated as a story. The Bourne Islanders' reverence to memory and its cultural transmission validates the importance of the ritualistic events in the Caribbean. Living with a (re)memory of the past, these islanders experience re-birth each year (in the ritual), while simultaneously they celebrate and revel in their past. Additionally, *lieux de mémoire*, sites of memory "only exist because of their capacity for metamorphosis, an endless recycling of their meaning and an unpredictable proliferation of their ramifications" (Nora 296). Commemorating practices are viewed in terms of how a society sees its past, discovers its essence, learns from it, and educates its future generations to preserve the social identity of the culture. Marshall maps how cultural or commemorating practices as a society's tales have evolved from the rich blanket of memories. And the art of storytelling as a cultural practice will continue to thrive despite advancements in digital technology. Therefore, storytelling, despite the invasion of cinema, social media sites, online gaming, and virtual community networks, has survived and continues to motivate people across the globe.

Works Cited

Assmann, Jan. "Communicative and Cultural Memory." *Cultural Memories: The Geographical Point of View*, edited by Peter Meusburger, Michael Heffernan, and Edgar Wunder, Springer, 2011, pp. 15–27.

Barthes, Roland. *The Semiotic Challenge*. Translated by Richard Howard, Blackwell, 1988.

Casey, Edward S. *Getting Back Into Place: Toward a Renewed Understanding of the Place-world*. Indiana University Press, 1993.

Chamberlain, Mary. "Diasporic Memories: Community, Individuality, and Creativity—A Life Stories Perspective." *The Oral History Review*, vol. 36, no. 2, 2009, pp. 177–187.

Confino, Alon. "Collective Memory and Cultural History: Problems of Method." *The American Historical Review*, vol. 102, no. 5, 1997, pp. 1386–1403.

De Lamotte, Eugenia C. *Places of Silence, Journeys of Freedom: The Fiction of Paule Marshall*. University of Pennsylvania Press, 1998.

Ferguson, Moira. "A 'Nation of Diabetics' Meets Empire A Chosen Place, a Timeless People." *A Human Necklace: The African Diaspora and Paule Marshall's Fiction*, State University of New York Press, 2013, pp. 37–54.

Gates, Henry Louis Jr. "Introduction: Narration and Cultural Memory in the African American Tradition." *Talk that Talk: An Anthology of African American Storytelling*, edited by Linda Goss and Marian E. Barnes, Simon & Schuster, 1989, pp. 15–19.

Grant, Alder S. "Subverting the Hegemonic Ideology and Redefining the Identity of Paule Marshall's Heroines." *Revista De Lenguas Modernas*, no. 12, 2010, pp. 31–56.

Halbwachs, Maurice. *Das Gedächtnis und seine sozialen Bedingungen* [Les cadres sociaux de la mémoire] (Lutz Geldsetzer, Trans.). Suhrkamp Verlag, 1985 (Original work published 1925).

Heitkemper-Yates, Michael, and Ana Penjak, editors. *The Practice of Narrative: Storytelling in a Global Context*. Interdisciplinary Press, 2016.
Hirst, William, et al. "Collective Memory from a Psychological Perspective." *Trends in Cognitive Sciences*, vol. 22, no. 5, 2018, pp. 438–451.
Jörngården, Anna. "Presencing Absence: Ruin as Counter-Monument in Caribbean Literature." *Literary Landscapes of Time: Multiple Temporalities and Spaces in Latin American and Caribbean Literatures*, edited by Jobst Welge and Juliane Tauchnitz, De Gruyter, 2022, pp. 143–162.
Kansteiner, Wulf. "Finding Meaning in Memory: A Methodological Critique of Collective Memory Studies." *History and Theory*, vol. 41, no. 2, 2002, pp. 179–197.
Kim, Tae H. "Memory, Story, History: The Formation and Change of Collective Memory and Narrative of the Past in Early China." Doctoral Dissertation, University of California Berkeley, 2019.
Kraus, Wolfgang. *Identität als Narration: Die narrative Konstruktion von Identitätsprojekten* [*Identity as Narration: The Narrative Construction of Identity Projects*]. 2000.
Marshall, Paule. *The Chosen Place, the Timeless People*. Harcourt, Brace & World, 1969.
Marshall, Paule. "Shaping the World of My Art." *New Letters,* vol. 40, no. 1, 1973, pp. 97–112.
Meuter, Norbert. "Die Ausbildung narrativer Identitäten: Paul Ricoeur." *Narrative Identität: Das Problem der personalen Identität im Anschluss an Ernst Tugendhat, Niklas Luhmann und Paul Ricoeur* [*Narrative Identity: The Problem of Personal Identity Following Ernst Tugendhat, Niklas Luhmann, and Paul Ricoeur*]. J.B. Metzler, 1995, pp. 122–175.
Nora, Pierre. "Between Memory and History: Les Lieux de Memoire." *History and Memory in African-American Culture*, edited by Genevieve Fabre and Robert O'Meally, Oxford University Press, 1994, pp. 284–300.
Opondo, Rose A. "Oral Storytelling and National Kinship: Reflections on the Oral Narrative Performance in the Kenya Schools and Colleges Drama Festivals." *Tydskrif Vir Letterkunde,* vol. 51, no. 1, 2014, pp. 118–131.
Rosca, Florentina. "Silent Sites of Memory in Paule Marshall's *The Chosen Place, The Timeless People*." *Papers in Arts and Humanities (PArtsHum)*, vol. 3, no. 2, 2023, pp. 75–88.
Schachtner, Christina. *The Narrative Subject: Storytelling in the Age of the Internet*. Palgrave Macmillan, 2020.
Shamail, Ashma. "(Re)Dressing the Cultural Wounds: Memory, Healing, and Survival in *Praisesong for the Widow*." *Dialog,* no. 30, 2017, pp. 16–31.
Shamail, Ashma. "Ritualistic Carnival: Storytelling, Remembrance, and Celebration of History in Paule Marshall's *The Chosen Place, the Timeless People*." *The IUP Journal of English Studies*, vol. 16, no. 2, 2021, pp. 7–22.
Slappey, Lisa A. "Writing Off the Map: The Postcolonial Landscapes of Pynchon, Marshall, Silko, and Vea." Doctoral dissertation, April 2001. Rice University, proquest.com/docview/250671564?accountid=136546&parentSessionId=Qt9mH%2B2fVUaQ4hrrMK1FOcpFKnqFLNMZ3M%2B6aDoYZWs%3D

2 In Search of Fragments of Recollection

Cultural Memory and Identity in the Select Travel Narratives of Tahir Shah[1]

Divyasree J. S. and B. Sajeetha

Introduction

The critical attention given to travel writing as a field of scholarly research is relatively new. Travel always brings new experiences, knowledge, and an understanding of other cultures. Over the centuries, travel narratives, in various forms, have enriched and educated the human mind. A travel writer has previously been an adventurer who recorded his objective observations. While travel writers like Thomas Coryate and John Taylor documented their travel experiences in the seventeenth century, the eighteenth century witnessed the attempt of writers like Jonathan Swift and Samuel Johnson to blur the boundary between travel writing and fiction. In the post-war period, travel literature took a different turn with the writers' formulation of theories based on travel narratives. Concepts such as identity, memory, diaspora, and colonial discourses have been studied in connection with travel literature.

Extensive research has been carried out in the field of travel literature. Previous research on Shah's works has been done on themes like border crossing, nostalgia, identity, etc. Rima Barua (2020) has analysed that Shah has digressed from the conventional treatment of the identity of a diasporic travel writer in his travel narratives. She has also studied the works in light of imperialism. Kamal Sbiri, in his article "Border Crossing and Transculturation in Tahir Shah's *The Caliph's House*", deals with the questions of "alterity, mobility, and negotiating differences when crossing borders" (2020: 12). There are seldom any studies done on the connection of travel literature with memory studies. Memory is not only an individual experience but also a societal and collective phenomenon. It plays a prominent role in the establishment of both individual and cultural identity. This chapter is an attempt to analyse the association of cultural memory and cultural identity in selected texts of Tahir Shah. The scope of this chapter lies in its treatment of the relation between memory and culture.

The texts selected for this study are *The Caliph's House: A Year in Casablanca* (2007) and *In Arabian Nights: In Search of Morocco* (2009), written by Tahir Shah. Tahir Shah is a prolific British writer of Afghan Indian descent who is credited with the authorship of fourteen books and many documentaries. Shah's works symbolise the multicultural background

DOI: 10.4324/9781003508564-4

(Anglo-Afghan Indian) to which he belongs. Born and brought up in Great Britain, he has travelled extensively, and in 2003, he moved to Morocco with his family. There are two levels in this study. This chapter will first analyse how the author represents the cultural identity of Morocco through memory, and second, at the personal level, it will show how he defines his identity through his experiences in Morocco. Both these works are about his settling and adaptation in a foreign land like Morocco.

Cultural Memory and Identity

Jan Assmann, in his essay "Collective Memory and Cultural Identity", has defined cultural memory as

> that body of reusable texts, images, and rituals specific to each society in each epoch, whose "cultivation" serves to stabilize and convey that society's self-image. Upon such collective knowledge, for the most part (but not exclusively) of the past, each group bases its awareness of unity and particularity.
>
> (1995: 132)

Travel narratives are active participants in creating and realising culture and identity. Memory is essential to existence as it helps an individual in the process of becoming and belonging. Travel narratives are remembrances of a travel writer's experiences with a host community. They are the result of recording an individual's memories in the larger process of becoming and belonging. As Sturken has said, "memories are part of a larger process of cultural negotiation, which defies memories as narratives and as fluid and mediated cultural and personal traces of the past" (2008: 76).

> Remembering is an active reconciliation of past and present. The meaning of the past in relation to the present is what is at stake here; memories are important as they bring our changing sense of who we are and who we were, coherently into view of one another. Remembering is not just an articulation of individual psychologies, but a performance rooted in lived contexts.
>
> (Keightley, 2010: 58)

Every social group develops a memory from its past experiences which will help preserve and pass it on to posterity. Collective memory is a socio-political construct and a version of the past. It is defined and negotiated through changing socio-political power circumstances and agendas. Sturken uses the term "cultural memory" as a memory shared outside formal historical discourse but imbued with cultural meaning: "Cultural memory as a term implies not only that memories are often produced and reproduced through cultural forms, but also the kind of circulation that exists between personal memories and cultural memories" (2008: 76).

Cultural identity refers to the shared sense of customs, traditions, rituals, beliefs, and language. It is a dynamic phenomenon that defines the soul of a nation. Cultural memory refers not only to the memories reproduced through cultural forms but also to the interconnection of personal and cultural memories. It foregrounds the connection between memory and socio-cultural contexts. Cultural memory can be analysed at social, material, or mental levels. Rituals and practices, myths, monuments, historical details, conversational recollections, organisation of cultural knowledge, etc., can be categorised under cultural memory. From ancient times, thinkers have inferred that identity is designed by the deeds of memory. For instance, the English philosopher John Locke has thought of the identity of consciousness as the essence of personal identity. It can also be considered a survey of the collective identity of a cultural community. The author travels across the Kingdom of Morocco in search of the cultural identity of the nation, and he attempts to define his own identity.

Socio-cultural Elements and Cultural Memory in *The Caliph's House*

Tahir Shah was born in London, but he and his family settled in Morocco. The heroic explorations of Tahir Shah into Moroccan culture entitle him to be a sentimental travel writer who narrates and describes the cultural elements and experiences as if they are a part of the dramatic performance. Morocco is called "the desert kingdom in Africa's north-west" (Shah, 2007: 1). His impulse to live in a land where traditions and family form an integral part of life and where his children can grow up learning the values of life leads him to buy a house in Casablanca. According to Shah, "tradition is the bedrock of life" (16) in Morocco. The reasons for choosing Morocco were many. There were some personal and emotional reasons for him to choose Morocco as the place to live. His emotional attachment to Morocco developed from his childhood days as his father took the family to Morocco to show them the fragments of his native land. The days spent in Morocco, he remembers, gave colour to his "sanitized English childhood" (7). To Tahir Shah, it was "a place of escape, [...] a place with a soul" (7) and he wished to pass on the cultural roots to his children as "a gift of cultural colour" (7).

Apart from the remote remembrances of his childhood and his deep desire to retire from the desolate life in London, his search for freedom and identity also contributes to his decision. His grandfather, who had spent his last years in a small villa in Tangier, after the demise of his wife, has been another reason. He has decided not to return to any place that reminded him of his wife and he wished to live in a land known for "the kingdom's mountains, its kasbahs, and the proud tribal traditions" (Shah, 2007:157). Even though the author had been to Tangier more than three decades before, he could still feel the pungent and intoxicating smell of orange blossom. He travels across

Tangier in search of the memories of his grandfather but realises that the resonance of Tangier is replaced with a sort of melancholy. He tries to analyse the cultural background of Tangier by connecting his childhood memories with his present travel experiences. His travel across Morocco helps him understand the social standing his grandfather and father had there. Both had friendly relations with the King of that time. He was the person destined to collect the last reminiscence of his grandfather – the diaries he had left behind.

Through the description of his explorations in Casablanca, he is trying to decipher the cultural code of Morocco. The first cultural element that he came across was the concept of Jinns among the Moroccans. Dar Khalifa, the house he bought in Morocco, was occupied by not only earthly pests but also by Jinns, magical spirits that love to haunt unoccupied houses. The house, Dar Khalifa, along with the three guardians, is the primary source of contact between Tahir Shah and the Moroccan culture. To the people of Morocco, jinns were a far more serious issue than suicide bombers. As per Muslim belief, a jinn is "a fraternity of spirits created by God from fire ... inhabit[ing] the world along with humans" (Shah, 2007: 354). Jinns or genies or *jnun* have supernatural power to take any form as they wish and are invisible to human eyes. All jinns are wicked and causing discomfort to man is their pleasure. The Moroccans believed that if a house is left empty for a long period, it will attract jinns and the master of the house should give them the blood they need. At first, Shah is incredulous about the existence of these supernatural elements. However, he is regarded with more respect only when he positively addresses the superstitious beliefs of the guardians. The Moroccans look for *baraka*, meaning "blessing", in whatever they do. The name of the jinn in Dar Khalifa is "Qandisha" and the guardians ask the master of the house to put out a plate of couscous and meat for Qandisha. They also believed that if a person keeps a frog in his pocket, fire will not harm him. Shah learned that everyday accidents like the breaking of a vase and a dog biting a child were considered the work of mystic forces "with the jinns at the centre of the belief system" (2007:173).

As Aleida Assmann, in "The Dynamics of Cultural Memory between Remembering and Forgetting", says:

> Cultural memory contains a number of cultural messages that are addressed to posterity and intended for continuous repetition and re-use. To this active memory belong, among other things, works of art, which are destined to be repeatedly re-read, appreciated, staged, performed, and commented.
>
> (2008: 99)

The architecture and planning of a city are material expressions of a culture and mirror its cultural identity. The narrative description of the city by the author is an indicator of the cultural standards of Morocco. The city of Fes which was once known for its wealth, scholarship, and trade, is described as follows:

> Our starting point was Fès, undoubtedly Morocco's greatest jewel. It is the only medieval Arab city that remains entirely intact. Walking through the labyrinth of streets that make up the vast medina is like stepping into A Thousand and One Nights. The smells, sights and sounds bombard the senses. A stroll of a few feet can be an overwhelming experience. For centuries, Fès was a place of impressive wealth, a centre of scholarship and trade. Its houses reflect a confidence in Arab architecture almost never seen elsewhere, their decor profiting from a line of apprentices unbroken for a thousand years.
>
> (Shah, 2007: 7–8)

The houses in Fes were an example of brilliant Arabic architecture. Shah also perceives "an exclamation of French colonial might" (2007: 40) in the buildings in Casablanca. The workshops in the alleys of the old city marked the existence of traditional skills of metalwork, leather tanning, mosaic design, weaving, ceramics, and marquetry. The interest among modern local Marrachis to sell their ancestral houses to Europeans for a large profit and to move into apartments in new towns reveals the cultural shift in Moroccan society.

Language is another concept that is closely knitted to cultural memory. It helps in shaping cultural identity and how the past is remembered. It also plays a pivotal role in transmitting cultural memory from one generation to another. The official languages in Morocco are Moroccan Arabic and Moroccan Berber. French and English are spoken in the urban areas of Morocco. The writer has used transliterated words from locally used languages. For instance, *jellabas* refer to traditional hooded robes. Certain examples of such words are Tarboosh (a round, velvet-covered hat), *bidonville* (French word for shantytown), *B'saf* (Moroccan Arabic word for a lot), *sehura* (sorceress), *tadelakt* (traditional Moroccan plasterwork), *moualem* (craftsman in a traditional Moroccan form of art), Merguez (spiced mutton or lamb sausages), *douane* (the French word for customs), *khobz* (bread), harem (a section of a traditional house reserved for women), sharif (noble), *jan* (a suffix added to a name), *souq* (market), etc. The use of vocabulary in the Moroccan way in the texts reveals the writer's attempt to adapt and adopt the cultural identity of Morocco. The writer glorifies bargaining as an honourable tradition in Morocco and stresses that it "has one of the most developed bartering economies" (Shah, 2007: 185).

Work culture is an element that defines the identity of a culture. The writer notices a difference in the work culture of the Europeans and the Moroccans. While the Europeans worked very hard and considered inactivity to be guilty, the Moroccans worked only when they needed to. Tahir Shah meets a French man working in the French Consulate in Morocco who sheds light on the

Orient–Occident dichotomy in the minds of the Europeans. According to François, the French diplomat, Morocco seems to be closer to Europe and Europeans but in the minds of the Moroccans, "they are Orientals" (Shah, 2007: 23), and he also adds that the only way to exist is "to appreciate the culture and to navigate through treacherous water" (24). The café culture in Morocco is entirely different from that of the European one. The writer, while in Europe, did not find it comfortable to spend much time in a café. In Morocco, however, spending time in a café is considered an honourable pursuit.

Various socio-cultural elements of Morocco have enriched the knowledge of the author thereby adding to the value of its cultural ethos. These socio-cultural acts are seemingly diminutive but are of high value in the field of cultural studies. These elements are bearers of cultural memory. Moroccan culture also gives importance to honour, especially honour of the family. Women belonging to respectable families were not allowed to go out to work, and they may take extreme actions to conserve the family's honour. Moroccan society is based on a system of helpfulness. In one instance, the author finds the Moroccan shopkeepers donating the best fruit from their collection to a beggar-woman. On the other hand, the writer also humorously presents the suffocation caused by the extreme helpfulness of the Moroccans. While searching for a maid and a nanny for the children, Tahir realised the quick spread of messages and news in Morocco was "like a fire tearing through the depths of Hell" (Shah, 2007: 38). The writer's first shopping experience also throws light on the difference he has felt between life in London and Morocco. Morocco had a lot of imperfections and irregularities in its production of goods, but was cheaper than the European market. The family is the centre of Moroccan life, and food is also a focal point in Moroccan social life. In Moroccan culture, an important man opening the door of his home for guests was considered a lowly action. The people in Casablanca, unlike other Moroccans, appreciated new and modern things. Owing to this reason, the centre of the town was moved from Casablanca to Maarif. Even though there was a cultural barrier, Tahir Shah was happy in his Moroccan life. The daily challenges at Dar Khalifa and the cultural and linguistic barriers in Morocco developed the writer's enthusiasm and problem-solving skills.

Stories, Memory, and Identity in *In Arabian Nights*

Tahir Shah's second book on Morocco, *In Arabian Nights*, through its stories and storytellers, not only presents a detailed exploration of Moroccan folklore but also establishes the restorative nature of the cultural memory. The art of storytelling and storytellers has nourished ancient Morocco for centuries. In the work *In Arabian Nights*, Tahir Shah investigates the repository of traditional stories narrated by a plethora of characters, including master masons, Sufi wise men who write for soap operas, and Tuareg guides addicted to reality television. The title of the work itself is based on the *One Thousand and One Nights*, also known as the *Arabian Nights*, a collection of folktales compiled in Arabic. These tales trace back their roots to ancient and medieval Arabian, Egyptian, Indian, Persian, and Mesopotamian folklore and literature. It is a towering monument in the history of the art of storytelling that is a source of inspiration for many artists and writers.

Storytelling as a universal cultural activity of sharing narratives within and outside a community helps in affirming the roots for growth. Storytelling has played a significant role in the development of a community since ancient times. Being a part of a cultural group, stories pass on with their narratives of the traditions, rituals, and beliefs of that group, thereby helping to identify both group and individual identity. Besides the entertaining nature of storytelling, it also aims to educate and instil moral values in the people and preserve cultural aspects. The oral tradition of storytelling can take many forms, like epic poems, chants, rhymes, songs, etc. It can encompass myths, legends, fables, religion, prayers, proverbs, and instructions. In many cultural communities, storytellers occupy honourable status in society. It not only preserves cultural practices and values but also serves to connect people to their cultural heritage, helping to shape their identity and sense of belonging. A sense of continuity between the past and the present helps in the sustenance of cultural identity and belonging. Stories make people capable of connecting to and understanding the experiences of their ancestors. They play a crucial role in moulding cultural identity by providing a space for collective memory. Storytelling is used as a bridge between knowing and understanding so that the members of a community can learn to connect the values of self and community. Shah writes, "To know about stories you must know people" (Shah, 2009: 99).

The role of performativity in the production of cultural artefacts and symbols has received serious attention in the field of Cultural Studies. Storytelling is a cultural practice that engages with the acts of remembrance in the production of cultural identity. This interconnection of storytelling and cultural memory is clearly found in Shah's statement at the beginning of the book, "For my father there was no sharper way to understand a country than by listening to its stories" (Shah, 2009: 9), and the assertion that the primary aim of the book is to share the author's understanding of Moroccan culture through its stories:

> The Berbers believe that when people are born, they are born with a story inside them, locked in their heart. It looks after them, protects them. [...] Their task is to search for their story, [...] to look for it in everything they do.
>
> (Shah, 2009: 7)

The art of storytelling is inherent in the lives of the Moroccans. Stories are given the status of powerful guides that transcend human existence to a spiritual realm. The author is in search of his own story, and he motivates the readers to join his journey. As it is mentioned in the book, "Some people find their story right away"; others "search their entire lives and never find it" – "it depends on 'perception'" (Shah, 2009: 48). To understand the stories of unknown cultures, people have to search for stories of their own. The *One Thousand and One Nights*, a collection of folktales compiled in Arabic, is a classic work in the history of the art of storytelling and has always been a source of inspiration for many artists and writers. His journey to find the lost ten-volume edition of *Alf Layla wa Layla*, *One Thousand and One Nights* from his father's collection is symbolic of his travels to discover his identity.

One of the experiences that transformed Shah's identity as a traveller was his prison days in Pakistan. He was imprisoned as they thought him to be a spy. He describes his torturous experience of imprisonment in Pakistan:

> As the days and nights in solitary passed, I moved through the labyrinth of my memories. I set myself the task of finding every memory, every fragment of recollection. They began with my childhood, and with the first moment I ever set foot on Moroccan soil.
>
> (2009: 4)

It is evident that he has used memory as a source of solace and inspiration for his own development. Here, memory becomes an instrument for the author to identify himself. In the work *In Arabian Nights*, Tahir Shah proposes his task to be "finding every memory, every fragment of recollection" (2009: 4), thus establishing his deep desire to trace the roots of his ancestry. These encounters, in fact, challenge him to question the stable nature of notions such as identity, nation, class, and gender. According to Bakhtin's theory, a text contains many different voices, and each of these voices has its perspective and validity without subordinating to the voice of the author. Similarly, *In Arabian Nights* contains many different voices of the storytellers of Morocco, and these voices contribute to the restoration of a devolving cultural memory of Morocco. The multitude of storytellers acts as a testimonial to the fact that they are the carriers of memory. For instance, when Murad, the storyteller, narrates the Tale of Mushkil Gusha, he remembers the moral he has learned from the tale "that the journey is nothing more than a path that leads to a destination" (111). From Idries Shah's stories, Tahir has also learned lessons of values like selflessness and the need to guide people to their paths. Thus, the author realises that his pursuit of the cultural identity of Morocco can help in revitalising his identity.

In Shah's search to dive deep into the cultural memorials of Morocco, the Café Mabrook becomes the "gateway into the clandestine world of Moroccan men" (Shah, 2009: 18) and he is asked to "root out the raconteurs" if he really wanted to get to know them (21). Events at home are interwoven with Shah's journeys across Morocco, and he perceives how the Kingdom of Morocco has a substratum of the oral tradition that has been almost unchanged for a thousand years. He also understands that it is a culture in which tales are a matrix through which values, ideas, and information are transmitted. Shah listens to anyone who has a tale to tell, and it is this curiosity that entitles him to be a good storyteller. He encounters professional storytellers, a junk merchant who sells his wares for no purpose but claims a high payment for the tale attached to each item, and a door-to-door salesman who can bring in anything. He compiles a treasury of stories rooted in *A Thousand and One Nights* as he travels through the labyrinthine medinas of Fez and Marrakech, the Sahara sands, and tastes the hospitality of ordinary Moroccans. These tales reveal fragments of cultural and collective memory and an oriental way of thinking.

Tahir Shah explains the origin of tales and their importance in the cultural memory thus: "stories are a communal currency of humanity. They follow the same patterns irrespective of where they are found" (Shah, 2009: 152). Stories can bridge cultural divides and promote understanding between different cultural groups. The writer's words reverberate the universality of stories from a humanitarian perspective. The beauty that attracts people across the world to Morocco is the art of storytelling. The culture of Morocco has flourished and developed through storytelling. To realise the beauty and importance of the culture of Morocco, one has to go through its rich tradition of storytelling. When Shah writesthe following, it is evident that he has assumed himself to be a participant in the cultural system of Morocco.

> In the south of Morocco people believe that there are streams running under the ground. [...] The streams don't run with water. [They run] With words. [...] The streams irrigate Morocco [...] like water on farmland, they have allowed the civilization to grow, to thrive. Why is Morocco what it is? Why does it mesmerize everyone who comes here, with its colours, with its atmosphere? [...] It's because of the streams.
> (2009: 382)

The tone of the author has now shifted from the gaze of a traveller to a familiar partaker in the cultural identity of the nation. Acculturation occurs with a continuous association with a foreign culture and its members, and it can apparently bring about changes in the beliefs, values, and conduct of the person. The journey of the author in search of his story culminates in his understanding of the role of storytelling as a cultural mnemonic tradition in the determination of its identity.

The author asserts the role of stories as a key, a catalyst, and a device to help humanity think constructively. The author states that "until their minds are stirred with stories, people are asleep" (Shah, 2009: 383). He also adds, "Stories are a way of melting ice ... turning it into water. They are like repackaging something – changing its form – so that the design of the sponge can accept it" (326). In *In Arabian Nights*, there are references to Shah's first book on Morocco, *The Caliph's House*, and to the stories from the collection

A Thousand and One Nights. Thus, the text, with its intertextual nature, is influenced by cultural and personal elements. When the author writes that stories are symbols and these symbols are around the people like a code, he is philosophising the aspect of storytelling in the lives of human beings. But he asserts that "the Oriental people can make sense of them, decipher them" (327).

His travel across Morocco acts as a symbol of the spiritual and cultural growth of his personality. Tahir Shah undergoes an identity transformation in his quest to unravel the mystery behind the art of storytelling. He is in search of his own alter ego and that makes up the story of his life. The recollection of the writer's torturous past in a Pakistani prison in between the narration of the pursuit of his own story reflects the conscious attempt to bring about an understanding of his identity. He is trying to rediscover his identity and the group identity to which his roots can be traced back. Shah's recollection of his family's first visits to Morocco and his father's insistence that traditional tales contain vastly undervalued resources are interspersed in his narrative. Shah's father has advised him to protect storytelling as it is a hereditary gift. As a father himself, Shah finally passes the baton on to his children.

Young Yun Kim has defined "adaptation as a fundamental life-sustaining and life-enhancing activity of humans [...] rooted in the self-organizing, self-regulating and integrative capacity in all living systems" (2001: 35). When a human being relocates to a new cultural surrounding, s/he attempts to establish a stable relationship with it. As "every cultural pattern and every single act of social behaviour involves communication in either explicit or implicit sense" (Sapir 78), communication plays a pivotal role in assisting someone in maintaining a mutual relationship with the host culture. The workings of stress, adaptation, and growth bring about an internal cultural transformation in the individual, and this transformation can be witnessed in the "functional fitness, psychological health and intercultural identity" (Kim 69). In Shah's attempts to acculturate with the new culture, he understands that tradition is the foundation of life in Morocco, where friendship, honour, pride, and heritage are highly valued. After describing his adventurous life in Morocco, the writer closes the narrative with the note that while adapting to an antique culture, compromises are inevitable, and the consequences are priceless. The final realisation of the narrator that they were accepted by Morocco, the guardians, and the Caliph's House marks the phase of growth. Thus, starting with a series of problems and challenges, and through compromises and communication, the narrator has finally reached a point of completeness.

Conclusion

According to Sturken, "Culture and individual memory are constantly produced through, and mediated by, the technologies of memory" (2008:

75). *The Caliph's House* and *In Arabian Nights* are documents that reflect the author's efforts to redefine and re-construct his identity along with the re-assertion of the cultural identity of Morocco. The places he travels in Morocco are described in relation to its present and the writer's present. There is an intricate connection between the cultural aspects of Morocco and the author's identity. These works not only provide a detailed presentation of Moroccan culture and folklore but also act as a testimony of the emergence of an intercultural identity of the author. Once adapted to a new culture, an internal transformation occurs in an individual; thereby, the original cultural identity will lose its dominance, and a new intercultural identity emerges. However, this intercultural identity is not based on belongingness but on a self-awareness of being a part of both the original and host cultures. The author's search for the story hidden in his heart is an example of the emergence of an intercultural identity. The new intercultural identity has increased the narrator's communication competence and has enabled him to maintain a dynamic relationship with the original and new cultures.

Consistent acts of remembering and recollecting stories and past incidents help in actualising both individual identity and cultural identity. Tahir Shah uses memory as a tool to re-affirm the cultural identity of Morocco, and in this process, he ascertains his personal and cultural identity as well. He has realised that the cultural identity of Morocco lies in the continuous use of cultural symbols like storytelling, language, architecture, and cultural practices. Moreover, he has negotiated with his past experiences to assert his identity.

Note

1 This article was first published in the journal *Sanglap*, Vol. 10, No. 1, December 2023. https://sanglap-journal.in/index.php/sanglap/article/view/252/424.

Works Cited

Assmann, Aleida. "The Dynamics of Cultural Memory between Remembering and Forgetting." *Cultural Memory Studies: An International and Interdisciplinary Handbook*, edited by Astrid Erll and Ansgar Nünning. Germany: De Gruyter, 2008, 97–108. Print.

Assmann, Jan, & Czaplicka, John. "Collective Memory and Cultural Identity". *New German Critique* 65 (1995): 125–133. Print.

Barua, Rima. "The Possibility of 'Counter Travel' in the Age of 'Belated Travelers': Tahir Shah as a Counter Traveler in *Sorcerer's Apprentice*". *DUJES* 28 (2020). DUJES. 140–154. Web. 29 October 2021.

Keightley, E. "Remembering Research: Memory and Methodology in the Social Sciences." *International Journal of Social Research Methodology* 13.1 (2010): 55–70. Print.

Kim, Young Yun. *Becoming Intercultural: An Integrative Theory of Communication and Cross-Cultural Adaptation*. New Delhi: Sage, 2001. Print.

Sapir, Edward. "Communication." *Encyclopedia of the Social Sciences* 4, edited by Edwin R. A. Seligman and Alvin Johnson. New York: Macmillan, 1937, 78–80. Print.

Sbiri, Kamal. "Border Crossing and Transculturation in Tahir Shah's The Caliph's House." *Open Cultural Studies* 4 (2020): 12–2. DeGruyter. Web. 09 December 2021.
Shah, Tahir. *In Arabian Nights*. New York: Bantam Books, 2009. Print.
Shah, Tahir. *The Caliph's House*. London: Transworld, 2007. Print.
Sturken, M. "Memory, Consumerism and Media: Reflections on the Emergence of the Field". *Memory Studies* 1.1 (2008): 73–78. Print.

3 Contextualising Memory Studies in Bedtime Stories

Understanding the Praxis of Formative Literary Frameworks

Rafid C.

Humans have evolved to seek patterns and establish general rules. The triumph of science, in its umbilical connection with the progress of civilisations, has inspired all disciplines to search for patterns and establish generally applicable rules. Literary studies is no exception. However, literature escapes the realm of general rules and concepts by enabling the perception of the singularity of things. According to Syed Sayeed's article "Being Seen Through Literature", literary reading focuses on the "extra-conceptual component in language" which "renders it unruly" (14). While literary studies have been (at least to an extent) fascinated by the general rules and patterns, literary reading focuses on the 'unruly' and singular dimension of perception. With the advent of interdisciplinary readings, the normative and rule-bound perceptions innate to sciences and social sciences are finding their way to literary studies as well. Certain aspects of memory studies will testify to this tendency. This leads to a tension between the unruly nature of literature and the rule-bound structures of interdisciplinary 'studies'. The chapter argues that this tension could be better explored in the context of bedtime stories. The chapter shows the formative nature of literary frameworks through the multiple retellings of the bedtime story "Red Riding Hood". Also, the chapter demonstrates how formative reading frameworks accommodate the understanding of literature as a singular 'event'. The following part explains what it means when I say 'formative frameworks' and 'event of literature'. After that, the chapter proceeds to the discussion of multiple retellings of "Red Riding Hood".

In the context of the chapter, 'Literary Studies' could widely include all the functions of different entities in literary studies departments. That is to say that 'Literary Studies' could be better understood as what literature departments do or perform. Literary Studies is conventionally understood as the discipline which informs or even 'instructs' the processes, modes, and forms of literature. From a historical perspective, the common understanding of Literary Studies involves the clash of different perspectives in critical theory. Andrew Goldstone and Ted Underwood talk about this: "The history of literary study is primarily remembered as a narrative of conflicting ideas.... Although scholars have complicated this simple history-of-ideas story in

DOI: 10.4324/9781003508564-5

recent decades with an emphasis on social and institutional struggle, generational conflict remains a central framework" (2014: 361). The dominance of critical theory in the Literary Studies departments has a crucial role in the portrayal of the discipline in terms of the conflict between ideas, scholars, and generations. However, isn't the history of Literary Studies also the history of the development in the history of literature as well? Or leaving the history question apart, what would be the nature of the relation between literature and Literary Studies?

On Practising *Poiein*

In a closer understanding, the relation between Literary Studies and literature is that of mutual interactions. By 'literature', I mean the acts of writing and reading literary works. Literary Studies on the other hand constitute the organised 'study' of literary works that happen primarily in literature departments. These two spheres are not mutually exclusive but interdependent. For example, the discussions in literature departments can influence the authors and their works. Subsequently, the works written by the same authors are studied in the departments resulting in a cycle of mutual influence. So the ideas discussed in literature departments shape and 'form' the authors' opinions and writings. And these authors' writings will in turn 'form' the discussions in the literature departments. To accommodate this mutual and cyclical 'forming', the critical frameworks in literature and Literary Studies should also be in a perpetually 'forming state'. Formative literary frameworks are capable of accommodating such mutual engagements between critical frameworks and literary works. For example, when a 'postcolonial critic' reads a novel, the critic's critical framework is 're-formed' by the act of reading. The idea of 'formative frameworks' could be elaborated with the concept of '*poiein*' proposed by Sthathis Gourgouris. *Poiein* is a 'practice transformed by its own process of formation'. As explained before, the practice of 'postcolonial reading' is transformed as the reading itself contests the imposition of categories and fixities. For example, as a reader I can have a 'fixed' notion of a 'postcolonial subject' as an individual belonging to the category of 'non-whites'. However, a novel that portrays the nuances of the post-colonial experiences can surprise me with the image of a white male protagonist undergoing the post-colonial experiences due to specific circumstances. Literature has the capability to unsettle the pre-given categories and fixed notions. Readers undergo such experiences of unsettling and reforming perpetually as they unravel new worlds and experiences within the literary work. Gourgouris sees this as a practice consisting of perpetual reworking: "Its working is a perpetual reworking, a thorough reworking, which would not spare even itself as an object of that work" (80). In the chapter, I have used the terms 'formative' and 're-formative' interchangeably. 'Re-formative' is used only to emphasise the perpetually 'formative' nature of the reading frameworks.

However, contemporary Literary Studies departments tend to organise critical frameworks into 'specialised departments' constituted by theorists who 'analyse' literary works. The surge in interdisciplinary interactions caused the birth of more specialised disciplines with hybrid methodologies. As Stathis Gourgouris argues, the "advent of interdisciplinarity" (76) resulted in the "excess of literary studies" (76). However, this excess and rigorous interdisciplinarity is "overstated and over estimated" (86) because literary studies have become "homeless at the core" (86). One reason for the 'homelessness' of literary studies is the failure to recognise the formative nature of reading frameworks. Towards the end of the chapter, we will address the problems and possibilities of interdisciplinary readings by taking the example of 'memory studies'.

Inherent to the notion of the 'formative reading frameworks' is the idea of the 'event of literature'. The chapter considers a particular understanding of a literary work as an event performed in the relation between the reader and the text. Derek Attridge presents this idea of a literary work 'coming into being' as an 'event': "we can't identify the work with any particular embodiment in a physical object.... The literary work comes into being only in the event of reading" (25). For Attridge, a 'text' could refer to any possible arrangement of words, but a 'work' is performed only in a reader's relation with the text. In this way, multiple readings of the same 'text' can perform plural 'works'. And at the same time, each reading is unique as it performs a singular work. For example, a Marxian critic can perform multiple readings of the same novel and each reading will be unique in its own way. Each reading modifies the notion of what constitutes a 'Marxian framework of reading', and gradually the plurality of readings modifies the idea of 'a/the Marxian framework'. In this manner, the understanding of literature as an event becomes foundational to formative reading frameworks. Bedtime stories would demonstrate the formative nature of literary works as they get 're-read' and 're-told' across time and cultures. Why the emphasis on bedtime stories? Unlike other forms of short stories, bedtime stories are frequently retold and 're-formed'. Similarly, critical frameworks about bedtime stories undergo perpetual 're-formation' as the stories contest all theoretical fixities and stagnancies.

'Retellings' in Need of Formative Frameworks

Even though the commonality among different bedtime stories across the world is striking, the modifications, additions, and deletions happening through the retelling of the stories are important. Usually, the claims for 'universality' and 'commonality' undermine the differences among the stories. As an important 'pre-sleep ritual' the stories were retold and 'reformed' frequently modifying the assumed temporal and spatial universality:

> The telling of bedtime stories to children has formed a pre-sleep ritual in cultures around the world, with the narrator usually being an adult,

> or, at times, an older sibling of the young listener. The source of such stories has ranged from mythology, fairy tales and popular folk tales, to the narrator's own creative imagination or even personal experiences. While such oral and written traditions have existed in extremely varied cultures, the themes of the stories have, interestingly, borne remarkable similarities.
>
> (Writer, 2018: 2)

Also, scholars across disciplines have emphasised the role of bedtime stories in shaping social perceptions as Shlomi Segall would even argue that bedtime stories are "intimate forms of parental partiality" (2011: 23).

The following section of the chapter looks at a bedtime story from James Finn Garner's book *Politically Correct Bedtime Stories: Modern Tales for Our Life and Times* (1995). A comparative reading of the story along with its other versions will reveal the plural possibilities of reading and retelling the bedtime stories. In the section, we will explain the plurality of readings by elaborating the nature of literary reading as an 'event'. The chapter considers the written versions of the story primarily and oral versions only if it is necessary. It is because reading and listening are two modes relating to the 'work', and intermixing the oral and written versions comes at the cost of undermining the subtle differences between those two modes. Following the comparative reading of the versions, the chapter looks at how the critical understanding of these stories evolves and re-forms. The politically correct retelling of the stories has indeed inspired the contemporary critical theory. Apart from the criticism of the stories. Instead of attempting a detailed introduction to respective theoretical frameworks, the chapter tries to show how the frameworks undergo the 're-formation' as they engage with bedtime stories.

Red Riding Hood and Critical Frameworks

James Finn Garner's work *Politically Correct Bedtime Stories: Modern Tales for Our Life and Times* is a satirical take on the contemporary tendency to impose political correctness over literary reading:

> Reviewers' reactions to the book suggest an interesting rhetorical point. All agreed on the appeal of the humor, but their analyses of the import of the satire differed. Some reviewers ... hailed the book as "a delightful and lucrative exercise in absurdist literature" and "a fresh breath of air and a well-deserved slap in the face for Hans Christian Andersen and the brothers Grimm." Labeling it "updated to account for modern political sensibilities,".... On the other hand, some praised Garner for producing "good political satire" and for "mak[ing] fun of current sensibilities by rewriting old fairy tales using seriously nonoffensive language." In short, the book's humor enabled diverse readings of its "meaning."
>
> (Gring-Pemble and Watson, 2003: 133)

Though Garner tried to offer a humorist's perspective about the imposition of 'political correctness' over literary works, the reception of Garner's collection varied considerably. Some reviewers even praised the work for producing stories that reflect the modern sensibilities of political correctness. Hence the chapter does not focus on Garner's intentions, and instead, our focus is on the insights provided by Garner's collections on the compatibility of literature with political correctness. Garner says why he wrote the stories:

> However much we might like to, we cannot blame the Brothers Grimm for their insensitivity to women's issues, minority cultures, and the environment. Likewise, in the self-righteous Copenhagen of Hans Christian Anderson, the inalienable rights of mermaids were hardly given a second thought.
>
> Today, we have the opportunity – and the obligation – to rethink these "classic" stories so they reflect more enlightened times.
>
> (Garner, 1995: 3)

As Garner argues in the introduction of the book, our more 'enlightened' time 'necessitates' politically correct versions of the stories. Garner's retelling is a part of the perpetual retelling process which accounts for the dynamic nature of reading frameworks. As each reader performs a singular version of work, each reteller articulates a unique version of the work. Though telling, writing, and reading are different modes of engaging with literary works, the 're-formative' nature of literary frameworks has a common effect on these modes. And even before 'our more enlightened times', the same stories evolved and retold differently according to respective cultural contexts. Importantly, the literary work never conforms to any particular theory but rejects all theoretical categories and fixities. Though the collection brings an appreciable change from the earlier versions of the stories, Garner's retelling, as an attempt to 'impose' political correctness over the stories, fails in its mission. Garner himself admits it in humility:

> If, through omission or commission, I have inadvertently displayed any sexist, racist, culturalist, nationalist, regionalist, ageist, lookist, ableist, sizeist, speciesist, intellectualist, socioeconomicist, ethnocentrist, phallocentrist, heteropatriarchalist, or other type of bias as yet unnamed, I apologize and encourage your suggestions for rectification.
>
> (1995: 4)

A reader, having a singular relation with the text, can still find politically incorrect instances in the work. According to the author's horizon of understanding, sanitisation from all the entities in the long list of 'isms' might constitute a politically correct retelling of the stories. But the reader has a different horizon and she engages with the work in a different way. That is to say that the reader and the author are constituted in different worlds.

And hence, by definition, the author's idea of political correctness is different from that of the reader. And two readers, despite belonging to the same 'modern and enlightened' times, can have totally different readings of the same story. The comparative reading of different retellings of the stories will help to elaborate the point.

The first story in Garner's collection is titled 'Little Red Riding Hood'. The book *Little Red Riding Hood: A Casebook,* edited by Alan Dundes, is a compilation of different versions of the story and respective criticisms. Dundes gives a brief introduction to the story:

> The story of a little girl who wears a red hood or cape and who carries a basket of food and drink to her grandmother is one of the most beloved and popular fairy tales ever reported. The girl, called "Te petit chaperon rouge" in French, "Rotkappehen" in German, and "Little Red Riding Hood" in English, invariably encounters a villainous wolf in European versions of the tale.
>
> (1989: ix)

The earliest known version of the story is from Charles Perrault's collection titled *Tales and Stories of the Past with Morals, Tales of Mother Goose* (1697). It was the first written translation of the orally transmitted versions of the story. Perrault introduced the red-coloured cap which was later criticised for its symbolic relevance. And Perrault gives the moral of the story towards the end and certain parts of the moral are more politically correct than Garner's version. And the addition of the story's moral was a key feature used by Perrault: "In short, although Perrault was no folklorist, he did address folktales in order to raise the morally worthy 'tales our forebears invented for their children' above the classic fables of the Ancients" (Perrault 183). And not only did Perrault argue for the value of those old women's tales "told daily to children by their nannies and grandmothers" (181–182), but he also offered the occasional folkloristic note (Da Silva 168).

In the part where the wolf eats the grandmother, Garner tries to sanitise the story from humanist and 'anti-animal' elements: "He burst into the house and ate Grandma, an entirely valid course of action for a carnivore such as himself" (1995: 6). While Garner puts the wolf into the category of carnivore and assumes human-eating as 'entirely valid' from the wolf's perspective, Perrault has a different solution. Perrault problematises such a general categorisation: "I say, Wolf, for all wolves / Are not of the same sort" (Dundes, 1989: 6). And Garner's tendency to generalise causes more troubles in the course of the narration. In the story, the woodcutterenters the home to save Red Riding Hood from the wolf and she asks: "'Bursting in here like a Neanderthal, trusting your weapon to do your thinking for you!' she exclaimed. 'Sexist! Speciesist! How dare you assume that womyn and wolves can't solve their own problems without a man's help!'" (9). Despite the good intentions to escape 'sexism' and 'speciesism', a reader can find the discrimination against Neanderthal problematic. Considering Neanderthals as thoughtless and blood-spilling creatures is a different form of 'speciesism'.[1] The point is that because of their formative nature, 'literary retellings' present themselves as perpetual misfits for the theoretical norms of correctness.

Another early version of the story appears in the book *Kinder- und Hausmdrchen* (1812) by Jacob Grimm and Wilhelm Grimm. The Grimm versions of the story and fairytales in general have an enormous importance in the western literary tradition. While highlighting the importance of the stories, Donald Haase quotes W.H. Auden: "In 1944 W.H. Auden decreed that Grimms' fairy tales are 'among the few indispensable, common-property books upon which Western culture can be founded.... It is hardly too much to say that these tales rank next to the Bible in importance'" (1993: 383). Instead of reproducing a single oral tale as such, the Grimm brothers collected different oral versions of the same story and combined them all to create a new story. As a result of this, the Grimm version of the story is more elaborate with a different ending. In the Perrault version of the story, the story ends when the wolf eats Red Riding Hood. However, the Grimm version introduces a huntsman who comes and saves Red Riding Hood and her grandmother. In the continuous formation of the story through multiple retellings, a 'reteller' might have faced the need to cheer up her listeners and add a new climax. And then, this climax along with the story evolved through different retellings. And yet it would be problematic to assume that the German peasant culture is reflected in the Grimm version because the retelling was not exclusively confined to the peasants. A direct source of the story mentioned in the collection is Marie Hassenpflug (1788–1856), whose background was partly French Huguenot. She was "hardly a peasant" (Dundes, 1989: 8). If we consider the story as continuously getting re-formed through multiple retellers, it would be impossible to find a specific element of the story as originating in a particular individual or culture. The Grimm brothers were inspired by nationalism and they "sought to document the existence of a body of authentic German traditions" (7). However as we saw in the case of "Red Riding Hood", many of the stories in their collection are influenced by other nations and cultures outside Germany. The plural and formative nature of the stories contest the imposition of any cultural or national categories. The chapter urges that Literary Studies should transcend any tendency to impose national, geographical, and cultural categories on literary works.

Paul Delarue is a folktale specialist who compiled the 35 oral versions of the tale in French. Some of his observations shed light on the dynamic evolution of the stories:

> And one discerns the error of those who have wished to find a symbolic sense in our tale, taking their departure from the name of the heroine with a red headdress in whom they perceive the dawn, the queen of May with her crown, and so on. Nor in most of the versions is the girl

> named; they begin simply: "une petite fille," "une petite," "la piteta," etc. (Dundes, 1989: 18)
>
> (18)

Symbolic reading has been a key tool in conducting the critical reading of texts in Literary Studies departments. However, as Delarue argues, it is problematic to generalise the symbolic reference. A specific reader, in a particular reading, can find the symbolic significance of 'red hat' fascinating. However, generalising that symbolism would mean fixing the meaning to one understanding. On the contrary, in the context of plurality, multiple readings can interpret and understand the symbol differently. A reteller, who is disinterested in 'red hat', can totally forget and omit it when she tells her version. This approach to the plurality of meanings would help Literary Studies departments to transcend the fixities of symbolic analysis.

Delarue's version of the story has an ending that is different from both the Grimms' version and Perrault's version. Here the girl tricks the wolf and finds a way back to her home: "the girl, perceiving that she is with a monster, pretends that she has to take care of one of nature's needs, lets herself be tied to a string, from which she frees herself when she is outside, in order to escape" (Dundes, 1989: 19). The girl does not depend on the woodcutter to escape. As we discussed in the beginning, Garner's politically correct version of the story also attributes certain independence to the girl: "Many people believed that the forest was a foreboding and dangerous place and never set foot in it. Red Riding Hood, however, was confident enough in her own budding sexuality that such obvious Freudian imaginery did not intimidate her" (1995: 5). Likewise, when the wood chopper comes to save the girl, she calls him a 'sexist' and claims that womyn[2] and wolves can solve their problems "without a man's help" (9). A reader of both Garner's and Delarue's versions can argue that Delarue's version is more politically correct because the independence of the girl is presented through her action, not just words. Arguing one version of the story is more politically correct than other versions would only mean that 'one version of the story seems more politically correct in a particular reading'.

Among other versions of the story, I will discuss the Chinese version before proceeding to the conclusion of the chapter. Unlike all other versions discussed here, the Chinese version is written by a sociologist as a result of elaborate data collection and analysis. Wolfram Eberhard conducted a field study in the Kuting section of the city of Taipei to collect data about four folktales. Among the four, "'Grandaunt Tiger,' was by far the most popular. Two hundred forty-one texts of 'Grandaunt Tiger' were collected" (Dundes, 1989: 21). The Chinese version, despite having multiple common elements, considerably differs from the European versions[3] of the story. Eberhard's role as a sociologist invariably reflects in his methods of collection and retelling:

> Not only was he concerned with the tale-teller, the audience, and the social context, but he also showed that the respective genders, ages, and

> family relationships of tale-tellers and audiences have a very marked influence on the transmission of a tale. (Cohen, 1990: 182)

So Eberhard's version takes notice of minute details and differences in the Chinese version when compared to other versions. The role of the wolf is played by a tiger in the Chinese version. Also the protagonist is not Red Riding Hood but a mother of two daughters. The tiger kills the mother and comes to her home to eat the two daughters. The rest of the story bears a remarkable resemblance to Delarue's version: the tiger disguises as the mother, the girl tries to escape saying urination as an excuse, the tiger ties her leg, and she tricks the tiger and escapes. The version is also rich with multiple cultural references. However, it is impossible to theorise the text using orientalism. Certain instances of the Chinese version could be read as gruesome and 'uncivilised'. For example, the tiger wants to tie the elder girl and prevent her from escaping. However, the tiger cannot find a rope and ties the girl with her sister's intestine. On the other hand, the girls ask the tiger many questions and figure out that the tiger is not their mother. The questions involve rigorous rationalisation of the tiger's voice, wrinkles of the hand, and patterns in the face. And a reader can argue that the Chinese version presents a more rationalised and civilised version of human beings. In short, the story confuses the theorist by challenging the fixed categories of East and West.

Fixed theories and categories constitute the rigidity of disciplinary frameworks in Literary Studies and related interdisciplinary domains. However, as we saw in the previous analysis, a work of literature embodied in the acts of reading and retelling is in a continuous state of formation. So as a framework that 'studies' literature, can Literary Studies and related 'interdisciplinary' domains adopt a 'formative framework' that is in sync with the nature of literature? In the following part of the chapter, we address this question by taking the example of 'memory studies'. Can memory studies adopt a *poiein* framework in its engagement with literary works? More specifically, in the context of the chapter, we are enquiring if memory studies can 'study' bedtime stories through a formative framework.

Contextualising Memory Studies in Bedtime Stories

Unlike other contemporary modes of literary expression, bedtime stories are inherently connected to our collective cultural memory. As primary tools of cultural transmission, tales told during bedtime, fireplace gatherings, or any other occasion play a crucial role in forming the cultural ethos of societies. Among other formats of storytelling, bedtime stories have sustained the modern times using new platforms and tools. So, for a memory studies student, bedtime stories carry the civilisational legacy of cultural transmission. However, given the formative nature of bedtime stories, two crucial questions need to be answered. First, is the idea of 'memory' in bedtime stories the same as the 'scientific forms' of memory such as history? Second, if the notion of 'memory' in the context of bedtime stories is different and unique, how does it change our understanding of 'memory studies'? Let us say that history involves the systematic study and validation of memories inscribed, recorded, or orally transmitted. Bedtime stories also embody recordings and recollections of memory. However, do we 'study' memory the same way in the domains of history and literature? If not, what is the 'job' of a memory studies student in the domain of literature? How is 'literary memory' different from other forms of memory? The following part of the chapter is trying to address these questions in the context of Pierre Nora's 'memory spaces' and David Berliner's 'abuse of memory'.

'Literary Memory: Space or Abuse?'

'Literary memory', as exemplified in bedtime stories, is different from other forms of memory because of the singular nature of literature. So a literary work does not embody memories the same way as a historical record preserves memories. Among the many qualities that contribute to the singularity of literature, we are focusing on the formative nature of literary works. Concerning the special nature of 'literary memory', Pierre Nora and David Berliner have different perspectives. For Berliner, when we start to validate all forms of memory including the literary forms, it becomes an 'abuse of memory'. And he criticises Pierre Nora for expanding the scope of memory to other domains: "Memory gradually becomes everything that is transmitted across generations, everything stored in culture" (Berliner, 2005: 203). This expansion of memory constitutes memory abuse and Berliner calls for more rigorous scrutiny to decide "what exactly memory is" (qtd in Berliner, 2005: 206). On the other hand, Pierre Nora asserts that strict methodological scrutiny and validation of memory reduces the 'sites of memory' to an "absence obsessed with objectivity" (Nora, 1989: 18). For Nora, history is by definition "suspicious of memory" and seeks to "suppress and destroy" it (9). Against the methodological scrutiny of history, Nora proposes the idea of the "sites of memory" (lieux de memoire) which compensates for the loss of the "environments of memory" (milieux de memoire). 'Environments of memory' would include many storytelling traditions and performances that became extinct with the emergence of modernity. However, few of those traditions managed to survive and adapt new forms as sites of memory. Bedtime stories constitute a prime example of such survived traditions which serve as memory sites.

However, what does it mean when we say bedtime stories are 'memory sites'? Can the Grimm brothers' version of "Red Riding Hood" be considered as a source to understand German history? As we mentioned earlier, the Grimm brothers have "sought to document" the body of "authentic German traditions" (Dundes, 1989: 7) through their collection of stories. But do the stories serve the function of a valid record of the past? If that is the case, Berliner's criticism becomes relevant when he says that "every little trace of the 'past in the present' is designated as memory" (206). He criticises Pierre Nora and Jan Assmann for being "the fathers of the memory craze among historians" (199) and hence responsible for the 'overextension of memory'. For a better understanding of this debate, let us put it in the context of bedtime stories.

What Do We Learn from Bedtime Stories?

Can we say that any reference to the past in the bedtime stories is invalid and hence an 'abuse of memory'? Or is it possible to see the stories as valid 'sites of memory'? Given the formative nature of literary works, we have already established that they transcend the objective scrutiny of theories and scientific principles. Hence it is impossible to 'validate' bedtime stories as authentic representations of our past. That is to say that the notion of 'validity' as prescribed by the (social) science methods cannot be 'applied' to the stories. In the same way as "Red Riding Hood" fails to be a pamphlet of political correctness, it fails to be a historical record as well. The principles and norms that govern the non-literary domains cannot be 'applied' to the domain of literature because of its formative nature. Practices of *poiein,* reading, and retelling will always, by definition, transcend the rules and theories. Hence, bedtime stories cannot do the archival function of a memory site. But it becomes an 'abuse of memory' only from the perspective of norms and theories to which the stories will always remain untenable.

When it comes to the question of discipline, 'memory studies' cannot 'study' bedtime stories as it studies historical and sociological records. The domain of literature is formative and unruly while the domain of 'studies' is often rule-bound. So the word 'study' refers to different activities in the context of these different fields. Hence any interdisciplinary engagement between literary studies and memory studies has to be mindful of this nuanced and yet radical difference between the methodologies. For literature, the 'methodology' is in a *poiein* state of perpetual self-transformation while for other disciplines, the scope of transformation is limited and rule-bound. So as students of memory studies, let us not reduce the stories to their cognitive content. But our 'job' is to let the bedtime stories amuse each of us singularly – thus providing a unique understanding of our past.

Notes

1 Anthropologists consider Neanderthal human as a distinct species within the genus 'Homo': Homo Neanderthalensis.
2 Womyn is a politically correct variety of the word 'women' used by some feminists. There are other varieties as well.
3 'European versions' does not mean that the stories have the quality of 'Europeanness'. In the chapter, the adjective 'European' only refers that those stories were identified as having the origin within the geographical boundaries of Europe. The same is the case with 'Chinese version'.

Works Cited

Attridge, Derek. *The Work of Literature*. Oxford University Press, 2015.

Berliner, David C. "The Abuses of Memory: Reflections on The Memory Boom in Anthropology." *Anthropological Quarterly*, vol. 78, no. 1, December 2005, pp. 197–211, https://doi.org/10.1353/anq.2005.0001. Accessed 20 September 2023.

Cohen, Alvin P. "In Memoriam: Wolfram Eberhard." *Central Asiatic Journal*, vol. 34, no. 1, 1990, pp. 177–186, https://www.jstor.org/stable/41927754. Accessed 17 November 2023.

Dundes, Alan. *Little Red Riding Hood: A Case Book*. University of Wisconsin, 1989.

Garner, James Finn. *Politically Correct Bedtime Stories: Modern Tales for Our Life and Times*. Macmillan, 1995.

Goldstone, Andrew, and Ted Underwood. "The Quiet Transformations of Literary Studies: What Thirteen Thousand Scholars Could Tell Us." *New Literary History*, vol. 45, no. 3, June 2014, pp. 359–384, https://doi.org/10.1353/nlh.2014.0025. Accessed 3 August 2023.

Gourgouris, Stathis. "The Poiein of Secular Criticism." *A Companion to Comparative Literature*, Wiley-Blackwell, West Sussex, pp. 75–87.

Gring-Pemble, Lisa, and Martha Solomon Watson. "The Rhetorical Limits of Satire: An Analysis of James Finn Garner's Politically Correct Bedtime Stories." *Quarterly Journal of Speech*, vol. 89, no. 2, January 2003, pp. 132–153, https://doi.org/10.1080/00335630308175. Accessed 4 August 2023.

Haase, Donald. "Yours, Mine or Ours? Perrault, the Brothers Grimm, and the Ownership of Fairy Tales." *Merveilles & Contes*, vol. 7, no. 2, December 1993, pp. 383–402, https://www.jstor.org/stable/41390373. Accessed 04 August 2023.

Nora, Pierre. "Between Memory and History: Les Lieux de Mémoire." *Representations*, vol. 26, Spring 1989, pp. 7–24, https://doi.org/10.2307/2928520. Accessed 19 September 2023.

Sayeed, Syed Abdul. "Being Seen Through Literature." *Academia.Edu*, 16 Apr. 2020, Accessed 18 June 2023.

Segall, Shlomi. "If You're a Luck Egalitarian, How Come You Read Bedtime Stories to Your Children?." *Critical Review of International Social and Political Philosophy*, vol. 14, no. 1, Jan. 2011, pp. 23–40, https://doi.org/10.1080/13698230.2010.518388. Accessed 25 September 2023.

Vaz da Silva, Francisco. "Charles Perrault and the Evolution of 'Little Red Riding Hood.'" *Marvels & Tales*, vol. 30, no. 2, 2016, pp. 167–190, https://doi.org/10.13110/marvelstales.30.2.0167. Accessed 7 September 2023.

Writer, Sharon. "The Bedtime Story: A New Chapter." *Indian Journal of Health and Wellbeing*, vol. 9, 2018, pp. 155–165, https://www.researchgate.net/publication/324506782_The_Bedtime_Story_A_New_Chapter. Accessed 18 November 2023.

Part II

Digital Technologies

A Powerful Medium of Memory

4 Remediating Karna

A Critique of the Canon and Caste

M. Subhasree

The Ramyana and the Mahabharata are two texts of paramount importance in the discourse of Indian culture and politics. As Barbara Stole Miller in her paper, "Contending Narratives—The Political Life of Indian Epics" states, the epic stories of both these texts have been fundamental "in the search for the commonality of the diverse groups that make up the Hindu majority of India" and "for drawing a vocabulary of Indian identity" (1991: 786). These humongous corpora of narratives also serve as the centre of many interpretations and imaginations that are reflected through myriad artforms, literature and rituals across India. Although these epics occupy the prime position in ordaining the culture of the nation, various debates on the authenticity of the events of the epics are an ongoing occurrence. Thus, the determination of whether these cultural texts are great epics of history or religious myths that are tools of mass instruction to endow values, is a question that is inescapable in the study of them. Keeping aside the true historical value of the epics/ myths, the most meaningful analysis would be the significance of the influence which the ethical value of these grand narratives have on the culture, therefore the masses.

These grand Indian narratives are quite distinct as firstly, they cannot be relegated to the rigid Western classifications of the genres of an epic or a myth. In her article, "The Mytho-epic Reimagination", Varsha Jha opines,

> Speaking of Indian epics, it is difficult to draw the line where the epic ends and where the myth begins. It is this interpenetration that makes them so susceptible to transmission and retellings. The magical and the mythical in the epics sustains them to a perpetual probing; while the epical in the myths "positions them in the contemporary world" to question its ideological relation to tropes of "nationalism, community, gender and identity".
>
> (2016: 189)

The blending of mythical and epic elements within grand narratives sparks various interpretations and explorations, showcasing their adaptability across different communication contexts. Therefore, from now on these narratives will be referred to with the hyphenated term epics-myths in this chapter.

DOI: 10.4324/9781003508564-7

Unlike other texts of antiquity that are contemporaneous to the epics-myths, the terms Panchamaveda (fifth Veda) and Adikavya (first greatest poem) are exclusive to the Mahabharata and the Ramayana respectively, owing to this multifaceted quality of their composition. The adaptability of these narratives has sparked countless ways of recalling and reinforcing them. This is amplified by a mnemonic process involving the careful selection of narratives, events and cultural artefacts, primarily by powerful institutions and agents, with the aim of preserving them for future generations—a process Aleida Assmann refers to as "canonization" (2010: 100). Grand cultural narratives, such as the Mahabharata, are then the products of this sanctification process that secures an everlasting place in the cultural memory of the community or the nation. The Mahabharata, as the Panchamaveda, is revered as a sacrosanct text which exudes 'messages' that are meant to enrich the values and morals of the societies, irrespective of their temporal or spatial demarcations. Therefore, the 'messages' or the 'dictum' of this sacrosanct text are deemed to transcend any forms of criticism, question or doubts.

It is also of immense importance to understand that the Mahabharata is not a 'canon' merely in the context of its literary richness or its religious value. There have been several artistic interpretations, representations and revisionings of the tales. This centrality of the epic-myth in every realm of communication and context clearly qualifies it as the 'lieu de memoire' or the 'site of memory', a term coined by Pierre Nora. Lieu de mémoire, he states, "is any significant entity, whether material or non-material in nature, which by dint of human will or the work of time has become a symbolic element of the memorial heritage of any community" (Nora, 1992: xvii).

The Mahabharata has attained the status of a lieu de mémoire, a powerful site of memory through "emphatic appreciation, repeated performance, and continued individual and public attention" (Assmann, 2010: 101) and is a source and part of several social, political and cultural discourses, each comprising their own agenda in influencing and altering the nation's cultural memory.

With its repetitive presentations, facilitated by many interpretations and reinventions across various media, time and contexts, the Mahabharata can be considered as a vast mnemonic hub, whose characters and narratives have evolved into cultural archetypes and mythical tropes. Jha states that, "although these archetypes are not a thing of history; their repetitive occurrence helps readers associate with the contemporary real-life situations" (2016: 188). Ultimately, these archetypes can be considered as the abstract representations of the situations of life that are intended to impart a 'lesson' or communicate a 'message'.

Among the popular cultural archetypes of Mahabharata, the one of Karna is of immense significance. Karna, the great warrior-hero, is known for his unwavering loyalty to Duryodhana, the 'adharmic' foil to the righteous Pandavas, and his tragic downfall credited to this affiliation. Born as a Kshatriya (warrior-class) and raised as a charioteer's son (oppressed class),

Karna is always recalled as the outcast character despite all his achievements as a warrior, king and as a loyal friend. The ostracisation of Karna, according to the grand epic-myth, is often linked to his befriending the immoral Duryodhana. At the least, this is the portrayal of Karna that popular media and culture have relayed across generations. Due to its status as a 'canon', any altercation against it would imply a threat to the current order of the society which is driven by the institutions that rely on certain values and systems of governance inspired from it.

The Mahabharata, as mentioned earlier, encompasses a long list of moral codes and value systems, of which caste is a primary aspect. Behind the popular cultural archetype of Karna as the tragic hero who is doomed because of his friendship with Duryodhana, its directives of caste must not be overlooked. John Wilson, in his book, "What Caste Is?", contends on the caste-centricity of the epic-myth as,

> In no work of classical literature of the Hindus, has so much been done by the interpolation and apocryphal additaments, to uphold caste as in the Mahabharata. That large work, with its numerous didactic episodes and interludes, is as a great stronghold of caste as any of the Indian law books to which, from its references to them, it is obvious that large portions of it are posterior. It may be characterised as the great fountain of Indian popular instruction. Its influence exceeds that of all the Puranas put together, though they themselves, to a considerable extent, harmonize with it.
>
> (1877: 277)

As a tool of mass instruction, the epic-myth creates an impression of a Greek tragedy through the Karna narrative, wherein the tragic hero Karna experiences the tragic fall due to his hamartia, which is often indicated to his friendship with the 'villainous' Duryodhana. However, if one were to traverse the life experiences of Karna, it can be noted that this epic hero's morbid state had begun much before the juncture of Duryodhana's alliance. The rigid system of caste withholds Karna from accomplishing his ambitions and receiving accolades for his incredible talent in archery. Disowned by his mother, who is ashamed to have borne a child through premarital conception, raised as a charioteer's son who had to face the perils of the caste system which was deemed natural and just by the institutions of power, Karna lived a life of struggles. The epic-myth's explanation of his disgraced state linked to Duryodhana, therefore, cannot be considered as the only tragic aspect that caused his downfall. Karna, even if not for his loyalty to Duryodhana, would still have led a life of the oppressed, filled with ordeals imposed by the caste system. Also, from the glimpses of his relationship with his biological mother Kunti in the epic-myth, it is quite doubtful if he would ever completely return to her, who had disowned him at his birth. Thus, it becomes evident that the status endowed on Karna, as an outcast hero of the epic-myth, is not merely because of his support to the adharmic (unjust) side of the war but predominantly due to the restrictions imposed by the caste system. It must also be noted that through the tragedy of Karna, the epic-myth focuses to impart a lesson, intended as a memoir to its consumers, who vicariously participate in the catastrophic consequences of befriending an immoral person. Similar to Augusto Boal's description of the coercive effect of Aristotle's tragedies on its spectators that states,

> the spectator has the great advantage of having erred only vicariously: he does not really pay for it. Finally, so that the spectator will keep in mind the terrible consequences of committing the error not just vicariously but in actuality, Aristotle demands that tragedy have a terrible end, which he calls catastrophe.
>
> (2013: 37)

Karna's great downfall, despite his good deeds, is thus magnified optimally, to achieve a strong remembrance of this lesson by posterity. But the adversities he faced because of the caste system does not form the centre of importance as the caste system is the law, the status quo of the period. The caste system, then, is only the 'milieu', the existing 'natural' social order of the epic-myth, which is beyond any interrogatory exercise. No matter how typical it is of Karna to have befriended Duryodhana, the only person who accepts him disregarding the caste restrictions, the epic-myth portrays that even this association is amoral as Duryodhana, despite his acceptance of Karna, is still a person of vice. This is the mass instruction that the Mahabharata canon aims to relay.

If the canon is the active, operative memory of a culture that becomes a lieu de memoire through constant repetitions and reinterpretations of those exclusive events of the historical or the mythical past, there is a vast body of cultural artefacts, events, monuments and narratives that do not qualify through this highly selective process of canonisation. These vast sources of memory that are cleared out of the spotlight form a huge repository and are called "archives" (Assmann, 2010: 102). The archival memory, also known as the reference memory, functions primarily to serve as a background for the canonical memory and they always belong to the institutions of power. They can be understood as the 'traces' that provide information to the gaps and ellipses found in the narratives of the canonical memory.

While the canon of the epic-myth portrays Karna as a tragic hero with his friendship with Duryodhana as his hamartia, there are many recontextualisations of this narrative, wherein the often sidelined or relatively less focused aspects of Karna are unearthed from the archives. These recontextualisations have probed into the outcast hero trope of Karna and have attempted to reconstruct the image of Karna as a generous, righteous warrior who met with his downfall unjustly.

There are many examples of such recontextualisations of the Karna narrative. Some popular ones include Kavita Kane's *Karna's Wife* (2014) which views the entire Mahabharata from the perspective of Uruvi, the wife of Karna who is among the lesser-known characters of the epic-myth. Even Chitra Divakaruni's *The Palace of Illusions* (2008), a retelling of the epic-myth from Draupadi's viewpoint, captures the untold characteristics of Karna, his unspoken love for Draupadi and his moral dilemma between Draupadi, the Pandavas and his friendship with Duryodhana.

Apart from literature, some television and filmic adaptations of the Karna story are also noteworthy. The popular television series, the *Mahabharat Katha* (Doordarshan, 1988) and *Mahabharat* (Star Network, 2013), in their attempts to digitise the grand epic-myth have, in the process highlighted the roundness of the character of Karna as a generous man, loyal friend and an able ruler. The series *Suryaputra Karn* (Sony Entertainment Television 2015) and the Chevalier Sivaji Ganesan starrer film *Karnan* (1964) have revisualised Karna as the protagonist and the hero of the epic-myth. A different reconstruction of the Karna story is director Mani Ratnam's film, *Thalapathy* (1991), wherein the mythological characters of the epic-myth are reprised in the modern-day context. The film focuses on the relationship dilemmas of Surya (played by Rajinikanth, the reprised version of the mythological Karna) with his mother Kalyani (played by Shrividhya, a modern equivalent to Kunti) and with his rogue friend Deva (played by Mammooty, the equivalent to the mythological Duryodhana). These reconstructions and recontextualisations helped in revealing the different contours of the mythic hero that were comparatively sidelined by the rigorous selection process of canonisation, which is focused on creating a certain cultural didactic.

These recontextualisations, as can be seen, are presented through different media. The different forms of media—literature, cinema, rituals, inscriptions, historical and political archives, and arts—act as the bridges between the past and the present, which in turn will determine the future. In fact, cultural memory relies on its transmission across centuries, only through these different media. Astrid Erll terms this medial quality of cultural memory as "remediation" and elucidates,

> With the term "remediation" I refer to the fact that memorable events are usually represented again and again, over decades and centuries, in different media: in newspaper articles, photography, diaries, historiography, novels, films, etc. What is known about a war, a revolution, or any other event which has been turned into a site of memory, therefore, seems to refer not so much to what one might cautiously call the "actual events," but instead to a canon of existent medial constructions, to the narratives and images circulating in a media culture. Remembered events are transmedial phenomena, that is, their representation is not tied to one specific medium. Therefore, they can be represented across the spectrum of available media. And this is precisely what creates a powerful site of memory.
>
> (2010: 392)

It is this process of remediation that had been the cause of the texts like Mahabharata to evolve into a 'lieu de memoire', a powerful site of memory. The reenactments, repetitive discourses, debates and performances have resulted in stabilising the canon of the Mahabharata as the Panchamaveda (the fifth Veda) and as a supremely important cultural artefact of the Indian cultural ethos.

The remediation of any memory site is also based on the circulation of the pre-existing media and their representations that models the future remediations, a process Astrid Erll terms as "premediation" (2010: 392). In the context of Mahabharata's Karna narrative, the aforementioned literary works, television series and films are themselves the products of the premediation processes of each other and their precedents. Thus, it is evident that premediation and remediation processes are cyclical and they continuously contribute in meaning production and modification of the sites of memory they are drawn from.

While the remediated versions of the epic hero Karna mentioned earlier in this chapter portray the unspoken, often less emphasised qualities of him, they never attempt to completely reimagine him, by estranging him from his mythical context. It could be said that Mani Ratnam's *Thalapathy* (1991) is by far the closest recontextualisation present in this matter of concern, that renders a modern but still a mythological saga of the well-known characters of the epic. These recontextualisations are the renditions of the hidden troves of the Mahabharata archives which are less explored, now brought to the forefront. So, they serve their purpose only within the framework of the Mahabharata.

Yet there are also many different forms of adaptation, reimaginings of the mythical narratives, tropes and characters that are repurposed to narrativise different experiences, initiate political discussions and thereby question the power of the canon. Some of the popular examples of these reimaginings include Mahashweta Devi's *Dopdi* (1978), a highly political retelling of the struggles of the tribal community and the brutality of the repressive government against them, narrated by the tribal woman Dopdi (a colloquial modification of Draupadi) who is victimised by the corrupt police force. Another example of such a reimagining is Sujatha Bhatt's poem, *What Happened to the Elephant?,* which raises the question of environmental conservation and criticises the institution of religion and the history of brutality and bloodshed behind its politics through the mythical tale of the birth of Ganesha, the elephant-headed god of the Hindu pantheon. In a similar approach, within the Karna narratives, the reimagined version of Mari Selvaraj's film *Karnan* (2021) is of immense importance.

Except for the names of its characters, the film *Karnan* does not in any means attempt to establish an association with the popular Mahabharata canon. Instead, it aims to utilise this popular cultural site of memory to modify and suit its agenda of questioning the caste discrimination prevalent in the society. The character Karnan (played by Dhanush) is determinedly different from the mythical Karna, except for the name. While the mythical Karna is shown to be a generous, sacrificial war-hero and a loyal friend who does not fight against the caste system in the hands of which he led a dismal life of discrimination, Mari Selvaraj's Karnan is unapologetically rebellious of the existing caste bias. His Karnan does not succumb to the fate of discrimination like the mythical Karna but transforms into a guardian of the village, educating and mobilising his people to retaliate against the repressive system and its agents.

Mari Selvaraj, through his Karnan, intends to challenge the cultural notion that the highly regarded names of the mythological characters are reserved only for the dominant caste groups. Apart from the protagonist Karnan, many of the film's characters are named after the heroes and heroines of the epic-myth, like Draupadai/Draupadi and Duryodhanan who are, unlike the mythological version, common people struggling to safeguard and establish their rights and identity from the perpetrators of caste hierarchy. In a manner similar to Gayatri Spivak's description of the marginalised tribal woman Dopdi of the Mahashweta Devi's short story as both a palimpsest and a contradiction (388), the mythological nomenclature of the characters of the movie *Karnan* (2021) serves as both an evocation of the mythical, cultural memory and also as a deliberate challenge to the expected norms of the caste hierarchy. Most certainly, this is a result of the remediation of the Mahabharata but also a critique of it and vice versa. Through the massively internalised medial constructions of the Mahabharata which are cultural memory now, the director externalises his political ideology through his craft and thus constitutes to a new meaning production that, in turn, integrates into the highly evolving symbolic vortex of the lieu de memoire, the Mahabharata.

The deconstructive critique of the canonical memory of the Karna trope intensifies in almost every frame of the film. The introductory scenes show Karna anointed by the community (notedly, not by any godman or a saint) for a fish slaying competition that shadows the episode of Draupadi's 'swayamvar' of the epic-myth. While the mythical Karna faces embarrassment and disdain from a society built on the hierarchy of caste, Mari Selvaraj's Karnan is a celebrated hero of the village in a similar contest. In this reimagining, the fish slaying event is not a marital contest but is conjoined with the pride of the village. In addition, the symbols of the sword and the horse, which are often considered as the birthright of the warrior-class, Kshatriya heroes like the mythical Karna and his colleague of warriors, the reimagined Karnan wields the sword and rides the horse as efficiently as his mythical counterpart would. In fact, the director also subverts the horse-riding warrior trope as he interposes the stereotypes of the 'warrior's horse' with the 'labourer's donkey' as Karnan owns both animals and considers them equally. This reconstructs the warrior archetype of the Sanskrit heroes of the epic-myths, as here, the hero is both a worker and a warrior, thus debunking the 'varna' ideologies that the canon of the epic-myth embodies.

The film also subverts the friction between the good and the bad through its sensational characterisation. While Karnan and the community are designated the names of the warriors from the epic-myth, the representative of state-orchestrated repression, the villainous police officer of the film is referred as 'Kannabiraan', a Tamil equivalent of the name 'Krishna', the revered divine incarnate of the epic-myth. It is this riveting attribution of mythological names that materialises the ideological caste bias into a brutal physical war between the community and the police force in the film, simply because Kannabiraan is unable to digest the designation of heroic names to, as what he considers, a community that is of a lower caste. With this the film simultaneously censures the trickster role played by Krishna in the epic for the occurrence of the great Kurukshetra war and, at the same time, condemns the present-day violations executed on the oppressed communities by the agents of power like Kannabiraan in the film.

The plot of *Karnan* (2021) is also loosely built on the sensational Kodiyankulam (1992) incident in Thoothukudi district, Tamil Nadu. This memory of the clash between the dominant and the oppressed castes and the horrors committed by the police force against the oppressed, instead of safeguarding them, is invoked by the director of *Karnan* (2021) through the nuanced utilisation of the cultural memory archetypes of the Mahabharata. This is, then, a double remediation that reinforces the remembrance of not only the manipulation of the caste didact of the canonical Mahabharata, but also of an event from a comparatively recent past. The Kodiyankulam incident stands as a testimony to the prolonged discriminatory practices of the caste system, the primal cause of which can be traced to the systematic remembrances of the 'messages' imparted by the canon, sponsored by the institutions of influence.

In conclusion, one can discern that the canon, the working memory of a culture, becomes a powerful site of memory through constant repetitions, continued inspiration, discussions and the resulting discourses, in short, through the remediation process. What is known about the great epic-myth Mahabharata and the reason for its canonisation is only through the medial constructions of the knowledge from the past. The mythical corpus of the Mahabharata, whose signs and symbols are repurposed to suit various meaning-making contexts across different media, are thus the products of a pre-existing, premediated cultural narrative. Roland Barthes articulates about this quality of mythical speech as follows:

> Mythical speech is made of a material which has already been worked on so as to make it suitable for communication: it is because all the materials of myth (whether pictorial or written) presuppose a signifying consciousness, that one can reason about them while discounting their substance.
> (Barthes and Lavers, 1972: 89)

It is then evident that the repurposing of the epic characters by Mari Selvaraj in his movie *Karnan* (2021) is a convenient way to capture the attention of the masses, through the archetypes and motifs of the familiar mythical speech, the Mahabharata, that is strongly etched in the cultural memory. These images, archetypes and motifs with their pre-assigned meanings that are easily relatable to the masses create a strong impact when extracted from their mythological framework and positioned in a different, contemporary milieu. It can then be concluded that the remediation of the Karna archetype is not completely alienated from its mythical world while also in its filmic context subverts the caste biases that are embedded in its mythological characterisation. Thus, the movie *Karnan* (2021) can be considered as a dialogue between the mythical and the cinematic versions of the character, the contexts and their respective media of propagation. These dialogic associations that are construed between the present and the past media by remediation enable in understanding and reinventing the elements of cultural memory.

It must also be noted that, even in the process of remediation of these powerful sites of memory, that can modify their meanings by placing them in different medial, socio-cultural contexts, the sites of memory do not degenerate into a cultural oblivion. As Astrid Erll states, "paradoxically, even despite antagonistic and reflexive forms of representation, remediation tends to solidify cultural memory, creating and stabilizing certain narratives and icons of the past" (2010: 393). It can be noted that even to retaliate the overarching dominance of the canon, the canon has to be referred to. So, the modern-day reimaginings of Karna as a flagbearer of anti-casteist society, aiming to dismantle the ideas of caste hierarchy embedded in the canon, actually build more layers into the huge symbolic corpus of the mythical narrative, now, with a more diversified but strengthened cultural rememberings.

However, these remediations must not be undervalued, as through the lenses of the different media, in different contexts, the events of the mythical or historical past are reconstructed and it is this reconstruction that forms the basis of 'what we already know', the popular idea and 'what we need to know', the repressed notions, that are deemed unfit for the political and/or cultural agenda of the power systems. For it is these reinventions that audaciously probe into the metanarratives of the culture and discern the course it must proceed on.

Works Cited

Assmann, Aleida. "Canon and Archive." *Cultural Memory Studies: An International and Interdisciplinary Handbook*, edited by Astrid Erll, Ansgar Nünning, and Walter de Gruyter, 2010, pp.100–101.

Barthes, Roland, and Annette Lavers. *Mythologies*. Vintage, 1972, p. 89.

Boal, Augusto. "How Aristotle's Coecive System of Tragedy Functions." *Theatre of the Oppressed*, Theatre Communications Group, 2013. ProQuest Ebook Central, http://ebookcentral.proquest.com/lib/amherst/detail.action?docID=1394257. Accessed 23 Jan. 2024.

Erll, Astrid. "Media and Cultural Memory: Literature, Film, and the Mediality of Cultural Memory." *Cultural Memory Studies: An International and*

Interdisciplinary Handbook, edited by Astrid Erll, Ansgar Nünning, and Walter de Gruyter, 2010, pp. 392–393.
Jha, Varsha. "The Mytho-Epic Re-Imagination." *Indian Literature*, vol. 60, no. 6, 2016, pp. 188–189, http://www.jstor.org/stable/44754735. Accessed 19 Jan. 2024.
Miller, Barbara Stoler. "Presidential Address: Contending Narratives--The Political Life of the Indian Epics." *The Journal of Asian Studies*, vol. 50, no. 4, 1991, pp. 783–792, https://doi.org/10.2307/2058541. Accessed 6 Mar. 2024.
Nora, Pierre. "Preface to the English- Language Edition-From Lieux de Memoire to Realms of Memory." *Realms of Memory: The Constructions of the French Past*, translated by Arthur, edited by Lawrence D. Kritzman Goldhammer, 1992, vol. I, Columbia University Press, 1996, pp. xvii.
Spivak, Gayatri. "'Translator's Foreword.' *Draupadi* by Mahashweta Devi. 'Writing and Sexual Difference'." *Critical Inquiry*, vol. 8, no. 2, Winter 1981, p. 388, https://warwick.ac.uk/fac/arts/english/currentstudents/postgraduate/masters/modules/femlit/gayatri_spivak_-_draupadi_by_mahasveta_devi. pdf Accessed 22 Jan. 2023
Wilson, John. "Caste in Indian Epics-The Ramayana and the Mahabharata." *Indian Caste*, vol. 1, What Caste Is? Times of India Office, Bombay, 1877, p. 277.

5 Ways of Remembering

A Study on the Use of Collective Memory in *Stranger Things* and *Miss Marvel*

Athira Manoharan and Aiswarya S. Babu

Stories that codify themselves into global, national, or regional history with the abutment of objective shreds of evidence cannot be appraised independently of the subjective whims of their creators, who may often occupy the loftiest positions of a hegemonic order. Contrary to the documented history is the collective memory, which is defined as

> the distribution throughout society of what individuals know, believe and feel about the past, how they judge the past morally, how closely they identify with it, and how much they are inspired by it as a model for their conduct and identity.
>
> (Schwartz, 2016: 12)

Ann Rigney in her essay "Cultural Memory Studies" notes, "Cultural artefacts, forms, and practices do not just provide a conduit for expressing already existing memories, as many studies have shown. They also play an active role in shaping what is to be remembered and how" (2016: 65).

The function of culture, as described by Rigney, is achieved through multiple apparatuses of hegemony that have the power to mould collective memory, which is consequently forged into an omniscient configuration through commemoration; a form of informal documentation in the form of songs, icons, eulogies, or monuments from the past, working in collaboration with the production of history (Schwarts 2016: 11). The term 'popular culture' is used in opposition to 'high culture' and is defined by John Storey as "culture that is widely favoured or well-liked by many people" (2018: 5). The term eludes definite characteristics in its productions as it is governed by spatio-temporal peculiarities.

Paul Grainge enumerates the potency of the motion picture as a new medium of commemoration when he comments that, "as a technology able to picture and embody the temporality of the past, cinema has become central to the mediation of memory in modern cultural life" (2003: 1). As a commemorative cultural artefact, cinema can also actively engage in the retention, deconstruction, and reconstruction of collective memory through the processes of keying and framing put forward by Barry Schwartz. In his essay "Rethinking the Concept of Collective Memory" Schwartz writes

DOI: 10.4324/9781003508564-8

that "keying makes this connection by aligning current events with happenings in the past, and by activating 'frames' that shape the meaning of these current events" (2016: 15). The frame of memory thus formed serves dual purposes within the community in question. They act both as a model of society by reflecting its ambitions, insecurities, needs, and amusements, and as a model for society by acting as a template into which members of a community melt their thoughts, sentiments, morality, and conduct. Thus, some events or perceptions are selectively remembered to accentuate and justify certain ideologies and prejudices of contemporary times. Popular cultural entertainment tends to pantomime hegemonic conditions by segregating memories worth remembering and not. The chapter seeks to explore the commemorative elements in the web series *Miss Marvel* and *Stranger Things* streamed on over-the-top platforms Disney+ Hotstar and Netflix, respectively, to study their repercussions in constructing and reconstructing collective memory.

Both *Miss Marvel* and *Stranger Things* are American science fiction drama television series that embody the postulations of commercial Hollywood production. Hollywood as a film industry has overshadowed every other film industry and diverse experience by imposing a singular American experience on every other fringe of imagination and endurance. Hollywood is often criticized for "tending to show the different groups as assimilated to the dominant white Anglo-Saxon Protestant (WASP) culture and values, or to promote such assimilation more or less explicitly" (Cortes 2013: 1492). Hollywood then acts as a cultural melting pot which promotes the singular American experience. Stereotypical images of early Hollywood films include,

> Irishmen are depicted as quick-tempered troublemakers and heavy drinkers ... Irish men were policemen, firefighters, or boxers, while Irish women were generally servants and washerwomen. Chinese people were depicted as mysteriously entranced in closed groups and devoted to underworld trades ... Jews were seen as greedy "penny pinchers," as depicted in *Levinsky's Holiday* (1913). During World War I, for propaganda reasons, Germans were portrayed as insensitive Huns capable of any atrocious crime.
>
> (Cortes 2013: 1492)

The extension of the market and the subsequent necessity of inclusivity demanded the deconstruction of some of these stereotypes. *Miss Marvel*, directed by Bisha Ali and produced by Marvel Cinematic Universe (MCU), engages to offer a deconstructive lens. Marvel has published superhero comics since 1961, but it was the 2008 *Iron Man* movie that brought Marvel heroes to the global audience. William Peitz relates the rise of superheroes and their relations with American ideals in his essay "Captain America: The Epitome of American Values and Identity." He notes that,

> The United States' entry into World War II gave superheroes a whole new set of enemies initiated a big push for patriotic superheroes, and supplied a complete working rationale and worldview for a super-patriotic superhero such as Captain America who epitomized American values during World War II.
>
> (2013: 8)

The story of the American-Muslim teenager Kamala Khan is an addition to this line of superheroes. Ali had to make a tremendous effort to conceptualize the first non-stereotypically depicted Muslim superhero of the MCU, whose "gender and race are foundationally incorporated into her narrative and experience as an American teenager, Muslim, and superhero" (Chung 2019: 3).

The web series *Miss Marvel* (2022) features the third alter ego of the 'Miss Marvel' superhero identity, Kamala Khan. Sixteen-year-old Kamala is introduced as an aspiring artist, an anonymous YouTuber, and an ardent fan of the Avengers, particularly Captain Marvel (Danvers). Iman Vellani, the star of the series who plays Kamala, says *Miss Marvel* "wasn't a story about a Muslim girl, it was about an Avengers-obsessed, fan-fic-writing nerd who just happened to be this Muslim girl" (Wittmer, 2022). Her opinion is substantiated by the mise-en-scène of Kamala's room which reflects her flamboyant American teenage character. The room is interestingly devoid of Pakistani elements, except of Kamala's ethnicity, which also makes her stand out from the rest of the family members. Nobel Laureate Malala Yousafzai's opinion that the series reflects the lives of Pakistani immigrant families (2022 Bureau) resonates with the transnational comic researcher Chung's observation that

> readers are introduced to Kamala as an ordinary teenager who is trying to figure out where she belongs. Because her identity is not framed as a spectacle, Kamala is not demonized or othered. Kamala Khan's story of growing up is relatable to vast audiences.
>
> (Chung 2019: 9)

Ali has made use of immersive narrative techniques to activate the Schwartzian 'frames' of collective memory which made the series relatable. Laura Karpman's music incorporates hip-hop, contemporary beats, and tabla beats to supplement the teen vigour while South Asian music accentuates the complicated diasporic position. It does not follow the conventional ethnic music that calls out 'Muslim' but rather reflects the nuances of the protagonist's thoughts as a misfit teenager and a superhero. When the plot of the story takes the prime protagonist to her homeland, whether in her fantasies or reality, it is accompanied by the rich flavours of South Asian music and instruments. While the contemporary American pop music that dominates the soundtrack of *Miss Marvel* contributes to the popularity of the series, the growing space occupied by South Asian music activates the frames of collective memory among the diasporic community.

The first episode of the series commences with a comic action video of the culmination battle of the *Avengers: The Endgame,* created by Kamala, establishing her artistic inclinations Art is another common ground that Ali has used to bring in different cultural frames. Kamala inherited her artistic virtuosity from her grandmother, Sana through her mother Muneeba.

Kamala's art complements her "cosmic head-in-the-cloud" (2022 Generation 00:05:50) personality which is assimilated into the WASP culture. She doodles all day, and flying superhero graffities follow her around in her fantasies and illustrate her battle plans. Her art resembles the calibre of superhero comic books and is unreservedly dissociated from her diasporic identity. Sana, on the other hand, premeditatedly uses art as a medium of conservation. She believes her paintings help her hold on to the past and has even recreated moments from her memory, including a painting of her mother Ayisha whom she lost during the partition. Sana's collection resonates with Ayisha's affirmation that "we can take memories with us" (2022 Time and Again 24:52) while leaving India during the partition. Sana has a collection of things from her homeland, India, that she was able to salvage through the partition. Her room is an informal, personal museum and it is where Kamala finds her identity as a Pakistani American-Muslim teenage girl with superpowers (Seeing Red 2022)

Muneeba is not explicitly depicted as an artist in the series, but it is she who fashions out the superhero outfit for Kamala. Inspired by a traditional Pakistani female apparel called the 'salwar kameez,' it carries around the heritage of her community along with her superhero in cognition. While Kamala and Sana, separated by a generation, engage in depicting the American and the Indian, through their art, the mediating Muneeba integrates both to form a hybrid culture which she embraces.

While Yusuf as the hardworking American asylum seeker prospering in the United States is a true testimony of the 'American Dream,' Muneeba's quest is realized through her discovery of the mosque and related community in her new world. Kamala, on the other hand, has integrated both her roots and her assimilated identity. The inevitable trip to the past as well as homeland expedites this integration which provides her strength to triumph through the problems of the present. It also coheres with the American trope of tracing the genes and realizing one's identity, facilitating the affirmation of the hyphenated identity that enables one to march forward, assimilating with the American whole to realize the American dream. The explicit connection made to the South Asian metaphysical idea of 'djinn' and the discovery of the ancestral bangle among Buddhist ruins rationalize Sana's explanation of magic in Kamala's genes. However, the realization of the magic requires a 'land' that can accommodate it, the lack of which made Ayisha undesirable. While Kamala is special due to the magic in her genes, she is a superhero as she is in the 'right place,' the United States. Each member of the diasporic family accomplishes their American dream and makes their existence richer and fuller.

Birds'-eye shots of culturally significant events are used by Ali to activate cultural frames of collective memory. The first season of the series accommodates three such events. The first two are euphoric celebrations of Eid and a grand wedding ceremony. Both these celebrations activate the frames of contemporary cultural memory while the third cultural event, the partition of India, activates frames of post-memory. The series directs Kamala's story right into the chaos of partition through the introduction of Ayisha. Kamala is transported to the railway station where Sana and her father, Hassan, attempt to board the last train to Karachi. She climbs up a train, delivering the viewers with an 'overhead shot' of the partition. In the ensuing episode, Kamala actively participates in it to save the infant Sana from being lost. The scenes are either middle shots or close-ups, immersing Kamala in the event. In her first transposition, Kamala takes up a position that is distanced from her cultural trauma, the partition of India and Pakistan, and the second time, she integrates into it.

The conversation between Kamran and Kamala, in which movies of Shah Rukh Khan are discussed, is as much Indian as it is Pakistani. Bollywood becomes a convergence point in the collective memory of these sibling nations. The use and recreation of classic Hollywood movements are also evident in the series. The sequence in the final episode where Kamala is supported and accepted by the public while defending Kamran mirrors a similar sequence in MCU's *Spider-Man 2* when the teenage superhero stops a train. The final episode of the series brings together friends and foes into the framework of the *Home Alone* trap references against a greater evil, racial prejudice. The series has thus, employing popular culture references, music, and art, carefully amalgamated American and South Asian cultural memories, to tap into both sections of possible spectators.

Clandenstines, the supernatural beings from an alternative dimension, are associated with Djinns, the enormously powerful magical beings of the *Arabian Nights* and with considerable significance in Islamic legends. This association is astutely connected with the colour purple which evokes a close reference to the Genie who appears in Disney's *Aladdin*. Kamala's superhero costume is red and blue, and her wardrobe is dominated by purple chrome. The colour of her costume orients with the colour of her eyes and the colour of pulsating energy emanating from her as she gains cosmic powers. Kamala inadvertently becomes the Genie of the Marvel Cinematic Universe and reaffirms her Islamic origins.

The framework within the collective memory is constructed by exploiting the elements of collective memory, which are compactly arranged throughout the series as aforementioned. The nuances of the plotline are conveyed through immersive storytelling techniques. According to Adrienne Resha, the live-action adaptation of the *Miss Marvel* comic satisfies the four criteria of environmental storytelling as elaborated by Henry Jenkins (Resha 2022).

She points out that "the show enables immersion not just in Kamala Khan's world but also in her story through its environmental storytelling" (Resha 2022).

The story unfolds largely through first-person shots which helps the viewer identify with the prime protagonist, Kamala. *Miss Marvel* engages actively with the menacing issue of Islamophobia. Agent Deever from the Department of Damage Control is the personification of prejudices against the Muslim community and is visibly shaken by the confusing identity of the new non-white superhero. The characterization of Bruno Carrelli is in stark contrast to that of Deever. The integration of Bruno into the cultural specificities of Pakistani celebrations and his genuine interest in it is both a deconstruction of South Asian culture as alien and the white man's interest in other cultures and his acceptance of it.

The white teenager is the voice of reason, civilizing the riskier tendencies of the brown girl, Kamala. He also provides her with intelligence and equipment, establishing the trope that the brown girl can save the world, but not without the help of the white American brain and it acting as the civilizing voice of reason to manoeuvre her power the right way. The group of brown Clandenstines, who are presented as friends turned foes, are in dearth of such a civilizing voice and are subjected to coercive submission. Kamran is then presented as a redeemable yet wayward other to Kamala's superhero self. It is the combined effort of the assimilated superhero that shows the possibility of second chances to him. *Miss Marvel* is thus reiterating and reinstalling the American dream on the othered South Asian antagonist.

The series employs certain cinematographic techniques like over-the-shoulder shots, jump cuts, and montages to construct the world of Kamala. The first episode of the series shows Kamala in her handmade Captain Marvel outfit, uneasily inspecting her reflection in the mirror with a poster of Carol Danvers in the background. The last episode parallels the shot with a confident Kamala, in her superhero outfit. Together, the two shots narrate her growth from a self-conscious teenager to a young adult superhero by accepting her diasporic identity.

By instigating the origin and growth of a superhero from a globally mistrusted community, MCU deconstructs the cynical consciousness that evolved through the collective memory of terrorism perpetrated by Muslim extremist groups. The first and third *Iron Man* movies are founded on the American stand against terrorism, with Tony Stark representing a patriotic American. In his essay "With Great Power Comes Great Responsibility: Cold War Culture and the Birth of Marvel Comics," Robert Genter relates the evolution of superhero comics such as *The Fantastic Four*, *The Incredible Hulk*, *Iron Man*, and *The Amazing Spider-Man* with the immediate necessities of Cold War culture in America (Genter 2007) After 9/11, America's communist peril was replaced by the defensive stand against Islamic terrorist groups (Gerges 2003: 79). MCU reflects American policies as it condemns Islamic terrorist organizations in some of its movies and has spoken out against the othering of the Muslim community in other movies. While America is forced to act like a secular agency of world peace, it has to hide its mistrust towards everything other than white and American, behind a red-blue shield of diplomacy. MCU, being the biggest advocate of American policies, follows the same suit to obtain audiences from all over the world.

It is not just the superheroes that use memories to instal themselves in the hearts of their viewers. The recent Netflix series *Stranger Things* unabashedly rose to the top of the most popular series on the platform by manipulating and building on the cultural memory of the American population (2023 Stranger Things Wiki). Written and directed by the Duffer brothers, the series is not only about forces of good and evil but also about the geek culture of the 1980s. *Stranger Things* pilots its viewer through a nostalgic journey with science and is permeated with references to Spielberg, Carpenter, Cronenberg, and Hughes classics, melted into the pop hits of the 1980s. According to Kyla McCarthy:

> The 2016 Netflix series *Stranger Things* exemplifies this consumerist convergence through its use of consumer artifacts from the 1980s, which help define the show as geek metafiction and also facilitate nostalgia for a specific brand of mediated past. If *Stranger Things* and its popular media contemporaries indeed recall 1980s geek culture through consumer goods, then they also reveal how American consumerism shapes individual identities and collective memory.
>
> (McCarthy 2019: 664)

The series is set in Hawkins, an imaginary town in Indiana that facilitates a commodious space for the creation of Schwartzian frames which can be broadly divided into two, the conspiracy theories on human experimentation and American hatred towards the Soviet Union which characterize the Cold War paranoia of the 1980s. The plot revolves around a group of teenagers, Michael and Nancy Wheeler, Dustin Henderson, Lucas Sinclair, Will and Jonathan Byres, Steve Harrington, and Max Mayfield. The prime protagonist of the series is Eleven, who is a genetically mutated human being with telekinetic power. She is a product of scientific research conducted at Hawkins National Laboratory which is operated under the United States Department of Energy.

The Duffer brothers have made staggering efforts to study the costumes, hairstyles, music, television shows, and vehicles that are featured in the series as indisputable replications of the trendiest fashion of the 1980s satisfying the nostalgic aspiration to relive the time. The first season of the series begins and ends in a game of *Dungeons and Dragons,* a geek cultural reference from the 1980s placed in the basement of the Wheelers.

The second season breaks the dominating low-angle shots of Hawkins Laboratory in the first season to replace them with eye-level shots of Sam Owens, who replaces Dr. Brenner. Hawkins Laboratory is endowed with a humanist relatability in the second season thus providing a space for another dominating, negative power structure. The USSR takes this space of dominating, negative power structure in the third season which begins with a panoramic shot of a Russian facility and a close-up shot of the Russian flag, flying in the wind. The scene is followed by a montage of different shots from Hawkins ending with a dropped American flag. The season has a newly constructed 'Star Court' mall, under which an illegal Russian facility operates, as the locus of action.

Kenneth T. Jackson traces the growth of socio-economic implications of American shopping centres in his essay, "All the World's a Mall: Reflections on the Social and Economic Consequences of the American Shopping Center"(Jackson 1996) The season brings every character to the mall for the final fight, thus relocating the centre of the action from private spaces to public spaces. The fourth season moves out of Hawkins as the Byers leave for California. It brings out the urban and suburban conflicts that place Eleven in a bleak predicament. It also incorporates the Soviet paranoia through a parallel narrative that takes Joyce Byers and Murray to Russia.

While the first season revitalizes the popular distrust in the US government authority, the subsequent ones rationalize the austere governmental policies with a greater impending problem. The representatives of authorities are forced to take away children to create human weapons as they face similar threats from an antagonistic nation. The narrative has the potential to remind people of how terrible the Cold War era was and warn them that Russia and an impending threat of war might force the US government to use such measures once more. Thus, the antagonistic position of the US government, built on the popular discontent against the use of its people to create bioweapons, is overshadowed and taken up by the larger and bigger threat from Russia that forces them to do so (Ayu 2022)The paranoia of the time is apparent in the seemingly comical confiscation of the *Dragons and Dungeons* game board along with El's used clothes and that of the police searching for absconding little boys using helicopters (S1E7 "The Bathtub" 00:16:23).

The cultural references of the 1980s are not limited to the storyline. Sarah Hindgaul, the hair stylist of *Stranger Things* for eight years, elaborately defined the characters through the fashionable hairstyles of the 1980s. Eleven's (Millie Boby Brown) buzz cut in the first season and short hair in the second and third is followed by an antiquated style of long curls and bangs in the fourth season.

There is ample reference to the popularity of *The Terminator* and the growing interest in science fiction writers such as Kurt Vonnegut. Mike, Dustin, Lucas, and Bill are ardent fans of *Dungeons and Dragons*. They also dress up as Ghostbusters for Halloween. The series also features the 1985 American science fiction film, *Back to the Future* in the third season.

Pop music of the 1980s has a salient role in reproducing retro culture. In season one, Will clings to The Clash's "Should I Stay, or Should I Go?" to maintain his composure when his life is jeopardized, foreshadowing Max in season four. Max is pulled back into reality with the help of her favourite piece of music, *Running Up That Hill* by Kate Bush. The series chronologically places the popular punk rock band The Clash, Kate Bush, and the heavy metal band Metallica in the series to indicate the progressive timeline of the series along with the character formation of the protagonists (Blake 2021)

The title of *Stranger Things*, 'ITC Benguiat,' has sinister-looking block letters inspired by the cover pages of books by Stephen King (Ferria). The characterization of the kids has a close resemblance to the characters from Spielberg's *E.T.* The bicycle chase in the first season is also reminiscent of a similar shot from *E.T.* (Heckman). The Duffer brothers have also incorporated popular cultural artefacts as a background for the blooming friendship of the young adult protagonists. While the friendship between Mike, Luke, Dustin, and Bill is founded upon their combined love for *Dragons and Dungeons,* Max Mayfield impresses the team with her high score in the game *Dragon's Lair* and introduces Eleven to the *Wonder Woman* comic books.

While pop culture references primarily have helped in placing the series within the nostalgia of the American and world populations, it is the Soviet paranoia that legitimizes the contemporary relevance and renewed interest in the series. Though the hints of Soviet advancement are laid out in the first season, it is in the third season that they become the centre of the plot. By the third season, the Cold War fear of illegal human experimentation is replaced by an impending Soviet invasion. Season three characterizes the Red Army as a spitting image of their characterization in American history books not excluding the 'elephant,' a notorious torture device used by them through a subplot featuring Jim Hopper.

The Duffer brothers have recreated a suburban American town of the 1980s through popular cultural references, hairstyle, costume, and appropriate characterization. They framed the science fiction plot of *Stranger Things* into pop culture, keying the memories of Cold War paranoia and conspiracy theories to the contemporary scenario of anti-Russian sentiments reignited due to the current war with Ukraine. The Cold War frame of Soviet peril is retained through such an antagonistic depiction of Soviet military research.

While the MCU series *Miss Marvel* actively speaks against the growing tendencies of islamophobia and suspicion against the Muslim community around the world, *Stranger Things* upholds the ruthless image of the Soviet Union during the Cold War and scientific experiments. Though the dual perception might seem unrelated, it can be paralleled with the foreign policies of the United States. With the unprecedented growth of Eastern powers like Russia and China, Western supremacy is jeopardized and requires cultural reintegration. *Stranger Things,* as a product of the popular culture industry, has the power to invoke this reintegration. America considers Pakistan an ally against India and China, and its cultural industries also reflect this policy. By giving Kamala Khan a similar template to that of one of the strongest Avengers, Captain Marvel, the MCU is vouching for the migrant Muslim community and their equality, which can impact the global perspective.

In both *Stranger Things* and *Miss Marvel*, the reaffirmation of trust in government authorities is brought about through an intervention of a neighbourhood cop, represented by Hopper and the sensible higher officer, respectively. Both series also reaffirm the position of family as the basic unit of social formation in American culture. While Najma disowns her son, Kamran, for choosing a different path, the parents from WASP culture, including Muneeba, Yusuf, Joyce Byers, and Hopper are shown fighting for the preservation of their families and thus for a richer life.

Thus, the two seemingly distant, yet similar Hollywood productions boil down to the old notion that the good one in the government is doing the right thing. It also reaffirms the faith in the United States as being there for its honest and good-at-heart citizens and even vigilantes. Kamala, Hopper, and the kids tinker with the law to some degree so that they can serve the law better against the outsiders, be it Russians, Djinns, or the 'Russified' military elements. Both series have subtly played into and within the cultural memory of the American as well as the world populations to frame and key their plots to suit contemporary national requirements.

Works Cited

Ali, Bisha K, director. *Miss Marvel.* Marvel Studios, 2022, Disney +, https://www.hotstar.com/in/home?ref=%2Fin. Accessed 8 Oct. 2022.

Ayu, Galuh Anissa Sekar. "The Evil Russian on American Screens: Stranger Things Season Four Short Review." *Modern Diplomacy*, 7 July 2022, moderndiplomacy.eu/2022/07/08/the-evil-russian-on-american-screens-stranger-things-season-four-short-review/. Accessed 26 Oct. 2022

Blake, Emily. "Unpacking the '80s Nostalgia of the 'Stranger Things' Soundtrack." *Mashable*, 29 Oct. 2021, https://mashable.com/article/stranger-things-soundtrack-netflix#:~:text=The%20show%20is%20set%20in,caressed%20%22Fields%20Of%20Cor al.%22. Accessed 10 Oct. 2022.

Bosch, T. E. "Memory Studies, A Brief Concept Paper." *White Rose Research Online*, University of Leeds, Jan. 2016, eprints.whiterose.ac.uk/. Accessed 30 Sept. 2022.

Bureau Entertainment. "Malala Yousafzai Gives a Shout out to Ms. Marvel for Reflecting 'The Lives of a Pakistani Immigrant Family'." *News18*, 8 June 2022, https://www.news18.com/news/movies/malala-yousafzai-gives-a-shout-out-to-ms-marvel-for-reflecting-the-lives-of-a-pakistani-immigrant-family-5330311.html. Accessed 17 Oct. 2023.

Chung, Erika. "Ms. Marvel: Genre, Medium, and an Intersectional Superhero." *Panic at the Discourse: An Interdisciplinary Journal*, vol. 1, no. 2, July 2019, pp. 5–16, https://doi.org/ISSN 2562-542X. Accessed 19 Oct. 2023.

Cortes, Carlos E, editor. "Motion Picture." *Multicultural America: A Multimedia Encyclopedia*, vol. 1, *Sage Publications*, 2013, pp. 1491–1495.

"Generation Why." Arbi, Adil El, et al., directors. *Miss Marvel*, created by Bisha Ali, season 1, episode 1, Disney +, 8 June 2022. Accessed 22 Oct. 2023.

Genter, Robert. "'With Great Power Comes Great Responsibility': Cold War Culture and the Birth of Marvel Comics." *Journal of Popular Culture*, vol. 40, 1 Dec. 2007, pp. 953–978, https://doi.org/10.1111/j.1540-5931.2007.00480.x. Accessed 21 Oct. 2023.

Gerges, Fawaz A. "Islam and Muslims in the Mind of America." *The Annals of the American Academy of Political and Social Science*, vol. 588, July 2003, pp. 73–89, https://www.jstor.org/stable/1049855. Accessed 22 Oct. 2023.
Grainge, Paul. "Introduction: Memory and Popular Film." *Memory and Popular Film*, edited by Paul Grainge, Manchester University Press, 2003, pp. 1–20.
Hirsch, Marianne. "The Generation of Post Memory." *Generation of Postmemory Writing and Visual Culture after the Holocaust*, Columbia University Press, 2012, pp. 103–125.
Jackson, Kenneth T. "All the World's a Mall: Reflections on the Social and Economic Consequences of the American Shopping Center." *The American Historical Review*, vol. 101, no. 4, Oct. 1996, pp. 1111–1121.
Manoharan, A. "The Popular Tale: A Study on Retention and Deconstruction of Collective Memory in Duffer Brothers' Stranger Things and Bisha Ali's Miss Marvel." *Sanglap: Journal of Literary and Cultural Inquiry*, vol. 10, no. 1, Dec. 2023, pp. 46–57, doi:10.35684/JLCI.2023.10105.
McCarthy, Kayla. "Remember Things: Consumerism, Nostalgia, and Geek Culture in Stranger Things."The Journal of Popular Culture, vol. 52, no. 3, June 2019, pp. 663-677, https://onlinelibrary.wiley.com/doi/10.1111/jpcu.12800. Accessed 26 Oct. 2023
Peitz, William. "Captain America: The Epitome of American Values and Identity." Senior Capstone Theses, Arcadia University, 2013, https://scholarworks.arcadia.edu/senior_theses/6. Accessed 31 Oct. 2023.
Resha, Adrienne. "Ms. Marvel's Mise-En-Scène: How the MCU Uses Environmental Storytelling to Adapt the Comics." *The Middle Spaces*, 20 Dec. 2022, themiddlespaces.com/2022/12/20/ms-marvels-mise-en-scene/. Accessed Oct. 24. 2023.
Rigney, Ann. "Cultural Memory Studies: Mediation, Narrative and the Aesthetic." *Routledge International Handbook of Memory Studies*, edited by Anna Lisa Tota and Trever Hagen, Routledge, 2016, pp. 65–75.
Schwartz, Barry. "Rethinking the Concept of Collective Memory." *Routledge International Handbook of Memory Studies*, edited by Anna Lisa Tota and Trever Hagen, Routledge, 2016, pp. 9–21.
"Seeing Red." Arbi, Adil El, et al., directors. *Miss Marvel*, created by Bisha Ali, season 1, episode 4, Disney +, 8 June 2022. Accessed 22 Oct. 2023.
Storey, John. "What Is Popular Culture." *Cultural Theory and Popular Culture: An Introduction*, edited by John Storey, 8th ed., Routledge, 2018 pp. 1–17.
"Stranger Things Wiki." *Fandom*, https://strangerthings.fandom.com/wiki/Stranger_Things_Wiki. Accessed 24 Oct. 2023.
"Time and Again." Arbi, Adil El, et al., directors. *Miss Marvel*, created by Bisha Ali, season 1, episode 5, Disney +, 8 June 2022. Accessed 22 Oct. 2023.
Wittmer, Carrie. "The Dawn of Iman Vellani." *Elite Daily*, 7 June 2022, https://www.elitedaily.com/entertainment/iman-vellani-ms-marvel-kamala-khan- interview. Accessed Oct. 16. 2023.

6 Memory Studies in Korean Drama

Exploring the Intersections of Memory through a Theoretical Interdisciplinary Lens

Rashmi Naik and Geetha Bhasker

Media, particularly television dramas, play a vital role in shaping personal and societal identities by intertwining viewers' personal experiences with the narrative. These dramas not only help in recalling and narrating collective and individual histories, but they also encourage reflection through diverse or contrasting narratives and shared experiences. Myra Macdonald notes that television fosters shared cultural memories by highlighting significant cultural and national events, re-broadcasting shows to bridge generations, exploring historical topics, and acknowledging its role in shaping national history (Macdonald 2006: 327–345).

Memory involves the processes of encoding, storing, and retrieving information. Information from external stimuli is captured by the sensory organs and transformed into neural impulses in a process called encoding. This information is then stored in the brain for future use, a phase known as storage. Finally, during retrieval, the stored information is accessed to perform tasks such as problem-solving or decision-making. Memory can retain information for durations ranging from a few seconds to many years (NCERT 2021: 133).

The development of memory theories has evolved significantly since the late 1960s. Richard C. Atkinson and Richard M. Shiffrin first introduced the Stage Model in 1968, dividing memory into three systems: Sensory Memory, Short-term Memory, and Long-term Memory (Atkinson and Shiffrin 1968). In 1972, Endel Tulving expanded on this by categorizing memory into Declarative (Episodic and Semantic) and Procedural memories. The concept of Implicit Memory was identified by Elizabeth K. Warrington and L. Weiskrantz in 1974 while studying patients with Korsakov's amnesia. The term Flashbulb Memory was proposed by Roger Brown and James Kulik in 1977. Later, in 2000, Martin A. Conway and Pleydell-Pearce introduced the concept of Autobiographical Memory. In 2004, Alison Landsberg discussed the impact of mass media in forming "prosthetic memories" that influence our collective identity and memory construction in her text on American remembrance. This field has seen considerable growth and the development of diverse theories since its early stages, particularly during a significant expansion in the late 1970s (Stony Brook University 2012).

DOI: 10.4324/9781003508564-9

South Korean television dramas, or K-Dramas, have become a focal point for global audiences and scholars, serving as a multidisciplinary research area that explores the complex nature of memory. These dramas intricately blend various memory theories into their narratives, engaging viewers by resonating with their personal experiences and cultural contexts. Korean Dramas[1] delve into historical events, personal and collective traumas, and the inter play between the past and present, contributing to discussions on the role of memory in society. They demonstrate how media can act as a tool for remembering and reinterpreting the past, and show the impact of personal and collective memories on society and cultural practices. An example of this could be seen in the Korean Drama *Bridal Mask* (각시탈), a period drama based on the Japanese colonial era in the 1930s, set in Seoul, Korea. The drama served as a reminder to the Korean population of their historical past under Imperial Japanese rule, highlighting a period of oppression and resistance in the 1930s. And episode 13 from the drama *Tomorrow* (내일) delves into the history of comfort women, a topic that had been largely erased from South Korean collective memory until the 1990s, when these women began to share their narratives publicly. These dramas illustrate the dynamics of memory, where its influence on individual perceptions is shown, as well as societal change and cultural practices.

Korean dramas effectively engage viewers worldwide, allowing them to gain an understanding of Korean history that can rival academic learning. These dramas exemplify the power of media to cross cultural and geographical boundaries, fostering a shared sense of history and identity among diverse audiences. By incorporating theories from cognitive psychology, sociology, cultural studies, and more, K-Dramas explore the mechanisms of memory formation, recall, and the emotional impact of memories. They highlight how memory contributes to the construction of narratives and identities, shaping our understanding of memory's role in society.

Knowledge is acquired through three ways. Perception is where knowledge about the world in our immediate vicinity is obtained; memory is where one retains knowledge about the world; and lastly, it is through nature and nurture where knowledge is gained through experiences and interactions with the environment. These methods operate under several assumptions: the predictability and systematic nature of the world, the predictability of humans as part of this physical world, and the preference for physical explanations over magical or mystical ones (Willingham 2019, pp. 8-9). Korean dramas provide a unique avenue to explore these assumptions about human behaviour and the world, offering insights without direct involvement. The chapter focuses on analysing K-Dramas as a tool within memory studies, highlighting their potential impact and the role of popular culture in shaping cognitive experiences. This approach provides a new perspective on how media influences our understanding of memory and cognition.

The rise of Korean drama, or K-Drama, in East Asia began in the 1990s as filmmakers and independent producers in South Korea sought to project a positive image of their country during a period of economic and socio-political change. This cultural export phenomenon was first recognized as the "Korean Wave" or "Hallyu" by a Chinese newspaper in 1999, a term that encompasses the widespread popularity of Korean cultural products like TV shows, K-pop music, animation, and digital games since 1997 (Yoon and Jin 2017). Notable dramas like *Winter Sonata* (겨울연가) in the early 2000s gained acclaim across Asia and globally, while *Jewel in the Palace* (대장금) made significant inroads into the Indian market. Since then, over 500 Korean dramas have been exported to East Asian markets alone (Oh 2013). These dramas, often formatted as miniseries with 10 to 25 episodes, have taken over prime-time slots and are available on OTT platforms like Netflix, Amazon Prime, and Hotstar, enjoying a global audience.

Television dramas are deeply rooted in the socio-political, cultural, and historical contexts of their creation, serving as cultural artefacts that reflect societal conflicts and challenges. According to McLuhan in *Understanding Media: The Extensions of Man* (1964), these shows are powerful tools for depicting real-life scenarios, revolving around human experiences that are meaningful to viewers. The relevance of these dramas to their audiences is fluid, changing as social conditions evolve, which affects the texts and audience tastes (Fiske 2005, p 6). Korean dramas, in particular, draw from their surrounding environments to highlight everyday life aspects, including their relevance to memory, illustrating how they adapt and remain significant over time by engaging with contemporary issues and societal dynamics.

This could be illustrated through the recently popular drama *Extraordinary Attorney Woo* (이상한 변호사 우영우). This drama is a narrative about a person suffering from Asperger syndrome, which is an autism spectrum disorder, and the drama shows the exemplary memory the character possesses. Another drama, *Good Doctor* (굿 닥터), looks into Savant syndrome, where the character is able to recall everything about the human body. In the drama *Find Me in Your Memory* (그 남자의 기억법), the character suffers from Hyperthymesia, a condition that lets the character remember every detail of his life experience in detail. It's important to recognize that Korean dramas may not be entirely precise, yet they emulate aspects of life.

This chapter analyses the portrayal of memory in Korean dramas, focusing on the use of flashbacks, amnesia, and repressed memories to enhance storytelling and character development. The chapter specifically examines three dramas, *Healer* (2014), *Kill Me, Heal Me* (2015), and *Shopping King Louie* (2016), each exploring different aspects of memory loss. *Healer* deals with a main character whose identity is deeply affected by her memory loss. In *Kill Me, Heal Me*, the protagonist is aware of her memory loss but manages to navigate her daily life effectively. *Shopping King Louie* features a lead who remains largely unaffected by memory loss and continues to lead a fulfilling life. While the chapter focuses on these three dramas, it acknowledges that they represent only a fraction of the diverse narratives available in Korean dramas and uses additional examples to support its analysis.

Methodology

This chapter adopts a qualitative research method, combining narrative and interpretive analysis, to explore the complex depiction of memory in Korean dramas. It focuses on specific episodes from selected dramas to analyse how memory influences storytelling and character development. The chapter leverages theories such as Atkinson and Shiffrin's model, Baddeley's working memory model (2012), Daniel L. Schacter's "The Seven Sins of Memory," and Dr Julia Shaw's *The Memory Illusion* (2016) to provide a theoretical framework. The goal is to identify nuanced elements within the narrative that arise from the thematic exploration of memory, thereby deepening understanding of character psychology and narrative construction in K-Drama.

Overview of the Dramas

Healer (힐러) aired on KBS2 from December 2014 to February 2015, starring Ji Chang-wook, Park Min-young, and Yoo Ji-tae, and follows the story of Seo Jung-hoo, a night courier, and Chae Young-shin, a tabloid reporter, as they uncover a complex case from 1992 involving deaths and hidden pasts, revealing repressed memories and traumas. *Kill Me, Heal Me* (킬미, 힐미) aired on MBC from January to March 2015, stars Ji Sung and Hwang Jung-eum, and focuses on Cha Do-hyun, a *chaebol* heir with dissociative identity disorder. The series depicts his journey alongside psychiatric resident Oh Ri-jin, as they address his repressed memories and childhood traumas, integrating his multiple identities. And *Shopping King Louie (쇼핑왕 루이*), starring Seo In-guk and Nam Ji-hyun, aired on MBC from September to November 2016. It narrates the story of Louis, a *chaebol* heir who loses his memory in an accident. The series portrays his amnesiac state with a positive light as he rediscovers himself and forms new relationships in Seoul.

Role of Memory in K-Drama through Psychological Theories

Individuals are exposed to a vast array of sensory information, but only a small fraction is retained and can be effectively recalled. The Atkinson-Shiffrin memory model, which includes sensory memory, short-term memory (STM), and long-term memory (LTM), explains this selective retention. Korean dramas skilfully apply these elements of the memory model to enrich character development and the complexity of their narratives (Human Memory pp. 89–195). By focusing on how characters process and store emotional experiences, especially traumatic or significant memories, these dramas illustrate the practical workings of the memory model in shaping both individual behaviour and broader story arcs.

In *Kill Me, Heal Me*, the character Oh Ri-jin revisits a traumatic memory of fire, storing this vivid but fragmented recollection in her long-term memory, which is initially inaccessible. Conversely, Cha Do-hyun repeatedly experiences distressing memories of child abuse, which persistently linger in his short-term memory due to their repetitive and intense nature, ultimately contributing to the development of his multiple personalities, such as Shin Se-gi, who embodies these painful memories.

Similarly, in *Healer,* Seo Jung-hoo's triggered memory of a childhood game called "Secret Secret Island" resurfaces when prompted by specific auditory cues. This memory, linked to happier times before his father's tragic death and societal ostracism, remains buried deep within his long-term memory, illustrating how significant emotional experiences are retained and can resurface under certain conditions.

In 1974, Alan D. Baddeley introduced a tripartite memory model consisting of a central executive system and two supporting subsystems for articulatory and visual-spatial processing. In 1996, he expanded this model by adding an "episodic buffer," a component that acts as a multimodal storage interface between these subsystems and long-term memory, holding integrated scenes or episodes. This buffer plays a crucial role in binding information across different codes, a process facilitated by conscious awareness and considered a key advantage of consciousness (Baddeley 2001; Baddeley 2012,). This concept is creatively paralleled in the Korean drama *Kill Me, Heal Me*, where the character Cha Do-hyun's alternate personalities, particularly Shin Se-gi, function similarly to the episodic buffer. These personalities protect Cha Do-hyun from painful memories by emerging during stressful situations or when he faces potential harm, thereby shielding the main character from psychological distress.

To analyse these complexities of memory as explored in Korean dramas, drawing on insights from Daniel L. Schacter's "The Seven Sins of Memory: Insights from Psychology and Cognitive Neuroscience" and Dr Julia Shaw's *The Memory Illusion: Remembering, Forgetting, and the Science of False Memory* is necessary. Schacter's work examines the common errors and distortions in memory, providing a psychological framework for understanding memory functions. In contrast, Dr Shaw explores the concept of false memories and the dynamic nature of memory, which is susceptible to various influences such as emotions and external suggestions.

Dr Julia Shaw explores the profound implications of memory loss on identity and self-perception. She highlights a dichotomy: while losing memories can evoke fear of becoming a shell of one's former self, it can also offer a sense of liberation from past constraints and a chance for a fresh start. This concept is illustrated through the character Louis in the Korean drama *Shopping King Louie*. After losing his memory, Louis experiences both a cognitive decline and a newfound freedom, questioning his identity but also embracing the possibilities of redefining himself without the burden of his past. He suggests that living in the present and creating new memories is more important than clinging to the past. This reflects Shaw's idea that forgotten memories may not be essential, highlighting the fluidity and selective significance of memory in shaping our lives and identities.

The prospect of memory loss presents a complex mix of fear and potential liberation. Although dramatic memory loss is rare in real life, our memories are prone to various errors, distortions, and modifications due to factors like emotions, external influences, and time. Memory is not a fixed and flawless record but is instead dynamic and adaptable, shaped by cognitive and environmental factors (R Wood et al. 2012, p.104). This flexibility underscores the inherent imperfections in our memory system and highlights the importance of understanding how our memories can evolve and change over time.

Dr Shaw discusses the role of semantic memory, which involves recalling meanings, concepts, and facts, and its relationship with episodic memory, which captures specific events and gives a sense of reliving those moments. These episodic memories are vital for shaping our identities as they encompass the personal stories and experiences that define us. Shaw also highlights the concept of false memories, where individuals recall events that never happened, which can have profound emotional impacts, including joy, distress, or trauma. Daniel Schacter's work on the seven sins of memory further explores the complexities and potential errors in how we remember, emphasizing the significant influence of memory on our emotions and identity.

Daniel Schacter explores the imperfections of memory through his concept of the seven sins of memory, which categorize common memory issues. These include transience, where memories fade over time; absentmindedness, marked by lapses in attention; blocking, a temporary inability to access information; misattribution, where memories are incorrectly linked to wrong sources; suggestibility, the impact of external influences on memory; bias, where current beliefs affect how past events are recalled; and persistence, the troubling inability to forget unwanted memories. These sins are further shown through instances from K-Drama to have a better understanding.

Schacter says, "The loss of information over time may be particularly likely to occur when people do not use a memory" (pp. 184). This is known as transience, which is the tendency of memories to fade or diminish over time. In *Healer,* Seo Jong-hoo has forgotten the memories from his childhood, including significant events like the games and the meetings between Oh Ji-an and Kim Moon-ho's families. Similarly, Chae Young-shin, as a seven-year-old, forgets her mother's intention to stay put and search for her once the violence subsides. Additionally, in *Kill Me, Heal Me*, Cha Do-hyun forgets the crucial detail that the accident leading to his father's coma was, in fact, his own fault.

The concept of absentmindedness, as one of Schacter's seven sins of memory, refers to memory errors that occur due to lapses in attention during the encoding or retrieval processes, or when information is superficially processed. This type of forgetting can significantly impact both event-based and time-based memory tasks. Event-based tasks depend on external cues to trigger a remembered action, whereas time-based tasks require self-generated cues at specific times. An example from *Healer* illustrates this concept through the character Chae Young-shin, who temporarily forgets her professional role as a tabloid reporter. As she approaches an apartment to uncover a scandal in episode 3, she only then remembers her journalistic duties when she sees other reporters, highlighting how external cues can suddenly trigger memory recall.

The concept of blocking, another of Schacter's seven sins of memory, describes situations where memories are present but temporarily inaccessible, often exemplified by the "tip of the tongue" phenomenon. In the Korean drama *Shopping King Louie*, the protagonist Louis experiences this when he cannot retrieve memories of Ko Bok-shil despite feeling a sense of familiarity. His difficulty in accessing specific memories is attributed to a head injury. However, his repeated encounters with Ko Bok-shil throughout the episode gradually build a subconscious trust, indicating that even when specific memories are blocked, repeated exposure can reinforce emotional connections.

The fourth sin of memory, misattribution, involves incorrectly assigning a memory to the wrong time, place, or person. This error is common in narratives such as Korean dramas, where it often forms a central plot element. For instance, in *Healer*, Chae Young-shin mistakenly recalls being abandoned and chased amid violence, instead of the true memory of waiting for her mother. Similarly, in *Kill Me, Heal Me*, Cha Do-hyun incorrectly believes he was the victim of child abuse he witnessed. It is these instances of misattribution which drive the drama's storyline forward.

The concept of suggestibility describes how external influences, such as misleading questions or societal pressures, can alter one's memories, leading to inaccuracies or false narratives. In the Korean drama *Shopping King Louie*, the protagonist Louis becomes convinced he might be responsible for a tragic death due to intense police questioning and the stressful circumstances of an investigation. This leads to self-doubt and acceptance of a potentially incorrect version of events. Similarly, in *Healer*, Chae Young-shin develops a false memory of abandonment, believing she is unloved by her biological family, which affects her self-perception and causes her to blame herself for unrelated adult issues. This sin of suggestibility can significantly impact personal memories and perceptions, particularly under distress.

The sixth sin of memory, bias, involves the distortion of past memories through the lens of current knowledge, beliefs, and emotions. This is evident in *Kill Me, Heal Me*, where Oh Ri-jin, despite a traumatic history, recalls her childhood as idyllic due to her current perception of having a happy family. This biased recall significantly alters her understanding of her past. Similarly, in *Shopping King Louie*, Louis's preference for cheap coffee and local food leads Bok-shil and her neighbour to wrongly assume he is not wealthy, showing how present behaviours can skew perceptions of someone's background. Louis also adopts the belief that he comes from a poor family, influenced by his neighbours' assumptions. This illustrates the intricate interplay between current knowledge and the formation of biased perspectives when trying to piece together someone's history or social standing.

The last sin identified by Daniel L. Schacter is persistence. This refers to the situation where some memories remain despite the efforts to forget them. Over time, these memories can transform into recollections of dramatic events, evolving into chronic fears and phobias. In the context of K-Dramas, such as *Healer* and *Kill Me, Heal Me*, this concept is evident in the characters' persistent fears. Chae Young-shin's fear of violence and any act of aggression (ep 3), as well as Oh Ri-jin's fear of underground basements and fire (ep 4), serve as examples of how memories, especially those associated with traumatic events, can persist and manifest as enduring fears, influencing the characters' emotions and behaviours throughout the storyline. This showcases the profound impact that persistent memories can have on an individual's mental and emotional well-being.

Memory in K-Drama through Sociological Perspectives

Michael A. Hogg (2018) presents identity as both influencing and being influenced by social interactions, highlighting its dynamic nature. Memory acts as a catalyst in this process, shaping how individuals respond to and are shaped by their social environment. Korean dramas, while striving for a balance between authenticity and entertainment, explore the powerful role of memory in shaping present realities, even when these memories may not be entirely accurate.

The portrayal of trauma in Korean dramas does not strictly follow the academic definitions provided by scholars like Cathy Caruth (1996), Kai Erickson (1994), or Arthur Neal (1998), but effectively uses narrative to explore the impact of traumatic memories. Trauma, affecting individuals and communities, often leads to distorted memories and identity crises, which can escalate to amnesia or societal identity crises (Abdullah 1). It is depicted as a complex phenomenon that intersects with history, literature, and culture, persisting in the unconscious and compelling individuals to relive painful events until they can narrate and control these memories (ibid, p 2). Korean dramas illustrate these themes through their characters, showcasing the enduring influence of trauma on personal and collective identities.

Traumatic memories, which are often fragmented and vivid, play a crucial role in shaping identity, as they are deeply intertwined with an individual's self-perception. According to Christianson (1987), victims of trauma often struggle with a distorted memory of their experiences, which can lead to amnesia or an identity crisis. These memories not only form a significant part of one's narrative identity but also have a lasting impact on how they are stored, recalled, and integrated. Korean dramas effectively highlight the profound and enduring effects of trauma on an individual's sense of self, demonstrating how these experiences can fundamentally influence personal identity.

In *Healer*, Chae Young-shin transforms into a hyperactive child due to a traumatic memory of abandonment, affecting her adult behaviours as she seeks validation and overextends herself to prove her worth. Her trauma manifests in distorted memories and a mistaken belief of being abandoned because of her autism, which is later corrected, bringing her relief and understanding of her past. In *Kill Me, Heal Me*, the character Shin Se-gi, an alternate personality of Cha Do-hyun, displays deep mistrust towards adults stemming from childhood abuse, impacting his ability to form trusting relationships in adulthood. This mistrust and the fragmented personalities illustrate the disruption trauma can cause in maintaining a coherent identity, as seen through Cha Do-hyun's struggles with his alternate personas which affect his daily life and professional responsibilities. *Shopping King Louie* depicts how Louis's subconscious memories of a wealthy lifestyle influence his interactions and self-perception, even when living in modest conditions. His keen attention to detail, preserved despite memory loss, aids his career advancement, demonstrating how some aspects of memory can remain influential even when not fully conscious.

These dramas skilfully depict the complex relationship between memory, trauma, and identity, illustrating how traumatic memories, whether conscious or subconscious, persistently shape individuals' lives and interactions. These narratives not only reveal the characters' personal challenges and development but also offer broader insights into the effects of trauma at various stages of life and within different social contexts.

Role of Memory through Visual Narratives and Cinematography in K-Drama

Korean dramas effectively use vibrant visuals, detailed camera work, and thorough attention to detail to capture the essence of their narratives, enhancing both the visual appeal and the immersive experience for viewers. This quality presentation contributes to the dramas' emotional and visual engagement, with actors delivering performances that add to the charm of these productions. According to Landsberg (*Prosthetic Memory* p.29), this leads to a phenomenon he describes as "emotional possession" or prosthetic memory, where viewers internalize the narratives so deeply that they feel as if they have lived those experiences themselves. This intense connection can make the impact of a drama as significant as actual life experiences (ibid p.30). Furthermore, the creation of memories from media is influenced by viewers' existing memories, creating a dynamic interaction where personal experiences and the drama's narrative intertwine (Forde p.68). Consequently, the visual elements of Korean dramas serve not only as entertainment but also as a means to preserve and recall memories, allowing viewers to continuously engage with the content and the emotions it evokes over time.

The drama *Kill Me, Heal Me* skilfully utilizes close-up camera angles to capture and amplify the emotional intensity experienced by its characters in episode 1. This technique is particularly effective in scenes of intense emotional distress, such as the one described where a character is undergoing a traumatic attack. By focusing closely on facial expressions and subtle emotional cues, these shots allow the audience to perceive even the smallest nuances of the character's feelings. As the camera gradually zooms in, it peels back layers of pain, enhancing the suspense and fostering a deeper empathetic connection with the viewer. A notable moment is the climax of the scene, where a reddened eye not only indicates physical duress but also deep emotional suffering, leaving a lasting visual and emotional impact on the audience.

In *Healer*, cinematography is crucial in portraying the emotional depth of Kim Moon-ho's nightmare, effectively separating his present self from his past through distinct changes in lighting and colour grading. This visual differentiation emphasizes the passage of time and the haunting effects of past experiences. Flashbacks are skilfully woven into the narrative, providing essential background that deepens character understanding, motivations, and forthcoming plot developments and are marked by visual cues like colour tone shifts, hazy filters, and unique transitions, helping viewers differentiate between the current storyline and past events. Additionally, Moon-ho's dream sequences in episode 3 delve into his subconscious, utilizing visual distortions and surreal imagery to explore his inner fears, desires, and unresolved issues. This approach enriches the narrative, allowing Moon-ho's emotional and complex past to resonate with audiences, deepening their connection to his character and shaping their engagement throughout his journey.

The Use of Audio Elements to Enhance Memory

In the first episode of *Kill Me, Heal Me*, the original soundtrack (OST) of the drama, "Auditory Hallucination" by Ang Jae-in and NaShow, becomes important as it creates a moment that resonates intensely with the audience as the temporal time lasts longer than the screen time. The entire sequence unfolds within a brief span of 5–8 seconds. This song is strategically used in key episodes and it not only enhances scenes but also adds layers to the narrative, conveying both suffering and beauty and illustrating how music can leave a lasting impact on audiences. The soundtrack triggers the memory of it in the audience, for music is said to improve episodic memory (Ferreri, 2015; Herget 2019). By meticulously constructing scenes and sequences and the carefully chosen soundtrack, the drama evokes powerful emotions and forges a strong connection between the audience's memory and the narrative. These moments serve as emotional anchors, making sure that the viewers become invested in the characters and the story, enhancing the overall impact on the memory of the drama.

The Circle Digital Chart, a prominent record chart in South Korea, underscored its popularity by ranking it among the top 12 in 2015. This success extends to online platforms like YouTube, where multiple videos of "Auditory Hallucination" had millions of views, and three of four videos have 11 million (PTimur), 21 million (Riak Official), and 7.5 million views. This significant online engagement showcases the lasting memory and impact of the OST beyond the confines of the drama, deeply resonating with and retaining a strong presence in the audience's collective memory. This is evident in viewers' comments, such as "Who is here in 2020 or 2024?"

The audio-visual elements in Korean dramas significantly enhance the viewer's experience, making it memorable both domestically and internationally. By integrating multisensory elements with audio-visual cues, these dramas effectively boost memory retention and deepen emotional engagement. This immersive approach ensures that audiences remember the stories, characters, and underlying messages well after viewing. Moreover, specific cues like a song or scene can instantly reconnect viewers with their memories of the drama, reinforcing the lasting impact of these elements.

Conclusion

Korean dramas are renowned for their complex plots and intricate character development, focusing significantly on psychological and sociological themes, particularly memory, identity, and trauma. Throughout the early 2000s to 2018, themes of memory loss were prevalent in dramas such as *Autumn in My Heart* (가을동화, 2000), *Blade Man* (아이언맨, 2014), *Who Are You* (후아유: 학교, 2015), and *While You Were Sleeping* (당신이 잠든 사이에, 2017), where main characters often grappled with forgotten memories. These narratives not only delve into the psychological aspects of memory but also incorporate social identity theory to examine the effects of memory on social behaviour. The immersive viewing experience is further enhanced by meticulous cinematography, including vibrant visuals and strategic use of music, which adds emotional depth and helps anchor the drama's narrative and associated personal memories more deeply in viewers' minds.

Korean dramas go beyond mere entertainment. They offer a profound exploration of the human psyche, memory, and societal dynamics. With their sophisticated visual and musical elements, these dramas provide rich material for academic research, particularly in the field of memory studies. This interdisciplinary field benefits from analysing how Korean dramas portray and influence collective and personal memory, including their formation and representation.

Perhaps the greatest testament to the malleable nature of personal and collective memory can be the remarkable transformation of South Korea's image from a country devastated by war just 70 years ago to a developed country today, from grappling with economic challenges to the most sought-after tourist destination today. This dramatic change in perception can largely be attributed to the influence of the Korean Wave, which has influenced the international popularity of Korean dramas, movies, music, and culture. Korean dramas have played a crucial role in reshaping and improving the global image of South Korea, showcasing the country's vibrant culture, technological advancements, and economic development. This phenomenon showcases how human memory and perceptions can be significantly influenced and altered over time by media and cultural exports, demonstrating the fluidity and reconstructive qualities of memory.

Note

1 Throughout this article, "Korea" refers to South Korea unless stated otherwise, and "Drama" refers to the television prime-time dramas.

Works Cited

Abdullah, Md Abu Shahid., editor. *Trauma, Memory and Identity Crisis: Reimagining and Rewriting the Past.* Cambridge Scholars Publishing, 2022. PDF

Atkinson, R. C., and R. M. Shiffrin. 'Human Memory: A Proposed System and Its Control Processes'. *Psychology of Learning and Motivation,* Elsevier, 1968, pp. 89–195, https://doi.org10.1016/s0079-7421(08)60422-3.

Baddeley, A. D. 'Is Working Memory Still Working?' *The American Psychologist,* vol. 56, no. 11, American Psychological Association (APA), Nov. 2001, pp. 851–864, https://doi.org10.1037/0003-066x.56.11.851.

Baddeley, Alan D. 'Working Memory: Theories, Models, and Controversies'. *Annual Review of Psychology,* vol. 63, no. 1, Annual Reviews, Jan. 2012, pp. 1–29, https://doi.org10.1146/annurev-psych-120710-100422.

Caruth, Cathy. *Unclaimed Experience: Trauma, Narrative, and History.* Johns Hopkins University Press, 1996.

Christianson, S., et al. 'Memory for Traumatic Events'. *Applied Cognitive Psychology,* vol. 1, no. 4, 1987, pp. 225–239, https://doi.org/10.1002/acp.2350010402.

Erikson, Kai. *A New Species of Trouble: The Human Experience of Modern Disasters.* W.W. Norton, 1994.

Ferreri, Laura et al. 'The Positive Effect of Music on Source Memory'. *Musicae Scientiae* 19 (2015): 402–411. https://doi.org/10.1177/1029864915604684.

Fiske, John. *Reading The Popular.* Routledge, 2005.

Forde, T. 'Television Dramas as Memory Screens'. *Image & Narrative,* vol. 12, no. 2, May 2011, pp. 66–82, https://www.imageandnarrative.be/index.php/imagenarrative/article/view/146.

Herget, Kristin. 'On Music's Potential to Convey Meaning in Film: A Systematic Review of Empirical Evidence'. *Psychology of Music,* 2019, https://doi.org/10.1177/0305735619835019. Accessed 4 Mar. 2024.

Hogg, Michael A. 'Chapter 5 Social Identity Theory'. *Contemporary Social Psychological Theories,* Stanford University Press, 2018, pp. 112–138, https://doi.org10.1515/9781503605626-007.

Landsberg, Alison et al. *Prosthetic Memory: The Transformation of American Remembrance in the Age of Mass Culture.* Columbia Press University, 2004, https://doi.org/10.2307/30036756.

Macdonald, Myra. 'Performing Memory on Television: Documentary and the 1960s'. *Screen,* vol. 47, no. 3, Autumn 2006, pp. 327–345, https://doi.org/10.1093/screen/hjl025

McLuhan, Marshall. *Understanding Media: The Extensions of Man.* 1964. Edited by W. Terrence Gordon, Critical ed., Gingko Press, 2003.

NCERT. *Psychology: Textbook for Class XI.* National Council of Educational Research and Training, 2021. PDF

Neal, Arthur G. *National Trauma and Collective Memory: Major Events in the American Century.* M.E. Sharpe, 1998.

Oh, Youjeong. *Spectacular Cities, Speculative Storytelling: Korean TV Dramas and the Selling of Place*. UC Berkeley, 2013, https://escholarship.org/uc/item/6722g87r.

Schacter, D. L. 'The Seven Sins of Memory. Insights from Psychology and Cognitive Neuroscience'. *The American Psychologist*, vol. 54, no. 3, American Psychological Association (APA), Mar. 1999, pp. 182–203, https://doi.org10.1037//0003-066x.54.3.182.

Shaw, Julia. *The Memory Illusion: Remembering, Forgetting, and the Science of False Memory*. Random House Books, 2016.

Stony Brook University. 'Provost Lecture - Jeffery Olick: What Is Memory Studies?' *YouTube*, 23 July 2012, www.youtube.com/watch?v=FdU_hYosb4o.

Willingham, Daniel T., and Riener, Cedar. *Cognition: The Thinking Animal*. Cambridge University Press, 2019.

Wood, R., et al. 'A Review of Long-term Memory in Natural and Synthetic Systems'. *Adaptive Behavior*, vol. 20, 2012, pp. 103–181, https://doi.org/10.1177/1059712311421219.

Yoon, Tae-Jin, and Dal Yong Jin. 'The Korean Wave: Twenty Years, Retrospect and Prospect'. *The Korean Wave: Twenty Years, Retrospect and Prospect*, edited by Yoon, Tae-Jin and Dal Yong Jin, Lexington Books, 2017, pp. xi–xix.

Television Dramas /Videos

Healer , directed by Lee Jung-sub and Kim Jin-woo, written by Song Ji-na, featuring Ji Chang-wook, Park Min-young, and Yoo Ji-tae, aired 8 Dec. 2014 to 10 Feb. 2015, KBS2.

Kill Me, Heal Me, directed by Kim Jin-man and Kim Dae-jin, written by Jin Soo-wan, featuring Ji Sung, Hwang Jung-eum, Park Seo-joon, Oh Min-suk, and Kim Yoo-ri, aired 7 Jan to 12 Mar. 2015, MBC.

"[*Kill Me, Heal Me* OST] Jang Jae-in - Auditory Hallucination, 장재인 - 환청, DMC Festival 2015." *YouTube,* MBCkpop, 9 Sept. 2015. www.youtube.com/watch?v=CB_WiL05ByQ. Accessed 8 Mar. 2024

"[MV][*Kill Me, Heal Me* OST] Auditory Hallucination 환청 (ENG+Rom+Han.SUB.) Jang Jae In. *YouTube*, PTimur, 4 Sept. 2015. https://www.youtube.com/watch?v=Gg0P9yd0noE. Accessed 8 Mar. 2024

"[Official]킬미 힐미 *Kill Me, Heal Me* OST Part.1- 환청 Hallucination (Feat.나쑈 NaShow) - 장재인 Jang Jane." *YouTube,* Riak Official, 14 Jan. 2015. https://www.youtube.com/watch?v=tVoE9_eN8TE. Accessed 8 Mar. 2024

Shopping King Louie, directed by Lee Sang-yeob, written by Oh Ji-young, Seo In-guk, Nam Ji-hyun, Yoon Sang-hyun and Im Se-mi, aired 21 Sept to 10 Nov. 2016, MBC.

7 Making the Village Alive in the City

Understanding Village-ness among Gurjars in Madanpur Khadar

Vishesh Pratap Gurjar

Caste and village have been considered the defining characteristics of Indian society (Jodhka). Although villages existed in India for a long time, their importance grew with the arrival of British rule whose administrators constructed an image of India as a land of 'village republics'[1] (Inden 132). In the words of Dr V. Nath, former Chief of Urban and Regional Planning at the Planning Commission, "both the village and caste have also been understood as the two foci of community feeling in rural India. The average villager feels that he belongs to these two entities...In much of our thinking on rural development, it is assumed that the 'village' is the 'community'" (Nath). The framing of policies for development works in post-independence India has further entrenched the imagination of India as the land of villages. However, in recent years scholars such as Dipankar Gupta have asked if the village is still surviving (Gupta). According to such studies the village has lost its traditional resonance economically but the village continues to operate as a form of the community shaping individual behaviours and patterns of life. The present chapter is an attempt to understand how the idea of a village as a community survives within the city of Delhi and how it gets reproduced by individuals in contemporary times with the use of collective memory and oral history.

Village as a Form of Community?

A village in India was not simply considered to be a residential settlement, rather it was perceived as a perennial socio-cultural unit, having its separate customs, rituals and a unique lifeworld organized around the agrarian reality. Since the Indus Valley civilization, the villages came to be understood as the cradle of Indian civilization, which survived over the years without any big changes affecting them. Most often, this story of the timeless existence of the village existence is propagated by oral histories of the village told by its residents ("Changel: Three Centuries of an Indian Village") (Das 1987). It is also interesting to note how the British colonial authorities like Charles Metcalfe eulogized villages as 'Republics' and saw an image of medieval Europe in the Indian village (Inden). Along with the colonial anthropologists, the village as an idea was taken up by Indian nationalists and re-signified as

DOI: 10.4324/9781003508564-10

a unit of pristine and unique Indian culture (;Cohn; Jodhka). It is through this encounter with the 'modern' British rulers and the Indian nationalists that the village, as a separate socio-cultural unit took shape (Cohn). Such a construction of the village was also reflected in the post-independent policies for development even though the leaders of the national movement did not have an agreement on the importance of the village in Indian society. Surinder Jodhka has explored the idea of the village that was present in the thought of Nehru, Gandhi and Ambedkar (Jodhka).

Post-independence, development schemes like the integrated child development scheme placed Indian villages at the centre stage further consolidating the idea of the village community. With the enactment of the 73rd and 74th constitutional amendments by the Indian Parliament in 1992, the ideal of 'a village republic' as a decision-making model was the foundation of the world's largest democracy (Dumont). Thus, the constitutional recognition of villages as building blocks of Indian democracy that placed trust in the collective wisdom of the grassroots community in the form of village panchayats for development and social change reinvigorated the ideal image of India as a country of villages.

Although this village community is nothing more than an ideological construction, the fractures within the 'village community' came to the surface with the inclusion of villages in the political structure as it heightened competition among various castes for gaining political power at local levels.

Besides politically induced changes, urbanization has also brought many changes to the rural areas. These changes are reported in many studies such as Oscar Lewis's study of Rampura, a report on marriage and kinship, caste relations, religious customs, rituals and factions, disease causation and cure, emphasizing diseases like malaria, smallpox, etc. (Lewis). The government of India also produced detailed surveys of the villages as part of the census survey of 1961; these surveys had details of individual villages concerning land revenue, work and culture of people that reside in these villages (Kashmir Singh and Raj). These studies produced the village as a separate site, different from the urban. However, in some sociological works the urban impact on rural Delhi was also captured, like in the writings of M.S.A Rao, who noted the social consequences of economic changes. He argued that change in occupation gave way to the associated social changes, like the transformation of the Jajmani system, where services are offered on the basis of patron-client relations and payments were made in kind but now have seen a shift to payments made in cash by the patrons (Rao 402). In a similar manner to Rao, Johan Bentick has pointed out that the traditionally dominant agricultural activities were under increasing pressure, although new opportunities for market-oriented agriculture were emerging. There was greater differentiation among villagers concerning resources and opportunities, leading to interesting new patterns of livelihood (Bentick). An important piece on the social life and changing gender relations due to urbanization was written by Sunil Khanna in his study of 'Shahr-Gaon' village; he highlighted the increasing conservatism among the Jat community leading to increasing control on women's agency. Sunil Khanna argued that Jat women faced more control whereas men gained freedom from urbanization (Khanna). In this tradition of studying the interaction of urban with the rural in Delhi, Radhika Govinda recently wrote on Shahpur Jat urban village in Delhi; she has focused on the changing dimensions of gender within the erstwhile village of Delhi after its inclusion in the city. She concludes that the Jat men from the village are engaged in a diversity of practices to recover the hegemonic masculinity that they lost due to the loss of land to the government (Govinda 12). Furthering this tradition of studying the changing rural settlements due to urbanization, the narratives below present a story of how the village is getting reproduced as a form of community in the everyday practices of the erstwhile villagers.

Life of Community in an Urban Village of Delhi: Understanding Village-ness through Collective Memory

In this section, I would like to draw attention to the various practices that help the revival of village community in the city. To do so, I look at the narratives of the construction of 'village-ness' by the residents of Madanpur Khadar village in Delhi. I argue that the construction of the 'village' in contemporary Delhi is partly a reflection of the agrarian/rural past, and in parts, the village gets constructed with newer everyday practices adopted by its residents. I employ the category of collective memory to understand the construction of 'village-ness' in the everyday practices of village residents. The past of the village and caste is invoked repeatedly by the young ones in their routine life thereby creating a sense of community around the past of the village. To understand this social process of construction of the village I employ the concept of 'collective memory' developed by Maurice Halbwachs in his works that are collectively published in the book *On Collective Memory* (1992). Halbwachs argues that besides the individual memory, there also exists a collective memory of the groups about the past, which is passed on to the next generation as tradition. Taking a cue from his ideas I argue that the 'collective memory' in the village is shaped and reshaped not only through the usual practices and performances that once existed in the caste and village system in the past, but also through the performance of collective acts that are done based on the collective memory which provides collective identity to its people. He also highlights the important role of space in the existence of collective memory, as he argues,

> every collective memory unfolds within a spatial framework. Now space is a reality that endures: since our impressions rush by, one after another, and leave nothing behind in the mind, we can understand how we recapture the past only by understanding how it is, in effect, preserved by our physical surroundings. It is to space – the space we occupy, traverse, have continual access to, or can at any time reconstruct in thought and imagination – that we must turn our attention to.

> Our thought must focus on it if this or that category of remembrances is to reappear.
>
> (Halbwachs 1950: 7)

In this sense, collective memory provides a way to understand the continuance of village and caste identities from a different perspective.

Collective Memory and the Prevalence of the Village Community

The members of the Gurjar caste in the village of Madanpur exhibit their allegiance to three types of community, one being the village as a physical space, then their caste/clan as a social relationship and further their separate family lineage. As explicated from the narratives of the origin stories of the Bhats, each family of the village has a relationship with each other in the generation of their ancestors. So, even though a great deal of change has taken place with population increase and urbanization, people act as a community based on their collective memory of the past of the village, by acting on social relationships and through the performance of the specific rituals of birth, death and marriage, etc. The collective memory of an ordinary Gurjar resident of the village would have something collective about their presence as Bidhuri (clan) and something as Gurjar and some other things as a resident of the village. The collective memory of people exists in a convergence of their clan, caste and village.

The Memory of Built Spaces

There are three ways in which the current generation of the village of Madanpur Khadar makes use of this collective memory. Almost every resident of the village, Gurjar or non-Gurjar, does have a certain collective memory of the built spaces of the village; it is exhibited in people's conversations about the places that have existed in the village for a long time. Almost all the residents of the village have a collective memory of the Chaupals (assembly place) in the village; it is a common space that is used by everyone for organizing their family functions or sometimes for the assembly of the villagers on important matters. Similarly, various other structures exist in the village whose collective memory from the past is passed on to the following generations of the residents through their social functions. In this category of village amenities comes the Khari-Kuan, a well, which is no longer used for pulling out water but is used for the ritualistic practices of the people. For example, after the birth of a son in the family the women usually get together in a group and go for prayer at this well. Also, during the festival of Holi, the villagers gather around the well and perform traditional songs with the beating of the nagadas (drums). Another important infrastructure aspect of community space is the location of the village god (Kheda-Devta). The village god has been given a separate abode on the common land of the village and

Gurjar residents usually go on Sundays to offer milk and prayers. On occasions like Deepawali, Holi and other such important events, the residents of the village have special offerings of porridge and deep-fried sweet fritters. As explained to me by the old man who takes care of the cleaning of the village god abode,

> he is the guardian of the village, everyone comes here when something good is about to happen or something bad has happened with them. He likes Daliya (porridge) very much, without him nothing could change, it is important to think about his happiness.
>
> (field notes)

Urusula Sharma, writing in a different context, has discussed these public religious places of villages in detail. She points towards numerous places that belong to separate castes and how only a few such places could be recognized as 'public' in terms of belonging to everyone in the village (Sharma). There are other built spaces which become part of the collective memory of the villagers, such as big, ruined traditional houses known as Havelis; old houses of usually the rich families of the villagers are used by people as a map to understand the past of the village community. Along with the built infrastructure of the village, the natural surroundings like an old banyan tree in the village or the image of the clean water flowing in the close by Agra canal also navigate in the collective memory of the villagers.

The Memory of Relations, Rituals and Events

Besides the collective memory that people have of the village's spaces, existing social relationships also reinforce a collective memory of being a village. This is usually invigorated through events, sometimes critical but otherwise ordinary and usual events. Critical events, like the murder of a notorious big man in the village by someone from the village, linger strongly in the collective memory of villagers. Anything that the villagers did collectively in the past is also kept in the collective memory of the villagers; for instance, when a private school was constructed on the lands acquired from the villagers, the villagers, largely Gurjars, mobilized themselves against the school authorities and asked them to add the name of the village in the school address. This mobilization also became part of the collective memory of a generation of young people, who now take pride in the collective identity of their caste and village. This collective memory of being powerful is used often by the people of the village, like Vinayak, a middle-aged man who took pride in telling me that "I often hurl abuses at the bus drivers of this school, if I see them parked on road blocking traffic, they have to understand who we are [the local villagers]" *(field notes)*.

The collective memory also gets shaped not just by the critical events in which individuals participate as a community; usual events like rituals of marriage, birth and death which are performed collectively, and daily interactions in evening 'baithak' (public grouping) also help in creating a collective memory. The collective memory therefore is a work in progress which accumulates through practices like rituals of marriage, which are many. In marriage, one can see that formal invitation cards are not distributed within the village. Instead the invitation for every ritual is sent out for the village community orally by the person of the barber caste from the village; he goes door to door and invite villagers as per the customary relations with the family. He goes to families and invites them in three ways: to some he gives invites to the full family, called the 'chulha nyot', to some he gives invites to only male members called the 'tagdi bandh', and then gives invites to the head of the family. Even though the agricultural economy has declined, the Jajmani system continues to operate in these rituals. These rituals, along with elaborate festivals which are performed in distinct ways, go down in the collective memory as markers of distinct cultural identity. Even though the culture or festivals that the Gurjars practise are not specific to them but to the larger agrarian system, yet to the individuals of the Gurjars' community they take them as unique practices of being a Gurjar and a villager. The presence of Jajmani rituals though without a Jajmani system in these erstwhile villages confirms how the village identity remains present in the city of Delhi.

Acts for Construction and Continuation of Collective Memory

The third way in which the collective memory is shaped and to some extent constructed is by using social media and consumption of content from mass media and through collective celebration and ownership of important village personalities. In all such celebrations, the identity of Gurjar village men is invoked and thus passed over to the next generation of the community. Events like the celebration of the birth centenaries of the personalities of the Gurjars caste from India's Freedom struggle like Vijay Singh Pathik, the farmer leader from Rajasthan, and Dhan Singh Kotwal, the Gurjar leader from Meerut of the 1857 revolt, are attempts to give shape to the collective memory of the Gurjars in the village. The members of the caste through such celebration identify themselves as a part of a large collective identity, that has had a glorious past and is now in search of new ideas for motivation. It is through such identification that village Gurjars associate with the Gurjars around the country. Some educated young men like Vikki who is a lawyer by profession (field notes) in the village feel that they need to take the lead in educating the new generations about the rich past of the village and their caste.

In the village, the youngsters use social media and mobile internet technology to give shape to collective memory, Facebook pages with names like 'Madanpur ke Models', and songs like 'Madanpur ke cheete', are used to assert village identity. Similarly, groups of people are formed on WhatsApp chat messenger applications with names like 'Jaharvir baba group', 'Yuva

Shakti' and others. While these groups are usually used for passing on forwarded messages, they also become a means of communication and staying united in a changing environment. In a group of 30 members, information on birthday parties, marriage arrangements, and wishes for the newborn are forwarded. Occasionally, some people also share content related to the Gurjars' history or thc viral vidcos of somc Gurjars in any part of thc country. Λ young man from the village who is educated has taken up the task of giving names to the roads and parks of the village on Google Maps, he has named all the major roads after the names of Gurjar leaders and has also given the name to the roads that are of different castes. As he explained to me,

> I named these roads because it is important for giving a good identity to the coming generation, it is necessary that they know which great man existed in this caste, to tell you the truth, I feel really happy and proud when a cab driver plying on these roads ask me if this is Umaro bhati marg, this way I contribute to my community.
>
> (field notes)

This naming of roads and parks on Google Maps, and the use of technology to assert the identity of caste along with the village, is the next step in pushing towards the construction of collective memory that has not really been part of the village but might become a part of it soon, since the names given to roads and parks are not really of the village leaders but of other Gurjar leaders from the country. In addition to the collective memory that belongs to the village from the past, such acts of naming also try to build horizontal solidarities among the caste residing in other villages of Delhi or the country. The young Gurjar men are imbued with two kinds of feelings, one of caste and the other of their village.

Politics of Space and the Recovery of Village Identity within the City

The efforts like the above one, where the young ones have been engaged in the active construction of a separate village identity, are the reasons for a resurging village identity in the city to be found in the unfolding of the urbanization process itself. In the nearby planned colonies, the emergence of resident welfare associations (RWAs) has been a cause of concern for the village residents. The RWAs have been trying to block traditional routes and alleys that pass through the colonies and connect the village with main roads. The politics of such appropriation of space by the means of RWAs is well captured by Sanjay Srivastava in his book *Entangled Urbanism.* He notes, "RWA are crucial to the process of consolidating an urban consensus around middle-classness, and the politics of space is crucial to the making of this consensus" (Srivastava). Thus, it is due to the construction of a distinct middle-class identity that the RWA practises exclusion through various means. The first strategy of making such a distinction with the village is to erect walls around the whole space and put gates for regulating the entry and exit of the people. The underlying reasons for putting gates on every street have always been the concern of security from the acts of theft and burglary. Thus, the practice of transforming oneself into a gated community is an act of carving an exclusive space for oneself by denying entry to non-residents. After the RWAs blocked the passages, the villagers had to dig up new paths. The digging for new paths was not only difficult but it also created a lot of problems for the villagers. As Shravan tells, "our village did not have any second way to get out from the village, it was like entering into a cave, with the kind of traffic we have today, we would have been choked to death". The then-local MLA Ramvir ji, who also belonged to the Gurjar caste, came to help with the construction of a new pathway for the village. Shravan further adds, "Now you can enter from the other side and can easily get out from the recently open side, this has kept the village thriving". Every village person felt the impact of such appropriation of the space by the RWAs; however, they could do nothing to stop it and negotiated their way through it. The urban residents thus occupy a central role in the lives of the village residents and play a critical role (via othering) in keeping them as villagers.

"You Are a Villager; You Can't Mix with Us"

In my interviews with the respondents of the village, the distinction between village and city remained a prominent theme. The village residents, who otherwise are rich and could be even richer than most of the urban residents in terms of wealth, have complained about the discriminatory attitude of the city residents. Chaman Singh (name changed), who belonged to the family of Zaildars, a reputed position in the colonial administration, remarked:

> Mai flat mein bhaut acche acche logon ko janta hu, sabhi hamare ghar bhi aate hain, kabhi paise wagrah ki dikkat mein bhi unhe madad de dete hai, magar meine dekha hai ki ye log hamare yaha to aajate hai magar kabhi bhi hame apne gharo mein upar nahi bulate. 90 per cent log hame Ghar ke niche hi ya raste mein hi baat karke chalta kar dete hai, matlb aaj bhi ye log hame Gurjar [might even mean a villager] ki tarah hi dekhte hai.
>
> (I know a lot of people from the nearby urban colony, they all come to our home in the village, we also sometimes help them with money but one thing that I have noticed is that they will not invite us to their homes. In 90 per cent of cases, if we happen to be in their locality, they will talk to us and deal with us only outside their home, despite all the exchanges, they only look upon us as 'Gurjars' and 'villagers'.)
>
> (field notes)

This feeling of distinction is based on the everyday experience of this man, who has seen the flats being built around their houses and may have known many residents for a very long time. Yet, there remains a distance in social relationships between the urban and rural residents of the same area. The primary axis of discrimination seems to be the rural-ness and class distinction enveloped in caste identity. In another case, a woman from the village was obstructed by the residents of the colony while she was taking a walk in the public park around the colony. The women from the colony asked her to not come to their park as it belonged to only city dwellers and not the villagers. The women from the village also responded quickly, "Tamara Park! tumhara to ghar bhi nahi hota, agar hum apni zameen na dete to". (Your park! You would not even have a home if we villagers hadn't given up our land to the authority.) Such incidents tell us how the boundaries of public spaces are maintained and the appropriation of space happens in everyday life. The binary of urban and rural along with the notion of forwardness and backwardness also carries the notions of status discrimination that are based on the notions of education, work and wealth.

Erased Memories and Subordination of Village

The discriminatory attitude does not only remain at the individual level, but it also takes the form of the collective consciousness of the city dwellers and takes root in the minds of the administration, civil society and the market. All these institutions also bend towards the demands of the city dwellers which leads to the subordination of the village in material ways. The first level of subordination begins with the lack of piped water supply from the state's local bodies; the village suffers from the problem of water and most residents of the village have to dig their borewells. The government and municipal bodies have almost failed to provide proper water supply to the village. Along with the non-availability of water, the village also faces frequent electricity cuts, which is a very unusual experience in the flats of the city dwellers in the vicinity. As Ashok remarks,

> I do not know what is it with us only, we don't get water and electricity properly in the village, it is because of the nearby river that we can get our water, I know many villages where they have to purchase water tanker every day, I wish we don't become like them one day.
>
> (field notes)

The problem is not only with the drinking water supply, other public amenities like the parks and roads are also not well maintained in the village area. Such subordination of the village not only remains at the level of materiality but also permeates into the domain of cognitive recognition of a village. The rapid increase of the markets and shops that cater to the high consumer demands of the urban area around the village has now reduced the village boundaries and it has become difficult to understand the village boundaries.

As explained by Vikram,

> A few years back, a new public school was built on the land that was acquired by the DDA from the farmers of the village, when the school was built, they gave it the name of the colony, you see, the building stands on our land yet our village has no identity.

The attempt to subordinate the presence of a village thus completes the cycle when the material negligence of the village by the local authorities is compounded by the penetration of the market and private capital which essentially utilizes the resources that once belonged to the village to undermine the presence of the village itself.

Negotiations, Preservation and Reclamation of Space

The efforts of subordination of the village by the city are not easily accepted by the residents of the village. The residents of the villages engage in the cultural reproduction of the village in their everyday practices and negotiate with the city life and residents. The nature of such negotiations is at large individualistic yet sometimes it takes the form of collective action by the village residents. While the RWA seeks responsibility for local works in their area, the residents of the village also utilize their political power wielded mostly through the caste politicians of the area to plead for development work in the area. These development efforts include petitions for better drainage, water, and the facilities of common spaces like the Panchayat Ghar (space for village assembly), Chaupal (community hall), Baarat Ghar (marriage halls) and open parks with better conditions.

Most often the negotiation over the space brings private benefits to a few powerful individuals. As it happened in 2013, a renowned school opened its branch that was once part of the village; the villagers wanted that since it is part of the village now, it should suffix the name of the village in the address instead of using the name of the flats. The school being a school of global repute did not like the idea; however, to come out of the crisis and dissipate the angry villagers, the management agreed to take admission of 5–10 students of the villagers every year. The villagers felt that they had been heard and that they had won the battle of negotiations. As Lalit enthusiastically explains, “Bhaiyaa, the whole village became one that time, I don’t know of the old people, but I have seen almost every young one during those protests, after all, it was an issue of our respect”. This incident gave confidence to the villagers that negotiation over space is possible and must be done. As Chaman feels, “I don’t fear these school authorities anymore, whenever I see their buses blocking the passage of our village, I get down and hurl abuses at their drivers to remind them of our last protest”. Along with these small negotiations, the villagers have now begun to take pride in their ‘village-ness’ and do engage in the practice of preservations that they think are necessary to preserve their culture and identity against the aggrandizing city on the one hand and the sprawling slums on the other.

This is leading to the eulogization of village life, caste identity and increasing belief in the community of both. The youth population which is not much educated and has no jobs to do, sit in large and small groups together with the youth of their village and smoke 'hukka', which they think is part of their tradition and separates them from the urban crowd who rely on cigarettes.

The villagers continuously discuss the caste history and listen to folk songs of the caste men to continuously feel proud about it. The educated youth also make use of the internet to take on the task of preservation. As Vikki told me,

> Bhai, I have put the name of our local village streets on the name of great personalities of our caste or some of our ancestors, every time a cab drivers take the name of a road while plying through our streets, I feel proud and happy to have contributed to something better for our village and our caste.

The internet has given space to the villagers and a few educated individuals to write and make people aware of their caste identity. Many young people in the village not only engage in preservation but have been working to reclaim the space that belonged to them in the recent past. These efforts are further complemented by content creation on social media around the village identity. Young people registered pages like 'Madanpur ke Cheete', or 'Gurjars of Madanpur' on Facebook to mark the presence of villagers onto the social media site. Vikki, who is an advocate by profession, started a Wikipedia entry with the name of the village highlighting the importance of the village in the past along with the name of important people of the village. The internet in this sense has made it possible to reclaim the identity of the village that was waning and vanishing with time and urbanization.

Note

1 The idea of 'village republic' was given by Sir Charles Metcalfe (see Inden 1990: 132).

Works Cited

Bentick, J. *Unruly Urbanisation on Delhi's Fringe: Changing Patterns of Land Use and Livelihood*. Netherlands Geographical Studies, p. 270. Groningen: Rijksuniversiteit Groningen, 2000.

Cohn, B. *Colonialism and Its Forms of Knowledge*. Oxford: Oxford University Press, 1997.

Cohn, B. "The Pasts of an Indian Village." *Comparative Studies in Society and History*, vol. 3, no. 3, 1961, pp. 241–249.

Das, A. N. (1987). Changel: Three centuries of an Indian village. *The Journal of Peasant Studies*, *15*(1), 3–60. https://doi.org/10.1080/03066158708438351

Dumont, L. *The 'Village Community' from Munro to Maine in Religion, Politics and History in India*. Paris/The Hague: Mouton Publishers, 1970.

Govinda, R. "'First Our Fields, Now Our Women': Gender Politics in Delhi's Urban Villages in Transition." *South Asia Multidisciplinary Academic Journal*, 2013, pp. 1–15.

Gupta, Dipankar. "Whither the Indian Village: Culture and Agriculture in 'Rural' India." *Economic and Political Weekly*, vol. 40, no. 8, 2005, pp. 751–58.

Halbwachs, M. *On the Collective Memory*. Chicago: Chicago University Press, 1950.

Inden, R. B. *Imagining India*. Bloomington: Indiana University Press, 1990.

Jodhka, Surinder. "Nation, Anthropology and the Village." Understanding Indian Society: The Non-Brahmanic Perspective, edited by S.M. Dahiwale, Rawat Publications, 2005, pp. 51–85.

Kashmir Singh, & Raj, B. *A Socio-Economic Study of Village Gazipur*. New Delhi: Government of India, 1961.

Khanna, S. "Shahri Jat and Dehati Jatni: The Indian Peasant Community in Transition." *Contemporary South Asia*, vol 10 (1), 2001, pp. 37–53.

Lewis, O. *Village Life in a Northern India: Studies in a Delhi Village*. Urbana: Vintage Books, 1958.

Nath, V. "Village, Caste and Community." *Economic Weekly*, vol. 14, Issue no. 49, 1962, pp. 1877–1882.

Rao, M. "A Rural Community on Delhi's Fringe." In *A Reader in Urban Sociology*, edited by M. Rao, C. Bhat, & L. N. Kadekar, pp. 389–410. New Delhi: Orient Longman, 1991.

Shah, A. "The Rural-Urban Networks in India." *South Asia: Journal of South Asian Studies*, vol. 11, no. 2, 1988, pp. 1–27.

Shah, A. "Caste in the 21st Century: From System to Elements." *Economic and Political Weekly*, vol. 42, issue no. 44, 2007, pp. 109–116.

Sharma, U. "Public Shrines and Private Interests: The Symbolism of the Village Temple." In *Sociological Probings in Rural Society*, edited by K. L. Sharma, pp. 257–277. New Delhi: Sage Publications, 2013.

Srivastava, S. *Entangled Urbanism*. New Delhi: Oxford University Press, 2015.

Part III

Self/Other, Self-Memory and Analysis of Identity

8 Memoirs Doubting Memory

An Exploration of Tara Westover's *Educated*

Vishnu Priya T. P.

Introduction

Literary and narrative approaches contribute significantly to our understanding of memory by exploring storytelling in literature and personal accounts, shedding light on how narratives shape the construction and communication of individual and collective memories. A collection of influential works delves into the intersection of literary and narrative approaches within Memory Studies. *Acts of Meaning* (1990) by Jerome S. Bruner emphasises the significance of narrative in constructing meaning, while *Autobiographical Memory and the Construction of a Narrative Self: Developmental and Cultural Perspectives* (2003) explores the developmental and cultural aspects of autobiographical memory. Additionally, Habermas and Bluck's framework of global coherence in life narratives, particularly their emphasis on temporal, causal, and thematic coherence, provides valuable insights into how life stories are structured to create meaning across extended time ranges and diverse contexts (8). These works, among others, contribute to the rich tapestry of Memory Studies by highlighting the literary and narrative dimensions of memory construction. The contemporary landscape of memory studies encompasses emerging trends that delineate the evolving contours of scholarly inquiry, from advancements in neuroscience to the impact of the digital age on memory preservation. In this diverse and expansive field, Tara Westover's acclaimed memoir *Educated* (2018) is a compelling narrative deserving scholarly scrutiny. The memoir unfolds against the backdrop of rural Idaho, primarily set in the environs of Buck's Peak, and chronicles the experiences of Tara, the seventh child of Gene and Faye. Tara's journey from an insular, ideologically driven upbringing to her academic achievements at Cambridge forms the crux of her narrative.

In the context of this complex landscape, this chapter scrutinises Tara Westover's *Educated* through a dual lens. The first lens involves a conventional analysis through the categories of genre, family, and self. The second lens, however, adopts a more critical approach, engaging with the memoir's central theme of doubting memories. This dual reading framework enables a comprehensive exploration of the narrative's complexities, offering insights into traditional literary elements and the nuanced, introspective examination

DOI: 10.4324/9781003508564-12

of memory within the memoir. This chapter employs a structured approach to unravel the complex dimensions of memory within the context of Tara Westover's memoir. It begins with examining the contemporary literary landscape to understand genre modulation and self-critique prevalent in memoirs, setting the stage for understanding the evolving nature of the memoir as a literary form. Subsequently, it delves into the private sphere, unravelling the dynamics of trauma within family narratives and elucidating the unique power paradigms embedded in familial relationships. Navigating the transformative landscape of memory, education, and authentic existence portrayed in Westover's narrative, the exploration engages with the ethical considerations inherent in testimonial narratives and decodes memory as a complex textual tapestry.

The methodology adopted in this study embraces a pluralistic orientation, integrating diverse analytical tools such as content analysis and narrative analysis. An interdisciplinary approach draws on interpretative frameworks from Genre Studies, Ethics of Memoir Writing, Autobiographical Memory, and Trauma and Healing. By intertwining these themes with chosen theoretical frameworks, the research aims to offer a comprehensive and innovative perspective on Tara Westover's *Educated*, challenging traditional notions of memory and genre while contributing to the broader discourse on memoir writing, autobiographical memory, and the portrayal of trauma in literature.

Memoirs in Flux: Genre Modulation and Self-Critique in the Contemporary Literary Landscape

The composition of memoirs has emerged as a prominent literary pursuit in contemporary discourse. The term 'Memoir,' rooted in the French word *mémoire*, transcends linguistic and cultural boundaries, representing a significant genre in modern literature. Memoirs and autobiographies share a common lineage, yet each possesses distinct characteristics within the literary spectrum. Autobiographies typically follow a chronological narrative of an entire life, whereas memoirs selectively concentrate on specific phases. Noteworthy memoirs, such as Ernest Hemingway's *A Moveable Feast*, Vladimir Nabokov's *Speak, Memory*, George Orwell's *Homage to Catalonia*, and Art Spiegelman's *Maus*, have indelibly shaped the literary landscape. These memoirs, revered by a diverse readership, serve varied purposes. Notably, *Maus* by Art Spiegelman, presented in graphic novel form, exemplifies the adaptability of memoir as a contemporary genre, responsive to the preferences of the reading public. As a genre, memoirs can explore the nexus between external events and their impact on the author's psychological landscape. While some memoirs engage with historically significant events, others delve into the complexities of familial relationships or childhood experiences. The contemporary era witnesses a substantial proliferation of memoirs authored by individuals ranging from celebrities and writers to survivors of illnesses and non-celebrities. This surge underscores the genre's efficacy as a medium for narrating diverse life stories and experiences. This chapter aims to explicate the distinctive features of a noteworthy memoir that delineates the upbringing of a daughter within a dysfunctional family. Through a scholarly examination of this selected memoir, the objective is to shed light on its inherent qualities and contribute to the broader understanding of the evolving landscape of memoirs in contemporary literature.

The act of individuals documenting their life experiences has a longstanding tradition, yet the genre of memoir, reflective of the zeitgeist, encapsulates the prevailing spirit of its era. Notably, the contemporary landscape has witnessed a discernible surge in the publication of memoirs and testimonies. A perusal of literary history reveals ongoing discussions about the selection of subjects deemed worthy of narration. In contrast to earlier genres such as epics, which narrated tales of heroes within an immanent world, more recent literary forms, exemplified by novels, have depicted individualistic characters involved in the quest for meaning within a transcendent world. Michael Bakhtin's discourse on certain genres, particularly the novel, as apt expressions for a multicultural world, underscores the dynamic relationship between literature and society (Bakhtin 11). The evolution of literature, serving as both a reflection and counter-voice to dominant ideologies, is inherently tied to societal transformations. As we examine this relationship between literature and society, it becomes essential to acknowledge the significant impact of contemporary digital technologies and social media platforms. In today's digital landscape, platforms like Instagram and Facebook have democratised the narrative documentation process, providing individuals unprecedented opportunities to chronicle their lives. This shift is particularly evident in the proliferation of micro-narratives within the LGBTQIA community, where digital platforms serve as powerful tools to question and subvert normative ideologies. These narratives extend beyond mere communication tools; they function as discourses of individualistic expression and mechanisms for negotiating societal norms. In this context, the contemporary memoir, as a literary form, exemplifies the power dynamics inherent in textual discourses, serving as a locus for the negotiation of individual and collective identities within the tapestry of societal ideologies.

The contemporary evolution of the genre of memoir has manifested in diverse forms, each reflecting unique thematic and stylistic attributes. One such manifestation is the emergence of the 'stunt memoir,' wherein individuals undertake a temporary lifestyle experiment, offering readers insights into unconventional experiences. Another category, the 'nobody memoir,' delves into personal encounters with illness or disability, shedding light on the subjective dimensions of such experiences. Additionally, 'postmodernist memoirs' acknowledge the constructed nature of the narrative, introducing a self-awareness that challenges traditional notions of autobiographical truth. A more recent classification, the 'relational' memoir, centres on narratives of intimate relationships, particularly those involving family members, navigating the complexities of unequal power dynamics, such as parent-child relationships. While these distinct categories highlight the genre's versatility, it is imperative to recognise that the boundaries between them are not rigid. The multiplicity of memoir modes often intertwines, giving rise to hybrid forms that challenge conventional classifications. This interplay of diverse modes underscores the fluidity inherent in memoir writing, emphasising the genre's capacity for adaptation and innovation. Despite the various modes, asserting that these categories exist in isolation would be untenable. The essence of memoir as a contemporary genre lies in its capacity to transcend rigid categorisations, fostering a space for individuality and originality. The hallmark of memoirs, in their myriad forms, is the exploration and expression of unique personal narratives, contributing to the rich tapestry of contemporary literary discourse.

Memoirs often delve into philosophical reflections, contemplating ontological and epistemological inquiries, whether implicitly or explicitly. While renowned philosophers such as Plato, John Locke, Immanuel Kant, and Bertrand Russell have extensively explored epistemology, one can argue that memoirs also wrestle with certain epistemological quandaries as they seek to comprehend the potency and mechanisms of human understanding. Additionally, these narratives may grapple with ontological questions, contemplating the nature of reality. The inherent fascination of memoirs lies in their exploration of the meaning of life, a shared human pursuit that adds a layer of intrigue to the narrative process, signifying a parallel journey with life itself. In contrast, autobiographies often project a sense of certainty and absoluteness in their narration. Works like *Long Walk to Freedom* by Nelson Mandela (1994) or *The Story of My Experiments with Truth* by Mahatma Gandhi exemplify this assertive narrative style. Autobiographies typically present a linear and assured account of one's life, adhering to a structured narrative conveying conviction. Conversely, memoirs embrace uncertainties and engage with the realm of possibilities. The narrative process in a memoir mirrors the complexities of life, where individuals grapple with ambiguities, reflecting the nuanced and dynamic nature of human experience. This inherent openness to exploration and contemplation of life's uncertainties distinguishes memoirs from the more assertive and definitive nature often found in autobiographical narratives.

In his seminal work, *Kinds of Literature: An Introduction to the Theory of Genres and Modes*, Alastair Fowler posits that "genres are actually in a continual state of transmutation" (24), a concept particularly applicable to the genre of memoirs, which mirrors the evolving trends of our era. In the contemporary landscape characterised by multiculturalism and globalisation, where traditional genres like Epics have given way to the prominence of novels, the genre of memoirs exhibits a notable fluidity. Fowler's notion of modulation becomes particularly relevant, underscoring the idea of generic blending and evolution. 'Modulation,' as defined by Fowler, is the process through which a genre extends its generic qualities to other genres over time (191). Fowler utilises terms such as 'kind' and 'mode' to discuss genres, highlighting the potential for a text to be tragicomic in kind yet pastoral or elegiac in mode. According to Fowler, in 'modulation,' the proportions of the modal ingredient may vary widely, resulting in various effects, from overall tones to touches of local colour (191). The generic qualities may not completely merge, allowing for the identification of elements belonging to a particular genre even after modulation has occurred. Bakhtin, too, acknowledges the influence of genres like novels on others, terming this phenomenon as 'novelization.' Bakhtin argues that 'novelization' liberates other genres, making them more flexible, incorporating extraliterary heteroglossia, and injecting a semantic open-endedness and living contact with contemporary reality (323). The remarkable characteristic of memoirs is their capacity for self-critique, signifying their continual development as a genre. This trait is particularly evident in memoirs like Tara Westover's *Educated*, which challenges the conventional expectations of the genre.

Tara Westover demonstrates a keen awareness of the complex terrains of memory. The initial chapter of her memoir, *Educated*, commences with the assertion, "My strongest memory is not a memory" (12), revealing that it is a product of imagination that she later "came to remember as if it had happened" (12). Tara's recollections are deeply intertwined with the imaginative constructs inspired by her father's narrative versions of incidents within the family. Notably, one such incident revolves around Randy Weaver, a self-proclaimed white separatist with anti-government views. Tragic events unfolded, leading to a siege that claimed the lives of Weaver's wife, Vicki, his 14-year-old son, Sammy, and U.S. Marshal William Degan. However, Tara's memory of the Ruby Ridge incident of the 1980s diverges from the factual record. Furthermore, another imagined memory permeates young Tara's consciousness, wherein she substitutes Randy Weaver's family with her own. The fear and suspicion instilled by her father regarding the government serve as the bedrock for these cognitive constructs, which consequentially shape her thought processes. While memoirs and autobiographies are conventionally expected to prioritise factual accounts over fiction, when a memoir questions the reliability of human memory, which forms the bedrock of the genre, it exhibits a novelistic quality. This novelistic quality does not imply a departure into fiction; rather, it reflects the genre's ability to engage in introspection and self-criticism, highlighting its dynamic and ever-evolving nature.

Familial Spaces: Unravelling the Dynamics of Trauma in the Private Sphere and Its Unique Power Paradigms

The discussion on family within the context of the memoir aims to establish a connection between the exploration of familial dynamics, the exercise of power, and the experience of trauma. Privacy and sentiment are often perceived as defining characteristics of the modern family, yet family spaces can also serve as arenas for unchecked exploitation and the infringement of basic human rights. The nuanced discourse surrounding 'childhood' and the challenges faced by children has emerged relatively recently, as highlighted by Philippe Aries in his influential work, *Centuries of Childhood*. Ariès suggests that the decrease in communal sociability allowed for the development of stronger emotional bonds within families, facilitated by a retreat into private, domestic life (375). Scholars, in their attempts to construct a comprehensive history of the 'private sphere,' have delved into themes of individualism to comprehend the evolution of family dynamics. The nineteenth century is widely recognised as a pivotal period for delineating the nuances of the intimate private sphere. While public archives readily facilitate the writing of a history of the public sphere, access to pertinent archives for tracing the evolution of the private sphere is notably restricted. Many scholars acknowledge the Renaissance as a critical juncture marking the foundational shift towards individualism (Perrot 2). James Marten notes, "One of the favorite preoccupations of historians of childhood has been the extent to which families have always loved and appreciated their children" (24). The familial space, far from being ahistorical or apolitical, has been significantly influenced by historical events such as the Renaissance and Protestant Reformation, altering the conceptualisation of childhood. Philosophers like John Locke assert that children are akin to blank slates, and Rousseau's novel *Emile* exemplifies the shift in the understanding of childhood during the Enlightenment. Despite the romanticised depictions of childhood in various discourses, reality often diverges from these idealised portrayals. The exploration of the familial space reveals a complex chemistry of privacy, sentiment, historical events, and evolving childhood conceptualisations that shape family dynamics.

In Michel Foucault's *Security, Territory, Population: Lectures at the Collège de France, 1977–78*, he introduces the concept of 'pastoral power' to elucidate a distinct form of power operative in modern societies. Described as benevolent, pastoral power acts from within the social body, particularly manifesting itself in intimate spheres such as the family, where it assumes the guise of pastoral care (127). The operation of pastoral power involves unique methods, with confession as a pivotal aspect. The individual's innermost secrets become subject to confession, marking a significant departure from the traditional exercise of power 'above' a social body. Unlike territorial dominance, pastoral power centres on individuals, and its origins trace back to Christian practices, albeit adapting to more secular goals from 'salvation' to contemporary parameters (126). Foucault's exploration of pastoral power sheds light on the distinctive nature of trauma within familial spaces. The incorporation of 'beneficial care' in the power dynamics adds complexity to the experience and witnessing of trauma, rendering it markedly different from its public counterpart. The familial context, where power operates through pastoral care, complicates the process of unlearning established behavioural patterns for the subject. Key elements of pastoral power, such as 'obedience' and the art of 'conducting' a subject, provide avenues for manipulation when necessary. However, Foucault's nuanced perspective refrains from portraying pastoral power as absolute, emphasising its coexistence with possibilities of freedom. Modern power, according to Foucault, necessitates these possibilities of freedom for its existence. The educational process within the memoir is related to engaging with these possibilities of freedom, highlighting the dynamic relationship between pastoral power and the pursuit of emancipation.

Tara Westover's memoir offers a penetrating examination of traumatic recollections within the private sphere, instigating a nuanced inquiry into the divergent treatments and conceptualisations of trauma within public and private domains. Publicly, trauma often undergoes commemoration through tangible artefacts such as tombs and monuments, functioning as collective symbols that encapsulate shared historical pain. The excerpt below vividly illustrates a cyclical pattern of abuse perpetuated by Shawn, the protagonist's brother, and the subsequent apologies through gestures or gifts, underscoring the complexity of trauma within familial relationships.

> I AWOKE WITH NEEDLES in my brain. Thousands of them, biting, blocking
> out everything. Then they disappeared for one dizzying moment and I got my bearings...
> "SLUT!"
> "WHORE!"
> Then another sound. Mother. She was crying. "Stop! You're killing her! Stop!"...
> I was yanked to my feet. Shawn grasped a fistful of my hair—using the same method as before, catching the clump near my scalp so he could maneuver me—and dragged me into the hallway. My head was pressed into his chest. All I could see were bits of carpet flying past my tripping feet. My head pounded, I had trouble breathing, but I was starting to understand what was happening. Then there were tears in my eyes.
> *From the pain,* I thought.
> "Now the bitch cries," Shawn said. "Why? Because someone sees you for the slut you are?"...
> Mother was sobbing, clawing at her hair.
> "I see you for what you are," Shawn said. His eyes were wild. "You pretend to be saintly and churchish. But I see you. I see how you prance around with Charles like a prostitute." He turned to Mother to observe the effect of his words on her. She had collapsed at the kitchen table.
> "She does *not,*" Mother whispered.
> Shawn was still turned toward her. He said she had no idea of the lies I told, how I'd fooled her, how I played the good girl at home but in town I was a lying whore. I inched toward the back door.
> Mother told me to take her car and go. Shawn turned to me. "You'll

> be needing these," he said, holding up Mother's keys.
> "She's not going anywhere until she admits she's a whore," Shawn said.
> He grabbed my wrist and my body slipped into the familiar posture, head thrust forward, arm coiled around my lower back, wrist folded absurdly onto itself. Like a dance step, my muscles remembered and raced to get ahead of the music. The air poured from my lungs as I tried to bend deeper, to give my wristbone every possible inch of relief.
> "Say it," he said.
> But I was somewhere else. I was in the future. In a few hours, Shawn would be kneeling by my bed, and he'd be so very sorry. I knew it even as I hunched there.
>
> (Westover 131)

The passage opens with a disorienting scene, employing visceral language to convey the aftermath of a violent encounter. The protagonist's awakening, described as feeling like needles in her brain, sets the tone for her intense and distressing experience. The immediate physical pain and emotional turmoil are depicted with raw and unfiltered narrative techniques, immersing the reader in the harsh reality of the abuse. Shawn's use of derogatory language, labelling the protagonist as a "slut" and a "whore," adds a layer of emotional brutality to the narrative. This verbal abuse complements the physical violence, emphasising the complex nature of the trauma inflicted upon the protagonist. The portrayal of the mother's involvement in the confrontation further complicates the family dynamics, revealing the power structures at play. The cyclical pattern of abuse becomes apparent as Shawn typically follows these episodes with gestures or gifts as a form of apology. This cycle, characterised by abuse, reconciliation efforts, and temporary relief, highlights the manipulative nature of the relationship. The gifts and gestures serve as a temporary reprieve, momentarily shifting the power dynamics, but they do not address the underlying issues or promise genuine change. Westover's narrative techniques, such as vivid imagery, metaphorical language, and sensory details, contribute to the immersive depiction of trauma. The cyclical nature of the abusive relationship adds depth to the overall narrative, symbolising the complexity of the protagonist's experiences and the challenges she faces in breaking free from the toxic dynamics within her family. The memoir invites readers to reflect on broader themes of resilience, trauma, and the long-lasting impact of familial relationships on individual development.

Conversely, the private realm shields traumatic experiences from external analysis and scrutiny, safeguarded by the confines of personal and familial privacy. Historically, the family is a social entity subject to delimited state intervention, as its categorisation within the private sphere implies constraints on external interference. Positioned as the foundational unit of society, the family serves as an emotive space, yet it remains an integral component of the power structure. Louis Althusser's proposition that the family, alongside the

Church, operates as an Ideological State Apparatus rather than a Repressive State Apparatus akin to the government elucidates its role in disseminating and reinforcing ideology within the private domain (17). This Ideological State Apparatus functions by transmitting and perpetuating cultural norms and values. Westover's narrative underscores the complex interaction between private and public spheres and beckons readers to contemplate the entwined dynamics of power, ideology, and trauma within familial spaces.

Rediscovering 'Self': Navigating the Transformative Landscape of Memory, Education, and Authentic Existence

The development of a robust 'sense of self' holds paramount importance for an individual's overall well-being, encompassing both physical and mental dimensions. Scholars, recognising the prevalence of a deficient 'sense of self' among individuals grappling with various mental disorders, delve into the relationship between self-awareness and mental health. Veronica O'Keane, a prominent scholar, expounds on the concept of "Meta-consciousness," characterising it as the act of "looking at yourself looking at yourself" (90) in her work *A Sense of Self: Memory, the Brain, and Who We Are*. These scholarly insights extend beyond the correlation between a 'sense of self' and mental well-being to illuminate the relationship between narration and consciousness. I argue that, in *Educated*, genuine education pivots on unlearning unhealthy relationship dynamics and reclaiming selfhood through adept narrative and autobiographical reasoning. Memory is pivotal in this transformative journey, involving the negotiation and reconciliation of one's memories. Relational memoirs often grapple with collective family memories, posing challenges for individuals attempting to reconcile their personal recollections with those of their family members. Instances where family members deny the occurrence of certain events compel individuals to confront emotional turmoil stemming from the uncertainty surrounding the veracity of their memories. This environment may also provide opportunities for narcissistic family members to engage in gaslighting. However, the utilisation of narrative reasoning emerges as a powerful tool for the author to reclaim their 'reality' and defy the gaslighting tactics imposed upon them. Through the complex interactions of memory, narrative reasoning, and the assertion of individual reality, the memoir becomes a transformative space for reclaiming and reconstructing a robust 'sense of self' amidst the challenges posed by familial dynamics.

Tara Westover's portrayal of her relationship with her elder brother, Shawn, unveils a complex dynamic marked by abuse and manipulation. Despite Shawn's abusive behaviour towards Tara, he skilfully maintains a façade of benevolence in the eyes of their parents. This is evident in their mother's praise, describing Shawn as someone who has always protected "angels with broken wings" (Westover 123). The discrepancy between Shawn's public image and his private conduct contributes to the distortion of

Tara's perceptions and memories. In the chapter titled "My Feet No Longer Touch Earth," Tara grapples with self-deception as she attempts to convince herself that Shawn's cruelty is a recent development. She reflects on her journal entries from that period, recognising the evolution of a narrative where she rewrites her history to fit a constructed reality.

> Reflecting on it now, I'm not sure the injury changed him that much, but I convinced myself that it had, and that any cruelty on his part was entirely new. I can read my journals from this period and trace the evolution—of a young girl rewriting her history. In the reality she constructed for herself nothing had been wrong before her brother fell off that pallet. *I wish I had my best friend back,* she wrote. *Before his injury, I never got hurt at all.*
>
> (147)

Tara's admission of doubt regarding her memories raises poignant questions about the reliability and malleability of personal recollections. Her struggle to reconcile the past reflects the interaction between memory, self-perception, and the transformative power of narrative construction.

The fear of being forever confined to a specific identity haunts Tara, particularly the image of the young girl in men's jeans working in the scrap yard on Buck's Peak. In the chapter "What We Whispered and What We Screamed," Tara embarks on a journey to reclaim control over her memories and narrative.

> This half-knowledge works in me like a kind of possession, and for a few minutes I'm taken over by it. I rise from my bed, retrieve my journal, and do something I have never done before: I write what happened. I do not use vague, shadowy language, as I have done in other entries; I do not hide behind hints and suggestion. I write what I remember: *There was one point when he was forcing me from the car, that he had both hands pinned above my head and my shirt rose up. I asked him to let me fix it but it was like he couldn't hear me. He just stared at it like a great big jerk. It's a good thing I'm as small as I am. If I was larger, at that moment, I would have torn him apart.*
>
> (215)

She confronts the half-knowledge that has been imposed upon her, recognising it as a form of possession. In a significant departure from her previous entries, Tara articulates a decisive narrative, describing a specific incident with Shawn in unambiguous terms. This newfound assertiveness in recounting her experience signifies a pivotal moment of self-empowerment and autonomy. The act of writing becomes a transformative tool, enabling Tara to challenge the imposed narratives and assert her version of events. These instances in Westover's memoir underscore the relationship between memory, narrative construction, and the assertion of personhood. The analysis of these quotations illuminates the ongoing struggle for autonomy over one's memories and the profound impact of narrative agency on shaping self-perception and overcoming the denial of personhood.

Education unfurls as an enduring journey, and Westover's foray into formal education at Brigham Young University stands as a transformative chapter in her continual odyssey of learning and self-discovery. Initially grappling with the unfamiliar lexicon of academia, where even the concept of an 'essay' feels foreign, Tara undergoes profound disorientation in adapting to the structured educational system. Amid this internal struggle, she contemplates the wisdom of her decision, pondering whether the path of home education might have been more viable. Tara's initiation into formal education acts as a catalyst, fostering an awareness that prompts critical reflection, especially concerning her brother Shawn's derogatory 'nicknames' such as "wench," "wilbur," and the racially insensitive term "nigger" (Westover 196). The discomfort Tara experiences, particularly regarding the racial slur, illuminates the transformative power of education in shaping one's social consciousness and sensitivity to language. Her enrolment in an introductory Psychology course further amplifies this transformation. Tara's realisation that some symptoms align with her father's behaviour underscores the interdisciplinary nature of education. This revelation extends beyond individual introspection, offering a broader commentary on the potential insights gained through education, transcending traditional academic boundaries. The philosophical underpinnings of education take centre stage in Emily Robertson's assertion that education, in its pursuit of knowledge, necessitates truth and justification as integral epistemic goals (2). This aligns with the well-established correlation between knowledge and power in philosophical discourse. Tara's journey underscores the significance of specific memories as repositories of knowledge, particularly when intertwined with power dynamics within familial relationships. A nuanced philosophy of education emerges, challenging the notion of education as mere indoctrination and advocating for it as an initiation—a process that extends beyond the mere acquisition of information to encompass knowledge that is both significant and organised in patterns contributing to perspective and understanding. Drawing from the insights of scholars like Elgin and Siege, the overarching goal of education extends to the development of intellectual judgement (Robertson 12). Tara's narrative thus becomes a testament to the versatile aims and transformative potential embedded in the pursuit of education, with the rediscovery of the 'self' as an integral part of this evolving journey.

Heidegger explores the idea of 'authentic' (*eigentlich*) and 'inauthentic' (*uneigentlich*) modes of existence, in his seminal work *Being and Time.* According to Heidegger, to exist authentically is to choose one's possibilities of being and, crucially, to take responsibility for one's existence (Gorner 105). Tara's narrative unfolds as a poignant illustration of the challenges inherent in choosing an authentic existence, distinct from the constraints imposed by her familial environment. The chapter delves into the complexities of Tara's existential choices, emphasising the centrality of 'memory' in this transformative process. Choosing authenticity for Tara entails rejecting the predetermined path set by her family and taking control of her own narrative. However, the consequences of this choice are profound, encompassing episodes of depression, financial instability, and becoming the family scapegoat. Tara's journey exemplifies the inherent struggles and sacrifices required in the pursuit of authenticity. Her ongoing trials and tribulations are situated within the broader human experience, suggesting that individual suffering is a microcosm of collective human anguish. This perspective aligns with existentialist philosophy, which contemplates the complexities of freedom and existential crises. By viewing personal tragedy through the lens of shared human suffering, the narrative invites a deeper sense of compassion. Ultimately, Tara's story underscores her quest to find her place in the world, acknowledging that alienation is an inescapable aspect of life. It is through the acceptance of this reality that Tara finds a pathway to an authentic existence.

Testimonio and Ethical Complexities: Decoding Memory as a Textual Tapestry

The intersection of testimonio and the unreliable narrator raises complex ethical considerations, particularly concerning the veracity of the narrative and the privacy rights of those implicated in the narrator's life. These ethical quandaries become especially pronounced when the narrative assumes the role of a testimonio, as is often the case with memoirs. Memoirs inherently possess the potential to serve as a testimony, whether on an individual or communal level. Thomas Couser, in his work *Memoir: An Introduction*, delineates the concept of testimonio, wherein an individual attests to the reality or truth of events experienced by one's community (86). In certain instances, memoirs classified as 'relational' may feature children narrating their experiences with toxic narcissist parenting. Within this context, the narrator not only shares their personal narrative but also serves as a spokesperson for all children grappling with the trauma associated with toxic parenting. Couser underscores the potency of testimonio, stating that its impact is derived not only from factual truth but also from its authenticity (92). Tara Westover's memoir, *Educated*, aligns with the testimonio genre as she attests to her experiences and challenges the authoritative voices that once dictated her life. Westover's narrative serves as a form of speaking truth to power, an act of authenticity that goes beyond mere factual accuracy. The ethical implications surrounding the portrayal of personal and familial experiences within the testimonio framework prompt reflection on the delicate balance between truth-telling and the preservation of individual and familial privacy. The nuanced exploration of testimonio and the unreliable narrator underscores the intricate ethical landscape inherent in the genre of memoir.

In contemporary discourse, the ethical ramifications stemming from the composition of potentially 'false' testimonio have assumed a significant gravity. The repercussions extend beyond the literary realm, encompassing legal consequences, prize retractions, and the tarnishing of an author's credibility, particularly when the author is politically active or takes a stance against oppression. Memoirs such as *Fragments: Memories of a Wartime Childhood*, *I, Rigoberta*, and Misha Defonseca's *Surviving with the Wolves* (2005) stand as noteworthy instances where the authenticity of the testimonial narrative has been subject to scrutiny. An equally crucial facet involves the ethical considerations inherent in crafting a relational memoir.

In recounting a poignant incident from her childhood, Tara Westover reflects on the inherent complexities of memory and the potential for divergent recollections within a familial context. At the age of ten, Tara's brother Luke experiences a harrowing accident in the junkyard, where his leg catches fire, prompting a desperate return home for assistance. While Tara provides a detailed narrative of the event, she candidly acknowledges the existence of inconsistencies in certain specific details. One such discrepancy revolves around the aftermath of the incident, where Tara recalls that Luke inadvertently spread the fire to the mountains. However, uncertainty arises regarding who extinguished the fire in the mountains. Upon questioning her brother Richard about this aspect, he asserts that their father played a pivotal role in extinguishing the mountain fire.

> Since the writing of [the story of Luke's burn,] I have spoken to Luke about the incident. His account differs from both mine and Richard's. In Luke's memory, Dad took Luke to the house, administered a homoeopathic for shock, then put him in a tub of cold water, where he left him to go fight the fire. This goes against my memory, and against Richard's. Still, perhaps our memories are in error. Perhaps I found Luke in a tub, alone, rather than on the grass. What everyone agrees upon, strangely, is that somehow Luke ended up on the front lawn, his leg in a garbage can.
>
> (87)

The quoted passage exemplifies Tara's introspective analysis of the fluid nature of memory. She grapples with the realisation that her recollection of the event may not align with those of her siblings, introducing the notion of subjective perspectives in familial narratives. Tara's transparency in acknowledging potential errors in her memory showcases a profound self-awareness and an openness to the inherent fallibility of individual recollections. Upon further reflection and dialogue, Tara engages with the variations in memory surrounding the incident. Subsequent conversations with Luke reveal divergent recollections, adding another layer of complexity. In Luke's memory, their father took him to the house, administered a homoeopathic remedy for shock, and then placed him in a tub of cold water before leaving to combat the fire. This version contradicts Tara's and Richard's recollections, challenging the notion of a singular, objective truth in memory. Tara contemplates the possibility of errors in her memory, considering the prospect that Luke may have been found in a tub rather than on the grass. Strikingly, amidst the variations, a shared element emerges—the consensus that Luke eventually ended up on the front lawn, with his injured leg placed in a garbage can. This exploration of disparate memories within the family not only underscores the inherent subjectivity and malleability of individual recollections but also serves as a testament to the intricate nature of familial narratives and the elusive quest for an absolute truth within the realm of memory. Tara's nuanced analysis invites readers to reflect on the dynamic and subjective nature of memory, challenging preconceived notions of objective truth and highlighting the role of individual perspectives in shaping family narratives.

For discerning readers, the reliability of a narrator constitutes a cardinal determinant in evaluating the authenticity of a memoir. Recent advancements in Memory Studies have yielded essential insights that bear significance in elucidating the complexities inherent in the genre of memoir. Eric Kandel, in his seminal work *Memory: From Mind to Molecules*, delineates the multifaceted nature of memory reconstruction, highlighting the presence of "creative errors, deleting some parts of the story, fabricating other parts, and generally trying to reconstruct the information in a way that makes sense" (Kandel 85). While considerable scholarly attention has been directed towards the intersection of Memory Studies and literary analysis, the discourse on the textual essence of memory transcends the conventional association of memoirs solely with the act of remembering. Avishek Parui, in *Culture and Literary: Matter, Metaphor, Memory*, posits that Memory functions as a narrative category characterised by fluidity and discursiveness (98). The discursive quality of memory manifests through the inherent involvement of interpretation in the act of remembering (98). Scientific investigations also delve into the role of 'metaphor' as a pivotal narrative instrument in the interpretative processes associated with memory (101). Consequently, the process of remembering and the construct of memory exhibit characteristics analogous to a text, contingent upon the interpretative act. These scholarly observations necessitate a reconsideration of the veracity of memoirs or autobiographies. Authors demonstrating an acute awareness of the textual quality of their memoirs not only recognise the tricky dynamics of memory but also manifest a consciousness that contributes to the authenticity of the narrative. This consciousness underscores transparency on the part of the author, emphasising the dynamic and interpretative nature of memory.

Conclusion

In the culmination of this chapter, the focus narrows to the transformative potential embedded in the act of narration, particularly within the context of unravelling trauma in the private sphere. The exploration centres on Tara

Westover's memoir, *Educated*, as a case study, delving into the multifaceted layers of testimonial narration. The study illuminates the often-overlooked impact of private emotional distress, underscoring its comparable intensity to physical pain. The evolution of the concept of family over time is emphasised, revealing that recognising dysfunction within familial structures requires a prolonged process of unlearning and education. The narrative argues for the acknowledgement of testimonies related to familial trauma, positioning them as contributors to genuine pain and post-traumatic stress disorder with tangible repercussions for the individuals involved. While acknowledging that testimonies are sometimes appreciated for the novelty of suffering, the conclusion raises a crucial concern regarding the risk of false narratives for personal gain. The transformative potential of narration takes centre stage, with a focus on its therapeutic value for both narrators and readers. Tara Westover's *Educated* is presented as a poignant example, offering catharsis to readers by sharing her traumatic experiences. The memoir becomes a conduit for exploring the intricacies of memory manipulation, the profound impact of identity loss, and the gradual journey towards healing. Narration is contextualised as a dynamic tool in the healing process, facilitating the stages of overcoming denial and achieving acceptance. The act of narrating private experiences is posited as a means of transforming them into collective knowledge, contributing to a shared understanding of human suffering. The conclusion underscores the ambivalence inherent in memory, with the acknowledgement of its fluid nature. The narrative emerges as a performative act, actively shaping and solidifying the evolving sense of self for the author. In this existential journey, the chapter asserts that existence precedes essence, encapsulating the profound transformative power of testimonial narration in the realm of trauma in the private sphere.

The dual reading framework introduced in this exploration reveals two distinctive modes: the conventional, which methodically analyses through the lenses of genre, family, and self, and the critical, which courageously engages with the memoir's profound theme of doubting memories. Through this bifocal approach, the narrative's complexities are laid bare, inviting readers into a nuanced understanding of Westover's transformative journey. Memoirs and autobiographies, traditionally regarded as bastions of factual representation, encounter a fascinating metamorphosis when a narrative probes the reliability of human memory—the cornerstone of the genre. In *Educated*, this venture into questioning memory imparts a novelistic quality, not as a deviation into fiction but as a testament to the genre's capacity for introspection and self-criticism. Far from diminishing its authenticity, this novelistic quality underscores the dynamic and ever-evolving nature of memoirs, inviting readers to reevaluate their expectations and engage with the narrative on a deeper level.

The narrative's exploration of the private sphere becomes a catalyst for contemplation on the complex dynamics of power, ideology, and trauma within familial spaces. Westover's memoir, beyond being a personal narrative, emerges as a reflection on broader societal constructs, urging readers to interrogate their assumptions about familial relationships and societal expectations. Genuine education, as posited in *Educated*, transcends traditional notions by becoming a transformative process of unlearning unhealthy relationship dynamics and reclaiming selfhood through adept narrative and autobiographical reasoning. Memory, a central theme in this transformative journey, assumes a pivotal role that extends beyond mere recollection. It becomes a terrain of negotiation and reconciliation—a dynamic interplay between past and present, self and society. Authors who demonstrate a keen awareness of the textual quality of their memoirs contribute not only to the complexities of memory but also manifest a consciousness that significantly enhances the authenticity of the narrative. This awareness, palpable in Westover's work, underscores transparency on the part of the author, emphasising the dynamic and interpretative nature of memory. In conclusion, *Educated* stands as a testament to individual resilience, challenging conventional norms of memory and memoir writing. By beckoning readers to delve into the complexities of the narrative, Tara Westover opens avenues for innovative approaches in the study of memoirs and recollection, enriching scholarly discussions on the interplay between memory, narrative, and the construction of personal histories. The memoir's profound impact lies not only in its individual resonance but also in its potential to reshape our collective understanding of the genre of memoir.

Works Cited

Althusser, Louis. *On Ideology*. Verso, 2008.

Ariès, Philippe. *Centuries of Childhood: A Social History of Family Life*. Jonathan Cape, 1962.

Bakhtin, Mikhail. *The Dialogic Imagination: Four Essays*. University of Texas Press, 1987.

Couser, G. Thomas. Memoir: An Introduction. Oxford University Press, 2012.

Fireman, Gary D., et al. *Narrative and Consciousness*. Oxford University Press, 2003.

Foucault, Michael. *Security, Territory, Population: Lectures at College De France, 1977–78*. Edited by Michel Senellart, Palgrave Macmillan, 2009.

Fowler, Alastair. *Kinds of Literature: An Introduction to the Theory of Genres and Modes*. Harvard University Press, 1982.

Gorner, Paul. *Heidegger's Being and Time: An Introduction*. Cambridge University Press, 2006.

Habermas, Tilmann, and Susan Bluck. "Getting a Life: The Emergence of the Life Story in Adolescence." *Psychological Bulletin*, vol. 126, no. 5, 2000, pp. 748–769, https://doi.org/10.1037/0033-2909.126.5.748.

Kandel, Eric R. *Memory: From Mind to Molecules*. Roberts & Company Publishers, 2009.

Marten, James. *The History of Childhood: A Very Short Introduction*. Oxford University Press, 2018.

O'Keane, Veronica. A *Sense of Self Memory, the Brain, and Who We Are*. W. W Norton & Company, 2021.

Parui, Avishek. *Culture and Literary: Matter, Metaphor, Memory*. Rowman & Littlefield, 2022.

Perrot, Michelle, editor. *A History of Private Life: From the Fires of Revolution to the Great War*. Translated by Arthur Goldhammer, The Belknap Press of Harvard University Press, 1990.

Robertson, Emily. "The Epistemic Aims of Education." *The Oxford Handbook of Philosophy of Education,* edited by Harvey Siegel, Oxford University Press, 2010, pp. 9–35.

Westover, Tara. *Educated: A Memoir*. Random House, 2018.

9 Memory in Question

Decoding the 'Self' in Select Indian Penal Autobiographies

Ananya Parida and Shashibhusan Nayak

Introduction

Prisoner-narrators write about themselves not only to express their feelings but to motivate, to cry out loud in anguish, to unravel the hidden truth, and to create a body of text equally important as other subjects. In modern times, prison literature is one of the emerging fields of world literature. In India, prison literature can be recorded from the time of Sangam.[1] George Misch, the founder of modern autobiography, begins his seminal book *The Conception and Origin of Autobiography* (1950: 1) with the definition of autobiography as 'a repository of inner experience and historical reflection,' asserting its existence since antiquity. There are numerous writers who are incarcerated for different political, social, and religious reasons. But still, it is proved that their confinement has only physically incarcerated them; their throbbing heart and imaginative minds had broken through the high prison walls to express themselves through writing. Under harsh circumstances and strict surveillance, they could manage to motivate their fellow compatriots strategically. The history of the Indian freedom struggle movement has a long list of such prisoners who were put behind bars in solitary confinement, denied reading and writing materials, denied natural sunlight, and lived in unhygienic cells yet could produce religious texts and poetry of love and autobiography. Their staunch conviction can be put into words through Richard Lovelace's often-quoted lines from *To Althea, from Prison*: "Stone walls do not a prison make / Nor iron bars a cage."[2] It is evident from prison narratives discussed in the next sections that one can restrict one's body only, never the curious, imaginative mind that can record and recollect events in captivity to use later. Memory supports them in the process of releasing the trauma off their tormented soul and imprisoned body through words. They recollect the carefully or naturally compiled memory to express their views on various issues connected to imprisonment. This not only helps to defend themselves from allegations that led to their jail-going, also they establish an altogether different identity for themself. Prisoner becomes a writer. Richard Terdiman claims that the exercise of memory seeks to heal the same traumas whose capacity for disrupting our existing memory itself perversely sustains while understanding Freud's explanation of memory that is paradoxical

DOI: 10.4324/9781003508564-13

(1993). The memory that haunts someone is the same memory that comes to rescue the bleeding heart by easing the burden through letters. It is also evident that the prisoners took the aid of mnemonic methods to memorise events by writing on walls and stones. Also, letters were smuggled to transfer information amid the horrors and traumatic conditions of the prison environment. Gusdorf has rightly mentioned "Each man matters to the world, each life and each death; the witnessing of each about himself enriches the common cultural heritage" (1980: 30)

Self and memory intersect and interact in the process of auto-writing. In prison narratives, both complement each other in such a manner that the line of difference blurs to the point of being granted as true. Sherif Hetata lucidly explains that autobiography:

> Should tell the reader how the author became a self; it should tell of experiences, choices in life; it should reveal the things we suppress or fear or hide or show under false colours; it should present the truth of the individual Self, how the Self relates to the world, to society, to family, to a spouse or a lover, to friends and rivals, to the system and values that govern life. These are the treasures autobiography can open up for us, the insights it can provide.
>
> (2003: 124)

Gopabandhu Das: Radicalising the Social

Utkalamani Pandit Gopabandhu Das was a nation-builder. A lawyer, poet, educator and social reformer, Das showed a ray of hope for freedom through his social activities. He brought modernity to Odisha with his complete dedication towards redressing the suffering of others. He dedicated his life towards spreading consciousness among the Odia people to strive for a society free from poverty and ignorance that would ultimately bestow a respectful life to its people (2014: 48). There are numerous turning points in his social-political career. In the year 1909, when the whole of India was gaining strength to stand against the British and militancy was the new norm, Gopabandhu Das started Satyabadi Vana Vidyalaya in Puri, a coastal district of Odisha. He believed that education is the most effective tool to make people aware of their innate freedom as well as their obligations towards their motherland. The school was open for all castes and creeds to sit, dine, or study together for their holistic development—physical, moral, mental, and societal—in an open-air teaching-learning system. It was an experiment in the field of education that subsequently succeeded in its goal of cultivating ideals of patriotism in the hearts of students while at once challenging Brahminical orthodoxy. The famous lawyer and freedom fighter Madhusudan Das continued to help him carry forward his movement to awaken the Odia people, to accelerate their demands for a separate province for Odias through the Utkal Union Conference. They strove hard to secure and strengthen the cultural, literary, and linguistic heritage and independent identity of Odias living in the then Bihar, Bengal, and Orissa Provinces. In order to save Odia language and literature from the Bengali *Bhandraloks* who believed Odia to be a part of their language, and to prove its linguistic significance, he started weekly *The Samaj* on 4 October 1919. Also, he started an Odia M.E. School at Bahadaguda for the same purpose.

Das's leadership motivated the educated middle-class people, and in this programme, he was assisted by a group of educated people. Among them were Nilakantha Das, Acharya Harihara, Godabarish Mishraand Krupasindhu Mishra. Das wrote extensively in *Satyabadi* and *The Samaj* to motivate people chiefly to revolt against the British rule and to address matters related to contemporary social, political, and literary situations. In the year 1915, he wrote in *The Satyabadi*: "The good of the individual lies in the good of the collectivity, and the perfection and full realisation of life lies in his securing the good of the society, its progress and liberation." In an editorial of *The Samaj* in 1927, he writes:

> National unity can never last long and be strong unless communalism is completely banished from politics. The country and nationalism, not religion and communalism, should form the basis of the politics of the people. True unity among the people can thus be achieved.

Apart from being a successful educationist, he was an inspirational writer who inspired thousands of people to participate in the freedom struggle movement. His life is a beautiful journey from being a lawyer to an educationist, social activist, and freedom fighter. And also a glorious Odia prisoner of the colonial era whose writing during imprisonment had become a symbol of Odia strength and honour of the land. Interestingly, his poetry had a purpose. His poems are nature-inspired, personal, and emotional in tone; motivated by his deep understanding of religion and nationalistic temper; and written in a conversational mode with the common people. Most of his well-known poems, such as "Kara Kabita" (Prison Poems) and "Bandira Atmakatha" (The Autobiography of a Prisoner), were written during his spells of imprisonment in Cuttack and Hazaribagh Jail.

His "Bandira Atmakatha" (The Autobiography of a Prisoner) and "Kara Kabita" (Prison Poems) were published in 1923 and 1928, respectively. They were written when he was imprisoned for participating in the non-cooperation movement. For his rebellious zeal, he was initially imprisoned in Cuttack Jail only to be shifted later to Hazaribagh Jail in present-day Jharkhand. It was the usual practice of the British government to relocate the agitators to a remote place so that they wouldn't be able to participate in any rebellious activity. Gopabandhu Das was one such prisoner. But even after putting him behind bars, he continued to motivate his people to strong opposition through his poetry and articles. "Bandira Atmakatha" is a long poem written in autobiographical mode running into six sections, spreading to 782 lines.

This poem narrates his plight during a short stay in the Cuttack Jail. Also, he writes about his transportation to Hazaribagh Jail by train. It provides a testament to the distressed socio-political environment that he had experienced behind bars. He remembers that he still had faith and conviction for a better time. He writes with strong conviction that all must unite, and he shall be the first one to show that unity.

The poet vows that whatever may happen, the end should only be complete Independence or Purna Swaraj:

> Make my heart strong!
> Oh, my Lord – Lord of Truth!
> Let my whole attention be on achieving Swarajya
> Bharat's Swarajya is a blessing to the world

These lines echoed in streets during the first half of the twentieth century. Another poetry collection named "Kara Kabita" (Prison Poems) is similar in tone and order as a continuation. The collection contains 13 poems focussing on his plight in Hazaribagh Jail and his socio-political disorder outside. Poems with titles such as "Bandira Swadesh Chinta" (The Patriotic Thoughts of a Prisoner), "Bandir Sandhya Bhakti" (The Evening Prayers of a Prisoner), and "Bandira Sandhya Bhavana" (The Evening Thoughts of a Prisoner) directly harp on imprisonment, whereas others focus on the excitement of love, an anxiety of loss, and a dissatisfaction questioning his destiny. The poem "Bandira Swadesh Chinta" is a lengthy autobiographical poem of 131 stanzas and is the most famous one among the 13 of them. It addresses the south wind that touches his cell in the Hazaribagh Jail and makes him intensely homesick. This homesickness is prevalent in all the three prisoner-writers the chapter deals with. Both "Bandira Atmakatha" and "Kara Kabita" are autobiographical in nature and give testimony to his creative craftsmanship and patriotism in modern Odia literature that powerfully express a need for change in the turbulent 1920s of India.

Interestingly, the poems were written and published during the same period. "Bandira Atmakatha" was published while he was in jail, as Cuttack Jail had less stringent rules. But his "Kara Kabita" was published later, and this collection is extensively dependent upon his memory of the trauma. Nevertheless, the publication date of his first poem puts forward a question: How under strict surveillance could he smuggle his poems that could be published in the same year he was in jail? The case can be otherwise. Either the date of publication is wrong, or it had been strategically published by others who were in close contact with him. These are the questions that position the autobiographical texts under doubt, and readers are left with confusion propagating questions on their authenticity. This can open up fresh scope of research related to the politics of publication. Though the present study is not concerned about it.

Barindra Ghose: Personal is Political

In the second decade of the twentieth century, the political prisoners who were behind bars and in fetters began their protest against "this life of suffering and sorrow, of vice and pollution" through hunger strikes and refusal to work (Ghose, 1922: 128). The heartrending narratives of degraded treatments flood the autobiographies of the political prisoners such as Baridra Kumar Ghose who was convicted in Manicktolla Conspiracy Case (1908), and subsequently transported to be imprisoned in the Andaman Cellular Jail. He wrote aboutthe manual jobs that were forced upon them, such as coir-pounding and oil-grinding. And they contributed to a history of penal workforce desired for productivity. The system of punishing and disciplining the prisoners led to the formation of an alternative space, away from the 'mainland,' highly deviating the moral and social codes of conduct by and large. Soon the educated prisoners took to hunger strikes and presented their agony, which was later stimulated by various political movements demanding their repatriation. While the settlement advocated for equality among prisoners, it simultaneously challenged the notion of sanctity among educated prisoners. To stand at par with the facilities extended to political prisoners in Indian jails, the prisoners transported as 'political' prisoners demanded the same position to ascertain those privileges and facilities.

Andaman Cellular Jail, unlike mainland jails, strategically curated a culture of penal inequality and perpetual servitude which remains unrecorded in the colonist texts. Yet its deep impact can be traced from the first-hand narrations of convicts who had experienced the trauma of transportation for life. How did they handle the trauma of living away from their homeland? How, with that trauma, could they memorise the events? What necessitated them to retrieve their memory and write years after their release? Responses to these questions can explain the culture of penal servitude. And their living condition can be assessed through a handful of penal narratives available in archives in the form of juridical literature such as letters to and from home, memoirs, and petitions, and in libraries in the form of auto/biographical texts. Autobiography of political prisoners remains a vital nerve to explain the crucial time. The writings—self-critical and self-analytical—testify the growth of nationalism that can hardly be articulated in any other from but autobiographical narratives. Although political prisoners were considered privileged, they formed an alternative category of prisoners that was deprived of all penal favours. The gruesome episodes narrated by these political prisoners—about the size of cell, the convict food, and the labour system—sharply contrast with the reformation project of the imperial government. These narratives serve as a distinct category of text to put forth the history of the penal culture and the psychology behind imprisonment. But, because they were written after release, they have to depend heavily upon their memory, putting the text under doubtful veracity concerning its truthfulness and authenticity.

Barindra Kumar Ghose, in his autobiography *Dwipantarer Katha* (1920), translated into English as *The Tale of My Exile* (1922), speaks loudly of the vicious jail atmosphere and how the jail itself instigated "unnatural crimes" to happen. Ghose introduces his autobiography by trying to remember the exact date of his deportation. He recounts,

> It was perhaps on the 11 December 1909, there has been a complete overhaul of things during my twelve years' exile...This faculty seems to be fallen in a moribund condition and can only groan at its best. All the past events have come there shadowy and uncanny images, as it were, parading in a drunken brain.
>
> (1922, 1)

This state of mind is justified as he lived aloof from the world outside the Alipore 44 Degree Jail for a long time. This was his experience at the time of transportation to the Andamans that he recalls after years of repatriation from the Andaman Cellular Jail. The gap can be overseen because memory re/construction is "about consistency with pre-existing knowledge and only secondary about 'what happened'" (Conway and Howe: 2022). He defines the state of convicts as "there was no such thing as gentleman, not even perhaps a thing as man, here were only convicts" (46). Imprisonment involved a process of disciplining by instilling shame and fear in the prisoners. He remembers that the jailers were the lowest kind of 'brute force.' He recounts:

> When it becomes physically impossible to grind out 30 lbs of oil, one is forced to seek the aid of the more robust ruffians in order to avoid punishment and that means to sell, in return, one's body for the most abject end.
>
> (108)

Without family, they experienced the void. This condition is expressed in his autobiography: "The want of home influence, the shutting of all ways of natural satisfaction turns a man gradually into a sheer brute" (109). They lived in the putrid atmosphere of 'sin,' 'vice,' and 'misery.' Ghose felt the need of a religious life, which he perceived to be the only immediate solace to the miserable life: "There are a thousand ways in the prison leading to vice, but not the least arrangement to instil knowledge, to evoke the higher susceptibilities" and "the prison shuts out all these wholesome influences and opens to the unfortunate prisoner the gate of heaven or hell?" (127). Strict prison rules and constant supervision could not repress the natural 'hunger' of the mind and body. He also memorised and wrote about the 'real criminals' who had no sense of nationalist or patriotic feelings.

Barindra Ghose states: "There was no hope for anyone to keep body and soul together and return to his country. Some would die by hanging, others would die by going mad" (85). He also writes:

> There is no arrangement for proper ventilation in these cells, except through a very small skylight. Even a healthy man feels suffocated in such a place and the feeling that one has, when ill and left alone, should better be experienced than described.
>
> (131)

Consequent upon inhuman treatment, seven political prisoners, namely, Bimal Kumar Das Gupta, Probodh Chandra Roy, Sushil Kumar Das Gupta, Prabir Goswami, Barindra Kumar Ghosh, Bimlendu Chakravorty, and Subodh Roy, went on hunger strike (2003: 90). The demands included, but were not limited to the provision of light in their cells till 10 pm, weekly and monthly newspapers, the right to petition under both central and local governments, a diet including a choice of vegetables, and toothpowder, toothpaste, and sandals, etc.[3] In addition to personal motives, a significant political phenomenon emerged from these hunger strikes. Devoid of facilities to write, the prisoner-narrator often memorised the events. Subsequently, he/she has to rely upon the information they have stored to write after years. Reliability poses a matter of concern in these texts, and they are put under doubtful veracity as the information is too personal to be examined. Darby and Sloutsky argue that a particular information gets diluted with other instances of memory with the passing of time. Forgetting indicates a failure in memory retrieval. Even if the instance is stored in long-term memory, with a gap in time it will be difficult to recall. The length of time between the information learned and information retained/recognised determines the amount of decay of the same memory. This study critically evaluates the fact that memory lies somewhere between forgetting and recollecting,[4] and asserts that the political prisoners carefully share their memory with a motive. The study of Barindra Ghose's case substantiates the argument that among prisoners who specifically had demanded to be called a 'political' prisoner, there was a political motive behind writing the autobiographies that Uma Ram and K.S. Ram call "historic nostalgia" (2014: 84).

As nonviolent action of the fast includes rationality and emotion to challenge structural conditions defining political opportunities, a hunger strike may be considered a well-planned counter-political action. Moreover, considering the biological aspect of the fast, it breaks reserved body fat to produce energy for survival and in a personal/political context, hunger strikes lead to self-consumption and ultimately to death. Such a death is a consequence of resisting the oppressor and his oppressive ways and poses violence by drawing the attention of people within and outside the country and challenging the concepts of humanity.

In keeping with Foucault's assertion that where there is [coercive] power there is resistance (1978), the attempt to reject food and work among the political prisoners of the Andaman penal settlement implies that power and influence do not flow in one direction but are distributed in a complex manner throughout the social system. Moreover then, self-starvation is a structurally isolating concept of human behaviour, and by its nature, where the prisoner does not take anything into the body, in a way splits himself from the world. Cutting the subject out of reach of the world, it contains the notion of placelessness and timelessness. It becomes historical through collective experiences, and political through representative or symbolic ones. Making his body a site where the national body-state can identify the shared suffering, the isolated individual prisoner bleeds into the national, historical, and also communal at once. It thus serves as a testing model where both the political prisoner and the body-state claim hunger as their own, and the enduring desire for freedom would do away with the claims of both the entities. It served as a tactic usually employed by the powerless against the powerful. If the defendant allowed the political prisoner to die of starvation, he would not only have to compensate for the death but also would invite fear and extreme consequences, even to the point of shaking the establishment of the subjugating authority.

Autobiographies project that the Cellular Jail hardly provided any opportunity to the political prisoners, unlike that provided to the other ordinary ones. The title 'political prisoners' does not have a particular definition other than implying their revolutionary or political activities. But they suffered much more than the criminals in the Cellular Jail. Ujjwal K. Singh rightly relates prison to a stage to showcase the mighty power of the colonial state and a place where "the colonised lost and found their freedom," and terms it as "an already politicised space" (1998: 7). For prisoners such as V.D. Savarkar, Barindra Ghose, and Bhai Parmanand, the Cellular Jail became a political platform. Their ideology was shaped in the 'mainland,' but it culminated as a political theory after transportation. Their life-narration became a weapon after their repatriation that tells about their sacrifice and love for their country. Their petitions and the subject of repatriation were highly debated topics, though the demand for their repatriation proved their strength and role in the Indian nationalist discourse.

Aurobindo Ghose: From Extremism to Spiritual Nationalism

The decades following 1857 changed people's perception of India as a nation. A national sentiment developed among people gradually. The Black Acts (1849), the Vernacular Press Act (1879), and the Ilbert Bill Controversy (1883) catapulted the existing doubt of the natives upon the British. Ideas and suggestions were put forward for better governance of the Empire. In the meantime, Swami Vivekananda returned from his first tour of the West in January 1897. His return marks the beginning of the first phase of a socio-cultural revolution in India.[5] With a spiritual outlook, Vivekananda preached a nationalist ideal. Sister Nivedita, Lokamanya Tilak, Sri Aurobindo, and Lala Lajpat Rai were among the active revolutionaries during the end of the nineteenth century (Majumdar, 1966).[6] Bal Gangadhar Tilak and Anne Basant initiated a new wing, 'extremism,' and

Aurobindo Ghose became the guiding principle of extremist ideal. Inspired by Vivekananda, Aurobindo wrote in 1907 that the nation "must aim not only at a national government responsible to the people but a free national government unhampered even in the least degree by foreign control" (1966: 18).[7]

After the partition of Bengal (1905) and the formation of the Muslim League (1906), people in India believed that freedom could not be achieved by passive methods of resistance, and there was a growing need for a strong blow to the government's economy. One of the methods applied for this was to boycott all British goods. This became the first expression of aggression of the native population against British policies. In public utterances, Gangadhar Tilak and Sri Aurobindo preached a bloodless revolution but secretly supported nonviolent substances through armed agitations. For instance, the speeches delivered by Aurobindo Ghose were thought to instigate the common people to unite and agitate. One speech reads:

> The storm that swept over us, sweeping over the national edifice that we were rearing over the mother…it is the hammer of God that is beating upon us to build this nation into a mighty and a perfect instrument for His purpose.[8]

His Uttarpara speech after his return to Alipore 44 Degree Jail remains a significant one. In the Bengali journal *Suprabhat*, he wrote a series of articles about his imprisonment experiences and the spiritual journey he undertook during his imprisonment.

Aurobindo Ghose was convicted for the Alipore Bomb Case or Manicktolla Conspiracy Case, the same case for which his brother Barindra Ghose was convicted and transported to the Andamans. Aurobindo Ghose spent a year in Alipore jail from 5 May 1908 to 6 May 1909. His experience of imprisonment is different from his brother's, although they lived in the same conditions. Barindra Ghose was later transported to the Andamans, whereas Aurobindo Ghose was released with lifetime surveillance. Aurobindo begins his narration by recalling the exact date of arrest: "The year of 1908, Friday, 1 May" (2013: 1), unlike his brother Barindra Ghose who was unable to recall the exact date of transportation in his autobiography. The striking difference in the ability to remember may be denoted to varrying mental conditions. Barindra Ghose was already imprisoned in Alipore Jail when his narration begins, whereas for Aurobindo Ghose this was his first imprisonment. In his autobiography Aurobindo Ghose moves forward, providing a description of the British jailors as "thick-headed Britons" (4), a picture of the prison and prisoners. From the very first few pages, he declares his spiritual faith, and he accepts the confinement with a heart full of love for God. Yet he makes it clear that the prison atmosphere was not conducive for the people concerned about hygiene. He writes about the condition:

> Solitary imprisonment is supposedly a special form of punishment, predicated on the deprivation of human company and curtailment of freedom to breathe freely under the open skies, to the extent possible. As arrangements for excretion outside the cell would violate these sacred principles, two tar-coated baskets were provided in the cell itself.
>
> (20)

He describes the educated convicts in jail as young men having bright faces, clearly expressive of intelligence and personality and also having the soiled clothes and lustreless visage of the average convicts (36). His autobiography moves back and forth many times, making distinctions among the prisoners and praising the prison system as it promotes the equality that he dreams of seeing in his country. But at times, he also speaks ill of the system as it promotes inequality in treatment among the class of prisoners. While ordinary prisoners were allowed to move freely outside their cells, convicts such as Aurobindo were given a 'six decree cell' as he was pronounced the leader of a group of murderers. Harsh words, hostile prison authority, demeaning treatment, contaminated food, and unhygienic conditions could not create a hurdle on his path to God. He states, "During solitary imprisonment, the mind did become restless at first. But after three days of prayer and meditation, an immobile peace and unshakable faith was again established in the being" (13). There was a point when he ignored the prison environment. He devoted his time to meditating and praying for the well-being of all the inmates. Positively, he found his way to a spiritual world. He writes that he was affected only for the first few days. Later, his mind transcended these sufferings and got away with any feeling of hardship. He asserts: "This is why memories of prison life, when they re-surface, evoke a smile instead of rancour or sorrow" (25). And, he continues:

> I felt a little happy as no distinction was made between myself and the common uneducated masses of our country; primarily this arrangement served as a sacrificial offering at the altar of Matri bhakti (love of the motherland). On my part, I accepted this as a unique means and conducive conditions for yoga-sadhana and transcending the sense of duality.
>
> (26)

He also dreams of the dawning of a day when people of all classes in the country will march together as one living mass. Concluding his autobiography, he writes:

> When I was asleep in the Ignorance, I came to a place of meditation full of holy men, and I found their company wearisome and the place a prison; when I awoke, God took me to a prison and turned it into a place of meditation and His trysting ground.

Penal inequality, penal favours, and perpetual servitude are chapters in penal culture that are often ignored in the colonist texts. But this culture has a deep impact on society which can be located from the narratives of native convicts who experienced its trauma. To be naked while cleaning in front of other fellow prisoners, timely or supervised urination, and excreting as per the prison timings were afew deragotory practices that resulted in mental turmoil, which the autobiographical literature possibly narrates properly. This treatment told upon their self-respect leading to serious self-critical analysis of penal misfortune. There are multifarious forms of nationalism that found an emblematic expression during the Indian freedom struggle movement. While spiritual leaders such as Swami Vivekananda and the Irish Elizabeth Noble or Sister Nivedita showed the way of spiritual nationalism, Aurobindo Ghose's *Jugantar* and *Bande Mataram* and Gangadhar Tilak's *Kesari* became serious texts articulating the potency of aggressive resistance. Expression of nationalistic rhetoric through media and public speeches resulted in the growth of nationalistic ideas.

Conclusion

The autobiographical records deal with the lives of political prisoners and develop a new perspective to understand the cause of the 'freedom struggle.' They provide an exclusive insight into the penal suffering the political prisoners received and the quality of life they lived. The prisoner-narrator utilises his memory to construct, deconstruct, and reconstruct history from their own viewpoint. Foucauldian 'counter-memory' is at work in the case of prison narratives. A whole new set of memory clusters pertaining to prison experience does not naturally occur but is rather constructed in the process of remembering in a socio-political context. Unremembering through writing sanctions these prisoners a novel and noble place in society to be identified later by their patriotism, which is validated through their own writings. They create an identity for themselves, from freedom fighters to prisoners to life writers, and also get sympathy from the public. Hence, their position is elevated. All the three autobiographical narratives lack proper coherence. Repetition, grammatical errors, improper chapterisation, breaks in the flow of narration, and haphazard sequence of time and place are noticed. The language used is also not that of educated young men but rather colloquial and very simple to the point of immaturity. Ideas seem to overflow without sequence and chronology. In fact, these imperfections are language markers proving the autobiographer's authentic remembrance as memory cannot be arranged to appear in order; they flash. In the article "The New Model Autobiographer," John Sturrock claims that in those "obsessional structures of the mind that alone guarantee the consistency of a personality" (1977: 54).

The experiences in prison are often harsh and condemn the usual working of the penal system. Often questioned and contested, the writings by prisoners are seen as different from the prison authority's statements. While the prison exercises its hegemony to rule over the prisoners, the prisoner who records the incidents remains on the other end, criticising and evaluating what is often granted by the public. When their writing comes out with alternative histories and contradictory views, the narrator holds the power to create a new chapter of knowledge. The writer makes way for a major socio-political change in twentieth-century literature, specifically in prison and subaltern literature. In this way, the hegemonic power of the ruling prison administration is destabilised. They encourage people to raise their voices against the dominant group. The writings of the political prisoners in question are examples of counter-hegemony. For Larson "the very effort to write is thus an act of political ressurection, a re-envisioning of the narrative of justice" (Larson:147). In the context of Odisha, Gopabandhu Das's poems serve as pamphlets of awakening for the middle-class Odia population. Soon after Das's imprisonment, women of Odisha also took the path of revolution, raising slogans against the British. Barindra Ghose and his compatriots' multiple hunger strikes and letters from the Andamans provoked the common men and the media to pressurise the British government for their repatriation to the mainland. The liberal nationalist leaders who opposed the militants had to support them instead in order to unite for a common goal of freedom from the British. Aurobindo Ghose, through his spiritual essays and speeches, motivated people to such an extent that his militant engagements were forgotten. Nationalism and spiritualism served one meaning. Thus, the prison narrative becomes a performative utterance of one's lived experiences and suppressed feelings from the past as George Gusdorf maintains that autobiography is a scripture of the self (1980)

**The chapter is an outcome of OURIIP-22 research project funded by the OSHEC, Odisha.

Notes

1 The poetry of Kancharla Gopanna or Bhadranchala Ramdasu is an example of the presence of prison literature in the Sangam period. It was written in the seventeenth century in quest of Lord Rama. Ramadasu or Ram Das was a devotee of Rama who had diverted government funds towards building a lavish temple for his God Rama; he was subsequently imprisoned. His poems written in the cell of Golconda Fort became some of the finest songs in Bhakti poetry (Ram, Uma and K.S. Ram: 84-92).
2 "To Althea, from Prison" by Richard Lovelace (1642: 25–26).
3 Letter No. 1417, 7 June 1933. "From Home Department, Government of India to Secretary of State for India." NAI PB.
4 Refer trace decay theory of forgetting and interference theory of forgetting. Also refer K.P. Darby and V.M. Sloutsky, 2015: 410–431.
5 This period is notorious for two murders. W.C. Rand, the British plague Commissioner of Pune and then chairman of a special plague committee, and his military escort, Lt. Ayerst, were murdered by the Chapekar brothers, Damodar Hari Chapekar, Balkrishna Hari Chapekar, and Vasudeo Hari Chapekar. They were termed the first among 'militant nationalists' in India who resisted the British when Pune was hit by the bubonic plague in 1896.

6 Bimanbehari Majumdar. *Militant Nationalism in India and Its Socio-Religious Background (1897–1917)*. Calcutta: General Printers & Publishers Pvt Ltd, 1966.
7 Sri Aurobindo. *The Doctrine of Passive Resistance*. Sri Aurobindo Ashram: Pondicherry, 1966, 18.
8 The speech was delivered by Aurobindo Ghose on 19 June at the District Conference at Jhalakati. Record No. 338C. 21 June 1909. From W.J. Reid to the Govt. of Eastern Bengal and Assam. NAI ND.

Works Cited

Acharya, Snigdha. "Paradigm of Socio-Economic-Cultural Notion in Colonial Odisha: Contemplation of Gopabandhu Das." *Orissa Review*, September 2014, pp. 48–54.

Aurobindo Ghose. *Tales of Prison Life*. Kolkata: Aurobindo Institute of Culture, 2013.

Conway, Martin A., and Mark L. Howe. "Memory Construction: A Brief and Selective History." *Memory*, vol. 30, no. 1, 2022, pp. 2–4.

Darby, K. P., and V. M. Sloutsky. "The Cost of Learning: Interference Effects in Memory Development." *Journal of Experimental Psychology: General*, vol. 144, no. 2, 2015, pp. 410–431.

Das, Gopabandhu. *The Prisoner's Autobiography*. Translated by Snehaprava Das, 1st ed. Bhubaneswar: Bird Nest, 2017.

Foucault, Michel. *The History of Sexuality Volume 1: An Introduction*. Translated by Robert Hurley. New York: Pantheon Books, 1978.

Ghose, Aurobindo. *The Doctrine of Passive Resistance*. Pondicherry: Sri Aurobindo Ashram, 1966.

Ghose, Barindra Kumar. *The Tale of My Exile: Twelve Years of Prison Life*. Edited by Sachidananda Mohanty. 1922. Pondicherry: Sri Aurobindo Ashram Publication, 2011.

Gusdorf, Georg. "Conditions and Limits of Autobiography." *Autobiography: Essays Theoretical and Critical*, edited by James Olney. Princeton, NJ: Princeton University Press, 1980, pp. 28–47.

Hetata, Sherif. "The Self and the Author." *Modern Language Association*, vol. 118, no. 01 Special Topic: "America: The Idea, The Literature," 2003, pp. 123–125.

Larson, Doran. "Toward a Prison Poetics." *College Literature*, vol. 37, no. 3, 2010, pp. 143–166.

Letter No. 1417, 7 June 1933. "From Home Department, Government of India to Secretary of State for India." NAI PB.

Majumdar, Bimanbehari. *Militant Nationalism in India and Its Socio-Religious Background (1897–1917)*. Calcutta: General Printers & Publishers Pvt Ltd, 1966.

Misch, George. "Conception and Origin of Autobiography." *A History of Autobiography in Antiquity*, translated by E.W. Dickes. London: Routledge and Kegan Paul, 1950, pp. 1–18.

Ram, Uma, and K.S. Ram. "The Prison Route to Rama: The Songs of Bhadranchala Ramdas." *Prison Writing in India*, edited by C.N. Srinath. Delhi: Sahitya Akademi, 2014, pp. 84–92.

Singh, Ujjwal Kumar. *Political Prisoners in India*. New Delhi: Oxford University Press, 1998.

Speech delivered by Aurobindo Ghose on 19 June at the District Conference at Jhalakati. Record No. 338C. 21 June 1909. From W.J. Reid, to the Govt. Of Eastern Bengal and Assam. NAI ND.

Srivastava, Pramod. "Resistance and Repression in India: The Hunger Strike at the Andaman Cellular Jail in 1933." *Authority and Resistance in the Penal Colonies*, vol. 7, no. 2, 2003, pp. 81–102.
Sturrock, John. "The New Model Autobiographer". New Literary History 9 (1). USA: John Hopkins University Press, 1977, pp 51–63.

10 Affect

Human Libraries as an Intersection of Memory and Affect Archiving

Kavya R. K.

The sociality of human existence has forever been an evolving phenomenon. And evolution in any sphere is inevitably linked to survival. Whatever changes a process of evolution entails can be assumed to be directed towards enhanced growth and co-existence at both individual and collective levels. Like how the technical developments are aimed at material progress, consistent social development is necessary to improve the quality of human life. To strike a balance between maintaining one's social status and healthy social life has become the need of the hour.

As much as material developments characterise the status of a society, the underlying affective networks of social connection play a decisive role in its development. A study that concerns social dynamics cannot happen without an understanding of the affects that are at play within. As a microcosm of the larger world of human interactions, the human libraries manifest as spaces that constitute a range of affective exchanges rooted in the processes of recollection, the modes of which will be explored in the chapter.

Being able to connect with each other is a prerequisite when it comes to understanding the social dynamics around us. Often, people situate themselves in the cosy bubbles of knowledge they have built, contentedly feeding on their own choices of stigma and stereotypes. These cocoons then transform as projections of their understanding of the world. The Human Library, as a new initiative in the 2000s, was envisioned on the grounds of dealing with such prejudices and stereotypes that govern people's attitudes towards each other ("Human Library").

It began in Denmark in the year 2000, as part of a festival in Copenhagen ("Human Library"). The people who gathered for the event became the books chosen to be read by others. The concept of the human library borrows the terms and ideas from that of the normal library, the difference being that the books here are people themselves. The event then gained momentum and was extended to other countries as well.

The focus is on the affectivities associated with the whole idea of the human library as a safe space to accommodate differences. The major constituents of the human library are the "human books" and the "readers". The process of reading a human book takes the reader through the intricacies of the book's modes of recollection, and thereby, an exploration into the memories of their

DOI: 10.4324/9781003508564-14

experiences. According to Andaleeb Qureshi, founder of the Human Library in India, the Human Library comes off as a reassurance to the insecurities faced by people for being different from what is perceived as the normal and the ordinary. The Human Library, she says, "is a social platform intended toward social integration and building empathy in Humanity, emphasizing the fact that you are absolutely fine as you are, however different that is" ("What is Human Library Mumbai?").

Affect, in a basic understanding of the term, is an underlying state of experience that pre-supposes, or pre-determines every life action. Affect as a theoretical framework began to gain momentum post the 1990s, after what came to be identified as the affective turn. Philosophers like Deleuze and Guattari were among the major figures who laid the roadmap to the various definitions and understandings of affect that exist today. The philosophical roots of affect theory lie in the work *Ethics* (1677) of Baruch Spinoza, where he distinguishes the terms "affectus" and "affectio", as the "capacities to affect" and "to get affected", respectively (qtd. in Ott 2). This power enables the body to either perform increased action or decrease the momentum of the action, depending on the degree of the affective charge.

Explored mostly in the fields of sociology and cultural studies, "affect theory" accounts for the several non-representational aspects of life that have an impact on everyday existence. It is the dominance of the linguistic domain that gets challenged in a study of perceiving the world through affective registers. Affect Theorists argue that apart from trying to make sense of the world from a linguistic dimension, affects enable the creation of a worldview that arises from giving attention to the details of the physicality of existence. "Affective susceptibilities and attunements bound up with sociality give judgments direction, signifcance, and urgency" (Wehrs 3). The sensations of the body, and the subsequent responses to the environment that constitute experience, interest the affect theorist.

Reading alongside the theory of affect, it could be argued that the human library initiative proves to be a very effective means to conduct a discourse on affect and its pivotal role in forging social connections. Qureshi mentions that the books are usually people who have faced some difficulty, stereotyping, or prejudice in their lives and have positively evolved from the experiences ("Human Library"). The acts of affective expression of the books, both in narration and in the non-verbal cues that accompany recollection, would be studied to understand the impact of affect in shaping human experience. Here, I understand the act of remembering as a mutually constitutive affective phenomenon, in that both the reader and the book undergo processes of remembering that could be connected to strong emotional experiences. The attempt is to also understand the ethical aspects of listening to a human book, a total stranger, and how the book's willingness to be vulnerable is received and perceived by the reader.

A study of bodily affects in the expression of vulnerability would be incomplete without the intervention of memory, as the very act of recollection can be considered as quite rooted in bodily dynamics and affect. "Memory", according to Astrid Erl, is an umbrella term for all those processes of a "biological, medial, social nature, which relate past and present (and future) in sociocultural contexts" (7). The human library, here, unites people from different social and cultural backgrounds to form social connections through indulging in acts of recollection. For the reader to engage with the book, the books must effectively traverse through their processes of remembering, and bring out the memories that can be most associated with understanding them and their individuality. In *Memory in Culture*, Astrid Erl reasserts the consensus on memory across all disciplines that "memory is an outcome of the process of remembering" and that "only through the observation of concrete acts of remembering situated in specific cultural contexts can we hypothesize about memory's nature and functioning" (8). The books in the human libraries come from diverse socio-cultural backgrounds. Their narration gives way to a synthesis of memories and affective experiences that result in nuanced cultural intersections.

The attempt of the books is to make the readers aware of their life experiences and the difficulties they have had to overcome, thereby giving the reader an insight into a world that they might not have been exposed to before. There is an active process of recalling that happens from the part of the book. This could involve tonal escalations, posture changes, hand gestures, and facial expressions, all contributing to the affective field of intrigue, curiosity, and sometimes even fear, and anxiety. Here the memories of the book about their own life function to shape the affective responses of the reader. Kayleigh Bateman in her article on Human Libraries refers to the concept of "contact hypothesis" which states that "contact between groups can help promote tolerance and acceptance when they are brought together under the right conditions"(qtd. in Bateman) to buttress the Libraries' effectiveness in influencing human relationships. The groups formed thus, embody within the spaces of the libraries possibilities for bodily and dialogic exchanges that create larger social impact.

In the case of the human books, situating them in the cultural and social contexts where their identities get challenged is crucial for the reader, the contours of which may be unfamiliar to them. This is where the reader is expected to shed off their prejudices and be open to the stories of the book. The concept of listening to/reading a human book needs to be scrutinised to understand the working process of these libraries. Humans inevitably experience, although to different degrees, the need to be heard, recognised, understood, and appreciated by others. It is intuitively connected to the fact that humans are basically wired to live in/as communities. However, when this need to be acknowledged becomes one-sided, then people tend to speak more and not listen. Listening to another person then becomes reduced to the level of mere hearing, aimed only at grabbing the right pause to interfere and speak about oneself. Transactions of this kind are futile and lack the empathy that is foundational to such a process of mutual exchange.

Looking at the human libraries from the reader's point of view, reading/listening comes with some level of responsibility and accountability. The book that has been loaned to the reader is a world that has expressed consent and interest in sharing a part, or sometimes, the whole of their life story with the reader. The emotional investment expected from the listener bestows on them the need to be fully involved and open to the book at hand.

Primarily, this openness must be cultivated from a personal level, where the readers, prior to getting introduced to the books, introspect on their lives, beliefs, and choices. This helps enhance the level of trustworthiness the book will have on the reader during the interaction. Although the interactions are not carried beyond the space of the libraries, the role of the listener in improving the quality of the time they spend within the library could be enhanced if this openness is achieved, thereby positively impacting the affective exchange that happens in the context. The books voluntarily offer to tell their stories in the attempt to push themselves out of the constraints of their traumatic life experiences. This willingness to be vulnerable is what opens up the explorations into the affectivities concerned with it.

Ben Anderson, in his essay "Affective Atmospheres", talks about the concept of atmosphere in relation to affect. He conceives of atmosphere as an "affective quality" (Anderson 79) that does not really come from the objects or subjects involved but influences them, nonetheless. "Atmosphere creates a space of intensity that overflows a represented world organized into subjects and objects or subjects and subjects" (79). Affective atmospheres are those sensations that are felt by the body but do not emanate from or culminate in it. Every setting can be affectively charged in terms of its atmosphere.

Therefore, in the case of the human libraries, the storytelling happens in an affective atmosphere that is charged with an air of curiosity, to name one, as the readers and books anticipate entering into the worlds unfamiliar to them. There is an aura of unfamiliarity that comprises the affective atmospheres of human libraries. The comfort derived from the strange or the unfamiliar becomes the outcome generated by the affective atmosphere(s) therein. Therefore, the "intensive space-times" (Anderson 80) created by affective atmospheres, in the case of the human libraries, can be conceived as comprising anticipations, reluctance, pauses, interruptions of feelings, and so on, that encompass the affective fields surrounding both the reader and the book. The bodies, here, of the book and the reader respond to these affective atmospheres. "Atmospheres are perpetually forming and deforming, appearing, and disappearing, as bodies enter into relation with one another. They are never finished, static, or at rest" (Anderson 79). In the kind of relation mentioned here, the bodies permeate in and through the affective qualities of the atmosphere.

Anderson presents affective atmospheres as an answer to the question, "how to attend to collective affects that are not reducible to the individual bodies that they emanate from?" (80). In a space like the human library, there is an inevitable interplay of such collective affects. The setting of the library is an influential factor in determining the atmosphere. Some libraries have conducted the events in open spaces like gardens and parks. Some others have facilitated face-to-face seating arrangements separate for each book and reader combo, creating the feelings of both security and proximity.

In addition to the impact that the spaces have on the interactions, the bodily sensations which are shared during the narrations also contribute to the formation of collective affects. Sara Ahmed, cultural theorist, discusses the concept of "affective economies" where "emotions *do things*, and they align individuals with communities—or bodily space with social space—through the very intensity of their attachments" (Ahmed 118). She says that rather than seeing emotions as psychological dispositions, "we need to consider how they work, in concrete and particular ways, to mediate the relationship between the psychic and the social, and between the individual and the collective" (118). In affirmation to this thought, it could be said that the bodily sensations shared during the human library interactions are quite decisive in forming the affective engagements therein. Like how the body responds through affects, the life experiences of the books are intricately connected with bodily/embodied memory.

For instance, one of the human books is a man who keeps modifying his body through tattoos and piercings. He conceives of the act as a product of the ultimate freedom and access one has to one's own body. The memories associated with his everyday life would be quite aligned with the making of such bodily memories. Similarly, some other books like a woman who cannot conceive, an amputee, are all people whose memories of their life experiences are inevitably connected to their bodies. So, the experiences they have had with their bodies account for being non-representational as they are all connected to the sensations of the body. These individual memories which have a collective bearing, when shared in a space like the human library, throw light also on the impact of such non-representational affects in the shaping of human memory and its permeation into the society.

In a session of the Human Library in Goa in 2018, Moumita Pal, who introduced the same in Goa, notes,

> Around eighty percent of the people who came said they want to be books and shared their stories on subjects like alcoholism, tattoos, body piercings, homelessness... it's great that people are talking about things that are bothering them, to make real conversations about things that genuinely matter.
>
> (D'Souza 2018)

As a space that discusses matters fundamental to the existence of individual and social lives, the human library, when read through the framework of affect, draws attention to the different ways in which it is perceived. The stories of the human books centre around the social consequences of experiencing a life that does not fit into the normative standards of the society. What happens here is an encounter between otherwise estranged bodies, bodies that would not have undergone similar experiences. The affectual realms that encompass the interactions embody the need to have empathetic associations to these experiences. An affective reading of the human library recognises and re-establishes the significance of bodily encounters in everyday lives, the need to embrace the vitality of the human bodily experiences and the memories that get constituted through them.

In his work on Collective Memory, Maurice Halbwachs draws on the concept of "social frameworks" (qtd. in Erl, 17) which are, simply put, "the people around us" who influence our acts of remembering. According to Halbwachs, without other humans, an individual is denied access not only to such obviously collective phenomena like languages and customs, but also to his or her own memory (18). The personal memories that form the narratives of the human books, therefore, form collective recollections that can also give us an idea about the cultures of the societies the books belong to. Also, a space like the human library not only gathers readers who are new to the stories of the books, but also creates chances of people meeting others who have been through traumatic and difficult situations like them.

The dialogic aspect of memory studied by several memory and cultural theorists—recollection as an active process that involves both the narrator as well as the listener—can be exploited well in the functioning of the human libraries. The book's memory opens an array of new perspectives to the reader, which the latter then combines with their own repertoire of memories. The interaction then takes the path of past events in the lives of both the reader and the book. Sometimes, this gives the reader an opportunity to connect with the book through similarities that can be drawn from the reader's past experiences. Or, the reader gets to hear a set of new experiences which could possibly be intertwined into their future memorial realms. This in turn creates an opportunity for the reader to accommodate the shared knowledge and take it further into the society.

The other important aspect that shapes the affective exchanges in the human libraries is concerned with the ethicality of the whole event. As an integrative activity, the human library involves the coming together of diverse people, most often total strangers, under a single roof with the simple, yet complex intention of knowing each other. The act of trying to actually know someone is intricately associated with certain ethical and moral responsibilities. And most of it lies with the listener/reader as they are the ones being confronted and conflicted with their belief systems on listening to the book.

When a book opens to the reader, the reader is vested with the responsibility to feel the book in all its essence, setting aside all judgements and biases. In most cases, the books are people who have confidently come out of their bounded lives, breaking open the stereotypes that have shackled them all their lives. The narration of their experiences then become revelatory for the listeners who probably have not had first-hand experiences of the same kind, or can be relatable to some others, who might have had closeted lives all along, out of the fear to overcome their insecurities. Listening is a revolutionary act, and a highly ethical one indeed. Through the act of listening, a person sets aside a valuable share of their life in selfless involvement with a totally different and distinct part of the world, that is, here, the human book. Effective listening forges connections, and aspects of relatability unfold as the interaction furthers, buttressing the fact that humanity is, by and large, a diverse, yet unified thread.

In an essay differentiating Affect, Feelings, and Emotions, Eric Shouse says,

> For the infant, affect is emotion, for an adult, affect is what makes feelings feel. It is what determines the intensity (quantity) of a feeling (quality), as well as the background intensity of our everyday lives (the half-sensed, ongoing hum of quantity/quality that we experience when we are not really attuned to any experience at all).
>
> (Shouse 2005)

This reinforces the role of affect as inseparably linked to the unfolding of everyday life activities. In the setting of a human library, the feelings and empathetic associations that the listener and the book develop for the stories being narrated, arise from the unconscious realm of affect that intensifies the need to feel. Prior to developing feeling/s, affect buttresses the innate intensities that develop in relation to the context. The involuntary gestures like twitching of hands, switching their positions, etc., are indicators of the affective exchange that takes place in the context. In the next level, the bodies sometimes interact more explicitly by expressing their emotions through crying, embracing, tapping on the shoulder, holding hands, etc.

A human book is "someone who volunteers to represent a stigmatised group in the community and based on his or her personal experiences can answer questions from readers to help them understand the issues being faced by the volunteer better" ("Human Library Goes Rural"). Further,

> each human book describes a summary of their experiences, describing their daily activities, what they do in their spare time, one thing that may surprise people, an example of discrimination they have faced and their values; they also choose a title for their story which can help facilitate the discussion.
>
> ("Human Library Goes Rural")

The platform enabled is interactive by all means, and productive listening reflects the book's effort. The book feels acknowledged and understood, the whole scenario then turning into a harmonious state of acceptance.

Zoya Hussain, in her article on Indiatimes, talks about the relevance of Human Libraries in a post-pandemic context. "Despite the fact that physical places were closed due to the epidemic, the Human Library Chennai conducted its first session online, with 17 books and around 150 readers" ("What is a Human Library"). There are two aspects which need to be emphasised here—first, the fact that the human libraries symbolise the need for preserving human connection even in the direst of circumstances. The Human Libraries materialised the necessity for human interaction despite the lack of proper resources and facilities for physical contact. Second, the digital organisation of the event throws light on how memory and narration can be effectively synthesised to forge human connections even on virtual platforms.

This is also where archiving of affect and the memory of the events take a digital phase. There are social media pages and websites which store information about the books, publish news of the library events and gatherings, and store the feedback of events. Memory and affect circulate, first, through the recollections of the books and readers, and second, through how they get further archived in digital and print modes. Through this concoction of traditional as well as digital remembering and archiving, memory of human experiences acquires and retains multiple affective dimensions.

However, alongside the merits it is also important to acknowledge the limitations of a system that tries to work in and through understanding vulnerabilities. The applicability of "unjudging someone" (as the motto of the human library says) is questionable on some level. It is difficult to overlook and overcome the preconceptions and prejudices that every individual harbours in their lives. In an open interaction with a stranger, these are bound to arise and impact the approach and attitude of the listener towards the book. The question of whether it is possible to keep off all judgements while engaging with a human book has been one of the criticisms against the human libraries. This is where listening has to be consciously made constructive and involved. In approaching the interaction as a process of productive affective exchange, the role of the listener in addressing and managing their biases becomes pronounced. The listener's capacity to affect the book, through active participation as well as meaningful silences, becomes part of the web of affective dynamics that characterise the process. Affect, primarily, works at a level prior to conscious involvement and, therefore, is intricately connected with the bodily responses that happen in an encounter.

The Human Library is, thus, an effective platform for potential affective exchange. The books sometimes let their hearts out, cry, and embrace the reader. These affectively charged acts of exchange are then taken out into the society when these readers and books go out and intermingle. The power of a person's everyday life to knit an invisible thread of affective connection-making in society becomes visualised through the concept of the human libraries. In the post-pandemic context, when physical interactions and connections have reduced in response to the universal distancing demanded by the pandemic, the human libraries could prove to be an effective resource to restore that lost balance in the society. Moreover, an inclusive space that attempts to negotiate traumatic experiences has become the need of the hour, in order to help ourselves cope with the unprecedented changes brought out by the pandemic. In a space like the Human Library, the ethics of understanding the world outside one's own limited knowledge and experiential base is revisited, and consequently, attempts are made to revise and unlearn the dictums of age-old prejudices and stereotypes.

Works Cited

Ahmed, Sara. "Affective Economies". *Social Text*, vol. 22 no. 2, 2004, pp. 117–139. *Project MUSE,* muse.jhu.edu/article/55780. Accessed 7 June 2023.

Anderson, Ben. "Affective Atmospheres". *Emotion, Space and Society*, vol. 2, 2009, pp. 77–81. Pdf. Accessed 29 May 2023.

Bateman, Kayleigh. "Human Libraries Can Break Down Prejudices, Foster Diversity and Inclusion. Here's How". *The Print*, 13 Dec. 2021, https://theprint.in/features/human-libraries-can-break-down-prejudices-foster-diversity-and-inclusion-heres-how/780871/. Accessed 11 June 2023.

D'Souza, Flexcia. "A Library in Goa Where Books Talk! - Times of India". *The Times of India*, 5 Dec. 2018, https://timesofindia.indiatimes.com/entertainment/events/goa/a-library-in-goa-where-books-talk/articleshow/66997933.cms. Accessed 13 June 2023.

Erll, Astrid. *Memory in Culture.* Translated by Sara Young. Palgrave Macmillan, 2011. Pdf file. Accessed 5 July 2023.

"The Human Library". *YouTube*, uploaded by MCPLIndiana, 13 June 2019, https://youtu.be/3YT1XiGc-KA. Accessed 3 June 2023.

"Human Library Goes Rural". *Telangana Today*, 18 Feb. 2021, https://telanganatoday.com/human-library-goes-rural. Accessed 17 June 2023.

"Human Library in India: Setting a New Trend of Storytelling". Best Line Producer and Fixer in India – New Delhi, Varanasi, https://www.filmingindo.com/blog-post/human-library-in-india-setting-a-new-trend-of-storytelling/. Accessed 20 June 2023.

Ott, Bryan L. "Affect in Critical Studies". *Oxford Research Encyclopedia Communication*, edited by Jon Nussbaum, pp.1–26, Oxford University Press, 2017. Pdf. Accessed 3 June 2023.

Shouse, Eric. "Feeling, Emotion, Affect". *M/C Journal*, vol. 8, no. 6, 1 Dec. 2005, https://journal.media-culture.org.au/mcjournal/article/view/2443. Accessed 5 June 2023.

Wehrs, R. Donald. "Introduction: Affect and Texts : Contemporary Inquiry in Historical Context". *The Palgrave Handbook of Affect Studies and Textual Criticism*, edited by Donald R. Wehrs and Thomas Blake, Springer International Publishing, 2017. Pdf. Accessed 29 May 2023.

"What is Human Library Mumbai?". *YouTube*, uploaded by Gav Achpalea, 9 July 2017, https://youtu.be/aOMvh7OpXRE. Accessed 7 June 2023.

11 An Analysis of Emotional and Media Factors of the Flashbulb Memory on Recollection of YSR's Demise

A Comparative Study

G. Haritha

Introduction

Brown and Kulik's seminal work in 1977 defined flashbulb memories as remarkably vivid and enduring recollections of impactful events and the specific circumstances in which individuals became aware of them (Bohannon, 1988). The events referenced in their work were the assassinations of Martin Luther King, John F. Kennedy, and Malcolm X as examples to trigger flashbulb memories. The research of Brown and Kulik highlighted that people don't just remember the event but also vividly recall the most intricate facts of the reception context (Bohannon & Symons, 1992) like the specific period and place they received the news from, their action at that moment, the individuals present with them, the information source, and the aftermath of the incident that happened (Bohannon, 1988). Flashbulb memories include intense memories that were confidently held and lasting recollections of discovering significant events (Conway, 1995). The actions that evoke these memories include the earthquake at Marmara in Turkey, the assassination of John F. Kennedy, the US president (Kulik & Brown, 1977), and the terrorist attacks of September 11, 2001 (Rubin & Talarico, 2003).

The powerful and long-lasting recollections of these events that were emotionally charged go in line with traditional cognitive learning mechanisms (Christianson,1989). Many research studies on flashbulb memories focused on major global events, extending the analysis beyond the United States (Conway, 1995). The research (Schaefer, 2011) reveals that individuals form curiously intense memories not only in response to international events but also in connection to significant incidents within their cultural, local, and national contexts (Zelizer, B., 2008).The present study serves a local context by taking into consideration the demise of a famous political leader who served as a chief minister of two Telugu states of India (i.e. Telangana and Andhra Pradesh) to understand flashbulb memory through the emotional and media factors. The study focuses on the details of flashbulb occasions

DOI: 10.4324/9781003508564-15

remembered because they serve as links between individual histories and experiences (Bohannon & Symons, 1992).

Review of Literature

Flashbulb memories are those that are exceedingly precise photographs over time (Bohannon & Symons, 1992). After a gap of a decade, the research in this domain has shifted its focus to investigate flashbulb memories that are influenced by two key factors (Neisser & Harsh, 1992), namely the surprise of the initial event and the importance-consequentiality of the initial event to the contemporary life. When an event elicits a high level of surprise and is deemed consequential, it is anticipated to be etched in memory for an extended duration (Neisser & Harsh, 1992). Brown and Kulik (1977) studied exemplified flashbulb memories among African-American and Caucasian participants related to the deaths of Martin Luther King and Malcolm X. The findings revealed that African-American participants exhibited higher flashbulb memories over their Caucasian counterparts (Brown & Kulik, 1977). The findings presented a specialized encoding mechanism in the human brain that is activated by the initial event.

The special encoding hypothesis, proposed by Brown and Kulik (1977), faced criticism from scholars who emphasized the significance of reconstructive post-encoding factors, also known as constructivist theory. Neisser (1982) states that the original experience of memory plays a vital role in the formation and maintenance of flashbulb memories (Neisser & Harsh, 1992), which comes in contrast to the notion of memories that are vivid and stable, which are inherently inaccurate and susceptible to decay (Neisser, 1982). This modification of flashbulb memories occurs through rehearsal processes, which condense distortion and bias over a period similar to the transformation observed in ordinary memories (Neisser & Harsh, 1992).

Rehearsal involves various processes, which include being engaged in discussions triggered by media that are related to the event, holding a conversation with others about the experience, and reflecting upon the original event (John, Robinson,1980 . In this perspective, emotion maintains its impact on memory even after the occurrence of the original event through social sharing and rumination about the experience (Finkenauer et al., 1998). Throughout history, the exchange of information has relied heavily on social interaction.

Flashbulb memories usually involve details about how and when the participant remembers certain events. Rubin and Kozin (1984) investigated various aspects related to the participants' reactions upon learning the news. The researchers examined factors such as the participants' location, the presence of others with them at the time, and their activities both during and immediately after receiving the news. In a study conducted by Bohannon et al. (2007), it was discovered that the group informed by the media recalled a greater number of factual details, while the group informed by personal accounts provided more information about their specific circumstances.

Media factors are an important part to study in flashbulb memory formation because they play a major role to process the initial encoding of the event that had happened, emotional arousal of the previous incident which can be juxtaposed with present situations, rehearsal of the actual event that happens with repeated exposure, social sharing through various memes and posts on various platforms and wide range of discussions that news channels hold.

Numerous investigations into the development and sustainability of flashbulb memories underscore (Nico & Frijda, 1987) the intricate connection between emotion and memory (Smith & Ellsworth, 1987) A critical inquiry revolves around the idea that individuals preserve distinct memories for identical emotional experiences. As posited by Brown and Kulik (1977), variations in individuals' responses to an event stem from the diverse levels of consequentiality attributed to it. In any given context (Nico & Frijda, 1987, the emergence of the flashbulb memory occurs when an incident is deemed highly consequential, or in other words, profoundly, Uric & Neisser, 1966) significant for the safety of individuals within that context.

Studies have explored a new model to underscore cognitive appraisals' role in evoking flashbulb memories (Finkenauer et al., 1998). This model highlights the implication of novelty and importance-consequentiality appraisals. While Brown and Kulik (1977) emphasized consequentiality, they didn't distinctly delineate it from the emotion itself. In the tested model by Finkenauer et al. (1998), novelty directly triggers surprise, while importance-consequentiality shapes emotional states, thereby influencing event rehearsal (Pillemer, 1984). These approaches collectively convey that flashbulb memories aren't solely products of individual recollection processes but rather genuine (Conway, 1995) social experiences shaped intricately by the contextual constraints within social media environments surrounding the original events (Conway et al., 1994)

Overview

In India, investigations incorporating flashbulb memories related to events such as the attacks by the terrorists in Mumbai, the brutal assassination of Rajiv Gandhi, and the Pulwama attack, provide valuable thoughts into the universality of these memory mechanisms. Although not much research has happened in recent years on this specific concept, this study makes an attempt to revive the importance of flashbulb memory in the present situation. The spread of media in varied forms highly influenced the retrieval of the emotions related to any events that have happened in the past, especially in a country like India where generational politics ruled Indians for over 75 years. The concept of flashbulb memory gets triggered if the present generational leader distorts the attributes carried by the generational head of the family. The study juxtaposed the rule of Rajasekhar Reddy and his son Jagan Mohan Reddy. The primary purpose of the study is to examine the concept of flashbulb memories among two distinct social groups. The research doesn't specifically test a model concerning the formation and maintenance of these memories (yet it acknowledges the well-established pattern to recall the attributes of encoding and rehearsal variables (Lazarus & Richard, 1988). Drawing from existing literature, flashbulb memories are defined using recognized categories of the reception context, encompassing factors like time, location, individuals present, contextual details, ongoing activities, and triggers in those incidents (Berntsen, 2009). The study emphasizes how ongoing activities trigger the flashbulb memory of past events (Blank, 2009).

The event for the study is the demise of Yeduguri Sandinti Rajasekhara Reddy, commonly referred to as YSR, who was a political figure in the state of Andhra Pradesh before the state was divided into Telangana and Andhra Pradesh with the Andhra Pradesh Reorganisation Act of 2014. YSR demonstrated a strong dedication to the betterment of society and social justice. He left a remarkable influence on the political ground through his groundbreaking health welfare initiative known as "Rajiv Arogya Sri". From 2004 to 2009, YSR served as the chief minister of Andhra Pradesh. In the domain of agriculture, YSR emerged as an advocate for the welfare of farmers, effectively introducing measures and schemes to waive agricultural loans on farmers. In his pursuit of various strategies aimed at upgrading the socio-economic conditions of the people, the visionary met an unfortunate twist of fate. YSR's journey came to an untimely end on September 2, 2009, when a helicopter crash occurred in the Nallamala Forest of Andhra Pradesh resulting in the sudden disappearance of his body without any trace being found. The unexpected passing of the great leader reverberated throughout the entire region, with a profound sense of astonishment and dismay. The untimely death not only created a significant void within the political sphere, but led to unforeseen political decisions of which state division into Telangana and Andhra Pradesh was one. The initiatives undertaken by YSR had a lasting and profound impact on the lives of individuals affected by social, economic, or political disparities.

Despite a dearth of recent comprehensive research on this phenomenon, I as a researcher closely observed the triggering of the concept and wished to unravel the episode of flashbulb memory in a local context. The omnipresence of media platforms ensures that experiences and events are constantly revisited, thereby compelling us to recognize and appreciate the significance and applicability of flashbulb memory in contemporary times. In the realm of political affairs in Andhra Pradesh, the election of YS Jagan Mohan Reddy, the son of the deceased YS Rajasekhara Reddy, to the position of chief minister (2019–present) has brought the significant comeback of the flashbulb memory. The expectations associated with Jagan's leadership, stemming from his family lineage, exhibit a notable contrast to the previously held admiration for his father. The government strategies, policies, and administrative approaches implemented by Jagan in Andhra Pradesh have generated a surge of dissatisfaction and pessimism among the people. As the 2024 general elections draw near, the fact that the majority of the population are contemplating on hypothetical settings as if YS Rajasekhara Reddy was alive, brought me to highlight the importance of flashbulb memory. The decisions and actions taken by YS Jagan have consistently brought out recollections and parallels with YSR that accentuate the notable disparities between these two leaders. With the social media trolling memes, ongoing discussions and collective recollections among various platforms reinforced past incidents. The discrepancy in memory retrieval serves as a clear demonstration that flashbulb memories influence formation of public opinions and assessments. The purpose of the study is to examine the notable disparities between the recollections of YSR's demise and the current administration of YS Jagan, thereby highlighting the significant occurrences on the recall of flashbulb memory among the common public.

The current political landscape and socio-economic conditions in the state of Andhra Pradesh prompted the public to reflect more on the legacy of YSR, whereas the impact of these factors on the population of Telangana appears to be comparatively less.

Research Method

The research methodology for the study involved the selection of 300 participants from both regions: 150 participants were considered from the state of Telangana and 150 from the state of Andhra Pradesh. The selection was made on the basis of benefits received from government schemes, especially the recipients of the Arogya Sri scheme and loan waiver for the agriculture scheme. The village volunteers were used to interact and collect responses from the selected responders. Of the 150 questionnaires, 103 questionnaires were returned from Telangana, 125 from Andhra Pradesh. To gather comprehensive insights, a questionnaire that encompasses the concepts of flashbulb memory (Finkenauer et al., 1998) was customized to suit the context and participants of the study, and was administered to the participants. The questionnaire included questions on the aspects of emotional and media determinants, confidence levels, memory of the primary event, emotional feelings, appraisal of importance, recall, and rumination. These aspects were individually studied with different scales of study to suit the specific outcome of the research.

The collected information from the questionnaires was meticulously tabulated and analysed to draw meaningful conclusions from the data. The percentage of responses and insights from participants in each region was a key feature of the analysis, contributing to a comprehensive understanding of the influence of the flashbulb memory traits in the context of the political and social landscape of Telangana and Andhra Pradesh. The flashbulb memory aspects under consideration for the research are as follows.

Flashbulb Memory Attributes

The study focused on examining how well participants could remember the details surrounding their initial exposure to the event. The study focused on gathering information about the specific details surrounding when participants received the news, such as the date, day of the week, and hour. It also examined the different sources of information, including family, friends, colleagues, and media. The study explored the various locations where participants were when they heard the news, whether it was in their country, city, room, or the village along with the people who accompanied them. The questions align with the established categories of flashbulb memories, as identified by various researchers (Bohannon, 1988; Brown & Kulik, 1977; Conway et al., 1994; Finkenauer et al., 1998). For the answers, a score of 1 was given if all the necessary details were mentioned, and a score of 0 if any details were missing. The results are displayed in Table 11.1.

The data from Table 11.1 shows Andhra Pradesh's and Telangana's recall accuracy regarding details of YSR's plane crash. In Andhra Pradesh, 125 participants were surveyed, with 109 displaying high recall proficiency who scored 1. In Telangana out of 103 participants, only 28 accurately remembered details, significantly lower than Andhra Pradesh. Telangana's study with 75 individuals showed an inability to recall, scoring 0. These discrepancies highlight variability in flashbulb memory preservation influenced by proximity, personal relevance, media exposure, and cultural significance, emphasizing typical flashbulb memory traits (vividness, emotional intensity, perceived accuracy).

Confidence Level

Confidence influences the emotional weight of flashbulb memories, intertwining with their vividness and clarity. Individual experiences and emotions heavily shape confidence that impacts perceived recollection accuracy (Blank, 2009). Rehearsals or discussions reinforce confidence and introduce accuracies. Although high confidence often accompanies flashbulb memories due to perceived significance, it doesn't guarantee flawless accuracy. The study evaluated the confidence levels using a 5-point scale (1. Not at all, 2. Slightly, 3. Moderately, 4. Very well, 5. Extremely well) for participants to rate each attribute of the flashbulb memories.

The data from the Table 11.2 shows the confidence level related to memories of YSR's plane crash from Andhra Pradesh and Telangana, focusing on how confidently the participants could recall the details of the incident. Participants rated their recollection confidence of the incident details on a 5-point scale from "Not at all" to "Extremely well". In Andhra Pradesh

Table 11.1 Scores of flashbulb memory attributes

Region	*Total people*	*Scored 1*	*Scored 0*
Andhra Pradesh	125	109	16
Telangana	103	28	75

Table 11.2 Scores of confidence level: Data collected through survey by the researcher

Region	*Total people*	*Not at all*	*Slightly*	*Moderately*	*Very well*	*Extremely well*
Andhra Pradesh	125	3	15	45	38	24
Telangana	103	28	20	25	25	5

notable confidence was rated as "Very well" by 38, indicating strong mental imagery; 24 rated it "Extremely well," suggesting precise recall; 45 rated intensity of confidence level as "Moderately," showing a significant emotional link. In Telangana, out of 103 participants, confidence levels were lower: 25 rated as "Very well," only 5 as "Extremely well," and 25 as "Moderately." The participants from Andhra Pradesh showed higher confidence in recalling vivid details and accuracy linked to flashbulb memory than Telangana with great confidence levels. Emotional intensity ratings were similar. Variations in vividness and accuracy ratings hint at potential differences in confidence level of memory attributes, due to involvement levels or exposure disparities to the event's details.

Memory of the Original Event

The original event's importance in the flashbulb recollection lies in its emotional intensity, distinctiveness, and personal relevance. These memories stem from emotionally charged occurrences, deviating from everyday experiences (Berntsen, 2009). Factors like the intensity of emotions, the uniqueness of the specific event, and personal connections influence everlasting recollections significantly. Social discussions that happen after an event impact memory formation and its subsequent evolution. Studies highlight the dynamic nature of the memory, which is notably influenced by social context (Blank, 2009). Flashbulb memories that are vivid and emotionally charged are initially believed to be highly accurate but tend to fluctuate over time or might etch in the memory depending on the impact that particular incident left. Understanding the event's significance and intensity to recall sheds light on the formation and behaviour of these vivid yet malleable memories.

For the assessment of memory of the original, temporal details, the event's location and the cause of death were required. Responses were scored based on the accuracy of details revealed: 2 for producing complete details correctly, 1 for partially correct information, and 0 for improper or missing answers. For example, "helicopter crash" received a score of 2 for cause of death, while a vague response like "accident" got a score of 1.

From the Table 11.3, in Andhra Pradesh, 125 individuals were contacted to evaluate their recall accuracy. Among the surveyed people, 51 achieved the highest score, 61 respondents provided partially correct information,

Table 11.3 Scores of memory of the original event: Data collected through survey by the researcher

Region	*Total people*	*Scored 2*	*Scored 1*	*Score 0*
Andhra Pradesh	125	51	61	13
Telangana	103	12	62	29

Table 11.4 Scores of emotional feelings: Data collected through survey by the researcher

Region	*Total people*	*Not at all*	*Slightly*	*Moderately*	*Very well*	*Extremely well*
Andhra Pradesh	125	12	22	29	49	13
Telangana	103	11	15	44	18	15

resulting in a score of 1, and 13 individuals received a score of 0 due to incorrect details. Data from the Telangana reveal that only 12 participants out of the total sample achieved a score of 2, signifying a low level of accuracy in recalling details accurately. A significantly larger proportion of individuals, that is, 62 respondents, obtained a score of 1, indicating partial recollections of the event; 29 participants received a score of 0, suggesting their memory completely erased the particulars of the incident as it was in no wayaffecting them. The comparative analysis brings attention to noteworthy differences in the precision and comprehensiveness of memory concerning the initial occurrences. The data tabulated recalls the original incident details with specificity surrounding the demise of YSR among people from Andhra Pradesh and Telangana. The information collected from the individuals is scrutinized to gather insights into the recollection of the event.

Emotional Feelings

The study investigated the vulnerability of flashbulb memories to emotional feelings. Upon knowing about an incident, it is a natural phenomenon that humans get highly charged or feel neutral about an event (Berntsen, 2009). Considering the impact of intense emotions on memory formation (Blank, 2009), the research used a 5-point emotional scale to understand the emotional intensity of the flashbulb memories. A 5-point scale from "Extremely well" to "Not at all" was referred to understand how emotionally charged up the participants were with the information of the event when it initially occurred and they got to know about it.

The data from Table 11.4 presents the affective reactions of individuals hailing from Andhra Pradesh and Telangana in the aftermath of YSR's plane crash, evaluated using a 5-point scale measuring their emotional levels. In

Andhra Pradesh, among 125 respondents, a diverse spectrum of emotional responses emerged—12 individuals indicated they were "Not at all" upset, 22 reported being "Slightly" upset, 29 felt "Moderately" upset, 49 were "Very" upset, and 13 were "Extremely" upset. Among the 103 respondents from Telangana, 11 individuals felt "Not at all" upset, 15 were "Slightly" upset, 44 reported being "Moderately" upset, 18 were "Very" upset, and 15 were "Extremely" upset. These emotional reactions in both regions emphasize the power of emotions connected with the incident, which in turn is a critical characteristic of the flashbulb memories. The variations in emotional responses between Andhra Pradesh and Telangana reveal a higher percentage of people expressing "Very" upset feelings in Andhra Pradesh, which implies more pronounced emotional impacts in that region.

Appraisal of Importance

The importance of appraisal in the flashbulb memories determines how strongly we encode emotionally significant events, making them more vivid and memorable to the circumstances happening in our lives (Berntsen, 2009). For the parameter, on a 5-point rating system, respondents indicated how significant the event was to them personally and in their lives (1. Not at all, 2. Slightly, 3. Moderately, 4. Very well, 5. Extremely well).

The data from the Table 11.5 was collected from respondents in Andhra Pradesh and Telangana regarding YSR's plane crash and the role of that event in their present life. Among 125 respondents in Andhra Pradesh, there was a notable divergence in perspectives: 34 individuals deemed the event moderately significant, while an split of 34 and 42 respondents, respectively, rated it as very and extremely important. Among 103 respondents in Telangana, a majority of 59 individuals considered the event "Not at all" important. In Andhra Pradesh, where the event held greater significance for respondents, there was a correlation with higher accuracy of impact in personal life, aligning with the typical traits associated with flashbulb memories. The stronger emotional attachment and perceived importance likely contribute to the creation of more vivid and intricate flashbulb memories. In Telangana, a considerable number of respondents viewed the event as less significant; this lower appraisal may correlate with decreased accuracy in the impact and vividness of flashbulb memories.

Table 11.5 Scores of appraisal of importance: Data collected through survey by the researcher

Region	*Total people*	*Not at all*	*Slightly*	*Moderately*	*Very well*	*Extremely well*
Andhra Pradesh	**125**	3	12	34	34	42
Telangana	**103**	59	13	14	15	2

Recall and Rumination

Recall is crucial for retrieving vivid details in flashbulb memories, providing a clear and emotionally intense recollection. Rumination influences the ongoing reflection and dispensation of these memories, potentially shaping their long-term retention and accuracy (Berntsen, 2009). Flashbulb memories are vivid due to the intense emotions tied to significant events, enhancing how our brains encode these memories initially. Accuracy can alter over time and this happens because of various factors influencing recall and perception (Blank, 2009). As a parameter for recall and rumination, participants were asked to identify triggers for recall and rumination and the given triggers are self-memory, media and information, personal reflection, interactions and conversations, and external stimuli, meaning events happening in the surroundings that are directly affecting the respondents.

The data from Table 11.6 shows that in Andhra Pradesh, respondents highlighted various stimuli contributing to their recollection of the incident. A large number, 47 individuals, associated their recall with external triggers, while a significant reliance on media for 40 individuals suggests the role of environmental cues and media coverage in evoking memories. Three respondents pointed towards personal reflection and 15 individuals to interactions and conversations as influential triggers for memory recall. In Telangana, different recall patterns emerged. Media and information remained primary triggers for 38 individuals, but a notable emphasis on interactions for 35 individuals suggests that discussions significantly contributed to their memory recall process. Interestingly, no respondents in Telangana identified memory triggers as significant contributors to their recall. These contrasting patterns highlight the diverse influences shaping individuals' memory recall processes related to YSR's plane crash.

Discussion

The study reviewed the literature on the formation, modification, and endurance of flashbulb recollections with the impact of emotional and media factors. The study aimed to understand the data collected and related it with the demise of YSR (the event) to understand the difference of opinion in

Table 11.6 Scores of recalls and rumination: Data collected through survey by the researcher

Region	*Total people*	*Memory triggers*	*Media and information*	*Personal reflection*	*Interactions and conversations*	*External stimuli*
Andhra Pradesh	125	20	40	3	15	47
Telangana	103	0	38	5	35	25

the perception between selected people of Andhra Pradesh and Telangana. It investigated the regional memory distinctions, hypothesizing that Andhra Pradesh residents possess stronger, more frequent recollections due to emotional ties and the current political situation of the state. The research supports this, by highlighting that the people from Andhra Pradesh had a notably higher recall accuracy of memories compared to Telangana. The parameter used shows that the flashbulb memory traits of Andhra Pradesh are of closer emotional proximity and are related to the event. The research also dissected how the event's perceived importance shapes regional disparities with the scrutiny of varying perspectives on the significance of the event by enriching the understanding of regional differences and offering insights to understand the impact of flashbulb memory. Focusing on emotional intensity, significance, and recall and rumination, it compares Andhra Pradesh and Telangana respondents. The research uncovers media and emotional differences in different cultural contexts and uses participant scores of memory specifics, and emotional intensity measures, revealing preliminary differences favouring Andhra Pradesh. For emotional links in memory formation, the study looks at the triggers of media influence for Andhra Pradesh and Telangana, showing distinct regional perspectives, where again Andhra Pradesh stands high. The role of environmental cues, social interactions, and reflections in flashbulb memory to ruminate, emphasizes the regional diversity in recall processes. The study explores disparities in memory accuracy, confidence, emotional responses, and importance appraisal related to flashbulb memories to unravel the intricate dynamics in their formation and recollection. It highlights emotional ties, personal relevance, and societal contexts in memory shaping, acknowledging societal and cultural influences, and being on the higher side among the people of Andhra Pradesh. The multifaceted factors of flashbulb memories show the importance and impact of emotional significance, media impact, and individual experiences' roles. The research outlines how an event of significance impacts shared memory and the role of various components of flashbulb memory on the comprehension of memory among diverse social groups, showcasing its higher impact on Andhra Pradesh over Telangana.

Conclusion

The study was effective to understand flashbulb memories linked to Yeduguri Sandinti Rajasekhara Reddy's demise in Telangana and Andhra Pradesh. It explored emotional intensity, media impact, and individual experiences' role in memory formation. The comparative analysis revealed the disparities in recall accuracy, emotional responses, and event importance between the regions. Andhra Pradesh participants showed higher accuracy and stronger emotional ties to the event than the people from Telangana. This suggests their superior retention and emotional connection, possibly influenced by cognitive abilities of emotional and media factors. The study uncovered the factors shaping flashbulb memories and individual experiences of a specific powerful event that left an impact on them. The study limits itself to the geographical specificity and subjective recall of a single event and the complexity of flashbulb memories in diverse social groups and contributes significantly to understanding memory dynamics around emotionally charged events. Examining emotions, media, and societal contexts enriches memory phenomena knowledge, particularly within regional and cultural settings. These findings pave the way for further exploration into memory formation complexities.

Works Cited

Berntsen, Dorthe. "Flashbulb Memory and Social Identity." *Flashbulb Memories: New Issues and New Perspectives*, edited by Olivier Luminet and Andrea Curci, Psychology Press, 2009, pp. 187–205.

Blank, Harold. "Remembering: A Theoretical Interface Between Memory and Social Psychology." *Social Psychology*, vol. 40, 2009, pp. 164–175.

Bohannon, James N. "Flashbulb Memories for the Space Shuttle Disaster: A Tale of Two Theories." *Cognition*, vol. 29, 1988, pp. 179–196.

Bohannon, James N., and Linda V. Symons. "Flashbulb Memories: Confidence, Consistency, and Quantity." *Affect and Accuracy in Recall: Studies of "Flashbulb" Memories*, edited by E. Winograd and U. Neisser, Cambridge University Press, 1992, pp. 65–91.

Bohannon, James N., et al. "The Effects of Affect and Input Source on Flashbulb Memories." *Applied Cognitive Psychology*, vol. 21, 2007, pp. 1023–1036.

Brown, Roger, and James Kulik. "Flashbulb Memories." *Cognition*, vol. 5, 1977, pp. 73–99.

Christianson, Sara A. "Flashbulb Memories: Special, but Not So Special." *Memory & Cognition*, vol. 17, 1989, pp. 435–443.

Conway, Martin A. *Flashbulb Memories*. Erlbaum, 1995.

Conway, Martin A., et al. "The Formation of Flashbulb Memories." *Memory & Cognition*, vol. 22, 1994, pp. 326–343.

Finkenauer, C., et al. "Flashbulb Memories and the Underlying Mechanism of Their Formation: Toward an Emotional-Integrative Model." *Memory & Cognition*, vol. 26, 1998, pp. 516–531.

Finkenauer, C., et al. "When Individuals' Memories Are Socially Shaped: Flashbulb Memories of Socio-Political Events." *Collective Memory of Political Events: Social Psychological Perspectives*, edited by James W. Pennebaker, David Paez, and Bernard Rime, Lawrence Erlbaum Associates Inc., 1997, pp. 191–207.

Frijda, Nico H. "Emotion, Cognitive Structure, and Action Tendency." *Cognition & Emotion*, vol. 1, 1987, pp. 115–143.

Frijda, Nico H., et al. "Relations Among Emotion, Appraisal, and Emotional Action Readiness." *Journal of Personality and Social Psychology*, vol. 57, 1989, pp. 212–228.

Hirst, W., et al. "A Ten-Year Follow-Up of a Study of Memory for the Attack of September 11, 2001: Flashbulb Memories and Memories for Flashbulb Events." *Journal of Experimental Psychology: General*, vol. 144, 2015, pp. 604–623.

Lazarus, Richard S. "Progress on a Cognitive-Motivational-Relational Theory of Emotion." *American Psychologist*, vol. 46, 1991, pp. 819–834.

Lazarus, Richard S., and Elizabeth A. Smith. "Knowledge and Appraisal in the Cognition-Emotion Relationship." *Cognition & Emotion*, vol. 2, 1988, pp. 281–300.

Luminet, Olivier, et al. "Predicting Cognitive and Social Consequences of Emotional Episodes: The Contribution of Emotional Intensity, the Five Factor Model and Alexithymia." *Journal of Research in Personality*, vol. 34, 2000, pp. 471–497.

Luminet, Olivier, et al. "Social Sharing of Emotion Following Exposure to a Negatively Valenced Situation." *Cognition & Emotion*, vol. 14, 2000, pp. 661–688.

Neisser, Ulric. "Snapshots or Benchmarks?" *Memory Observed*, edited by Ulric Neisser, Freeman, 1982, pp. 43–48.

Neisser, Ulric, and N. Harsh. "Phantom Flashbulbs: False Recollections of Hearing the News About Challenger." *Affect and Accuracy in Recall: Studies of Flashbulb Memories*, edited by E. Winograd and U. Neisser, Cambridge University Press, 1992, pp. 9–31.

Pillemer, David B. "Flashbulb Memories of the Assassination Attempt on President Reagan." *Cognition*, vol. 16, 1984, pp. 63–80.

Robinson, John A. "Affect and Retrieval of Personal Memories." *Motivation & Emotion*, vol. 4, 1980, pp. 149–174

Rubin, David C., and M. Kozin. "Vivid Memories." *Cognition*, vol. 16, 1984, pp. 81–95.

Schaefer, E. G., et al. "TV or Not TV? Does the Immediacy of Viewing Images of a Momentous News Event Affect the Quality and Stability of Flashbulb Memories?" *Memory*, vol. 19, 2011, pp. 251–266.

Schmidt, Susan R. "Can We Have a Distinctive Theory of Memory?" *Memory & Cognition*, vol. 19, 1991, pp. 523–542.

Smith, C. A., and P. C. Ellsworth. "Patterns of Appraisal and Emotion Related to Taking an Exam." *Journal of Personality & Social Psychology*, vol. 52, 1987, pp. 475–488.

Talarico, Jason M., and David C. Rubin. "Confidence, Not Consistency, Characterizes Flashbulb Memories." *Psychological Science*, vol. 14, 2003, pp. 455–461.

Zelizer, Barbie. "Why Memory's Work on Journalism Does Not Reflect Journalism's Work on Memory." *Memory Studies*, vol. 1, 2008, pp. 79–95.

Part IV

Partition – Analyzing the Bloodiest Chapter of the Indian Subcontinent

12 Challenges of Using Memory as a Tool in Oral Historiography

An Analysis with Respect to Urvashi Butalia's *The Other Side of Silence*

Chaithanya V.

Urvashi Butalia's *The Other Side of Silence* attempts to reinforce the significance of memories of survivors of the Great Indian Partition of 1947. Published in 1998, it is a collection of interviews narrated in the form of essays, dismantling the water-tight compartment of looking at history from the perspective of the historiographer. She therefore aims to present the less explored truths of the past through the experiences of individuals. By including testimonies from experiences shared by the then marginalised – women, children, the aged, and the Dalits – Butalia has focused on presenting an oral history deleting "the major players of history: Gandhi, Nehru, Patel, Jinnah, Liaquat Ali Khan, Mountbatten" (11). This analysis focuses on re-presenting oral historiography as a story-telling technique that subsists itself on the memories of the "storytellers". Stories are considered fiction and hardly as facts. Therefore, Butalia critiques the validity of the mainstream history that dwells on recorded facts. There have been multiple records on The Great Indian Partition of 1947 enlisting the number of casualties, number of women and girl children raped, and the number of people killed and displaced. Analysing these statistics under the pretext of the emotions of the survivors makes this methodology more relatable to the present citizens of India.

It is impossible for a historian to capture emotions in the historiographical process if facts are the only information relied upon. In some cases, emotions do not become part of history because they are a threat to the blinkered view offered by mainstream history. French historian Lucien Febvre called emotions "primitive feelings" and said that he urged his contemporary historians to beware of sensibilities and fundamental human emotions as they were capable of turning the world into a "stinking pit of corpses" (Frevert 29). This proves the capacity of emotions to generate meaning. Therefore, the absence of emotions in mainstream history leaves an unidentifiable gap.

When the nation-building process continued under the pretext of partition in 1947, two kinds of identities were formed – "Self" and the "Other". Therefore, the history of the partition should describe the histories of these two sects as they have different stories to convey. This negates the possibility of a singular, monolithic history and makes the historiographical process ambiguous. Butalia explains this by comparing the varied consequences of

DOI: 10.4324/9781003508564-17

partition in both India and Pakistan. She documents how Pakistan did not have its own banknote as the minting of currencies happened in India. There was an imbalance in the occupational sector when barbers, weavers, and tailors shifted from India to Pakistan, and the accountants, lawyers, and teachers shifted to India, both in the name of religion (97). Being raised in India, Butalia focuses mainly on the story of partition as narrated by an Indian.

Donald A. Ritchie, in his book *Doing Oral History*, mentions that in the case of oral historians, the source of information will be "first-person observations of witnesses of events great and small" in order to learn "what sense those people made of the events in their own lives. Motivations and objectives are especially important". A lot has been recorded under the mainstream partition history as facts. However, as Pippa Virdee records in her article "Remembering Partition: Women, Oral Histories and the Partition of 1947", it was in the early 1980s that a new historiographical school emerged that shifted its concern from the "great men of history" approach to a "history from below approach" (50). Ranajit Guha's contribution to the subaltern perspective of history and its impact on Regional Studies (shift of focus from national to regional history) is rightly acknowledged in this essay. However, Virdee acknowledges the role of feminists and social activists in helping history dig into an individual's traumatic past (50). This is what Urvashi Butalia does as she compiles the stories of the victims of partition in *The Other Side of Silence*. She says in the collection that the most suitable way to understand partition and its consequences is to analyse the event from the perspectives of people who felt it (13). Thus, Butalia explores the human element of emotions in her approach to history. It is the presentation of history, the facts that the historian chooses to present and the ones that are deliberately silenced, that shapes the future of a nation's ideology. Butalia ensures that the voices of the survivors or informants hardly leave any gaps in her presentation of history. However, the possibility of gaps arises when her version of history gets compared with mainstream history. One villain here is the unreliability of memory as a source of information due to various factors that will be discussed further in this chapter.

Butalia's decision to adopt the methodology of oral history and the dilemmas she faced as a result of it are discussed by Ira Raja in his review of the book. According to him, there are two reasons why Butalia chose this methodology: one is her urge to do right to the survivors of partition, and the other is to exhibit her inclination towards the postmodernist disposition of distinguishing the "truth" from opinion (102). Oral History is comparatively more inclusive. The voice of the oral historian will be felt by the reader when the historian filters and presents the information collected from the stories of the informants. Butalia reveals her role in choosing the narratives that were to be included in the book. She says in the book,

> And in the end I have chosen to use a rather arbitrary criterion. I have included the stories that meant the most to me, the stories of people

> with whom I have formed real friendships, or stories to which I keep returning again and again.
>
> (14)

Butalia collects these stories as information; she structures them in such a way in her book that they foreground their parallelism to mainstream history. She claims that the historical account she is producing is purely subjective, and the personal history will therefore be coloured by her political and emotional preferences (20–21). By pointing out the constructed quality of her "history", she associates history with the art of storytelling. This thought resonates with that of Richard Waswo, who believes that both histories and stories are narratives. He quotes Hayden White and says, "Recognizing this formal and etymological identity, Hayden White has argued with respect to nineteenth-century historiography that history itself is 'made' by the choice of tropological and narrative structures derived from literature" (304). R. F. Foster's elaboration of these narrative structures with respect to Irish history in his work *The Irish Stories: Telling Tales and Making It Up in Ireland* shows how the historiography of the Irish is influenced by the myths, legends, and folktales of Ireland. He showcases that the "Story of Ireland", when narrated, would adhere to Vladimir Propp's laws as mentioned in "The Morphology of Folktales" (5). Therefore he proves that Propp's narrative modes were sufficient to narrate Irish national history. In other words, the narrative modes of historiography can be similar to that of a fable or folktale. Since History involves telling/narration of stories, it is not just a product of "academic orthodoxy". The "Story of Ireland" is an interwoven narrative of "personal experiences and national history" (2). Therefore narrative mode can demote the status of History as "the collection of facts" and can present the same facts as a narrative from one perspective. However, these narratives contributed to the nation's story.

> The compelling notion of the Story of Ireland, with plot, narrative logic and desired outcome, reached its apogee in the later nineteenth century. The historiography thus created is intimately connected with the discovery of folktale, myth and saga as indices of national experience; the development of Irish nationalism is strongly influenced by the transference of these forms into a narrative of nationality.
>
> (Foster 3)

Narration can thus blur the distinction between a narrator and a historian. Butalia believes that it is important to express herself in the collective narrative as it is the implicit presence of the speaker in many histories that misleads the reader into believing that the facts presented as historical are the only truths (20). She also claims that such a history that has "written itself" would be "dishonest" (20). Unlike the mainstream history that presents the truth of the omniscient historian as facts, this personalised history presents itself as an alternative, showcasing the "truth" as the version of the teller or narrator. Therefore, "the teller is to us (audience) as the hero is to the tale. Defiant or solicitous, embittered or engaging, he and the shape of his story make the history that we recognize as ours" (Waswo 326). R. F. Foster's finding that Irish history implies a beginning, middle, and end like a plot of any other story, and the belief that "the formal modes of *Bildungsroman*, ghost story, deliverance tale, family romance have lent motifs to the ways Irish history has been told" (2), add on to the constructed quality of history as literature.

However, the product of oral history is very different from that of conventional history. In *Narrating Our Pasts*, Elizabeth Tonkin studies the power relationship between the interviewer and the interviewee in the active process of collecting oral testimonies. Viewing the interview as a dialogue between interviewer and narrator, she says that the history thus created is a mutual construction of reality in itself as the informants present facts, giving meaning to them in their own ways, which might even be problematic (85). She also adds that along with the data collection, calculating how the historian's interpretations and interests shape the construction of the text is also important, as it is these assumptions that will help the reader make sense of the narrative (80). Besides, "translation of the narrator's experience-near terms to the audience's vernacular puts a creative burden on the researcher" (86). *The Other Side of Silence* reveals that Butalia successfully overcomes this burden by taking the initiative of narrativising them (15). She says that while transferring words to text, so much gets lost. This results in "conscious shaping of the interview by the interviewer who is usually in a situation of power vis-à-vis the person being interviewed" (15). Therefore, the stories Butalia built from interviews of maternal uncle Ranamama, the only sibling of her mother who decided to stay back in Pakistan, and her mother Subhadra Butalia's version of it, of a scooter driver Rajinder Singh who explains the reluctance of people to displace themselves, of Damayanti who tasted only loneliness in life, till the story of Maya Rani, a Harijan who witnessed the violence of partition in her childhood – these were chosen and narrated by Butalia in a sequence that would fit in as sections in the book. The sections are titled "Beginnings", "Blood", "'Facts'", "Women", "'Honour'", "Children", "'Margins'", and "Memory", like that of an episodic novel. Thus, oral historiography adds multiple layers to the otherwise linear narrative of mainstream history.

The act of sharing stories is a means of making a connection with the present. "Storytelling is, in the words of historian David Blight, part of 'the human quest to own the past and thereby achieve control over the present'" (Walker 2). Oral history narrators use the tool of memory to build connections. Memory demands the survivor to remember and recollect the trauma, which is ironically wished to be forgotten. Since people locate their memories in different frameworks of space and time, different perspectives of the same incidents are obtained. Indira Chowdhary notes the difference between recording oral testimonies of other historical incidents and that of partition and says that, unlike other historical incidents that occurred in India, the great partition cannot be pinned down to a location or place. She feels that an effort taken to locate or "monumentalize" this incident would result in the creation of "sites of memory", which are "artificially created in order to eradicate memory and create and organise history" (39). Butalia compares the memories of the Great Indian Partition and the Holocaust memorials and the memorials of the Vietnam War to conclude that there is nothing called "institutional memory" for the former unlike the latter two. She claims that there is nothing at the border where masses migrated that could be marked as the site of partition (361–362).

> For people, for the State, what is at stake in remembering? […] No matter how much Indian politicians, members of Congress Party, tried to see themselves as reluctant players in the game, they could not escape the knowledge that they accepted partition as the cost of freedom. Such histories are not easily memorialized
>
> (Butalia 362)

But oral history functions against the conventional methods of documentation and rejects any effort to hierarchise the generally accepted truth. Like Butalia's narration, oral history tries to connect memories and their surroundings to history as perceived in general (Chowdhary 39). Therefore, memory is directly associated with history as a lens projecting the frame of mind of the contributors. As Butalia rightly points out in the book, though the memories of partition are never wished to be remembered, remembering becomes, unfortunately, an "essential part of resolving" (269). In an effort to reflect upon the ideology of the then Hindus, Butalia gives the example of one of her informants – Hoondraj Kripalani. He was hooked on the belief that the Hindus were abused by the Muslims. He explains how the Muslim women approached the Hindu household in the pretext of selling something and how they occupied the house and refused to leave (187–188). This account of aggressive Muslim women from the perspective of an individual's conception of the past offers a different framework of space and time that is absent in mainstream history. Similarly, interacting with people from different sects gives different perspectives on the same incident.

Dipesh Chakrabarty explains the difference between memory and history as "history seeks to explain the event and the memory of pain refuses the historical explanation and sees the event causing the pain as a monstrously irrational aberration" (322). He also says that besides the sentiment and trauma, the aspect of memory that contradicts the relationship of an individual's present to the past and to the collective memory of the nation concerns the oral historians. He says that the narrative structure of the memory of an individual who has undergone trauma is different from the conventional historical narrative, paving the way for new insights. However, for memory to be plausible, it has to be associated with the historical event, the general conception of trauma that validates the emotions and claims of the informants.

Therefore, the construction of the general past should coincide with the individual construction of memory (319). Therefore, the importance of collective memory in interweaving individual memories is high.

Frank de Caro claims that memory is not just a collection of facts but also a re-creation of meaning. He also feels that the "thematic thread" connecting the stories told by the informants can reveal significant information connecting their past to the present, as their once-lived experiences would have the potential to interconnect with the present. He believed that the stories that are narrated by the informants give hints to the readers to associate the past with their reality (263). Thus, the stories told by the informants of oral history are not just creative constructs and mere traumatic recollections but also linkers that make the past progressive. Butalia associates independence with the success of "anti-colonial nationalism" and the Great Partition with "the triumph of communalism", both having long-term consequences (192). This shows the relevance of the stories told by the informants of Butalia's works to date. It also proves that oral historiography is a systemic way of telling stories and not just recording facts. Memories surface in the lives of the survivors unpredictably. The haunting memory of visualising the murder of a kin, the trauma of an abducted woman who was raped, the pain of a child separated from his/her parents: all their stories continue even though the documented history of partition records only about the year 1947. By introducing the human element of memories and presenting "facts" in the form of stories, the reality faced by the victims in the past was felt by the readers in the present. Thus, presenting historiography as a storytelling method eased the transmission of information across time periods.

With memory playing the lead role, oral history brings two perspectives in front of the readers – the perspective of the insider (witness) and that of the outsider (historian). However, when the historian and the interviewee interact, there is a chance that their interpretations of the historical facts differ, leading to a conflict. Allen Barbara explains that when an oral historian asks the informants to explain their past, they "re-create" what was experienced (6). In other words, they are not "constructing" historical facts while describing the events to the historians but attempting to express the intensity of the trauma of their historical experience and to deliver a suitable "context" for the historian to approach history (6). Therefore, it is necessary that historians allow the interviewees to "recreate" their memories without establishing a relationship based on the hierarchy between the interviewer and the interviewee.

The interviewees are conscious of the subjective nature of the history they are contributing to the world. They realise that their stories will become part of the narrative of historiography. Their awareness that their perspective may alter the course of official history makes them nervous about the consequences. Therefore, their recollection of the past has an impact on the present and on their memories. This may be conscious or unconscious. Kenneth R. Kirby says that if it is unconscious, it is because the informants have faced changes in their outlook on life. Their growth in terms of experiences and their evaluation of the past changes their historical perspective (Kirby 30). This makes the pieces of evidence of oral history ambiguous.

The story of Mangal Singh, as described by Butalia, shows that the impact of a decision taken during a crisis stays for a lifetime. Mangal Singh was one of three brothers who killed seventeen of the women and children in their family during the partition. His is a "legendary status" in the locality, and he was adamant in naming this act as martyrdom and not murder (94). When Mangal Singh was asked the reason for their forced martyrdom, he replied that it was about pride and honour and not about fear (195). Therefore, it is the fear of conversion and the knowledge of its consequences that will last for a long time that makes Mangal Singh justify the killings. However, Mangal Singh initially refused to speak to Butalia, asking why he should dig up his past (194). This may be a conscious decision because he might be aware that the scenario has changed and that he may be accused of killing people of his own blood. Therefore, he emphasises the word "martyrdom" many times in the interview in order to hide his guilt and to make the killings context-specific. Such screening of information by the interviewees may mislead the historian from collecting authentic information from oral testimonies.

Storytelling demands coherence between sequences, so does historiography, which knits stories of multiple instances from the past. While trying to co-relate the various stories told by her informants (who belonged to various sections of society), Butalia struggled to find continuity. There were instances when memories of different individuals on the same incident provided varied information. Such information not only challenged the written evidence but also questioned the credibility of listening to only one version of "truth". This is referred to as the "Rashomon Effect" by historians. According to Sam Azgor, "The Rashomon Effect emerges, where people give significantly different but equally believable details of the same event. It describes a situation where the people involved in the same incident give conflicting interpretations or descriptions, while everyone's interpretation seems plausible" (Web). Karl G. Heider lists some of the possible reasons for the change of perspectives – the speakers may be looking at different cultures or subcultures, they may be referring to the same culture at different times, some speakers may have wrong information about incidents, they may be looking differently at the same culture, they may possess different value systems, etc. (75–76). One instance where Butalia provides two perspectives of an event is in her presentation of the story of Ranamama from his perspective and that of her mother, Subhadra Butalia. When Ranamama's story makes the readers sympathetic towards his helplessness as an unemployed youth who was forced to stay back in his motherland, the story of Subhadra, who had to take up the responsibility of the whole family by migrating to India, is equally justifiable (29–65). However, Butalia cleverly reduces the impact of the "Rashomon Effect" by making it less evident. This is one of the few incidents to which

Butalia does not offer an extensive interpretation, leaving it to the readers to be judgemental.

Retrieval is an important aspect of memory. "In discussing memory process and retrieval, researchers make a distinction between accessibility and availability" (Hummert 56). While some believe that "once information is understood and stored in long-term memory, it is always available", there are other oral historians who believe "in the constructive and reconstructive aspects of memory" (Hummert 56). Butalia mentions a number of times in *The Other Side of Silence* that her interviewees admitted that they forgot many things when they tried to recollect their stories. For example, her conversation with the record collector Savitri Makhijani ended with Makhijani saying that she could not recollect what happened to the girl who was returned to the NGO after adoption, saying that she was naughty (250). Hummert lists many reasons for such forgetting: "when we did not pay much attention to some incident and it never reaches our long-term memory", piling up of later events making it difficult to "recall an incident from the garbage", decaying of "memory traces" and "selective recalling" of memories are some of these (55). Another reason for forgetting could be the desire in the informants to "forget the frightening past, or the equally uncertain and fearful future, and live only for the present" (150). Butalia records Damayanti Sahgal's words on the abducted Muslim women born in poor families, who were exposed to "silken salwars, net dupattas and cold ice creams" (150), all of which they could not have enjoyed otherwise. Circumstances made these women forget their past after abduction, and retrieval of memories after the conscious forgetting becomes difficult.

Memory gets silenced when the informants in the partition historiography are women. The information given by the women survivors who were interviewed was either influenced by the presence of men in the household or by the fear of getting silenced by the patriarchal pillars at home. Butalia gave importance to the silences and gaps of women in her interviews. "Silence", according to Sherry Thomas, is another technique used by the historian to present the trauma faced by the survivors (53). He points out that "silence is terribly important and the significance of the sentence changes if you leave the pauses and silences in", giving it a poetic and emotional feel. However, for Butalia, silence is meaningful if uttered by the survivor. She describes "speaking to and with women as learning to listen differently, often listening to hidden nuances, the half-said thing, the silences which are sometimes more eloquent than speech" (16). But she also adds that a researcher may come across a dilemma of "whether is it better to 'allow' silence or 'force' speech?" (16).

Oral historians who came later found a methodology to gather information from such "silences", thus extending the credibility of voices from the survivors. The continuing research on this silence proves the need to know the "truths" beyond written pieces of evidence. Parul Sehgal, in her article "Seventy Five Years After Indian Partition, Who Owns the Narrative?" refers to Aanchal Malhotra's *Remnants of Partition* in which Malhotra devises a wise plan to collect memories from her silent grandparents who were Punjabi migrants from Pakistan. Since they were reluctant to share their stories, she asked them what they carried with them. Thus, the conversation that started from everyday objects that her grandparents carried with them during the journey to India produced stories of trauma and separation. "Her book is a history of Partition told in twenty-one possessions: a string of pearls, a sword. These objects are not relics; many are pointedly, movingly, still in use". Thus, the strategies to bring out "facts" from stories evolved as oral historians stressed the need for multiple perspectives.

However, the credibility of oral history also depended upon the type of informant contributing to the story. The story of Zainab and Bhuta Singh, described by Butalia, is a good example of how women were proved incapable of providing the right information to oral historiographers of partition. Zainab, who was abducted on her way to Pakistan, was sold to Bhuta Singh, a Sikh who fell in love with her. They lived happily with two children until the government decided to rescue the abducted women to help them find their roots. Zainab was asked to leave for Pakistan to reunite with her parents. She left with her second child, promising Bhuta Singh that she would return. However, she was forced by the relatives in her hometown to marry her cousin (so that the property in her name would not go outside the extended family). Bhuta Singh, who got the news, converted to Islam in order to get a passport and visa to Pakistan. After all the hardships, when Bhuta Singh met Zainab as Jamil Ahmed, he was rejected by Zainab. She had no choice like the thousands of women "who live their lives in silence" (127–131). The immediate surroundings and the patriarchal power controlled the voices of women, silencing them often and shutting them off from their past. Therefore, when it comes to women informants, the place of the interview and the presence of men/patriarchal agents at the site of the interview influenced the narration by women.

Butalia has also taken into account the "information" given by informants who were children during the time of partition; the reliability of the "truth" in it is more problematic. When it comes to the recording of the marginal voices, she questions the possibility of the voices of children who cannot speak on their own behalf when women's lives are silenced by patriarchy (286). If given a voice, Butalia also doubts the reliability of children's memories, assuming that the narration of children could be just fantasies (258). Listening to the stories of the "partition children", Butalia rethinks on the aspect of memory: "I could not help feeling that these were the words, and the interpretation of an adult [...] How else would memory have reconstructed the details?" (259).

The deepest emotions can only be felt and can never be expressed in words. The trauma of partition can never be translated into words by the survivors. Butalia records how the informants struggled to describe their experiences as the language seemed to lack expressions to convey what they suffered. The memory is often shunned as "indescribable" (360). "Partition, the word itself is so inadequate. Partition is a simple division, a separation, but surely what happened in 1947 was much more than that" (360). Therefore, memory only remains as an intangible reality in the minds of the survivors. Though the survivors wished to tell their stories of the past, the medium failed them. The stories go untold, leaving questions behind. Individual memory takes the upper hand here because stories get confined to the individual memory and never reach the collective memory. However, it is the realisation of the presence of a common past in these memories that connects the past to the present that instils a sense of unity among the nationals of both nations.

The scope of memory is not just limited to oral historiography. Stories and testimonials of partition have helped in documenting these memories in many other forms, re-creating history. Partition literature is one genre that comprises such stories. Though the victims of partition are presented as characters in stories, they can be any Indian/Pakistani who was part of the great migration. "Creative writers have captured the human dimensions of partition far more effectively than have historians", Parul Sehgal quotes the scholar Ayesha Jalal. Thus, partition literature not only emphasises the fact that history is another form of literature but also contributes to the documentation of the lesser-heard voices in the form of stories. Sehgal cites many examples: the realist narrative *Train to Pakistan* by Khushwant Singh, Yashpal's feminist epic *This Is Not That Dawn*, Manto's short story "Black Margins", Salman Rushdie's novel *Midnight's Children*, Bapsi Sidhwa's *Ice Candy Man*, Veera Hiranandani's American young-adult novel, *The Night Diary* are literature set in the background of the partition. Sehgal also feels that partition literature has chronicled the trauma and terror of partition like that of oral history:

> Two decades ago, Akash Kapur, writing in the *Times* about a landmark work of Partition oral history, directed the reader back to "the excellent fiction" of Partition, such as Khushwant Singh's "Train to Pakistan" (1956), which "does a far better job of evoking the terror, the bewilderment and the remorse that still shadow so many lives on the subcontinent".
>
> (Sehgal 2022)

When Geetanjali Shree's *Tomb of Sand* won the International Booker Prize in 2022, the story of lives torn apart by partition reached an even wider audience. This also highlights the fact that Partition Literature is preferred by readers across the world to acknowledge the experiences of the survivors. Therefore, academic history is not the only document revisited in the present to understand the facts. The importance given to the voices of the unheard is evident in the success of Partition Literature like that of *Tomb of Sand*.

The chapter has so far analysed how oral history showcases the gaps in written history and the challenges an oral historian has to go through while showcasing these perspectives. It is also important to acknowledge the emotions in history and the facts fictionally represented in Partition Literature. However, oral history is never independent of official history. There should be an officially written history for the oral historian to prepare questions for the interview. Besides, knowledge of the official history is the primary necessity to understand where the gaps are and how they are being filled by oral evidence. James E.Fogerty quotes Morrissey in his article "Filling the Gap: Oral History in the Archives", "Even the most ardent advocate of oral history cannot argue persuasively that interviewing is worthwhile if conducted independently of prior research in surviving written materials" (149). Butalia agrees with Morrisey as she explains in the book that it is the anger and dissatisfaction with the facts recorded in mainstream history that provoked her to explore the gaps in the former using the methodology of oral historiography (Butalia 6). This led to the world of oral evidence. Therefore, the project of oral history had its origin in the official history.

However, recent trends in documenting the past do not stop with reading the documented facts and listening to the stories of the survivors. Memories are archived by organisations like Guneet Singh Bhalla's 1947 Partition Archive and Sharmeen Obaid-Chinoy's Citizens Archive of Pakistan (CAP). Sehgal also mentions Project Dastaan, initiated by the students of Oxford University, which "not only collects testimonies but also offers refugees a chance to 'visit' their homeland using virtual-reality headsets". Thus, historiography is beyond the recording of the past. It is recovering the past to make meaning of the present. Therefore, historians nowadays are adding to the archives collected by oral historians like Butalia.

By admitting the inaccuracies of oral history and the limitations of its primary tool, memory, Butalia asserts that though memories keep changing, the fundamental certainty in them can help one arrive at a probable truth (13). She quotes James Young, who says, "Whatever 'fictions' emerge from the survivors' accounts are not derivations from the 'truth' but are part of the truth in any particular version" (13–14). This resonates with the words of Edward S. Casey, an American philosopher who believed that the memories of an individual will always be loyal to the truth of the past, though it need not exactly be the past (Kirby 32).

Urvashi Butalia, through her significant book of non-fiction, *The Other Side of Silence*, has tried to normalise the high status enjoyed by "History" as a form of literature by analysing the event of the partition of India (1947) through the stories told by its victims. The oral historiography and its results complement the official history and highlight the significance of storytelling in generating facets of truth. The reliability of using memory as a tool during the storytelling process is also analysed in the project. Though memory and storytelling based on it have their own drawbacks, this initiative by Urvashi Butalia has unveiled the hidden side of history, that of emotions and humanity. Her significant methodology of chronicling the emotions and experiences of the subaltern in parallel to the written pieces of evidence questions the superiority of the generally accepted truth. The chapter also mentions the role of Partition Literature in expressing the human elements of history, thus highlighting the power of literature in showcasing the past. By traversing through the stories told by the survivors and witnesses of the Great Partition of 1947, Urvashi Butalia not only connected the memories of the past to the perceptions of the present but also re-created history for the otherwise voiceless protagonists of *The Other Side of Silence.*

Works Cited

Allen, Barbara. "Re-Creating the Past: The Narrator's Perspective in Oral History." *The Oral History* Review 12 (1984): 1–12. *JSTOR*. Web. 20 August 2022.

Azgor, Sam. "The Rashomon Effect: A Well-known Problem of Eyewitness Infidelity." *Medium*. A Medium Corporation. 12 September 2021. Web. 18 August 2022.

Butalia, Urvashi. *The Other Side of Silence.* New Delhi: Penguin Books, 1998. Print.

Caro, Frank de. "Stories and 'Oral History' Interviews: A Thematic Analysis of 'Embedded' Narratives." *Western Folklore* 71.¾ (Summer and Fall 2012): 257-277. *JSTOR*. Web. 22 August 2022.

Chakrabarty, Dipesh. "Remembering Villages: Representations of Hindu-Bengali Memories in the Aftermath of the Partition." *Inventing Boundaries: Gender, Politics and the Partition of India.* Ed. Mushirul Hasan. New Delhi: Oxford University Press, 2000, 318–336. Print.

Chowdhary, Indira. "Speaking of the Past: Perspectives on Oral History." *Economic and Political Weekly* 30 (2014)

July 26): 39–42. *JSTOR*. Web. 22 August 2022.

Fogerty, James E. "Filling the Gap: Oral History in the Archives." *American Archivist*. Vol. 46, No. 2/Spring 1983. 148-157. Web. 24 August 2022

Foster, E. F. *The Irish Story: Telling Tales and Making it up in Ireland.* London: Oxford University Press, 2004. Print.

Frevert, Ute. *Emotions in History.* ProQuestEbook Central. Budapest: Central European University Press, 2011. *Inflibnet-ebooks*. Web. 8 August 2022.

Heider, Karl G. "The Rashomon Effect: When Ethnographers Disagree." *American Anthropologist* 90.1 (1988): 73–81. *JSTOR*. Web. 19 August 2022.

Hummert, Mary Lee, Howard E. Sypher, and Sheryl L. Williams. "Social Psychological Aspects of the Oral History Interview." *Interactive Oral History Interviewing.* Eds. Eva M. McMahan and Kim Lacy Rogers. London: Routledge, 2009. Print.

Kirby, R. Kenneth. "Phenomenology and the Problems of Oral History." *The Oral History Review* 35.1 (2008): 22–38. *JSTOR*. Web. 25 August 2022.

Raja, Ira. "Stories to Tell: Women's Agency, Activism, and Emancipation in South Asia." *Australian Feminist Studies* 17.37 (2002): 101–107. *Taylor & Francis Online*. Web. 20 August 2022.

Ritchie, Donald A. *Doing Oral History*. New York: Twayne Publishers, 1995. Print.

Sehgal, Parul. "Seventy Five Years After Indian Partition, Who Owns the Narrative?" *The New Yorker,* 26 December 2022. Web. 6 July 2023.

Thomas, Sherry. "Digging Beneath the Surface: Oral History Techniques." *Frontiers: A Journal of Women Studies* 7.1 (1983): 50–55. *JSTOR. Web.20 August 2023.*

Tonkin, Elizabeth. *Narrating Our Pasts.* New York: Cambridge University Press, 1992. Print

Virdee, Pippa. "Remembering Partition, Women, Oral Histories and the Partition of 1947." *Oral History Society* 41.2 (2013): 49–62. *JSTOR*. Web. 25 August 2022.
Walker, Melissa. *Southern Farmers and Their Stories: Memory and Meaning in Oral History*. Kentucky: University Press of Kentucky, 2006. Print.
Waswo, Richard. "Story as Historiography in the Waverley Novels." *ELH* 47.2 (Summer 1980): 304–330. *JSTOR*. Web. 22 August 2022.

13 Reconstructing Memoryscapes

The Role of Imagined Homelands in Post-Partition Bengali Memoirs

Sreya Mukherjee

Introduction

Within the Indian subcontinent, the political manoeuvres surrounding the Partition yielded profound social consequences. The resultant calamity was characterised by a psychological trauma stemming from the abrupt and coerced relocation, separating individuals from their homes, possessions, and kin. The recollections associated with the Partition evoke profound anguish and sorrow, as discerned in post-Partition literature. Conversely, an examination of non-fictional Bangla memoirs from the post-Partition era unveils a distinct narrative. Despite the palpable sense of loss and the trauma of displacement from one's place of origin, these memoirs reveal a constructive dimension. The contemplations within these memoirs prove to be resourceful, nurturing the creative essence of the authors. Amidst the physical dislocation from their homeland, these writers embark on a self-sustaining narrative journey, delving inward in pursuit of an imaginary homeland. The post-Partition Bangla memoirs, therefore, accentuate a space conceived within the writers' imagination—a space that encapsulates enduring images. Remarkably, through these memoirs, this conceptual space transcends mere backdrop status, assuming the roles of a character and a wellspring of rejuvenation.

The Indian Partition has been extensively explored through fiction, historical accounts, and documented records. However, unravelling its complexity, especially on the eastern side of the country, continues to challenge scholars and historians. The intricate politics and dialectics surrounding the dual partition hinder the development of a comprehensive canon of critical writings and reflections. Notably, the ongoing and continuous processes of dispossession, displacement and migration persisted well beyond the formation of the two nations, lasting nearly until the 1971 Liberation War and the eventual secession of East Pakistan into Bangladesh.

The Memoryscape of Memoirs

The genre of memoirs, recollections, and similar works inherently incorporates a sense of immediacy (Erll and Nunning 48). These narratives are characterised by a deeply personal tone, and their intensely individualistic

DOI: 10.4324/9781003508564-18

worldview often grants them the status of an ultimate personalised truth. The infusion of nostalgia further amplifies this effect. As a result, memory is fundamental in the formation of these narratives. The psychological wounds inflicted by these events, post-Partition displacement in this case, are often considered too sacred to be exposed to the public gaze, symbolising a violated and profaned private sphere. The written word, therefore, serves as a metaphorical body in conflict, navigating the delineation between personal and public spheres.

Once the initial wounds heal, these memories transform into markers for understanding and analysing the formation of identities. The written word becomes a metaphorical body articulating the language of loss and reparation, subjecting itself to study and scrutiny. Thus, the public and private realms engage in a compromised negotiation where the intrusive gaze is admitted under verified and sanctified codes of conduct. This chapter aims to unravel the intricate relationship between memory, imagination, and the notion of home by scrutinising representative texts such as *Romanthan* (1993) by Tapan Raychaudhuri, *Bishadbriksha* (2004) by Mihir Sengupta, *Oparer Chhelebela 1931–1947* (2005) by Jayantanuj Bandyopadhyay, and *Smritichitran* (1994) by Parimal Goswami.

Memory plays an integral role in such memoirs or narratives, transforming them from personal historical accounts into emotional analyses of the events surrounding the catastrophic partition of British India in 1947. However, it is important to acknowledge that personalisation of events poses a threat to the writer's narrative control, akin to a hazy lens obstructing clear vision. The limitation of perspectives comes into play as the politics of kinship and selfhood influence the narrative. It leads to the question, to what extent does nostalgia encompass genuine memory, and how much of it is a product of imagination and construction? Is nostalgia more aligned with fact or fiction? Additionally, can one perceive memory and imagination as opposing binaries, given that recollection often involves the use of imaginative faculties?

Is Nostalgia Real or Imagined? A Theoretical Framework

Svetlana Boym's theory of nostalgia provides a lens through which this chapter analyses the intricate narratives of post-Partition Bengali memoirs, revealing a nuanced interplay between personal memory, collective identity, and imaginative reconstruction. Boym distinguishes between reflective and restorative nostalgia, where the former embraces the pain of longing and the latter seeks to rebuild a utopian past. In these memoirs, authors navigate a delicate balance between the two forms, reflecting on the trauma of the Partition while engaging in a restorative nostalgia that reconstructs an idealised homeland.

The memoirs, encapsulating both individual and collective memories, align with Boym's idea of reflective nostalgia by acknowledging the irretrievable loss and trauma experienced during the Partition. The palpable anguish and sorrow echo the reflective aspect, resonating with the pain of severed connections and dislocation. Simultaneously, the authors delve into restorative nostalgia by creating an alternative space within their imagination, akin to Boym's "homeland of the mind" (Boym 36). This conceptual space becomes a source of solace, rejuvenating the writers and transcending the mere backdrop status to assume the roles of a character and a wellspring of creativity.

Boym's theory helps articulate the dual nature of the memoirs—a reflection on the painful reality of the Partition and an imaginative reconstruction of an idealised past. This interplay between reflective and restorative nostalgia enriches the narratives, demonstrating how authors grapple with the complexities of memory and longing. The memoirs, in essence, become a poignant exploration of Svetlana Boym's nostalgic paradigms within the context of post-Partition Bengal, weaving an intricate narrative of emotions, imagination, and a profound sense of loss.

Nostalgic Recreation of an Idealised Homeland

The poetic essence of Bengal unfolds through its lush riverine landscapes, intertwined with local customs, festivities, and the cyclical rhythms of life—embracing themes such as love, birth, death, marriage, labour, sustenance, libations, and family values. Tapan Raychaudhuri, in his memoir *Romanthan*, skilfully captures the recollections of Barishal, a district in undivided Bengal which in the present day has become a part of Bangladesh, with a wittily tongue-in-cheek narrative and the detached perspective of a critical observer (Gupta 173). Born in the village of Kirtipasha in Barishal, the distinguished historian reminisces about his childhood, marked by displacement from his ancestral home due to the political unrest surrounding the Partition. As implied by the English translation of the memoir, which is suggestively titled *Ruminations*, Raychaudhuri engages in a 'rumination' on the distinct culture and customs of the place he left behind in his formative years. Through his distinctive method of revisiting childhood memories, he portrays the temporal and spatial dimensions, along with the people who shaped his early years, all the while indulging in a critique of their idiosyncrasies. Behind his laughter, one discerns a subtle yearning for the bygone era, the spatial landscape, its inhabitants, and their languages. Raychaudhuri's anecdotes subtly convey a sense of pride in the courage and robustness inherent in Barishal society. This narrative not only brings the entire society of East Bengal to life but also illuminates its social structure, caste system, linguistic vibrancy, and an almost nihilistic philosophy of life. Furthermore, it reflects a vital idealism that embraces the celebration of earthly existence and confronts death without fear.

A consistent pattern is discernible across these narratives in their presentation of the concept of lost childhood. The remembrance of childhood accentuates the aspects of tranquillity and happiness within the idealised state, as exemplified by Mihir Sengupta in *Bishadbriksha*, wherein he reflects on the pre-Partition Bengal:

> If someone says that I liked that phase of my childhood only for nostalgic reason, I will rather say it was a wrong surmise. In fact, I never felt any kind of social anarchy in this phase. Those old aunts and grand aunts not yet gave away the society to anarchy. They always kept society in a festive mood with their worships, religious rituals and customs.... We accepted them with simple heart and believed, everybody would be happy and everything would be fine. These customs carried a strange philosophy of life that was not at all troubled by the lamentation of anarchy.
>
> (Sengupta 72)

Bakhtin's theoretical framework surrounding the idyllic chronotope proves highly pertinent for comprehending the portrayal of lost childhood within these memoirs. The idyllic settings are characterised by an intrinsic connection, an integration of life and its occurrences with a specific locale—a familiar territory encompassing its distinctive nooks, crannies, fields, rivers, forests, and the abode one calls home. Within this spatially confined realm, a continuous succession of generations becomes localised, fostering an uninterrupted organic bond. The unity of generations within an idyll is delineated by the 'unity of place,' signifying the enduring entrenchment of successive lifetimes to a singular locale, where life and its events coalesce seamlessly (Bakhtin 225). This unity of place diminishes temporal boundaries between generations and within the various phases of individual lives. A parallel sentiment is echoed in *Oparer Chhelebela* (*Growing Up on the Other Side*), as recounted by Jayantanuj Bandyopadhyay:

> It is here that I opened my eyes at the beauty of the Earth. It is here that my father and his father were born. I was born here along with most of my siblings. In a distant past in my early adolescence, cruel history dragged my uprooted being farther and farther from the periphery of Vajrayogini.... There is an unfathomable fissure of merciless cruel history between my geographical location and the dwelling of my soul. I am eternally homeless.
>
> (Bandyopadhyay, *Oparer Chhelebela* 7)

In his essay titled "Remembered Villages: Representation of Hindu-Bengali Memoirs in the Aftermath of the Partition," Dipesh Chakrabarty underscores the patrilineal nature of the *Bhite*, or 'homestead,' explaining that the *Vastubhite*, or 'foundation,' concept relied heavily on male ancestry across generations (Chakrabarty 2145). Residing on the *Vastubhite* was perceived as a symbol of good fortune, while displacement from it, or being designated as *udvastu* ('a refugee'), represented a significant calamity disrupting the stability of the *vastu* or the idyllic state. Tapan Raychaudhuri encapsulates the protective sentiment associated with one's homestead, articulating, "The earthen walls and the thatched roof must have been renovated time and again, and yet we believed that, that insignificant dwelling place constructed with very commonplace materials, bore ancestral blessings, and that blessing protected us in adversities" (Raychaudhuri 29). Chakrabarty, in his essay, aptly elucidates how the discourse of values is intrinsically linked to the native village, imparting an idealised character of an idyll or a panacea. These memoirs, composed in a spirit of mourning, convey a poignant sense of pathos, by depicting the native village as a cherished and revered space. As a result, communal violence is framed as an act of desecration and transgression (Chakrabarty 2145). Communalism is portrayed as a disruptive force that encroaches upon the pristine beauty of rural Bengal. Consequently, the authors of these memoirs, in their endeavour to overcome the trauma, seek solace in the recollection of a pre-Partition world, constituting a mental panacea described by Chakrabarty as an "eternal present" (Chakrabarty 2147).

The focal point of the temporal setting, particularly in the pre-Partition decades of the twentieth century, is established through recurrent depictions of rivers, nature, familiar topography, people, and their customs within these memoirs (Choudhury 129). Consequently, the space assumes an autonomous character, distinct and integral to the narratives. The verdant riverine landscape, a defining element of rural Bengal, was instrumental in moulding the region's way of life and shaping the emotional experiences of its people. The space, coupled with its nurturing watercourse, becomes ingrained within the identities of the writers, concurrently contributing to the constructive formation of their personalities. Parimal Goswami, in his memoir *Smritichitran*, articulates this symbiotic relationship, stating, "I have seen the river-course in monsoon in its many forms, felt with all my soul its indomitable prowess; each of its bubbling and whirling is entwined with my life" (Goswami 19).

Mihir Sengupta experiences a profound sense of loss as he recalls the watercourse of *Pichhara Khal* and the majestic rain-trees, a sentiment further heightened by the emergence of the metaphorical 'tree of despair' within his consciousness:

> In spite of all the factors keeping in mind, the greater canal and the canal of *Pichhara* and the two great trees at the bank of that canal, remain the irresistible and ever-conscious repositories of every atom of my memory that never leaves me even in sleep or waking, in dream or reverie.
>
> (Sengupta 12)

In titling his memoir *Bishadbriksha* (*The Tree of Despair*), the author appears to reference the ancient 'rain-tree-couple,' silent observers of the societal transformations—both physical and psychological—and the tribulations endured by its residents. The enduring tree-couple, symbolic of withstanding the test of time, is portrayed by the author as a source evoking both his joy and melancholy.

Jayantanuj Bandyopadhyay, on the other hand, associates his memories with a pipul tree that

> proudly stood at a road's crossing, at the middle of our village Vajrayogini.... Its shadow, the play of sunbeams and the movement of the seasonal cycle on its branches and leaves, and its endless murmuring still drag on the roots of my being.
>
> (Bandyopadhyay, *Oparer Chhelebela* 8)

The stimuli emanating from the present prompt a journey into the past for both authors, wherein the past becomes reminiscent of their idyllic childhood. Parimal Goswami aptly articulates this connection in his memoir, *Smritichitran*:

> In this way one becomes acquainted with a country and thus an intimate relationship grows with every dust particle of the land. The bond cannot be felt at that moment, but the moment one leaves the country, one feels not only separated but also uprooted from it.
>
> (Goswami 57)

Their compelled relocation instils a longing for an alternative space of revival, with memory and nostalgia serving as instrumental elements in creating this refuge.

Sacred Space of Memory: Navigating the Nostalgic Past

Patterns of nostalgia undergo an extensive gestation period between the initial experience and the subsequent process of recording, as articulated by Goswami:

> The images of memory do not consist of the things very near to you; their charm rather increases further they move. It requires a long passage of time. It should be kept under the earth for years like wine—"a long age in the deep-delved earth."
>
> (Goswami 214)

Parimal Goswami and adopt an interrupted fragmentary narrative pattern, aptly mirroring the arbitrary and associative nature of memory itself. Each segment reflects on the past, leads to contemplation, and ultimately coalesces into a sustained image. These fragments encapsulate distinct personal and, to some extent, imaginative space-time dimensions, collectively contributing to a broader canvas of historical time. Consequently, the voices of personal histories both complement and challenge the overarching narrative of political history. In the essay "Remembered Villages," Dipesh Chakrabarty underscores the disparity between history and memory, highlighting history's inclination towards explaining the Partition event through causality, while memory perceives it as an 'irrational aberration,' causing personal pain and loss (Chakrabarty 2144). Chakrabarty introduces two facets within this memory: a sense of trauma and a sentiment of nostalgia linked to native villages. He posits, "Memory is a complex phenomenon that reaches out far beyond what normally constitutes a historian's archives, for memory is more than what the mind can remember or what objects can help us document about the past" (Chakrabarty 2143).

In an idyllic state, the developmental stages and cyclical repetition of life processes serve as indicators, illustrating how "this narrow and reduced idyllic little world is the red thread running throughout the narrative, functioning as its resolving chord." According to Bakhtin, these pockets of warmth, filled with human emotion and compassion, scattered across the expansive, indifferent, and unfamiliar world, are vital within the narrative (Bakhtin 233). Subsequently, the trauma inflicted by the Partition transformed the world into an alien landscape, vividly experienced through communal riots on both sides of the divided land. This catastrophic event resulted in millions becoming homeless, thousands losing their lives, and numerous women enduring torment—a human calamity of immense proportions, transcending mere numerical accounts. In the memoirs, the ancestral village emerges as both an idyll and an ideal. The idyllic qualities of the lost homeland enable writers to juxtapose the trauma of communal violence sharply (Chakrabarty 2149). As a result, the memory of Partition, intertwined with violence, casts the long-lost homestead as "sacred and beautiful," creating a striking contrast (Chakrabarty 2145). The writers of post-Partition memoirs cling to this compensatory space, attempting to overcome the trauma of the Partition. Not only does the village become a repository of hallowed sentiments, but the city also serves to evoke precious reminiscences.

The space of compensation, evolving through nostalgic reminiscences in post-Partition Bengali memoirs, is both physical and psychological, aligning with Foucault's theory of heterotopias. According to Foucault, this state engenders an abstract conceptual space that is "other, another real space, as perfect, as meticulous, as well arranged as ours is messy, ill-constructed, and jumbled. This latter type would be the heterotopias, not of illusion, but of compensation" (Foucault 8). He further elucidates that such places exist "outside of all places, even though it may be possible to indicate their location in reality" (Foucault 4). Writers of post-Partition memoirs in Bengal, through their narratives, position themselves in a space where their physical presence is absent, superimposing themselves upon a scene where they are not supposed to be at that moment. This phenomenon can be termed as their "otherwise existence," a concept resonating with Foucault's characterisation of heterotopias as "other places" (Foucault 4). In alignment with Foucault's third principle, heterotopias possess the capacity to juxtapose multiple spaces and sites within a single real space, even if these spaces are inherently incompatible (Foucault 6). Similarly, post-Partition Bangla memoirs encapsulate a timeframe spanning the pre-Partition era and the Partition event, all while being written in the post-Partition era. The narratives critically examine the present in relation to the past, accommodating multiple spaces and timeframes within a single narrative—a concept that Foucault describes as "the rediscovery of time" (Foucault 7).

The deprivation of the tangible presence of the homeland heightens the post-Partition memoir writers' yearning for it, and the function of memory takes on a constructive role in the formation of an image—a psychological space for sustenance, as exemplified in the recollections of Jayantanuj Bandyopadhyay:

> I spent only the initial fifteen years of my life at my birthplace, Vajrayogini. Even before completing my sixteenth year, I went far away from the place of my birth. Subsequently, my life was spent moving even farther, in many distant lands of this Earth. But in the initial fifteen years Vajrayogini moulded in many ways the course of my life, my socio-political awareness, my ideological set up and my goal. The root of my existence lies here. That is why my eternal homeland Vajrayogini beckons me yet in the twilight of my life
>
> (Bandyopadhyay, *Oparer Chhelebela* 7)

Nevertheless, the act of recollection and nostalgic journeys into the past transcends mere romantic reveries, often leading to a discerning analysis. Mihir Sengupta's memoir, in particular, provides a critical commentary on the communal dynamics prevalent in post-Partition Bengal. Similar to Jayantanuj Bandyopadhyay's narrative, Sengupta's work can be construed as a personal account contributing to a broader understanding of the historical upheaval in Bengal. Although it does not adopt the detached stance of a social historian, it functions as the testimony of an individual profoundly impacted by the sweeping changes in history. Consequently, it serves as a firsthand source for constructing a socio-historical narrative of the era. Sengupta's documentation highlights the significance of regional songs (*Bhadugaan* and *Jarigaan*) and dialectal verses sung by individuals from the lower echelons of society. These expressions vividly convey a profound sense of despair in response to communal disharmony, a sentiment experienced universally regardless of religious affiliation (Sengupta 187–190). In this manner, these memoirs act as a cultural mirror reflecting rural Bengal's pre-Partition social structure and class relations.

Despite potential personal biases and exaggerations, these memoirs constitute a valuable resource, offering a rich documentation and analytical examination of facts. Through the expression of private emotions and intimate tones, they possess the capacity to construct a subaltern perspective on the momentous historical event of Partition (Guha and Chatterjee 79). For instance, Jayantanuj Bandyopadhyay's memoir, *Oparer Chhelebela 1931–1947*, provides an analytical commentary on significant historical events such as the Freedom Movement, the Great Famine of the 1950s, the Quit India Movement, World War II, the Civil Disobedience Movement, and the encroachment of communalism threatening the social fabric of his native village, Vajrayogini. Here, the interplay between the personal and the political is evident, as private memories serve as documents reflecting broader socio-historical shifts. The analysis of eminent historian Asin Dasgupta proves insightful understanding of the temporal relationship inherent in these narratives. In his book *Itihas O Sahitya* (*History and Literature*), Dasgupta delineates three facets of time in human life: Greater Time, governing societal and state dynamics leading to progress or distress; Smaller Time, constructing the real life of specific groups; and Personal Time, an entirely private, psychological, introspective, and mental experience imperceptible to others (Dasgupta 40–41). Drawing inspiration from Dasgupta, Sandip Bandyopadhyay aptly observes,

> But the individual has a personal, small history, which is substantiated by the memories of his own experience. That history has a different tongue/rhetoric, another voice. By paying heed to that voice, we may get a hint for moving towards the larger history.
>
> (Bandyopadhyay, *Deshbhag* 30)

Urvashi Butalia also shares a similar sentiment, "interpreting these painful and anguished memories as the 'underside' of this history" (Butalia 347). Similarly, Mihir Sengupta's narrative appears to encapsulate the collective emotions of the homeless populace:

> Perhaps, a thousand souls like me spent their entire life in a similar melancholy, keeping in their heart the void of their childhood streams. Does history remember them? People speak in general about the Partition and its cause and effect. That explanation forms history, but where is the space for our melancholy realisation in that history?
>
> (Sengupta 83)

Conclusion

In accordance with Boym's concept of reflective nostalgia, these memoirs serve as poignant reflections on the irreparable losses incurred during the Partition. The authors confront the painful reality of severed ties, forced relocations, and the traumatic upheaval of their lives. This reflective aspect of nostalgia is evident in the palpable anguish and sorrow that permeate the narratives. Authors like Mihir Sengupta, Jayantanuj Bandyopadhyay, and others in their extensive narratives explicitly acknowledge the profound impact of the Partition on their personal and communal identities. This reflective stance allows readers to witness the raw emotions of displacement, making the memoirs a testament to the deep scars left by historical events.

Hence, these memoirs unveil the narrative of a nation, wherein the nation is portrayed as a complex storytelling structure encompassing its people, social classes, genders, and castes. Through these narratives, a discourse of evocation is established, facilitated by creative self-expression and the faculty of memory. The erstwhile East Bengal, characterised by its profound folk customs, vivid imagination, and lush natural landscape, emerges as both the principal character and the predominant theme within these memoirs. Each of these accounts resonates with a distinctive tone of pathos, lamenting the loss of the homeland. Through creative expression, the authors engage in the imaginative reconstruction of a place they can never physically revisit—the long-forgotten and desolate mystical realm of Beauteous Bengal. Consequently, post-Partition memoirs grapple with fragmented human identities, seeking unity through the creative recollection and mental reconstruction of a lost idyll.

Works Cited

Bakhtin, Mikhail Mikhailovich. *The Dialogic Imagination: Four Essays*. Translated by Caryl Emerson and Michael Holquist, edited by Michael Holquist, Austin, University of Texas Press, 1981.

Banbyopadhyay, Jayantanuj. *Oparer Chhelebela 1931–1947*. Subarnarekha, 2005.

Bandyopadhyay, Sandip. *Deshbhag: Smriti Ar Satta*. Progressive Publishers, 1999.

Boym, Svetlana. *The Future of Nostalgia*. Basic Books, 2001.

Butalia, Urvashi. *The Other Side of Silence: Voices from the Partition of India*. Penguin Books, 2014.

Chakrabarty, Dipesh. "Remembered Villages: Representations of Hindu-Bengali Memories in the Aftermath of the Partition." *South Asia: Journal of South Asian Studies*, vol. 18, Jan. 1995, pp. 109–129, https://doi.org/10.1080/00856409508723247. Accessed 23 Aug. 2023.

Choudhury, Suranjana. *A Reading of Violence in Partition Stories from Bengal*. Cambridge Scholars Publishing, 2020.

Dasgupta, Asin. *Itihas O Sahitya*. Ananda Publishers, 1989.

Erll, Astrid, and Ansgar Nünning. *A Companion to Cultural Memory Studies*. De Gruyter, 2010.

Foucault, Michel. "Of Other Spaces: Utopias and Heterotopias." *Diacritics*, vol. 16, no. 1, 1986, pp. 22–27.

Goswami, Parimal. *Smritichitran*. Pratikshan, 1994.

Guha, Ranajit, and Partha Chatterjee. *The Small Voice of History: Collected Essays*. Permanent Black, 2009.

Gupta, Swarupa. *Notions of Nationhood in Bengal*. Brill, 2009.

Raychaudhuri, Tapan. *Romanthan Othoba Bhimratipraptor Paracharitcharcha*. Ananda Publishers, 2007.

Sengupta, Debjani. *The Partition of Bengal*. Cambridge University Press, 2015.

Sengupta, Mihir. *Bishadbriksha*. Subarnarekha, 2004.

14 Memories of 1947

A Journey from Oral to Digital

Mahuya Bhaumik

Memory is always suffused with emotions; it is essentially complex and is never abstract. When that memory is associated with both personal and collective recollection its connotation becomes far encompassing. As Urvashi Butalia observes: "Working with memory is never simple or unproblematic" (Butalia, *The Other Side of Silence* 10).

Partition memories are such, which are entwined with a sense of displacement, loss, horror, anguish and trauma. For the Partition victims, Partition itself is an unpardonable "mistake."

> "Who lives in Iran?"
> "The Iranians live in Iran."
> "Who lives in England?"
> "The English live in England."
> "Who lives in France?"
> "The French live in France."
> "What country is this?"
> "This is Pakistan."
> "The Pakistanis live here, don't they?"
> "No, the Pakistanis don't live here. The Sindhis live here. The Punjabis live here. The Bengalis live here. This community lives here. That community lives here."
> "But the Punjabis also live in Hindustan. The Sindhis also live in Hindustan. Why was another country created?"
> "Sorry, it was a mistake..." (Bhalla Vol II 105)

The Partition of India in 1947 is a cataclysmic historic occurrence whose impact has passed down from one generation to another. The intensity of the massacre is unfathomable and statistical data can only provide an idea about the carnage though the real picture is far more horrifying. "Between 500,000 to one million people are believed to have died, hundreds of thousands of children lost and abandoned, between 75,000 to 100,000 women raped and abducted" (Kaul 208). Family members were separated from each other; girls were raped in front of their mothers; violence, communal riots and mass slaughter were rampant. People had to leave their native soil, were

DOI: 10.4324/9781003508564-19

literally uprooted and had to undertake perilous journey across the border in search of a new home and find place in the inhospitable refugee camps. These are memories of terror. Damayanti Sahgal, an 80-year-old Partition survivor recollects: "Everyone was full of fear... they kept saying put your windows up.... Amritsar is coming and they're cutting people down there" (Butalia, *The Other Side of Silence* 116).

For filmmaker Supriyo Sen

> The Partition was not just about the Nehrus and the Jinnahs. It was about the people like my parents who had to forget their own identity and remain dissolved in the claustrophobic atmosphere of this city. They needed a passport to go back home and nothing could be more painful than this.
>
> (Mukherjee and Mandal 81)

A Muslim shopkeeper of Delhi makes the gruesome observation: "it was only in the bloodshed of Partition that ordinary people saw the shape of Independence" (Pandey 125). This remembrance is painful; yet it is essential because history can never be denied. Therein comes the role of memory. Partition memories are shared in diverse forms such as story-telling and recollection of personal experiences by the older generations in families. This sharing is oral in nature. Sometimes it takes the shape of memoirs and interviews. At times these memories evolve as an integral part of literature and cinema. Efforts have been initiated to preserve Partition memories in the shape of Partition Museums where artefacts donated by Partition survivors tell their own stories of suffering and the aftereffects of the dire event. Finally, there are online Partition archives which aim at preserving memories of the 1947 gruesome Partition history. Young generations of the present day have formulated their own memories of Partition sometimes by listening to anecdotes from the elders of the family, at times from books and movies, visiting Partition Museums but largely from online archives, blogs, Facebook, Twitter, Instagram. Thus, Partition memories undertake a journey from being oral to getting digitized.

These personal and collective memories have continued to torment the survivors of Partition since these haunting memories never got an opportunity to be shared or listened to properly. Yet, these memories existed and could never be erased. The choked voices, the muted memories have shaped identities and have formulated history. Partition memories represent "a trauma of such deep dimensions, that it has needed nearly a half century for Indians to acquire some distance, and begin the process of coming to terms with it" (Kaul 209).

The Partition of 1947 led to mass migration which resulted in 10–12 million people moving across borders being uprooted from their native soil leaving behind their homes. Almost one million people were victims of communal violence. Atrocities upon women knew no bounds. Abduction, rape, forced conversion were common lots of women during the time of Partition and during their journeys across borders. However, the border has never been able to wipe away memory on either side of the border. Kavita Puri, during her interviews with people settled in Britain who have survived the horrors of Partition, stated:

> I have seen descendants who keep earth in a jar from Bangladesh in their fireplace, or who wear a pebble from Pakistan around their neck every day, or who cherish a saved heirloom from India – all places their forefathers left 75 years ago. These objects are often their only connection to that time and place. It is proof their family once existed in that land too, and it is meaningful to these young people today.
>
> (Puri)

While narrating these stories, which Puri gathered during her travel across Britain, she recounted:

> I met a man with a 70-year-old scar indelibly etched on his arm from a poisoned spear. I cannot forget the sound of anguish he made as he explained he was left for dead, and almost died, as a mob entered his village. I listened as an elderly man sounded almost childlike as he described the horrors of waking up on a train platform full of dead bodies. A woman talked of overhearing her uncles planning to kill all the girls in her family to save them from dishonour, such was the fear of sexual violence. Her grandmother talked them down. So many stories like these had largely been hidden for decades, by people who live among us, and who still have nightmares from that time. And we never knew.
>
> (Puri)

These are not simply personal stories hidden within families; rather, they are integral to shared history.

Books based on Partition include literary pieces, reminiscences, interviews and even documentary evidences such as Assembly Proceedings which provide the readers with enough resources to delve deep into Partition history. Poignant fictional works written by several authors like Saadat Hasan Manto (*Mottled Down*), Kamleshwar (*Kitne Pakistan*), Khushwant Singh (*Train to Pakistan*), Bapsi Sidhwa (*Ice Candy Man*), Bhisham Sahni (*Tamas*), Attia Hosain (*Sunlight on a Broken Column*), Amrita Pritam (*Pinjar*), Salman Rushdie (*Midnight's Children*), to name a few, make shivers run down the spine. The readers have no difficulty to comprehend that all the fictional narratives are soaked in the blood of the contemporary times of Partition and this understanding gives them an idea about the chilling brutality of the Partition days. Heart-wrenching exposition of Partition memories has been made in books like *Partition: The Long Shadow* and *The Other Side of Silence: Voices from the Partition of India* by Urvashi Butalia. *The Long Shadow* is a sensitive handling of the abysmally dark and persistent shadow that has been cast over the lives of people of India, Pakistan and Bangladesh because of the borders drawn not only geographically but also amongst families and friends, which resulted in fragmented lives, permanent losses, ever-bleeding scars and memories of pain and anguish. *The Other Side of Silence* gives voice to those unheard and suppressed memories which could never get an opportunity to be expressed. It comprises testimonies and oral narratives of Dalits, women and children being supported by memoirs, reports, diaries, documents and official records thus making Partition memory personal. This memory turns into the voice of the marginal and helps us reread Partition from a new perspective.

The heart-wrenching depiction of the impact of Partition on children has been brought out by Butalia when she describes what Anis Kidwai found out in November 1948 during her visit to Irwin Hospital in Delhi. "Kidwai found a number of children of all ages in the hospital – someone had a head wound, another a broken leg, a third a broken arm" (Butalia *The Other Side of Silence* 259–260). One little girl not more than five years old, told Kidwai:

> "I came here with my aunt ... but she's dead now." And then, she introduced the other children. "This is Rashid ... everyone in his family is dead, and that is Zainab, her family is also dead, and over there is Nabu – they slit his mother's throat."
>
> (Butalia, *The Other Side of Silence* 259–260)

The trauma of Partition victims is palpable in short stories like "Weeds" or "Cold Meat" which are fictional representations of the horrors and nightmarish experiences of the times. Kulwant Singh Virk's description of a nameless woman is a poignant example of the silencing of the voice of innumerable Partition victims:

> Abducted, raped and humiliated, she lay quietly and still. There was no one from her caste, community, religion or village with her. No one had told her that she could once again be with the people who were dear to her. Perhaps even if someone had told her, she would have refused to believe him.
>
> (Bhalla Vol I 207).

The memories of homelessness, the memories of uncertainty, the memories of being uprooted, the memories of violence, the memories of rape, the memories of forced migration have loomed large in the mental landscape of millions of people and could not be obliterated even today. The trauma persists.

Cathy Caruth in her book *Unclaimed Experience: Trauma, Narrative, and History* explains the source of trauma: "What causes trauma ... is a shock that appears to work very much like a bodily threat but is in fact a break in the mind's experience of time" (Caruth 61). It is a disruptive experience and impacts the emotional core of the victim. Taking clue from Freud, Caruth points out the belated and inescapable impact of trauma: "Trauma is not locatable in the simple violent or original event in an individual's past, but rather in the way that its very unassimilated nature ... returns to haunt the survivor later on" (Caruth 4). In many instances the effect of Partition trauma is belated as in the case of Urvashi Butalia's uncle. He refused to come to India, severed all ties with his sisters and chose to stay back in Pakistan after Partition, converting himself to Islam. Hardly could he understand at that time what emotional turbulence this would create for him. Later he confessed, "I have not slept one night in these forty years without regretting my decision" (Butalia *The Other Side of Silence* 38). Caruth points out:

> the shape of individual lives, the history of the traumatized individual, is nothing other than the determined repetition of the event of destruction. In modern trauma theory as well, there is an emphatic tendency to focus on the destructive repetition of the trauma that governs a person's life.
>
> (Caruth 63)

The fright and anxiety involved in recapitulating Partition memories involves a trauma of its own. Somavanti, a refugee woman could not get rid of her traumatic past even when decades had passed by after the Partition, explains: "Even today there is no peace. No peace outside, no peace inside ... I don't sleep, there is a feeling of being unsettled" (Menon and Bhasin 204). For Somavanti it is a constant repetition in memory. As Kumar points out:

> There was a large number of women who were not recovered, women who apparently reconciled themselves to the new circumstances, but they carried within themselves a gnawing sense of the irreparable loss of a perfect past ... the past which counterposes itself with the present.
>
> (Kumar 99–100)

This repetition in memory is the truth of several Partition victims. Nalini Mitra, who had to leave her childhood home in Dhaka asserts: "after so many years, my heart still weeps for Dhaka. How can I ever forget my motherland? I still crave to go back there" (Bagchi and Dasgupta 142). The repetition of trauma in the mental landscape eventually leading to the fragmentation of psyche can be witnessed in the protagonist of Jamila Hashmi's short story "Exile" where the protagonist, an abducted young girl, having been compelled to get married and fulfil the role of a "Bahu" in the family feels like asking her brother in a completely disillusioned state: "Why does anguish never diminish?... Doesn't misfortune so disillusion human beings that they cease to hope for better days?" (Bhalla Vol I 38). She could never be a part of her in-laws' family and is consistently haunted by the truth that her present life is an exile far away from her loved ones, and she is forced to accept this bitter truth of life. Her trauma crushes her inner being and takes away peace from her. The traumatic brutality unleashed upon uncountable numbers of women during the time of Partition resulted in the permanent damage of their inner self. "They remained stuck in the memory of the harmonious past by obliterating the ugly present, thereby denying themselves a future" (Kumar 93). This denial of future and damage caused to psyche are brilliantly exemplified by Umm-e-Ummara in the short story titled "More Sinned against than Sinning": "How can one have any relationship with the present or dream of the future, by forgetting the past?" (Bhalla Vol I 106). It is this same denial that has been pointed out by Bagchi while discussing the plight of widows who took refuge in Brindaban during Partition. One of the inhabitants of "Amar Bari," a home for the widows in Brindaban, says: "We have had no ties with the outside world. No one has come to visit us, we know nothing. From 1947 to 2000, I have only chanted the name of God." Anusuya Roy, the matron of "Amar Bari" told Subhoranjan Dasgupta, the interviewer: "She weeps softly at night" (Bagchi and Dasgupta 188). There is a strong apathy to recall the memories of Partition days in several Partition victims. Gopika Saha, another widow from Brindaban says: "I do not want to recall Noahkhali and my life there" (Bagchi and Dasgupta 189).

This silencing of the voice and inability to express one's past speak of a scarred psyche which often leads to irreversible change of identity. Caruth refers to this feature of trauma as: "the silence of its mute repetition of suffering" (Caruth 9). Gopika Saha who used to take every challenge of life to raise her children "in the best possible way" lost all her determination and came to Brindaban as a completely transformed self, stating "I have lost everything" (Bagchi and Dasgupta 189). This inability to express trauma often leads to the "erasure of the violent past from memory" (Kumar 105) and hence several Partition victims employ "the strategy of forgetting" (Kumar 95). Hence, "tropes such as forgetting, discontinuity, exclusion and silencing have been used in the historical as well as many fictional narratives that record the phenomenon of Partition" (Kumar 95).

Butalia, during her interview of the Partition victims, witnessed this silence as the most common response of the interviewees who were unwilling to share their traumatic memories. "What, they asked me, is the use of remembering, of excavating memories we have put behind us?" (Butalia *The Other Side of Silence* 10). This process of remembering can be extremely painful as penned down by Butalia while narrating the experience of a Partition victim who shared her Partition memories after having suppressed them for several years. She lost her sleep as she was tormented and anguished by remembering the pain and loss. Thus "speech is not always cathartic, not always liberating" (Butalia *The Other Side of Silence* 54). Hence, silence challenges the limits of language and even if language expresses the pain there is a sense of disruption in it. This linguistic abnormality can be found in Kamlaben Patel's observation: "Partition was like a tandav nritya ... I have seen such abnormal things, I kept asking myself, what is there to write, why should I write it" (Butalia *The Other Side of Silence* 133).

Caruth observes that trauma journeys across generations and is transmittable. It traverses across generations through the process of remembering. She states that trauma "is never simply one's own ... (it is) precisely the way we are implicated in each other's traumas" (Caruth 24). The impact of Partition trauma is also found to be intergenerational. "Why is it that so many second and third generation Hindus and Sikhs after Partition have come to internalize notions of 'us' and 'them' when they have no reference of Partition – except through family and community memories?" (Butalia *The Other Side of Silence* 12). The trauma is unforgettable and is passed on from one generation to the next. The concept of this intergenerational memory has been brilliantly described in the short story "The Land of Memories" by Asif Aslam Farrukhi, where the narrator himself is surprised to identify his emotional bond with his ancestral house and questions: "I wondered what links I had with that house? I had never seen my ancestral home ... it was strange ... they hadn't been erased from memory" (Bhalla Vol III 49). The narrator further explains: "We had inherited those memories; they had been passed to us in our blood; they were a part of our genetic make-up; a chromosomic map which determined our character" (Bhalla Vol III 53).

The trauma of Partition has been depicted in several movies. Ritwik Ghatak's Partition movies are poignant depictions of compelled migration and despicable living conditions of the refugees. *Pinjar* (2003), directed by Chandraprakash Dwivedi, narrates the horrors encountered by a Hindu woman who is abducted by a Muslim man. Deepa Mehta's *Midnight's Children* is based on Rushdie's award-winning novel and depicts two babies who were born on the day of India's Independence being swapped at the hospital. *Garam Hava* (1973), directed by M. S. Sathyu, is a sensitive delineation of the challenges faced by a Muslim family which decides to stay back in India in the post-Partition days. *Tamas* (1988), *Earth* (1998) and *Train to Pakistan* (1998) also deserve mention as far as depiction of the ordeals of Partition are concerned. References to several other movies may be made in this regard. This suggests that there have been attempts to preserve the memories of terror shrouding the lives of millions of people, the trauma they suffered from and its aftereffect, through the medium of cinema, thus nullifying any possibility of erasure of the memories of those dark days.

Another endeavour to preserve Partition history is the establishment of Partition Museums. The Partition Museum of Amritsar is a storehouse of artefacts which were donated by Partition survivors. During the time of displacement people carried along with them whatever they could manage to gather and those very objects have turned to be memories of losses and sufferings incurred. The Museum displays artefacts ranging from jewellery boxes to utensils and preserves memories of people hailing from diverse social strata. These artefacts are loaded with emotions and each one of them has a story of itself. The Museum preserves paintings of painters like Krishen

Khanna, Satish Gujral and S. L. Parasher whose works bear unmistakable testimony to the trauma of the time. There are several galleries with audio-visual facilities which house interviews of Partition victims and give expression to those voices which had been muted for years. The Kolkata Partition Museum focusses on the specificity of Bengal's Partition and stresses not only the harrowing experiences of Partition; rather it tries to bring into the limelight the cultural amalgamation between West Bengal and Bangladesh. The Kolkata Partition Museum thus attempts to stress the continuity that is unmistakable in every sphere of life of the two Bengals – language, literature, song, food, fabric. This continuity has been shared throughout despite all ruptures and all the artefacts preserved in this museum have their own tales to be told.

An attempt to share Partition stories has been made at the Godrej India Culture Lab in Mumbai where a three-day event named "Remembering Partition: Museum of Memories" offered oral narratives, personal objects and files, all of which have personal and collective memories associated with them.

Apart from books, movies, conferences and museums trying to preserve Partition history and aiming to sensitize today's generation towards the same, several South Asian Digital Archives like the 1947 Partition Archive, the BBC Documentary on India Pakistan Partition, Indian Memory Project, The Citizens Archive of Pakistan and Facebook pages like Bolti Khidki have democratized the history of Partition and helped to reach out to people across the globe. The digital world has provided a space not demarcated by any borders to retell histories of and across borders. Today's cyber world offers "a collective memorial landscape" (Veale) to transform "personal bereavement to the memorialisation of collective trauma" (Parmar 1–14), thus blending personal and collective memories. Guneeta Singh Bhalla, founder of the 1947 Partition archive, asserts that several testimonies are unbearable. She recounts one Muslim family's 36-hour train journey from Delhi to Lahore. The interviewee is a woman of that family who recalls: "My baby cousin's mouth was stuffed with a cloth so that he may not make a sound.... Our uncle told us insurgents are sharpening swords on the platform. If we make a sound, they would massacre the entire train" (The New Humanitarian). The Stanford University digital library includes testimonies and personal stories where interviews have been conducted in various languages. There are brilliant documents of the times of the Partition in these online resources. In such an interview one of the Partition survivors, Taj Begum, says that she could never visit her birthplace in Delhi since Partition because "more than the love for my birthplace, I have fear of it. I can never forget those awful days of Partition" (Stanford Libraries).

Digitization has provided the Partition survivors the power to reach out to the world and make their stories heard. "At least half of the people we've interviewed, their family did not know their story because it was so harrowing," Guneeta Bhalla says.

> Then there's a cathartic element so they start talking about it more. I've seen some of them come out and write memoirs ... I think people felt that nobody cared, especially in the villages. It's very empowering to have somebody listen to their story.
>
> (The New Humanitarian)

Projects like Bolti Khidki and The Citizens Archive of Pakistan deserve mention in this context as they are priceless resources offering Partition memories and ensuring communication among India, Pakistan and Bangladesh. These are platforms where personal stories turn into collective and shared memories. "The idea is that we must bring our history to the forefront and talk about all that is not in the books. We are trying to make history more engaging and interactive through storytelling," says Aaliyah Tayyebi of The Citizens Archive of Pakistan (Kohli and Sreedhar). Bolti Khidki – The Speaking Window is a digital initiative and houses stories of Partition survivors from India and Pakistan on its Facebook page. Sandeep Dutt, one of the founders of this Facebook page, explains:

> Most Partition survivors are old and it will be difficult to trace them after four–five years. Our generation should know where they come from. We thought the best way to do this was by documenting these tales for the future generation through a photo series.
>
> (Kohli and Sreedhar)

These cross-border projects have a healing capacity. They not only embalm the scars of the Partition victims; they help to significantly reduce the spirit of animosity across borders. "When you hear these personal tales of Partition, you realize there's no hatred among the people on either side of the border," says Ritika Sharma, who works as an editor for Bolti Khidki (Kohli and Sreedhar]. A similar kind of cross-border initiative was adopted by The Citizens Archive of Pakistan and Routes2Roots, an Indian non-profit organization. The initiative was named the Exchange for Change (EFC) programme. EFC was an exchange programme where more than 2,000 children from ten schools on either side of the border were involved in an exchange of letters, postcards, posters and an oral history project. "And this made the children understand that people across the border were not as alien as they were made out to be," says Aaliyah Tayyebi of CAP (Kohli and Sreedhar). She further adds: "The idea is to have a friend, for if you have a friend, then you might not have hatred" (Kohli and Sreedhar].

Digitization of Partition memory has a palpable social impact. It creates a sense of democratization of history and provides a borderless digital world where history and memory are shared, thus generating a commonality of suffering, and generates a sense of unity. Thus, this borderless world has a significant impact and is a stark commentary on the geographical and political borders that have divided countries, nations, people and their histories. It helps in the creation of collective memory that transcends personal losses and unifies the suffering souls. It creates an alternate space where muted voices get a platform to tell their stories irrespective of their national identities. It helps in the formation of a South Asian community and a sense of solidarity amongst the younger generation who can relate with each other across borders and share a sense of belonging because of the digitization of Partition memories that enable them to understand the scale of loss, and also sensitize them to be compassionate towards the innumerable Partition victims across borders and geographical barriers. Thus, it creates a transnational South Asian identity where histories and memories are relatable and creates "a collective memorial landscape" (Veale). "Digital archives have allowed a level of interaction I haven't really seen between India and Pakistan," points out historian Ali Raza (Irfan), who is engaged in a digital project to assess the impact of abductions on women and children during Partition. Yadav points out that "much of our silence or lack of challenging state narratives around Partition comes from a collective, generational trauma that many in the region are suffering from" (Irfan). Yadav further explains:

> In the subcontinent indulging in the past and nostalgia was available only to a few, but now it is more a need. Now the new generation is saying we're not going to get to escape this trauma cycle until we relearn and move past it.
>
> (Irfan)

Apart from being more largely accessible in comparison to physical archives, it ensures democratization of history involving diverse perspectives, thus spreading power and agency to common mass. Writer and photographer Anusha Yadav, who founded the Indian Memory Project, says, "It's important to have as many stories out there with as many points of views because there's no one right history" (Irfan). Guneeta Bhalla, while stressing the need of digitization of Partition history, feels that raw and unedited versions of Partition experiences are essential and should be offered to people without any kind of bias of any author or historian. "Historians have very strong views but human beings all have limited views because all our views are shaped by our life experiences, and history and this event that is so major in our histories shouldn't be limited" (Irfan). Digitized preservation has assured availability of Partition anecdotes and narratives irrespective of political boundaries, archive restrictions and financial limitations. It helps to know the history of the "other" side and generate a sense of empathy for the "other." It enables sharing of experiences, inculcating a sense of understanding and investing human emotions in the Partition narratives. Digital archives interrogate the official history of Partition and subvert the politics of representation of memory, thus reshaping the existing history. Through the process of digitization history is negotiated and endowed with a fresh perspective. Digitization helps in the creation of post-memories of Partition for those who have not been direct victims of the horrors of Partition but have constructed those memories from second-hand experiences. The construction of these post-memories has been possible largely because of the availability of Partition memories in the public domain.

Thus, preservation of Partition memories has a long and sustained history and this preservation is a continuous process. It is this process which has helped the memories to evolve and provide a sustained narrative to trace the trauma of Partition victims and its intergenerational impact. It is this process that has offered articulation to the muted voices and provided a healing capacity. Partition memories have undertaken a journey from being oral to getting digitized. It is a journey of memory itself from being personal to collective and the diverse forms of preservation have served as repositories of personal and collective trauma of the Partition that occurred in 1947. This preservation is essential "to overcome new fear, to gradually rebuild faith and trust and hope and ... to conceive new histories – and new 'memories' that are in some reckonings, 'best forgotten'" (Pandey 15–16). This preservation of memory through digitization has unmistakably positive social impact which creates a sense of solidarity in a borderless digitized world and helps in the formation of a transnational identity that is achieved through the experiences of pain, loss, dislocation, suffering, and trauma and thus fosters unity across borders and encourages dialogue and healthy interactions across borders.

Works Cited

Bagchi, Jasodhara and Subhoranjan Dasgupta, editors. *The Trauma and the Triumph Gender and Partition in Eastern India*. Stree, 2003

Bhalla, Alok, editor. *Stories about the Partition of India Volumes I-III*. Manohar Publishers & Distributors, 2020

Butalia, Urvashi. *The Other Side of Silence: Voices from the Partition of India*. Penguin, 1998, edition 2017

Butalia, Urvashi, editor. *Partition: The Long Shadow*. Zubaan Books, 2015

Caruth, Cathy. *Unclaimed Experience: Trauma, Narrative, and History*. The John Hopkins University Press, 1996, https://joaocamillopenna.files.wordpress.com/2015/03/caruth-unclaimed-experience.pdf

Irfan, Anmol. "Digitizing Partition: How Oral Histories Cross Borders Online." *Logically*, https://www.logically.ai/articles/the-history-of-partition-goes-online-and-crosses-borders. Accessed 25 Aug. 2023.

Kaul, Suvir, editor. *The Partitions of Memory The Afterlife of the Division of India*. Permanent Black, 2001, edition 2011

Kohli, Divya and Nitin Sreedhar. "How Technology and Social Media Help Trace Partition Memories." *Mint Lounge*, https://lifestyle.livemint.com/amp/news/talking-point/how-technology-and-social-media-help-trace-partition-memories-111646985019398.html. Accessed 27 Aug. 2023.

Kumar, Sukrita Paul. *Narrating Partition Texts, Interpretations, Ideas*. Indialog Publications Pvt. Ltd., 2004

Menon, Ritu and Kamla Bhasin. *Borders and Boundaries: Women in India's Partition*. Kali for Women, 1998

Mukherjee, Srideep and Manan Kumar Mandal, editors. *Partition Literature: An Open Praxis*. Netaji Subhas Open University, 2016

"Oral Testimonies help Partition Survivors Break Taboos and Heal Old Wounds." *The New Humanitarian*, https://deeply.thenewhumanitarian.org/peacebuilding/articles/2018/05/21/oral-testimonies-help-partition-survivors-break-taboos-and-heal-old-wounds. Accessed 25 Aug. 2023.

Pandey, Gyanendra. *Remembering Partition: Violence, Nationalism and History in India*. CambridgeUniversity Press, 2001

Parmar, Maya. "Memorialising 40 Years since Idi Amin's Expulsion: Digital 'Memory Mania' to the 'Right to be Forgotten." *South Asian Popular Culture*, vol. 12, no. 1, 2014, pp. 1–14. Taylor & Francis Online, https://doi.org/10.1080/14746689.2014.879420

Puri, Kavita. "After 75 Years, the Hidden Memories of India's Partition Are Rising up through Britain's Generations." *The Guardian*, https://www.theguardian.com/commentisfree/2022/aug/06/75-years-india-partition-britain-generations-india-pakistan. Accessed 27 Aug. 2023.

Stanford Libraries. "Explore the Personal Stories of Partition." *The 1947 Partition Archive Survivors and Their Memories*, https://exhibits.stanford.edu/1947-partition. Accessed 28 Aug. 2023.

Veale, Kylie. "Online Memorialisation: The Web as a Collective Memorial Landscape for Remembering the Dead." *The Fibre Culture Journal*, http://three.fibreculturejournal.org/fcj-014-online-memorialisation-the-web-as-a-collective-memorial-landscape-for-remembering-the-dead/. Accessed 28 Aug. 2023.

15 Unravelling the Narratives of Partition

A Study of Individual and Historical Memories in Film

Maithry Shinde

The importance of remembering and recalling narratives by people who lived through the partition times of a nation brings in legacies of suffering, bitterness and hatred. This recalling manifest itself differently in different places, referring largely and overtly to the incidents that took place in the past and the consequences that still have a bearing on its members: individually, as a collective society or as a nation. It is still difficult to gauge the magnitude of the incidents and the psychological tremors that the victims of these two nations have been through. The stories are varied and reveal a multitude of ramifications. However, many spaces have opened up for the victims to give vent to their suffering and hatred, and present them to the society as truths. Such narratives have also gained validation and momentum because of varied reasons: academic interest and curiosity, role of popular culture, evolving disciplines of study, role of media, to name a few. Looking at the past with the lens of the present also brings forth several schools of thought to surface.

Jason Francisco, who worked on the partition of India in his anthology *In the Heat of Fratricide: The Literature of India's Partition Burning Freshly*, says that rupture, protest and rebuild form a natural response to partition—a continuum from pain to healing via stories of repair to the healing powers of memory. (Francisco, 2022) The Partition of India, a demarcation, clear or unclear, decided in the blink of an eye, has been extended for several reasons. The extreme events of war, political revolutions, abductions, sufferings, rapes and the interplay of political and sociological events are shared by the media drawing content from the mediated memory of its people and historical records. Amidst this ingloriousness of partition, neither did India nor Pakistan, their separate and linked histories, escape the gruesome realities of this divide. The riots of the times have been assimilated and perpetuated as communal hostility on either side of the border, although both India and Pakistan had shared a common cultural heritage and were subjects to a common imperialistic domination—a clear ugliness of the political motives of the times depicted. There were atrocities committed from all directions—the Hindus, the Sikhs and the Muslims. Historical evidences show frantic movement of people on trains that were burnt, people mutilated, women raped and children traumatized. All such episodes put us through questions like: Did we visualize freedom at such a heavy price? Did the political harbingers

DOI: 10.4324/9781003508564-20

of the country ever envisage such bloody and gruesome realities of partition? Would the losses encountered by the common public ever be repairable? And how much of these memories in differential capacities in their telling and re-telling have an impact on the grand narratives of partition? Do these memories fade or are obliterated completely with the passing time? Or does a new memory seek stance in its attempt for meaning-making in re-storying lives?

Avishek Parui in his work on Memory Studies says that memory is the story the brain tells to the self about what happened and what may emerge. He also puts forth that memory is stories enacted by things that are important and also menial, stories that are stored in the complex neural nets in the brain. (Banerjee, 2023) The liminal play between reality and possibility, between what is and what might have happened is an act of anticipation. Historical narratives of the Indian partition have been put forth by such memories: individual, society and the media. However, it is said that the cataclysmic realities of the times have been side-lined, or that selective narratives have been brought to the public that appeal desired objectives in a given society. It is to see "how these forms of remembering operate as collective representations of the past, how they constitute a range of cultural resources for social and historical identities, and how they privilege particular readings of the past and subordinate others" (Keightley and Pickering, 2013). According to the French sociologist Maurice Halbwachs (1925), identified as the founder of collective memory, for individuals to remember events outside their group context is impossible. This means that he rejects an individual approach to memory to make conclusions of incidents of the past and makes a clear distinction among different memories: autobiographical memory—memory of those events that individuals experience, historical memory—memory that reaches us through historical records, and collective memory—the active past that forms our identities. For writers who worked on the discourse of memory undermine grand narratives of history and power, as "memory, remembering and recording are the very key to existence, becoming and belonging" (Garde-Hans, 2011). This interplay of 'memories' and 'histories' of the partition times, their representations and adaptations in movies, give scope to analyse these stories from the discourse of memory and also consider its paradox.

It is seen that individuals and groups recalling the past depends upon what is consolidated as a memory. The three phases of memory as distinguished by psychologists—encoding, consolidation and retrieval—form the basis of all remembering (, (Philip) At the micro level, what seems as absolute memory is always subject to what an individual remembers to recall or retrieve and also what is supposed to be recalled. On the contrary, when there is encoding of information, there is also scope for decoding of information. This means that something is excluded from the memory or some events or episodes are forgotten by the memory. This forgetting is a natural instinct of humans. For meaning-making, what seemed a relevant and absolute memory in the past is pliable to take a nuanced memory in its retelling. In the testimonies of survivors of traumatic events, it is in the unreliability of these stories (as said by historians) that lie the deeply embedded experiences in all its variations. At times, these memories are not recalled as an organized narrative, but as sudden impulses, impulses that might have been evoked by a certain experience. In such a recalling, there could be memories that have been lying deep and seek an outlet or an impulse to surface. Therefore, the exclusions could be varied where spatial barriers, social and political structures and geographical divisions stand as strong agents for such forgetting. Such a paradox is sometimes catalysed by people in power and the choices they make on what has to be forgotten. "Some memories are elaborated, some elided, some never summoned up at all; thus, it is that from the totality of a life only a fragment is offered here, some part of the broken line" (Menon, Ritu and Kamla Bhasin, 1998). Forgetting is not always an innocent or passive activity of individuals or society; they could be culturally or politically motivated. At the macro level of remembering, recalling is sometimes governed by power factors to establish a desired and collective memory. Collective memory could be a manipulated memory that is socially and culturally constructed and established.

Given the interplay between individual, collective and historical memories, the mass media plays a key role in constructing and establishing of memory. The researcher attempts to analyse this discourse of partition through the lens of Memory Studies while referring to some of the individual narratives from *The Other Side of Silence* (1998) by Urvashi Butalia and also study the representations of these popular narratives in movies.

> Remembering is an active reconciliation of past and present. The meaning of the past in relation to the present is what is at stake here; memories are important as they bring our changing sense of who we are who we were, coherently into view of one another. Keightley and Pickering, 2013
>
> (Keightley and Pickering, 2013, p.58)

Bhutalia's work has chronicled real voices of the partition times that brings to the fore buried memories which lay deep rooted in the history of India. "These shaming histories—so long under wraps—are narrated with honesty and clarity and informed by compassion", says the Pakistani novelist Bapsi Sidhwa in her review of the book. It is said that the work does not question the veracity of the facts but provides adequacy to the truths as they are the telling of those human beings in real flesh and blood whose lives have been profoundly affected and mutilated. History books might have spooled in incidents of the past, giving numbers of those affected and recording stories of people who were viewed as mere informants. Many of the agonizing episodes of the victims have been pushed under the carpet, and no document can approximate the trauma and anguish or the confusion and insecurity that the Hindus, Sikhs and Muslims had been through.

Both men and women have their share of stories—from displacement and abduction to rape and killing. Revisiting these traumatic narratives, while placing them in the current context and reinterpreting them to draw an image, interweaves real stories and history through current understanding. As the cultural establishments vary, these narratives give rise to analyse these constructions from different perspectives. Carolyn Steedman (2001), the British historian, says that one must have a narrator, a voice and an identity to tell one's story, the self is not created in isolation, but through the perspective of the self in the society looking from the wider network of relations and identities. Therefore, narratives drawn from individual memory through the broader dimensions of a given society give these events an inter-subjectivity to interpret them from the tools of historical and social identities.

The Other Side of Silence recounts the stories of many victims—each distinguished from the other, as the bloody hues of suffering and agony bear a darker shade with the unfolding of each incident. The story of Rajinder Singh is about people from his family and village who crossed the border on foot in a 'kafila' (caravan), a journey that was without any direction. The unforgettable hardships and the never-ending path showed how everyone suffered; he recalls the many questions that they had—"Which nagar, which side, which direction.... We had no desire to eat, nor was there anything to eat" (Bhutalia 103). The victim's story is touching for its sense of inexorable and slow torturous movement, as people were beaten; women were raped, gave birth to children; the elderly were not spared either; yet they were forced into an unknown future.

The story of Damyanti Sehgal, another victim, recounts her journey from the times before Partition till her flight alone to a place from what became Pakistan to India. She, as a child, was forced to flee from her village Kotra, near Lahore, when the Sikhs had taken oaths to put an end to the Muslims. Fearing serious repercussions that the Muslims would kill the Hindus, and that she would be gutted in this fiery exchange, Damayanti went alone when partition started because her father did not budge; he believed that things would settle after some time. She failed in her attempts to move her father. During the course of her journey, she witnessed the gory incidents in Amritsar where people were being cut, and the eventual retaliation by the Muslims brought in episode after episode of killing, looting, wrath and hatred. Absolutely penniless, and in tattered condition, she moved wherever possible, from Dharamshalas to Ashrams, surviving on people's mercy. She, however, survived the times, and in her subsequent years, it's said that she worked in the Indian State's recovery and relief operation travelling in the interiors of Pakistan to locate abducted women and bring them to relief centres. Her descriptions retrieve the history of such violence—rape, forcible abduction and marriage—and a further violence inflicted by the state in its recovery operation. Damayanti's story reveals the history of those women who remained silent or whose stories were corroborated by men for many reasons. The author in an attempt to draw a complete picture from the incompletely woven stories says,

> There are, of course, no complete pictures. This I know now: everyone who makes one, draws it afresh. Each time, retrospectively, the picture changes: who you are, where you come from, who you're talking to, when you talk to them, where you talk to them, what you listen to, what they choose to tell you… all of these affect the picture you draw.
> (Bhutalia 126)

Multiple versions and perceptions of the same events by different people based on memories told immediately after the event and memories told after, say, fifty years, have a great bearing on the representation of a collective memory. While integrating historical facts, memoirs, stories of individual survivors, rescuers and witnesses, it's arguable whether all these would shed light on the manifestations of this traumatic experience and also on the nature of memory per se. Saulius Suziedelis, a prominent historian writes,

> In as much as the purpose of commemoration, the affirmation of a particular vision of a shared history, is the reinforcement of group loyalty, the exercise of the various solemn national remembrances, is, at heart, a political act. By its very nature, the act of remembrance is hostile to critical analysis—shades of grey are unwelcome. This is particularly true of historical events characterized by mass violence. Wars, revolutions and genocides have winners as well as losers, perpetrators as well as victims, and it is natural that irreconcilable memories will clash.
> (Suziedelis, 1995: 47)

To encode the silence of people through interviews and histories—transcripts, newspapers, memoirs and other sources—Bhutalia could piece together a story of love and of hate, a story of four lives and two nations, a story that brought her back to the histories of women: the story of Zainab and Buta Singh, a Sikh soldier who served in the British army during the Second World War. Zainab, a Muslim girl, was abducted while her family was moving to Pakistan in a 'kafila' during the partition riots. As she was passed from one hand to the other as an object of booty, Zainab finally came into the hands of a 'Jat' (one who traditionally belonged to rural ethnic groups of northern India and Pakistan) named Buta Singh. Buta Singh paid a price to save Zainab's life and secretly took care of her fearing vehemence and ostracism from his community. Eventually, the two fell in love with each other and the 'chaddar' (marriage) ceremony was performed so that their relationship was legitimized, although this was unwillingly accepted by the Sikh community in which they lived. It is said that during the following years, the couple lived peacefully bearing two children until a search party, on the lookout for abducted women, traced Zainab. An inter-dominion peace treaty signed by India and Pakistan, ten years after partition, stated that women who were forced to live on either side of the border should be expatriated to their homeland. Life took a different turn for the couple; like many other women, Zainab had no choice but was forced to leave for Pakistan—an event that was featured in the newspaper when the entire village had assembled to see Zainab go. Some narratives also say that Zainab's uncle had orchestrated the entire rescue operation, so that Zainab's property in Pakistan could be recovered, and her marriage with his son would secure the property within the family. In Pakistan, Zainab's cousin was reluctant to marry her initially because Zainab had lived with another man, and that, too, a Jat. However, the wedding did take place. On the other side of the border, and after a long wait, Buta Singh moved heaven and earth to reach Zainab. Consequent to the political dictates from the Pakistan government, he sold his land, got converted to a Muslim, and ultimately changed his nationality. Despite the persistent political silent warfare between the two countries, Buta Singh crossed the border and finally reached Zainab. His hopes were shattered when Zainab, besieged by her relatives, rejected him. She said: "I am a married woman. Now I have nothing to do with this man. He can take his second child whom I have brought from his house" Bhutalia 130). Totally shattered, Singh threw himself under a train with a suicide note in his pocket that read that his body should be buried in Zainab's village. This history shook people across the borders, and some filmmakers swore to produce sensational blockbusters.

Considering the larger picture drawn from individual memories as chronicled by Bhutalia, there are several questions that surface. If Zainab was truly in love with Buta, what was the reason for her to reject him? Had her memory of the partition riots faded completely, or did she compromise with circumstances and prefer to reconcile with her present condition in Pakistan? Or was she trying to construct a new meaning to her life and hence preferred to live in Pakistan? Could it be possible that what we consider as absolute memory has variations or fissures that society is unaware of? All these questions give much room to view an apparent interplay of history, psychology, polity and socio-cultural trajectories. Studies on memory say that while psychologists are more interested in memory from the individual perspective, the social and cultural bases are brought into the centre by sociological theorists. However, Halbwachs in his work *Social Frameworks of Memory* (1925) says that memories are social and passed on from generation to generation, they should be viewed beyond the individual phenomenon. *Freedom at Midnight*, a book by Larry Collins and Dominique Lapierre. features the events around the Indian independence movement and partition. It says,

> One unfortunate man, Boota Singh, the Sikh farmer who had purchased a Moslem girl fleeing her abductor, came to symbolize for millions of Punjabis the tragic aftermath of their conflict as well as the hope that

> ultimately man's enduring aptitude for happiness might overcome the hatreds separating them. (Collins and Lapierre,1976: 528)
>
> (Collins and Lapierre, 1976: 528)

This brings into perspective man's ulterior motive to be hopeful in life while glorifying Buta Singh and also portraying him as a man who purchased Zainab.

The movie *Gadar: Ek Prem Katha* (2001), based on the life of Buta Singh and Zainab, became a blockbuster hit where actors Sunny Deol and Amisha Patel featured in lead roles as Tara Singh and Sakina. Although the movie retains many of the real incidents of history, there are several other episodes that come together as sub-plots. In the gruesome and bloody mass killing of people in trains on either side of the border during the riots, it is said that Tara Singh happens to meet Sakina while he is on his mission of killing the Muslims. The movie spools in heart-wrenching stories of displacement on either side; it is also shown that Tara Singh's parents give their two daughters some poison, so that they can kill themselves before falling prey to the lust and anguish of the Muslim men. Unfortunately, Tara Singh's sisters are molested several times and killed—the result of an oath that the men had taken on either side of the border to bring disgrace to the 'other' group by molesting the women. The main plot of the story, believed to be an absolute memory, has events that are realistic. Tara Singh and Sakina after their eventual married life are caught up in the political strife between the two nations. What takes the audience by surprise, especially for those who had read history, is that there is a happy ending after persistent struggles by Tara Singh and Sakina; both come together and are united. Sakina's family and the government of Pakistan succumb to the circumstances created by the duo, and let them go free.

The movie *Partition* (2007), written by Patricia Finn and directed by Vic Sarin, a Canadian, is set in 1947, narrating the story of Buta Singh and Zainab as Gyan Singh and Naseem. During the partition riots, Gyan happens to meet Naseem, a young Muslim woman separated from her family, and saves her life. They face hardships in the village from the other Sikhs as they are unwilling to accept Naseem in the community. However, after they get married, situations come under control until one day they get to know that Naseem's family has been found in Pakistan. Naseem, overwhelmed with the information, leaves for Pakistan to meet her family. In Pakistan, Naseem's brothers lock her up in a room and vow to keep her away from the Jat. Gyan leaves for Pakistan after a long wait to reach Naseem. Gyan, dressed like a Muslim along with his son Vijay, reaches Naseem, but goes through several hardships in Pakistan. Naseem's mother, realizing the couple's commitment towards each other, releases her daughter. Gyan and Naseem are reunited and make attempts to come back to India. However, the story comes to a tragic end when the hero is pushed onto the tracks in a physical combat that takes place between Gyan and Naseem's brothers.

Another movie featuring this grand narrative is the Punjabi film *Shaheed-e-Mohabbat Boota Singh* released in 1999. Starring Gurdas Maan and Divya Dutta in the lead roles and directed by Manoj Punj, the film won the best feature film in Punjabi at the 46th National Film Awards. This movie is also internationally acclaimed for it being reviewed as realistic and also constitutes episodes glorifying the grand love story that evokes the emotions of the audience.

All the three movies feature history; the story of Buta Singh and Zainab is well situated among the grand narratives of love stories. To the partition crisis, Indian popular cinema responded with a good number of jingoistic films: *Mission Kashmir* (2000), *Roja* (1992), *Border* (1998), *Sarfarosh* (1999), *Maa Tujhe Salaam*, *Gadar: Ek Prem Katha* (2001), to name a few. Perhaps this particular historical narrative takes a celebrity status with media being a strong agency to communicate to the society a memory which would have otherwise remained a relic. There are some nuances or some episodes that have been fictionalized in the movies, trying to meet the desired agendas, individual memories and history as mediated through technology. Knowing the fact that the mass media plays a key role in the constitution of memory, negotiations between what exists and what is to be conveyed to the society is apparent.

In the current media-saturated environment, mediatization has become a significant concept to interpret social transformations. Mediatization is defined as an increasing adoption of the logic of media by other domains of life to make representation of narratives more impactful and relevant (Hjavard 2017). It is seen as a merger between media and other social institutions (politics, economics, education, arts, science, etc.) where the media has become an integral part of other institutional operations. With its integration into every aspect of life, society has submitted itself to or has become dependent on media and its logic.

In the present context, adopting nuances in the narratives of Buta Singh and Sakina, in the above referred movies, brings the theory of mediatization of history to the centre that makes re-construction of narratives more empirical. Such media representations of the past focussed more on the media side of the process of telling the story where the historian or individual narrators were overlooked or remained on the periphery.

At this point, a concept by Alison Landsberg, called 'prosthetic memory', comes to the fore where a new form of cultural memory is formed under the influence of media. Here the past is projected as part of the present rather than showing the past as simply past. Landsberg said that this new memory showed how films can produce historical knowledge while having the potential to awaken social responsibility among its public. (Landsberg, 2004)

Halbwachs saw history as "a dead memory, a way of preserving pasts to which we no longer have an 'organic' experiential relation" (1925). However, in favour of memory's meaningfulness, the inter-subjectivity that lies between individual and historical memory paves the way to form a new memory through media. So, the collective memory drawn through media is seen as an organic past that manifests itself through actions and statements of individuals and through history. The question, however, lies with how it is mediated. The negotiations that are carried by the media in its manifestation of a story bring several variables to the centre. Garde Hansen describes media "as the first draft of history as they record events as they happen, negotiating history and memory" (Garde-Hansen 2012).

Films try to connect emotionally past memories with the distanced audience to draw a picture in the form of a newly constructed memory. They try to blur the boundaries between the past and the present. Therefore, history is mediatized and for its aesthetics, fictionalization and dramatization are used as techniques to make the story more impactful and also to fit it into a certain cultural framework. (Horbyk et al. 2002) All the above referred movies take significant liberties skewing the historical events. However, in creating such a prosthetic memory, misrepresentations of these narratives, such as sensationalizing the violence and atrocities of the partition times, over-glorifying the romantic episode between Tara Singh and Sakina, portraying Pakistan as a one-dimensional antagonist, and concocting the climax scene, might all diminish the historical value of the narrative. In a conversation between film director John Sayles and historian Eric Foner, on whether filmmakers care about historical accuracy, Sayles says that if films "are true to the spirit of the story" (Jenkins 2), it becomes unnecessary to get all facts correct.

In its attempt to construct and reconstruct individual and historical memories, films have mediated facts to make narratives impactful to evoke desired impulses. A happy ending in the movie *Gadar: Ek Prem Katha* certainly deviates the audience from the real incident as history claims that Buta Singh had lost his battle against the government of Pakistan and also Zainab. He is a victim to the silent political warfare between the two nations, a gruesome reality that shook people on either side of the border. Can we justify a happy ending story as an attempt by the movie makers to romanticize history and instil a jingoistic attitude in the audience? As the titles roll, it is evident that the episodes of love stories supersede all others, specifically the horrifying experiences of the general public because of partition.

Stories of the past, when recalled as stories of the present, are reconstructed and are worthy of analysis as the frames of culture and society differ. However, this mediatization of past memories and contextualizing them to suit the cultural context can estrange the society from the original events.

A very unceremonious and tragic end to Gyan Singh under a train in the movie *Partition* is a glaring instance of selective storytelling by the media because after the mammoth struggles that Gyan is subject to, his death brought through Naseem's brothers under a train certainly puts Gyan into obscurity. The historical fact remains that Buta Singh's suicidal end summons a slew of questions to be addressed, not only for the victimized nations but also for nations who have been subject to the partition mayhem. History places on record Buta Singh's grave that is immortalized as a shrine called 'Shaheed-e-Mohabbbat'at Miani Sahib' in Lahore—a grave that spools in memories of pain and trauma. (Khalid, 2010)Can we discount these nuances as the logic of media in its retelling a memory to draw a new memory—a prosthetic memory that may or may not conform to the exactness of the events of the past? Memory certainly becomes 'adjustable' when the agency differs in its telling and retelling each time. But such an image driven by deliberate paradoxes certainly has an impact on the society to construct a collective memory of a very significant event, especially for the younger generation when movies become powerful agents for instilling learning. Also, such shared historical understanding is integral to a nation's identity formation, its history, culture and values. When media becomes such a strong agency of communication to the public, such memories might form a backdrop or framework for further interpretation and research.

Works Cited

Bhutalia, Urvashi. *The Other Side of Silence*. New Delhi: Penguin Books, 1998.

Collins, Larry, and Dominique Lapierre. *Freedom at Midnight*. Renaissance Literary & Talent, 1976.

Francisco, Jason. "In the Heat of Fratricide: The Literature of India's Partition Burning Freshly." *Annual of Urdu Studies*, vol. XI, 1996, pp. 227–250. https://jasonfrancisco.net/in-the-heat-of-fratricide. Accessed 10 Nov. 2022.

Garde-Hansen, Joanne. *Media and Memory*. Edinburgh: Edinburgh University Press, 2011.

Halbwachs, M. *Les Cadres Sociaux de la memoire*. Paris: Alcan, 1925.

Horbyk, Roman, et al. "Mediatization of History: Introducing the Concept and Key Cases from Eastern Europe." *Soviet and Post-Soviet Politics and Society*, vol. 239, 2022, pp. 179–184. http://dnb.d-nb.de abrufbar.

Jenkins, Kale A. "The Reel Truth: The Importance of Historical Accuracy in Films." Eastern University. Masters of Arts in History. Other Films and Media Studies Common, 2020. https://dc.ewu.edu/theses

Keightley, E. and M. Pickering. *Research Methods for Memory Studies*. Edinburgh: Edinburgh University Press, 2013.

Khalid, Haroon. "Shahhed-e-Muhabbat." 11 Oct. 2010. https://lahorenama.wordpress.com/2010/10/11/shaheed-e-muhabbat-by-haroon-khalid/*Lahore Nama*. Accessed 31 Dec. 2023.

Landsberg, Alison. *Posthetic Memory : The Transformation of American Mass Culture*. New York: Columbia University Press, Cop, 2004.

Mehta, Julie Banerjee. "Why Memory Matters through Abhishek Parui's New Book." https://www.telegraphindia.com/my-kolkata/lifestyle/slippages-and-lapses-why-memory-matters-through-abhishek-paruis-new-book/cid/1867943. My Kolkatta. Accessed 2nd Jan. 2023

Menon, Ritu and Kamla Bhasin. *Border & Boundaries: Women in India's Partition*. New Delhi: Kali for Women, 1998.

Smith, Philip. "Three Stages of the Learning/Memory Process." *Pressbooks.library.upei.ca*, pressbooks.library.upei.ca/upeiintropsychology/chapter/three-stages-of-the-learning-memory-process/.
Steedman, Carolyn. "The Space of Memory: In an Archive." History of the Present, vol. 11, no. 4, 2021.
Stig Hjarvard. *Mediatization*. Mar. 2017, pp. 1–20, https://doi.org/10.1002/9781118783764.wbieme0107.
Suziedelis, Saulius. *Landscape and Memory*. New York: Knopf. 1995.

Part V

Voices of Memory Studies from India

16 Memory of 1971 War in Indian Cinema

A *lieux de mémoire*

D. Sudha Rani

Introduction

Benedict Anderson, an Irish scholar, makes a significant mark in the discussions regarding "nation" and "nationalism." As we the scholars of the modern era understand, the idea of nation seems more and more "imagined." Anderson argued through his noteworthy work, *Imagined Communities: Reflections on the Origin and Spread of Nationalism* (1983) that nations have not existed (as they are seen today) since ancient times, they are rather modern and imagined political communities. Further, Anderson claims that the nation does not preexist nationalism. Rather, the nation is the product of modern nationalism. Contrary to nationalist claims, the nation was not rooted in ancient history and did not arise spontaneously. The nation was the product of decidedly modern political interests and dynamics that took a very specific but universal form that originated in the Americas and spread across the globe from there. Ernest Renan's popular lecture on "What Is a Nation?" proved that everything that a nation knows as a tradition has value. Duncan Bell (2003) also supported the idea that historical representation of anything would add value to nationalism. Nationalists for a long time believed that remembering and forgetting played a vital role in nationalism. Scholars belonging to memory studies began supporting the idea that memory is crucial in nation building and nationality building. As opined by Jeffrey K. Olick, the relationship between nations and memory is not only unique but it has a peculiar synergy (2003). Many scholars worked on the relationship of memory, nations, and nationalism and comprehended that questions of memory and its relation to national and other identities have gained significance in the past 10 to 20 years (Olick and Robbins 1998). Now that the connection between memory and nations is well established, we need to scrutinize how this influences nationalism. As observed by Berger (2004) and Coakley (2012), for a century and a half, professional historiography largely concentrated on exploration of the past of nation-states, or nations seeking to get their states facilitated looking at the usable past, that is, the most commemorated and sometimes also most debated historical episodes through nationalist lenses. Therefore nation-states took the memory making phenomenon seriously. Ernest Renan (1992) proclaims that "A nation is a soul, a spiritual

DOI: 10.4324/9781003508564-22

principle. Two things which, properly speaking, are really one and the same constitute this soul, this spiritual principle. One is the past; the other is the present." Using the past to influence the present assumes greater significance and this is done through many dynamic and strong ways by many, including historians (Hroch 1985; Suny and Kennedy 1999; Coakley 2012). Scholars of nationalism generally support the famous observation of Renan about "a heroic past" and particularly "suffering in common" as "the social capital upon which one bases a national idea" (1992, 19). The above argument summarizes the inextricable connection among nationalism, history, and memory.

It is a common site across the globe where the nation-states are encouraging, rather than mandating, the "patriotic history" and giving more significance to affirmative interpretation of history and celebration of select past achievements (Kończal and Moses 2023, 2). It is something regular to instill citizenship education and patriotic feeling by engaging the citizens in the narratives of the national history, which is a part of nationalism. The strategy here is nothing but eulogizing the national myths, pushing the historical truths aside, and these are possible with the stories of nations during wartime. The nation-states prefer to use these wartime narratives to stigmatize the outsiders as enemies and they do all that is possible to exclude the uncomfortable part of the past only to highlight the continuous history of national greatness. It is becoming increasingly clear that the rise of "patriotic" histories is a campaign waged by nationalists in the—real or imagined—culture wars (Didier Eribon 2013). While instilling patriotic fervour among the citizens, nation-states follow three aspects that stand out: "the ruthlessness of methods applied by many state authorities to impose certain interpretations of the past, the increasing discrepancy between professional and political approaches to collective memory, and the overall sociopolitical context in which post-truths gain ground easier than before" (Kończal and Moses 2023, 2).

Media plays a vital role in achieving this goal of nation- building and using narratives that safeguard the nation-states. Nation-states thus deem it their duty to safeguard the states and as Shek Moinuddin writes, "In a democracy, the legislative, executive, judiciary and media are considered as the main pillars to sustain the State and to assist the State in moving ahead" (2017, 30). As we know, the role of media is very critical but the pace at which it is growing in the modern technology-oriented world is noteworthy. Among all forms of media, television and cinema are very prominent in creating a mediascape. As rightly pointed out by Arvind Rajagopal in his book *Politics after Television: Hindu Nationalism and the Reshaping of the Public in India* (2001), television had a crucial role to play in the Ram Janamabhoomi Movement (RJM) and Babri Masjid (BM). Eventually, BJP came to limelight only after this incident. Rajagopal observes that Hindu nationalism shared their technologies and commodities (image) for expanding the market and reaching the audience, respectively. Referring to the power of media in creating mediascapes, Arjun Appadurai writes,

> Mediascapes refer both to the distribution of the electronic capabilities to produce and disseminate information (newspapers, magazine, television stations, and film production studios), which are now available to a growing number of private interests throughout the world, and to the images of the world created by these media. These images involve many complicated inflections, depending on their mode (documentary or entertainment), their hardware (electronic or pre-electronic), their audiences (local, national, or transnational), and the interests of those who own and control them. What is most important about these mediascapes is that they provide (especially in their television, film, and cassette forms) large and complex repertoires of images, narratives, and ethnoscapes to viewers throughout politics are profoundly mixed.
>
> (1996, 35)

He is very clear that the mediascapes are created and circulated among many and all those consuming it won't be able to distinguish between reality and fiction and they create imagined worlds from what they consume. Therefore, the nationality and patriotic message created through these mediascapes is not only powerful but reaches a multitude of persons within the shortest time.

Maurice Halbwachs (1920) initiated a discussion regarding the collective memory and its impact. Every individual at the individual level remembers/forgets individual or community memories. But the community on the other hand remembers/forgets many socio-cultural or socio-political memories based on dynamic factors. According to Astrid Erll,

> The second level of cultural memory refers to the symbolic order, the media, institutions, and practices by which social groups construct a shared past. "Memory," here, is used metaphorically. Societies do not remember literally; but much of what is done to reconstruct a shared past bears some resemblance to the processes of individual memory, such as the selectivity and perspectivity inherent in the creation of versions of the past according to present knowledge and needs.
>
> (2008, 05)

It is therefore natural that socio-cultural conditions influence the individual memory and similarly the socio-cultural conditions of a community equally impact the memories and memory-making process of an individual through various media. In nationalist discourses, representations of the historical past are typically focused on reinforcing a positive self-image of the nation (Coakley 2012, 94).

Such contexts of remembrances are called *points de vue* by Maurice Halbwachs; monuments, rituals, and books are some of them. In continuation to Halbwachs, Pierre Nora came up with a concept of *lieux de mémoire* which are basically mnemotechnical devices that are ideological in nature and nationalistic in purpose. These are not free from value judgement and are far from being neutral in expression. According to him, most *lieux de mémoire* were created, invented, or reworked to serve the nation-state. What Pierre Nora worked on played a crucial role in identity politics in France and imprinted a certain set of notions about the national history among its citizens. In Nora's words,

> *A lieu de mémoire* is any significant entity, whether material or non-material in nature, which by dint of human will or the work of time has become a symbolic element of the memorial heritage of any community (in this case, the French community).
>
> (2008, 5)

He observes that any place, object, or concept carrying some historical significance in the popular collective memory which also supplements and complements the national identity becomes a *lieux de memoire*.

The collective memory of a nation or community is culturally mediated through various media like texts, pictures, films, memorials, toponyms, museums, public holidays, symbols, and rituals. According to Erll, "Fictional media, such as novels and feature films, are characterized by their power to shape the collective imagination of the past in a way that is truly fascinating for the literary scholar (and somewhat alarming for the historian)" (389). She scrutinizes how the media and memories are interrelated in her seminal essay, "The Power of Fiction: Novels and Films as Media of Cultural Memory" (2017), in which she introduces the theory of mediality. According to this theory, whenever crucial parts of the past of a nation are communicated to its citizens, the choice of media plays a critical role. Erll propounds that in such contexts, media attempts four modes of "rhetoric of collective memory"—the experiential, the mythical, the antagonistic, and the reflexive mode. To begin with, the experiential modes of representation tend to represent past as a recent, lived- through experience. As Erll writes, experiential mode is almost like "communicative memory," where everyday life is clearly depicted. This mode authentically portrays the inner experientiality to the reader/audience. Literary or medial forms use the mythicizing mode by representing the past as a faraway mythical past which is Jan Assmann's "cultural memory." According to Erll,

> Typical of this tendency is Ernst Jünger's novel *In Stahlgewittern* (1920; *The Storm of Steel*), in which German soldiers are transformed into figures of Germanic mythology. But also, Francis Ford Coppola's highly acclaimed Vietnam War movie *Apocalypse Now* (1979) mythicizes the historical events by means of intertextual references and the creation of a primordial atmosphere, using an array of visual and sound effects.
>
> (2008, 392)

Antagonistic mode of representation of the past is a mode where one version is favoured rejecting the rest of the versions which includes representation of memories of one group as authentic refuting the other versions as false. Erll writes,

> Authors of the "lost generation," Ernest Hemingway and Richard Aldington for example, make ample use of these strategies. Resorting to we-narration may underscore the antagonistic potential of a novel. This is one of the most striking narrative features in Remarque's requiem on the lost generation, *All Quiet on the Western Front*. Here, we-narration creates a collective identity for a generation of young front-line soldiers, who are set apart from the old, war-mongering generation at home.
> (2008, 392)

Coming to reflexive mode, they are modes which draw attention to processes and problems of remembering. Writing about this mode, Erll says, "One of these forms is the explicit narratorial comment on the workings of memory, found, for example, in Marcel Proust's famous novel of memory, *A la recherche du temps perdu* (1913–27)" (392).

Erll analysed that memory of the past while traveling within one media strategizes in experiential, mythical, antagonistic, and reflexive mode, but the memory can travel from one media to another or proliferate in many media. It is not only interesting to study what happens when such a process happens, but it also allows us to understand how *lieu de mémoire* is created. According to her, remediation is a phenomenon that consolidates the memory of important contexts; she writes, "With the term 'remediation' I refer to the fact that memorable events are usually represented again and again, over decades and centuries, in different media: in newspaper articles, photography, diaries, historiography, novels, films, etc." (400). Erll also writes about how a certain media in a certain society or community presents a schemata for future experiences or events. She further analyses how these memories travel in multiple media to stratify the memory of the certain past to make it a,' *lieu de mémoire*. It is a common site across the globe where the nation-states are encouraging, rather than mandating, the "patriotic history" and giving more significance to affirmative interpretation of history and celebration of select past achievements (Kończal and Moses, 2023, 2).

Conflicts between India and Pakistan are as old as the partition of India. Scholars like Sisir Gupta (1972), Sumit Ganguly (2019), Sumita Kumar (2000), Smruti S. Pattanaik (1999), and many others worked extensively on this topic. After four wars and many encounters, the situation between India and Pakistan in the past 75 years remained stable in terms of conflicts. Reporting the current state, the Council on Foreign Relation writes,

> At the May 2023 Shanghai Cooperation Organization summit in India, the foreign ministers of India and Pakistan traded barbs over Kashmir,

> missing an opportunity to improve relations. Furthermore, actions of the Pakistani military against Imran Khan in early 2023 have raised concerns that Pakistani political turmoil will fuel the arguments of Indian hardliners and hinder peace.

The conflicts between India and Pakistan were more politically motivated and many forms of media give a lot of significance to it. An article appeared in the *Washington Post*, "Why India and Pakistan are fighting again—and the risks that remain: Rumors and misinformation add a new challenge" by Asfandyar Mir on 7 March 2019. According to him, the conflict continues and the governments on both sides are forced to react and show their might and opposition to each other. The animosity is being continuously supported by both nation-states and it has impacted every field of life including sports.

As Mohammad Zubair Iqbal and Shabir Hussain observe,

> Since separation as two independent states in 1947, both India and Pakistan have been at the loggerheads due to an array of unresolved issues, particularly the disputed territory of Kashmir. The two countries have fought four wars in 1947–8, 1965, 1971 and 1999 and still they are not at peace with one another.
>
> (2018, 140)

Though each war is equally eulogized on both sides for the valour and patriotism of their respective armed forces (with their side of the story), 1971 war is given a special place in Indian history and its victory is celebrated with a lot of respect for the soldiers who fought and who lost their lives in the war. This war attains the status of *lieux de mémoire* for all the Indians. The photo where the representatives of both the armed forces are signing the end of war and surrender of approximately 90,000 Pakistan soldiers gained much popularity. On December 16 of every year Vijay Diwas is celebrated across the army establishments in India to mark the victory of India over Pakistan in the 1971 war. So, Bangladesh formation is not only important for it but gained greater significance in India.

The collective memory of the 1971 war between India and Pakistan is presented in *Border* (1997—Hindi), *1971* (2007, Hindi), *1971—Beyond Borders* (2017, Malayalam) *Ghazi* (2017, Telugu), *Raazi* (2018, Hindi), *Bhuj—The Pride of India* (2021, Hindi), *Pippa* (2023, Hindi), *IB71* (2023, Hindi), *Mission Majnu* (2023, Hindi), *Sam Bahadur* (2023, Hindi), and some more films. Among many media forms, cinema is one the most powerful media (India is the largest producer of films) with a strong impact. Identifying this significance, spreading nationality through this medium and selecting Indo-Pakistan clashes, especially the 1971 war seems to be very precise. It is also very accurate in terms of economics as this subject is still in vogue in both the countries and among the Indian diaspora (major patrons of Indian cinema) as cinema is not only an aesthetic art, but it is primarily a commercial art. When *Border* (1997) was released worldwide on 13 June 1997, it not only became one of the highest grossing Hindi films with approximately ₹655.7 million, it also received a lot of critical acclaim and many awards like Film Fare awards along with Best Feature Film for National Integration by National Film Awards, etc. The film is all about how a company of around 120 Indian soldiers safeguarding the India-Pakistan border defend the Indian border as the Pakistanis are preparing an all-out assault on it. The film depicts the battlefield, border, grit, and the patriotic spirit of Indian soldiers. The film is based upon a real incident, the actors were great in their roles, and the filmmakers made these characters flesh and blood so that it could get an immediate connect with the audience. Not many films were made on this topic before *Ghazi* was released in 2017, but after this, a series of films were made on the 1971 India-Pakistan war. The mediascape they created is significant both in terms of spreading patriotism, nationality, and the capacity of the Indian army.

There are many works that represent the partition of India and Pakistan in different media. Books include *Aag Ka Darya* (*River of Fire*) (1959) by Qurratulain Hyder, *Midnight's Children* (1980) by Salman Rushie, *Kingdom's End and Other Stories* (1987) by Saadat Hasan Manto, *Tamas* (1987) by Bhisham Sahni, *Ice-Candy Man* (1989) by Bapsi Sidhwa, and *Train to Pakistan* (1990) by Khushwant Singh. Films include *Pinjar* (2003), adapted from the novel by Pritam Amrita and also made into a TV series broadcast on TV One Pakistan in 2018; *Meghe Dhaka Tara*, directed by Ritwik Ghatak (1960); *Garam Hawa*, directed by M. S. Sathyu (1973); *Partition*, directed by Ken McMullen, adapted from Saadat Hasan Manto's story *Toba Tek Singh*, by Tariq Ali (1978); *Earth*, directed by Deepa Mehta (1998); *Jinnah*, directed by Jamil Dehlavi (1998); *Hey Ram*, directed by Kamal Haasan (2000); *Gadar: Ek Prem Katha*, directed by Anil Sharma (2001); *Kaalapaani*, directed by Priyadarshan (1996); and *Partition*, directed by Vic Sarin (2007). Television series include ", *Lajwanti (2015)* by Rajinder Singh Bedi, *Dastaan(2010)* by Samira Fazal, and *Buniyad* (1986) by Ramesh Sippy. All these works act as premediation to the 1971 war because all these TV serials, feature films, and books that were produced over a period of less than half a century since partition prepare the audience to watch and understand the significance of the 1971 war that made an indelible mark on the psyche and memory of Indians. They also prepare the audience to understand the context and India's standpoint during those turbulent times.

Therefore, the conflicts between India and Pakistan during the 1971 war are also well presented through many works. The photograph where Lt. Gen. Jagjit Singh Aurora (General Officer Commanding-in-Chief of Indian Eastern Command) from India and Lt. Gen. A. A. K. Niazi (Commander of Pakistani Eastern Command) are signing the document Instrument of Surrender on 16 December 1971 is very popular. The celebration of Vijay Diwas on 16 December of every year also is a reincarnation of the memories, along with many novels like *Calling Sehmat* (2008), and many books written by Indians,

Pakistanis, and outsiders. This war is remediated both within the media like films and books, and a sizeable number of short films and feature films were also made. Therefore, stratification of the collective memory related to the 1971 war between India and Pakistan is seriously taken up by a series of films in India. As rightly pointed out by Erll,

> By the term "remediation" I refer to the fact that especially those events which are transformed into *lieux de mémoire* are usually represented again and again, over decades and centuries, in different media. What is known about an event which has turned into a site of memory, therefore, seems to refer not so much to what one might cautiously call the "actual event", but instead to a canon of existent medial constructions, to the narratives, images and myths circulating in a memory culture.
>
> (Erll, 18)

This phenomenon points out to what Pierre Nora terms *lieux de mémoire* and Ann Rigney calls "convergence," that is "Cultural memories tend to 'converge and coalesce' into a *lieu de mémoire*" (Rigney, "Plenitude" 18). Discussing this, Astrid Erll points out how stories, iconic images, and topoi about the past flow together and are conflated into a site of memory (Erll, 18). Similarly, the conflicts between India and Pakistan and the four wars they fought with each other, and the bloody partition, are presented through different media, like newspaper articles, official and unofficial histories, novels, photographs, and movies. They are presented through different periods of recent history—right from 1947 to as recently as 2023. Different cultural contexts, world media, Pakistani media, Bangladeshi media, and of course, Indian media represented the 1971 war in different perspectives. Therefore, the collective memory related to the 1971 war becomes a repository of memory worth becoming a *lieu de mémoire*. This war has given different memories to different people, but the collective memory created by these films produced in India creates a mediascape of nationality in recent decades.

Border (1997, Hindi), written and directed by J. P. Dutta, is an experiential film that opens to the battle field, where the Airforce of India is getting ready for the 1971 war. The entire story is set in 1971 and the complete action is around a battalion of 120 soldiers struck on the Rajastan-Pakistan border. The audience will learn how the war tanks work and how the soldiers need to adjust with limited food and water supply. Moreover, we will be introduced to the language, psychological condition of soldiers when they participate in war, bullets, guns and battlefield, and the challenges faced by the soldiers. One of the main protagonists, Major Kuldeep (played by Sunny Deol) is the mouthpiece of Indian patriotism and the interaction of characters in every scene attempts to establish nationality.

1971 (2007, Hindi), directed by Amrit Sagar, is a fictional war film based on the 1971 India-Pakistan war. It is a mythicizing remediation where a good number of prisoners of war from India are ill-treated by the Pakistani army.

The film is all about how their plans of escape fail and they are forced to die and suffer in the jails of Pakistan which are violating the Geneva Convention and ill-treating prisoners of war.

Ghazi (2017, Telugu), directed by Sankalp Reddy, is the first ever submarine-based war film based on true incidents from history. This film mythicizes the 1971 war with an audio introduction of how India and Pakistan participated in four wars and how the 1971 war is very crucial. This film is also an experiential one, where we are introduced to the political condition of 1971, and the plan of Pakistan to crush India by crushing *INS Vikranth*, the powerful submarine of India. The film is all about how the crew of *INS Vikranth* strived to save it and attack *Ghazi*, Pakistan's submarine.

1971—Beyond Borders (2017, Malayalam), directed by Major Ravi, is a fictional, reflexive memory remediation, where the sons of the soldiers who participated in the 1971 war from both India and Pakistan happen to meet in Georgia as part of a UN peace-keeping force. And the action then moves to the 1971 war where India and Pakistan are fighting on the border. It shows the battlefield, soldiers, tanks, and the travails of soldiers on both sides. The major protagonists are two army officers, one from India and the other from Pakistan. Though the film attempts to show the courage and great warrior abilities of Indian soldiers, it also eulogizes the Pakistani army and their strengths and discourages war as it only brings destruction to both sides.

Raazi (2018, Hindi), directed by Meghana Gulzar, is both reflective mythicizing in remediating the 1971 war. The opening scene of the movie shows a navy battalion being addressed by their leader approximately 40 years after the war. He begins to describe the valour of Indian soldiers in the wars that they participated in and then mentions the role of the Intelligence Bureau of India, especially a 20-year-old young Kashmiri girl who was instrumental in saving *INS Vikranth*, the submarine of India which attacked *Ghazi*, the Pakistani submarine. Towards the end of the movie, we are shown the news reel of the 1971 war, the victory of India over Pakistan and the formation of Bangladesh. Therefore, this film mythicizes the past and shows it in reflective mode and presents the conflict-ridden nations and how an average Indian was ready to sacrifice his/her life for the nation. This film was highly appreciated and received many awards including best film by Filmfare and earned 195 crore rupees at the box office. This film is based onl *Calling Sehmat,* a novel by Harinder Sikka, an army officer, who claimed that it is written based on true events.

Bhuj: The Pride of India (2021, Hindi) is a film directed by Abhishek Dudhaiya, set during the Indo-Pakistani War of 1971. It is an experiential film based on true events, depicting the resilience and grit of Indian soldiers. It is the story of Squadron Leader Vijay Karnik, in charge of Bhuj airbase. When the Indo-Pakistan war breaks out in 1971, the Pakistani airforce destroys Bhuj airbase in an unwarranted attack, then Vijay Karnik along with around 3000 local women reconstruct the airstrip. This grit and resilience of

Indians showcasing their patriotism is a story used to build nationalistic fervour among its citizens.

IB71 (2023, Hindi), directed by Sankalp Reddy, is an experiential remediation in which the audience understand the activities of the Intelligence Bureau of India during the 1971 India-Pakistan war. In 2023 alone, three films *Pippa* (2023, Hindi), *IB71* (2023, Hindi), and *Sam Bahaddur* (2023, Hindi) were released. All of them are experiential remediation where the films present the war from different perspectives. *IB71* (2023, Hindi) is not completely based on true events but the other two are based on true events. *Pippa* (2023, Hindi) and *Sam Bahaddur* (2023, Hindi) are experiential mediation but based on true events as both of them are biographical war films based on Balram Singh Mehta and Sam Manekshaw of Indian Army. *Pippa* (2023, Hindi) is the nickname of a war tank, the PT-76, imported from Russia. The protagonist of the film Captain Balram Singh, a young officer from the 45th Cavalry regiment is in charge of PT-76. The film depicts the war scenes, plight of Indian soldiers, dire predicament of Bangladeshis, and the bloody war of 1971 where this war tank helped Indian soldiers cross the border and engage in the Battle of Garibpur to a greater extent. This film is based on a book written by Balram Singh Mehta, *The Burning Chaffees: A Soldier's First-Hand Account of the 1971 War* (2016). The entire family of Balram Singh, his father, his brother, and his sister are patriots and served the Indian nation with great commitment. *Sam Bahaddur* (2023, Hindi) is directed by Meghana Gulzar and is the biographical sketch of Sam Manekshaw, India's first Feild Marshal. He is quite known for his pivotal role leading India in the success of 1971 war. The film showcases a lot of photographs and videos of the 1971 war including the iconic photo where the Pakistani army representative signs the surrendering treaty. As discussed already, this film not only depicts the battlefield, soldiers, their plight, and their lives, it also depicts the socio-political conditions of the 1971 war.

Conclusion

As discussed above, the 1971 war between India and Pakistan was the third war fought by both countries. The conflict between these two countries began ever since the partition. All the literature, books, films, documentaries, photographs, and memorials like museums of partition act as premediation to the 1971 war. Both the nations used these incidents to prompt nationalism among their citizens and primarily selected visual media. In India, this war is remediated deftly to make the iconic photo of Pakistani soldiers' surrender and the date of surrender prominent. The act of celebrating 16th December of every year as Vijay Divas across all army camps, celebrating the resilience and grit of the Indian soldiers through many media, gives it the status of a *lieu de mémoire*. All these feature films made in different languages of India are remediating the 1971 war. Many of these films are made based on novels, therefore remediation from one medium to another is also happening. Another significant point to be noted is, as India is a vast and multilingual country, these movies based on the 1971 war were made in different languages, more prominently in Hindi as it is being spoken by the majority of Indians. They are consolidating many true events of the war making them available for the millennials who might get motivated to showcase their patriotism. As discussed above, any action by India against Pakistan is always eulogized and celebrated by the citizens, so much so that even the cricket between these two countries is also viewed from the same perspective. The strong way of reinforcing patriotism among the citizens and developing nationality in India is done inevitably by proving that Indians are mightier and won many wars against Pakistan.

Works Cited

Anderson, Benedict. *Imagined Communities: Reflections on the Origin and Spread of Nationalism*. Verso Books, London, 1983.

Appadurai, Arjun. *Modernity at Large: Cultural Dimensions of Globalization*. University of Minnesota Press, Minneapolis, London, 1996.

Bell, Duncan S. A. "Mythscapes: Memory, Mythology and National Identity." *British Journal of Sociology* 54.1 (2003): 63–81.

Berger, Stefan. "Representations of the Past: The Writing of National Histories in Europe." *Debatte: Journal of Contemporary Central and Eastern Europe* 12.1 (2004): 73–96.

Coakley, John. *Nationalism, Ethnicity, and the State: Making and Breaking Nations*. Sage, Los Angeles, 2012.

"Conflict between India and Pakistan | Global Conflict Tracker." *Council on Foreign Relations*, Council on Foreign Relations, www.cfr.org/global-conflict-tracker/conflict/conflict-between-india-and-pakistan. Accessed 18 Nov. 2024.

Didier Eribon, *Returning to Reims*. MIT Press, Cambridge, MA, 2013.

Erill, Astrid. "The 'Indian Mutiny'as a Shared Site of Memory: A Media Culture Perspective on Britain and India." In *Memory, History, and Colonialism: Engaging with Pierre Nora in Colonial and Postcolonial Contexts*, 2009, Bulletin of Deutsches Historisches Institut London 117–148.

Erll, Astrid. "Literature, Film, and the Mediality of Cultural Memory." In *Cultural Memory Studies An International and Interdisciplinary Handbook*, edited by Astrid Erll and Ansgar Nunning. Walter de Gruyter, Berlin, New York, 2008, 389–399.

Erll, Astrid, et al., eds. *Cultural Memory Studies: An International and Interdisciplinary Handbook*. Walter de Gruyter, Berlin, New York, 2008, 1–18.

Ganguly, Sumit. *The Origins of War in South Asia: Indo-Pakistani Conflicts since 1947*. Routledge, 2019.

Gupta, Sisir. "Issues for the Indo-Pak Summit." *India Quarterly* 28.2 (1972): 126–131.

Halbwachs, Maurice. *On Collective Memory*. Edited and Translated by Lewis A. Coser. University of Chicago Press, Chicago, 1920.

Hroch, Miroslav. *Social Conditions of National Revival in Europe: A Comparative Analysis of the Social Composition of Patriotic Groups among the Smaller European Nations*. Cambridge University Press, New York, 1985.

Iqbal, Mohammad Zubair, and Shabir Hussain. "Indo-Pak Wars (1948, 1965, 1971, 1999): Projecting the Nationalistic Narrative." *Journal of Political Studies* 25 (2018): 139.

Kończal, Kornelia, and A. Dirk Moses, eds. *Patriotic History and the (Re) nationalization of Memory*. Taylor & Francis, New York, 2023.

Kumar, Sumita. "Trends in Indo-Pakistan Relations." *Strategic Analysis* 24.2 (2000): 221–246.

Moinuddin, Shekh. *Mediascape and the State*. Springer Geography, Cham, 2017.

Nora, Pierre. *Pierre Nora en Les lieux de mémoire*. Ediciones Trilce, Gallimard, Paris, 2008.

Olick, Jeffrey K. "Collective Memory to the Sociology of Mnemonic Practices and Products." In *Cultural Memory Studies An International and Interdisciplinary Handbook*, edited by Astrid Erll and Ansgar Nunning. Walter de Gruyter, Berlin, New York, 2008.

Olick, Jeffrey K., and Joyce Robbins. "Social Memory Studies: From 'Collective Memory' to the Historical Sociology of Mnemonic Practices." *Annual Review of Sociology* 24.1 (1998): 105–140.

Pattanaik, Smruti S. "Indo-Pak Relations: Need for a Pragmatic Approach." *Strategic Analysis* 23.1 (1999): 85–110.

Rajagopal, Arvind. *Politics after Television: Hindu Nationalism and the Reshaping of the Public in India*. Cambridge University Press, Cambridge, 2001.

Renan, Ernest. "What Is a Nation?" Text of a Conference delivered at the Sorbonne on March 11, 1882, in Ernest Renan, Qu'est-ce qu'une nation?, Paris, Presses-Pocket, 1992. (translated by Ethan Rundell)

Suny, Ronald Grigor, and Michael D. Kennedy, eds. *Intellectuals and the Articulation of Nation*. University of Michigan Press, Ann Arbor, 1999.

17 Stor(y)ing Memory and *Totam*

Perspectives towards Oral Narratives

Santhwana Santhosh and Joly Puthussery

The chapter is an attempt to provide an interdisciplinary approach drawing upon the theoretical premises of memory studies, narratology, folk culture studies, performance studies and digital humanities to look into how storytelling, memory, oral narratives, its performance and digital interweave in the complex of *Teyyam* of North Malabar of Kerala. The chapter is segregated into various sections. The initial section attempts to introduce *Teyyam* and the oral narratives related with it known as *totam*, followed by the role of storytelling in the phenomenon. In the following section, a performance-centric approach to the complex is looked into. Further, the intertwining of aspects of memory in the complex is discussed. The penultimate section tries to situate the phenomenon in the digital sphere followed by a conclusion.

Transmitted from generation to generation, oral narratives and performance traditions are inevitable to the understanding of culture. A reflection on the etymological roots of the word "narrative" suggests that the term is associated with the idea of knowing and meaning making. In Latin, *narrare* means to tell. Narratives make sense of the world we are living in, shape one's experiences and still let one's imagination run wild, ultimately to make sense of one's reality. A vast epistemology including collections, documentations, analyses and interpretations are devoted to the field. There is a remarkable shift from mere collection and documentation of oral narratives to scientific, theory-oriented methodological analyses and interpretations. A memory studies approach to the oral narratives and performance, in the backdrop of the phenomenon discussed here, reveals that these are not mere retrievals of survivals of the past, but valuable affective markers informing identities of individuals, communities and regions constructing worldviews. The chapter also tries to look into how communities of memory emerge in the context of the complex.

The entanglement of storytelling, performance and memory is inevitable in the context of *Teyyam* and the oral narratives associated with it. A spatio-temporal phenomenon of the North Malabar of Kerala, where a human is apotheosised into "god"/*Teyyam*[1] in a shared sacred space, aided by oral narratives, *totam*,[2] it creates a sense of collective belonging through "stor(y)ing," imagining and reimagining the narratives. *Teyyam* and the oral

DOI: 10.4324/9781003508564-23

narratives of it rejuvenate the lore and land, forging connections between the landscape and mindscape by weaving stories, forming a memoryscape. The shared sacred space, often known as *kaav* or shrine enclaved in sacred groves turns into a performative space as the human transcends to god, clad in intricately embellished elaborate red costumes and heavy headgears, grooving to drumbeat to shower blessings on common devotees/ audience from different walks of life. The narratives through acts of (re)membering go down memory lanes, celebrating and raising ordinary beings, once relegated by various social evils, to the positions of goddesses and gods, to glorify their extraordinary heroic feats.

In the *Teyyam* and *totam* complex,[3] stories are conveyed through orality. So, memory plays a vital role in its transmissions. The complex promotes group solidarity where cultural transmission happens through storytelling in a shared sacred space. The space becomes the locus of cultural and ritual practices maintaining a sense of community involved in active participation. The space then turns into an institution of collective remembrance. The narratives bridge the gap between the past and present. The stories become fundamental to the shared experience of recollections and eventually get ritualised for collective commemoration.[4]

The article "Communities of Memory and the Problem of Transmission" by Michael Pickering and Emily Keightley (2013) discusses the issue of memory transmission and introduces the idea of mnemonic imagination:

> along the two temporal planes in which it occurs: vertically, through time; and horizontally, in time. It is because we regard memory transmission as involving the mutual interaction of these two planes that we introduce the concept of the mnemonic imagination. The value of the concept is that it enables us to see, inter alia, how communities of memory emerge.
>
> (115)

The notion of dissemination and inheritance of memory across and within time can be extended to the spatio-temporal specific and calendrical patterns of the *Teyyam* complex. The transmission of knowledge vertically takes place through narratives, as it gets handed down to the next generation by the practitioners of specific communities, where the novices through observation and repetition aquire the intergenerational and traditional knowledge. And, horizontally in time, the stories get told in the traditional space shared by the commoners/devotees/audience/listeners.

The dynamic sees various levels at which memory operates, a spectrum merging individual acts of remembering and recollecting in a ritual and cultural context where past and present interact with each other. A framework of memory at different levels is considered here, following Maurice Halbwachs' foundational insights and social frameworks of memory to study the memory of a group based on a Durkheimian approach.[5] At the individual level, the narration manoeuvres verbal and non-verbal gestures of the narrators and performers to convey the stories across the audience. At the personal or individual level, memory can be traced as it takes shape as the memory of the practitioner who recalls the narrative and the memory of the devotee who recollects, reflects and empathises with the characters of the narratives who have survived trauma of the societal oppressions of various forms. For instance, among the many forms of *Teyyam*, well known among the commoners is *Makkamteyyam*, a poignant tale of Makkam[6] killed along with her children by her brothers, later venerated as a goddess. As the *Makkamteyyam* happens, her tale is retold and the devotees empathise with the character. It is conducted even at houses at times as a prayer for fertility and prosperity. Also, narrators' identities emerge out of the birthright to narrate, hereditarily, culturally and obligatorily. The narrators essentially are individuals who learn, memorise and remember the oral narratives imitating their predecessors for a sense of belonging. For example, the authority to perform *Makkamteyyam* customarily rests in the hands of specific people belonging to the caste called *Vannan*, who are initiated into performing *Teyyam*. At this level, the memory parallels private mnemonic practice when narrators learn and rehearse the narratives through repeated utterances, a trained memory, as opposed to the performance in a ritual event involving public commemoration. The level then transforms into collective memory, at which the individual sphere moves to a shared collective one with certain ritual convections, making sense of the past. And, at shared and collective level, it engages cultural and collective memory in shared sacred space, foregrounding a sense of nostalgia. The notion of nostalgia in the complex is discussed further later. The oral narratives of the complex can be considered as the literary texts or representation of remembrance and memory. The episodes in the narrative cue at the specific areas of the region and give a sense of where the events are taking place, demonstrating its validity. The interspersing of the names of the places in the narrative not only provides authenticity testifying to the past-present continuum in/of the narratives but also evokes geographical memory. In the case of another *Teyyam* form, *Kativanoor Veeran* narrates the heroic tale of a warrior born in a place called Mangadu and brought up in Kativanoor in Kerala. The hero who was unarmed and ambushed behind his back in a battle at Coorg in Karnataka is deified. Also, interesting in the narrative is the use of a series of flashbacks to describe the vivid memory of the hero and his deeds of the past to hail and venerate him as a god. The lore forms the corpus of knowledge, told and retold in the groves witnessed by mass audience and collectively stored and shared, thus rekindling the cultural and collective memory. The sacred groves and the shrines associated with it thus essentially turn into culturally specific sites of memory, a tangible point of reference. Jeffrey K. Olick (2008) notes "collective memory really refers to a wide variety of mnemonic products and practices, often quite different from another" (158). Further, stories and rituals could be considered as products and reminiscence and representation as mnemonic practices. To extend it further to the considerations in the chapter, *totam* and *Teyyam* qualify as mnemonic products and *Teyyam* as an event can be seen as a mnemonic practice. The mnemonic products and practices are produced, reproduced and consumed building a shared sense of a collective, sacred and creative process. As collective concerns are reiterated in the social space, a synthesis of memories is produced, that is, a confluence of memory inherited through generations and acquired through experiencing the complex. The interweaving of the levels forges a connection between socialisation and memory, in the lines of Maurice Halbwachs' idea on which Jan Assmann (2006) in the work *Religion and Cultural Memory* builds:

> The socialization process enables us to remember, but the converse is also true: our memories help us to become socialized. Socialization is not just a foundation, but also a function of memory. We can go so far as to speak of a "bonding memory."
>
> (4)

To understand the nuances of the how of remembering in the complex, a performance oriented turn to the oral narrative is geared toward. Performance as a medium to know how memory operates in the spatial and temporal bound traditional enactment of *Teyyam* is looked into. The oral text is not autonomous, relegated and secluded text but complements with the performance text in actualising a communicative event of/in the complex of *Teyyam*. In light of verbal art as performance, a conception of Richard Bauman, discussed in his work *Verbal Art as Performance, Teyyam* can be considered as a ritual and aesthetic communicative event and a collective representation. The narrator performs, recollecting through mnemonic formulae to the devotees who are the audience engaged in collective remembering at the event, *Teyyam,* where context specific cultural signs are sent, received and recollected. For instance, *varavili* or invocation that calls for prosperity by naming the land, the place and the people can be understood as a formulaic expression memorised and produced to communicate to the audience the commencement of the narrative. The communicative event gives scope to communicative memory, which accords well with the observations of Aleida Assmann that communicative memory is a synchronic memory space and tradition acts as a diachronic axis, and cultural memory can be considered to be a special case of communicative memory; as cited in the book, *Religion and Cultural Memory*, "Tradition can be understood as a special case of communication in which information is not exchanged reciprocally and horizontally, but transmitted vertically through the generations" (8). It is, thus, not just the ritual that gets performed but memory too. The practitioners as narrators and performers become agents of memory.

The article further draws on distinctions among different levels of collective memory borrowing from a cognitive taxonomy proposed by David Manier and William Hirst (2008), who based their work on human memory systems. In liturgical recitation of the oral narratives, the narrator in the case of *Teyyam* and *totam* undergoes a conscious experience of remembering, or what is described in the article as direct memory or a cued recall. The complex involves the transmission of oral narratives coded in bygone days, perfected through rigorous practice. To extend the classification, another description in the framework is that of the distinction between procedural memories and declarative memories, the former is knowing how something is done and latter is mere knowing or experiencing. The description suits the quality of the practitioners who learn from elders how *Teyyam* is conducted and how the narratives are rendered, making it a procedural *memory*. The description of declarative memory parallels knowing that *Teyyam* is conducted ritually and recalling attending *Teyyam* at some point. The categories transcend to a collective domain when witnessed by people of shared past forming a mnemonic community. Discussing the taxonomy of collective memories the authors opine, "no matter the composition of the community, shared memories of a community's experience can be constituted as a collective episodic memory" (257). In discussing the complex of *Teyyam* in this light, witnessing the event of *Teyyam* and listening to the oral narratives in a shared site as a community solidifies the collective episodic memory in the complex. Another category presented in the article is collective semantic memory, where facts about events and places are all over the place during commoners' recollection, "without necessarily remembering where they learned them" (257). For example, the commoners of the region connect to the narrative of *Makkamteyyam* even though they were not present during the time of Makkam; her tale, set in a distant past, is told, learnt, and experienced during the event blurring the categories of lived semantic memories and collective distant semantic memory. Further, the category described as collective procedural or implicit memory includes community rituals and practices. "Rituals and traditions, or more general, procedural memories, can serve as mnemonic tools that shape the collective identity of their practitioners, collectively reminding them of declarative memories" (259). *Teyyam* as living tradition falls under the classification of collective procedural or implicit memory and calls for empathy for the heroes, reiterating the search for a just society.

Another perspective in the interaction of oral narratives and memory is the memorisation of texts by the narrators making use of formulaic features to aid the process as the narratives are long and stretched to hours of rendering. The narrative portrays several episodes ranging from the origin, birth, childhood, challenges and resolutions of the heroes or the gods as the narrators through the format involving flow of words or *manipravala* and vernacular words or *vaachal*[7] foreground the orature of the complex. The article refers to the oral formulaic theory proposed by Milman Parry and Albert B. Lord to examine the composition and multiform structure of oral narrative poetry and comprehend the manner in which epics are composed, learnt and remembered. Albert B. Lord in his work, *The Singer of Tales*

(1960), examined the Serbian Yugoslavic oral epics in Turkish coffeehouses during the nights of Ramzan and noted key ideas related to the composition which aided memorising long verses such as formula, formulaic expression and theme. According to which, an oral epic song is composed of a formula, a regularly employed set of words having identical metrical conditions to express an idea, along with formulaic expression which is a line or half line based on the formula or 'multiform'[8] and consists of a theme that involves repeated episodes and descriptions in the narratives. A look at the oral narratives of *Teyyam* shows that the rendering incorporates sets of stories, narrative strategies of formulaic nature that are characteristic to the liturgical text of the complex. For instance, the *totam* of *Makkam* commences typically with an invocation with the formulaic opening, *polika polika* "let it flourish, let it flourish" and constitutes repeated themes such as the festival of *Pooram*[9] celebrated in North Malabar or the repeated scenes of wars fought between the chieftains.[10]

David C. Rubin examines the cognitive psychology of epics and ballads and notes that cognitive psychology reveals how oral traditions get maintained. The stable monotone, metrical and melodic rendering aid remembering, in which the words get elongated to ease recalling. Discussing serial recall, it is observed,

> Each word recalled provides cue for the next word. The cues involve all the forms of organization that might be involved in recalling the next word. Thus, part way into a ballad the next word to be recalled is being cued by schema, or forms of organization, that involve meaning, imager, spatial layout, rhyme, alliteration, assonance, rhythm, and motor movements accompanying the verbal output and melody.
>
> (1995, 280)

Similarly, in the case of *totam*, the process of recall is enhanced by beats on a drum; for instance the narrators often practice the verses with the help of the single drum or *otachenda* assists in maintaining the flow of the recalling. An interesting aspect that floats in the interaction of lengthy oral narratives and remembering is the aspect of forgetting. Jack Goody in *Myth, Ritual and the Oral* (2010), studying various versions of the LoDagaa myth of Northern Ghana, notes that imagination or fancy is not the prerogative of one culture and suggests that recitation is a cultural activity and to understand it, one needs some knowledge of the accompanying ritual, and the result of flexible creativity of oral culture is distinct from the fixity of written; and there is forgetting which requires invention and creation which probably requires some forgetting. In an interview with Kunjirama Peruvannan, a *Teyyam* practitioner and an expert in the field of oral narratives of *Teyyam* in the Kannur district of Kerala, conducted as a part of the fieldwork in relation to the research thesis, it is observed that though the rendering is tradition-bound, improvisation of the telling is inevitable. He remarks that forgetting is as human as it can get but it is the belief in the hereditarily assigned functional role to transcend into a god and to sing and evoke the god that strengthens the mnemonic faculties of a *totam* singer. He also refers to the concept of *manodarmam*, command of the mind, that shapes the rendering allowing creativity to seep in to develop the singers' repertoires.

To reflect upon the complex in light of digital mediation is inescapable as the complex focussed here has undergone inevitable changes in the due course of time. The emergence of the digital sees a widening of local consciousness to wider popular consumption. The potential that the digital opens up is immense as oral narratives get preserved, collected and documented and turn into a site of cultural repository. The verbal properties are sound-recorded and visual properties and the performance are photographed and filmed. A quick entry of "*Teyyam*" as the keyword in a search engine gushes out a great deal of information, plenty of images and heaps of videos of the complex. The kinesic and acoustic elements of the complex go around in the new media, mostly edited, streamlined and eliminated of extraneous noise. The scope of intermediality in the dissemination of the narratives and mediational space for knowledge production is enhanced in the digital sphere. The article "Between Local and Global: *Teyyam* Goes Cyber and Beyond" in *Cracow Indological Studies*, discusses "fading boundaries" of local-global praxis of *Teyyam* and opines, "*teyyam* is gathering strength to become, with the aid of new technologies, a traveling sacred space" and calls for "probing the local and global perceptions" (De Martino 23,44). The digital presence of *Teyyam* is remarkable in its externalisation inviting a global outlook at the phenomenon, especially in the promotion of tourism by the state. Also, transmediality has resulted in diffusion of folkloric aspects of oral narratives into popular entertainment[11] from organic[12] sacred domains to digital domains. However, the potential problems the sphere presents cannot be elided. In terms of linking digital to the complex of *Teyyam*, the digital revolution sees *totam* disseminated digitally transcending the oral quality, resulting in discontinuity of oral memory. In its wide circulation, the tendency of externalisation, manipulation and de-contextualisation of the complex is a concern among the practitioners as authenticity of whose voice is put out there in what context and the ethics related to its tellability get essentially called into question. In the digital arena, being-in-time gets problematised as context which is a distinctive essence of the complex gets reshaped and the amplitude of the vernacular of the complex attenuates. In its dissemination in the digital venues, though textual, visual and aural get transmitted, the immediate functionality associated with the complex conducted to commemorate and celebrate the local characters in a shared sacred space for prosperity and the notion of sacrality, spatiality and divinity in the physical realm get problematised. On the other hand, in the mental realm it is solidified through the virtual evoking a sense of nostalgia of the experienced and unexperienced. This notion holds true especially in the case of the *Teyyam* complex as the diaspora from North Malabar is ever growing. The digital aids the urge to visit and revisit in space and time, offering a simultaneity and continuity in/of space and time, an alternate spatio-temporality to the complex virtually. The longing for the local in the dispersed gets addressed as the digital quality transforms the spatial, experiential and embodied quality of the complex making it ubiquitous and space-bound at once as *Teyyam* is just a click away.

The article has tried to look into the interplay of oral narratives, memory, storytelling and digital, in its dealing with the phenomenon of *Teyyam* and the oral narratives related to it, *totam*. The attempt has drawn on multidisciplinary perspectives, especially drawing from memory studies situating the complex in various frameworks. The operation of memory at various levels in the complex is addressed, followed by a briefing on the mnemonic formulations of the oral narratives. The digital turn and its scope in the complex was also touched upon. The discussion of new media, oral narratives and memory presented here is somewhat amorphous in nature, seeking a liminality in the interaction, in hope of retaining the reach of the complex through digitalisation and yet not be ensnared in it.

Notes

1 The word *Teyyam* is a colloquial form of the word *deivam* in Malayalam, meaning god. One can witness the phenomenon from October till June in shrines of North Malabar in Kerala.

2 The oral narratives rendered in relation to *Teyyam* to invoke, praise and appease gods. According to *South Asian Folklore: An Encyclopaedia: Afghanistan, Bangladesh, India, Nepal, Pakistan, Sri Lanka*, edited by Margaret Ann Mills, Peter J. Claus and Sarah Diamond, the word is derived from a Dravidian root meaning "to make something appear".

3 The usage of the word "complex" is to indicate firstly that *Teyyam* is an aggregate of several aspects— rituals, oral narratives, and performances with drumbeats and gestures, involving interactions of human–nonhuman, tangible–intangible, fixed–fluid elements. Secondly, it is believed that there are hundreds of *Teyyam* forms, of which only a few are cyclically performed in ritualised contexts, often for prosperity. Also, these forms are particular to the certain communities who have the authority to perform based on their heredity and are entrenched in the caste dynamic of the region.

4 The shrines and groves are often connected to various communities. As far as the social organisation of the region is concerned, integral to it is *taravadu* or ancestral place, a locus, where a familial sense of belonging is instilled among the members who come together, near and afar (linked to the notion of diaspora and memory which is addressed towards the end of the paper) during *Teyyam*. The locus often consists of tutelary spirits protecting the place.

5 On discussing the term "collective memory", it is pointed out that Maurice Halbwachs assigned it to refer to mediate aspects of memory between individual and society on learning Emile Durkheim's psychosociological theory on "collective representations" (Olick 2008).

6 One of the various *Teyyam* forms, Makkam is a goddess who had to face the brunt of injustice caused by her own relatives and was killed out of jealousy. It is believed among the commoners that as her ancestral home burns down, her death is avenged and the holy aura around resulted in revering her as *Teyyam*.

7 The liturgical register specific to *totam*, colloquial in nature, is usually understood as a mix of words borrowed from Malayalam, Sanskrit and Tulu.
8 Lauri Honko in his study of Siri epic uses the term. (Kamppinen 2014)
9 The festival involves the ritual vow the young maidens offer by creating Kama's figure with the flowers celebrated in the region.
10 The political organisation of the region consisted of several kingdoms or *swaroopam*, such as the kingdoms of Cochin, Kolatunadu (presently regions specific to North Malabar), Quilon and Zamorin.
11 The folk elements of *Teyyam* ooze into popular songs. For example, see the YouTube link, https://www.youtube.com/watch?v=6HqMhkXddc4 to the song *Theyyam—The Storyteller.*
12 Lauri Honko puts forward the concept of the second life of folklore emphasising the recycling of folk elements and the withering away of its original context (Kamppinen 2014).

Works Cited

Assmann, Jan. *Religion and Cultural Memory: Ten Studies.* Translated by Rodney Livingstone. Stanford UP, 2006.

Bauman, Richard. *Verbal Art as Performance.* Newbury House, 1977.

De Martino, Giorgio. "Between Local and Global. *Teyyam* Goes Cyber and Beyond." *Cracow Indological Studies,* vol.18, no. 18, 2016, pp. 23- 54. https://doi.org/10.12797/cis.18.2016.18.03

Finnegan, Ruth. *Oral Traditions and the Verbal Arts: A Guide to Research Practices.* Routledge, 1989.

Goody, Jack. *Myth, Ritual and the Oral.* Cambridge UP, 2010.

Kamppinen, Matti. "The Role of Theory in Folkloristics and Comparative Religion." *Approaching Religion,* vol. 4, no. 1, 2014, pp. 3-12.

Lord, Albert Bates. *The Singer of Tales.* Harvard UP, 1960.

Manier, David, and William Hirst. "A Cognitive Taxonomy of Collective Memories." *Cultural Memory Studies: An International and Interdisciplinary Handbook,* edited by Astrid Erll and Ansgar Nunning, Walter de Gruyter, 2008, pp. 253-262.

Mills, Margaret Ann, *et al. South Asian Folklore: An Encyclopaedia: Afghanistan, Bangladesh, India, Nepal, Pakistan, Sri Lanka.* Routledge, 2003.

Namboothiri, Vishnu.M.V. *Totampatukal: Oru Padanam.* National Book Stall, 1990.

Olick, Jeffrey. K. (2008). "From collective memory to the sociology of mnemonic practices and products." *Cultural Memory Studies: An International and Interdisciplinary Handbook*, edited by Astrid Erll and Ansgar Nunning, Walter de Gruyter, 2008, pp. 151-162.

Ong, Walter J. *Orality and Literacy.* Methuen & Co. Ltd.1982.

Pearson, Mike. *In Comes I: Performance, Landscape and Memory.* University of Exeter Press. 2006.

Pickering, Michael, and Emily Keightley. "Communities of Memory and the Problem of Transmission." *European Journal of Cultural Studies*, vol. 16, no.1, 2013, pp.115-131.

Rubin, David C. *Memory in Oral Traditions: The Cognitive Psychology of Epic, Ballads, and*

Counting-out Rhymes. Oxford UP, 1995.

Tarabout, Gilles. "Malabar Gods, Nation-Building and World Culture: On Perceptions of the Local and the Global." *Globalizing India: Perspectives from Below*, edited by Jackie Assayag and & Chris Fuller, Anthem Press, 2005, pp. 185-210.

18 The Patua and Patachitra

Religiosity, Tradition and Memory in Scroll Paintings of Bengal

Soutik Chakraborty

India has a lot of folk art forms dispersed in its vast land. The art of picture storytelling is one among its many such art traditions. Known by different names in different places, this art form involves a display of painting and a narration of the illustrated story painted on a cloth canvas by the artists or the performer. In some places single pictures are used while in other places scrolls are used by the narrator/artist who narrates the story through a song. In some cases, the songs are accompanied by instruments while in some areas the artist sings all alone. In all the cases, the art form is rural and for generations it has continued to entertain people. The themes of these paintings include local myths, legends and stories of gods and goddesses, primarily taken from *Ramayana* and *Mahabharata*. The narrative art form of Bengal is known by the name patachitra. In the previous century, patachitra artists, calledpatua or chitrakar, could be found in several districts of Bengal but in the twenty-first century, the number of patuas has decreased. A major concentration of patuas in the twenty-first century can be found in the Naya village, located in the Paschim Medinipur district of West Bengal, India.

The themes of patachitra vary from mythological stories of gods and goddesses, tales of region-specific deities, stories of the origin of patua community to the description of modern-day important events like destructions caused by tsunamis, earthquakes as well as awareness campaign on AIDS and COVID-19. A peculiar observation regarding patuas of Bengal that has amazed the researchers and art enthusiasts, and which has been the issue of this study too, is the fact that a majority of the patuas drawing Hindu gods identify themselves as Muslims. A lot of academic studies, from the mid-twentieth century, examine the historical facts and the social position of these artists. With the advent of Turkish invaders in Bengal in the thirteenth century, the painters are assumed to have changed their religion. Islam offered them a better social position compared to Hinduism. Being a Hindu they had to lead a life of lower caste. It is also plausible that the social transition might have been a forced one. The previous researches on this field didn't fully address the tenacity of the art form that has denied altering its themes even when the religion of the artist is altered. Though the artists are Muslims, for quite a few generations they have been painting Hindu gods and goddesses. The art form travels from the older generation to the newer

DOI: 10.4324/9781003508564-24

generation of the family. The same themes are painted time and again while the songs are kept in memory.

The painting conventions and the performance procedures live in the memory of the artist and such a memory is transferred to posterity. When memory is taking an active part in the whole enterprise then a study of memory can provide insights on why the art form has refused to alter with social changes, particularly religious affiliations.

Published in 1973, Binoy Bhattacharya in his research made a detailed field study of all the villages of West Bengal where patua communities could be found. In the book *The Pats and Patuas of Bengal*, his chapter lists the socio-economic position and jobs done by patuas (95–97). They are chiefly idol makers and itinerant patachitra artists while a minority also practise snake charming. The patuas have two names, one Hindu name and another Muslim name. They are neither included in the Hindu community nor fully accepted in the Muslim community. Yet the Muslim community shows a certain degree of acceptance. Their marriage customs include both Hindu and Islamic rituals. The funeral rites are according to the Islamic rules. There are some patuas in Bhattacharya's study, who consider themselves to be fully Hindu. From the time of his research to the first half of the twenty-first century, the social structure hasn't changed.

There are various mythical stories within the patua community regarding their mixed religious identity. Atul Chandra Bhowmick in his article, published a few years later in 1995 in the journal *Indian Anthropologist*, collects all such mythical stories (40–41). A story, prevalent among the patuas, states that once a patua was cursed by god Shiva because he had polluted his brush with his own saliva and thus he and his descendants became *mleccha* (a Sanskrit word for people from foreign countries, in a degrading sense), or Muslims. Another story tells that a patua, while making an idol of goddess Durga, had accidentally dipped the brush in his saliva which he used to draw the eyes of the goddess. Durga cursed him and he became *yavana* (another Sanskrit term for a foreigner, someone not included within the Hindu caste system). A story with a different turn states that the patuas are Muslims because of a curse upon them as a patua had once painted a copulation scene of Shiva and Parvati. Yet another story follows the same format where the curse is given by a sage to one of his sons because of his greed for having beef and he is condemned to become a *mleccha* and earn his living as a painter. There is also an opinion among some of the patuas that they are originally migrants from Arabic countries. However, such a proposition of migration is rather fictitious and gathering proofs for such a hypothesis is not within the purview of this research. "From the study of the habitations and legends of the Patuas I am inclined to infer that in the past the Patuas was a caste of Hindu social system" (Bhattacharya 96). In cases where a logical conclusion is not possible because of a gap in historical knowledge, the instinctive opinion of the field researcher gets a plausible dimension. In this context, Binoy Bhattacharya's presupposition regarding the patuas' Hindu origin is undisputed. Yet Bhattacharya is not alone in his remark, but supported by Atul Chandra Bhowmick who writes, "Whatever real or fictitious ... but from the stories one thing is clear that they have Hindu origin" (41).

The dichotomy in religious practice and profession can be addressed to a past religious shift of the community. Such a proposition calls for a re-assessment of region-specific historical facts. Islam reached Bengal with the Turkish invasion in the thirteenth century. For two centuries, the literary output in Bengal was either none or insignificant due to troubled social and political conditions. The poets and priests found no patron among the new rulers and on the top of that, they had to flee to other regions like Nepal to save their lives and scriptures. From the fifteenth century onwards, the political upheavals settled down and a favourable environment for literature was sensed. The period marks the onset of Middle Bengali Literature. In the preceding dark period of Bengali literature, myths and legends of various communities began to assimilate and as a result gave birth to non-vedic deities Dharma, Chandi (also Caṇḍī) and Manasā. These texts, the three *Mangalkāvyas*, depict the creation of its gods and goddesses according to the Vedic tradition of describing the creation of universe and the subsequent birth of gods and goddesses. The three mythical stories are related to one another and altogether "a new myth of cosmology was evolved, which is different from the Sanskrit tradition but which has an unmistakable affinity with the cosmogonic hymns of the *Rigveda* and with the Polynesian myth of creation" (Sen 40). Alongside the Vedic deities, the indigenous deities of Bengal have found a special place in the religious thought and devotion of the people.

"The pundits and poets writing in Sanskrit were silenced but not the singers of mystic cults and rhapsodists of popular deities, who had no prominence" (Sen 39). The broad group of "singers" and "rhapsodists" can include a number of folk performers, but it is obvious that the patua is counted one among them. Poets might have suffered but not the folk artist whose presence would hardly have gained the notice of the new rulers. It is not surprising to observe that, in present times, the common themes of patachitra are the stories of Dharmaraj, Chandi and Manasā. Patachitra is the bearer of the mythical stories that have been the result of a mixture of different cultures. It also affirms the fact that the art form was active among other folk forms when a major social change was taking place both culturally and politically.

Atul Chandra Bhowmik opines that under the reign of Muslim rulers, the patuas changed their religion to evade Jizya poll tax imposed on non-Muslims (42). Richard M. Eaton in his book *The Rise of Islam and the Bengal Frontier, 1204–1760*, records the opinions of early British officers, working in the colonial government, regarding the presence of Muslim population in Bengal. He notes that among many theories proposed to answer the existence of a large number of Muslims in Bengal, one definite cause is the strict Hindu caste system which compelled men of lower classes to convert to Islam

(113–134). The patuas are regarded as a low caste by the Hindus and in the course of history, religious conversion might have fostered social upliftment.

Whatever may be the reasons behind a social change, the illustration of gods and goddesses denied any alteration even when the newly adopted religion forbids such paintings. To account for the stubbornness of art motifs, the memory of the shared culture can provide insights which had kept on accelerating irrespective of any dominating religious influence. To begin with, the memory that creates a patua identity needs emphasis. Maurice Halbwachs' concept of collective memory finds a suitable example within the patua community and their hereditary art. Out of our memories "the remembrances we evoke at will ... are always at hand because they are preserved in groups that we enter at will and collective thoughts to which we remain closely related" (Halbwachs 141). A patua at all times tethers to his identity of a patua through his community. The surnames of all patuas are either Patua or Chitrakar or Mistri, leaving aside minor exceptions. He carries forward the art and technique from their elders, and in turn carries the memory of the oral stories, the culture and the communal identity. "While the collective memory endures and draws strength from its base in a coherent body of people, it is individuals as group members who remember" (Halbwachs 142). To validate theoretical paradigms, it may be noted that a patua lives not discretely but in a community, if he is pursuing painting as his profession. "When it considers its own past, the group feels strongly that it has remained the same and becomes conscious of its identity through time" (Halbwachs 146). The element that sustains the memory of the individual as an artist, is the art itself. The scroll paintings are the texts that provide meaning to them as patuas. Jan Assmann in the Preface to his book *Religion and Cultural Memory* describes both of the meanings implied by the word "text," in the field of Hermeneutics and in the field of Memory Studies. Texts form with repeated iterations, through generations, with repeated incidents of the event. Passed on through generations, augmented or subtracted at the fringes but keeping the core intact, the message continues towards the future. In the Preface, Assmann reaches to a definition before expounding his treatise – "Being that can be remembered is text" (ix).

If patachitras are viewed as texts then the text is keeping its own historical memory in its pages or folds. The story of the origin of patuas lives within the painting and songs of patuas. The story says that once a giant was slain using the wits of a common man. The killing of the giant was a magnificent story to tell and people living far and near should know about it. In order to make people know about the heroic deed, a painting was prepared and taken to villages. The villagers watched the paintings and learnt about the deed through the song that was sung and slowly the patua community was born. Be it mythical or real, the story serves to bind an entire community. Some patuas still make patachitras on this theme and sing songs over it. There are alternative stories regarding their origin. The Sanskrit religious text, *Brahma Vaivarta Purana* presents a story of the origin of painters. According to the text, the first painter was a son of celestial architect Viswakarma. Due to a faulty painting a Brahmin cursed him and he was degraded to a *sudra* or the low caste. In another version of the story, he married a *sudra* woman. The patuas tethered their identity as descendants of Viswakarma and found a reason for belonging to the lower castes of society.

The acquired memory of the heritage, the craft, the style of narration, from the forefathers can be called "semantic memory." "Semantic memory (refers) to everything we have learned and memorised. It is called 'semantic' because it is related to meaning and reference" (Assmann 2). Nietzsche developed the idea that historic awareness shapes an individual. The memory of the culture exerts a pressure upon the individual which he calls "plastic power" because the individual comes out of himself and assimilates with the things of past which he has never seen (Ruin 801). The semantic memory continuously binds the patua to the community and the art form. The patua identity forms with the prior knowledge of their art form existing for centuries and the task of the community members is to carry it forward. The concept of a "bonding memory" comes to play as it is the society which forces an individual to its ways and bounds him within its framework. Borrowing from Freud, Assmann elaborates the functions of "bonding memory" and also adds that it is the "natural desire (of man) to belong and to develop a social identity. The bonding memory has its roots in man's desire to belong in his nature as a *zoon politikon*" or political animal (6).

As assessed, patuas are exposed to the community pressure of being a propagator of the art form. However, it should also be noted that some patuas in the past had abandoned their caste profession and shifted to a better economic opportunity. The community pressure, or rather caste calling, is always present but that doesn't mean any restrictive confinement. Whether the patua is continuing his profession or not, the memory never leaves.

"Religious rituals are without doubt the oldest and most fundamental medium of bonding memory" (Assmann 11) that ties the community members into a succinct group and the traditions are carried forward to the future. In order to connect and stay together, rituals play a great part. For the patuas, religion is a troubled phenomenon. A mixed identity, borrowed from two religions, can never provide a stable position. The Hindus ostracise them for their Muslim identity but their main work is to make idols and paintings of Hindu gods and goddesses. The patua identity is formed by taking rituals from both quarters. The religious anxiety may affect their social position or their reflection as individuals in society but not their art. The art carries a philosophy of its own.

Remembering the past brings cohesion among the members and the unity is founded upon a common heritage. The medium of invoking the stable past can take various forms, be it a ritual or a commemoration. In the case of the patuas, the stable past is the themes of their art; the stories of gods and goddesses. The art conventions, process of preparing the canvas, the preparation of colours, the motifs, the technique and all the artistry involved belong to the patuas and to no one outside the community. Patachitra is the identity of the patua. The identity is made using memories. The memories of medieval Bengali life depicted in the *Mangalkāvya* stories, the rituals of Bengalis reflected within the stories of *Ramayana* and *Mahabharata*, the familial memory of making patachitra and singing on it for generations, the realisation of the uniqueness of art form and the memory of its historical significance – all combine to form a memory of the patachitra art.

While examining the role of religion in memory making, Tuula Sakaranaho in his article "Religion and the Study of Social Memory" examines Halbwachs' observation of gospels as memories held by certain groups of people. He adds that "Halbwachs describes a process whereby certain events, taking place at a particular time and place, are remembered in testimonies and are thereby reconstructed into the form of a narrative, shared by a group" which continues to make meanings for those who haven't seen it in their lifetime (139). Shared by the patua community, patachitra serves this function at its best. The external references of the painter in society or the religion with which he identifies himself socially, might have changed but his internal memory, carried through the community throughout the course of history, has remained the same. There is no scope of forgetting the (pre-Muslim) Hindu memory as well as the memory of being the disseminator of the myths and legends. However, all these memories are not in the active consciousness of the community. It is precisely for this reason that a change in the religious affiliation of the patuas didn't bring a change in their art themes. In turn, the change in religion for reasons that are unclear helped in expanding the thematic vocabulary of the patuas. They included themes from Islam and painted patachitra on Gazi Pir (a Muslim saint believed to have spread Islam in Bengal) and even combined themes from two religions at hand and painted Satya Pir (amalgamation of Hindu god Vishnu and the cult of Islamic Pir). However, patuas are not singularly responsible for the evolution of the deity Satya Pir in between the fifteenth and sixteenth centuries.

The rigidity of the memory (the memory of the culture and art form) can be analysed by Danièle Hervieu-Léger's concept of religion that she proposes in *Religion as a Chain of Memory*. She describes religion as comprised of collective memories as a chain of memory that serves to bind groups rooted in tradition (83–111). The phrase "chain of memory" stands for the remembered memories by which members of the community members link their past and future. There are additions and modifications to this memory according to the demands of the present, as the patua incorporates new themes, but the newly acquired traits are linked to the historically continuing memory and included as a part of it. While explaining the functions of various esoteric arts in religion, especially Hinduism, Ajit Mookerjee in his book *Ritual Art of India* states that the Indian culture is open to imports in matters of art. The culture has assimilated foreign elements to suit the demands of the present. He comments, "This dynamic outlook has prevented cultural breakdown or the disintegration and extinction of the civilization. The incoming elements are absorbed into the old cultural pattern, and the old is widened ... to meet the needs of every type of person" (10). From Mukherjee's observation, the "dynamic outlook" in the context of culture can be re-framed as "dynamic memory" of the patuas that can assimilate diverse elements and not break down. Even if the religion at root on the subjective or individual level is changed, the memory continues in its own pace without any obstruction. To live with the ever-evolving cultural memory; forms the tradition and thus completes the patua tradition in its entirety. It is not the resistance to change but the power to include and expand that makes it possible for a Muslim patua to paint Hindu gods and goddesses.

However, this leaves one gap in the whole discussion. What will happen if the personal memory and the community (collective) memory are at odds? To put it another way, if the patua tradition comes in conflict with the Muslim identity carrying a separate set of cultural memories, then the collective memory may face a threat of disintegration. Such a dilemma can occur at the subjective level only because at its core it is the individuals in group formation who remember. Paul Ricoeur, in his book *Memory, History, Forgetting*, solves this dialectic by stating that "a person remembers only by situating ... herself within the viewpoint of one or several groups and one or several currents of collective thought" (121). It implies that the beliefs and memories of the patua at the individual level are formed with his/her interaction with the community. The community tradition is his/her own tradition. A new patua born in a patua family finds the Muslim identity and the patua identity going hand in hand as a tradition. The collective memory becomes his/her memory and thus conditioned, there is no scope of any revolutionary breaking away.

Tradition and memory often arrive at a hostile condition where the boundaries of each of the terms become important. It is pertinent to demarcate how much of tradition and how much of memory works behind a cultural artefact. In case of patachitra, the painting as tradition has to be situated within the periphery of memory; else the entire project will suffer with the internal contradiction of what refers to the memory of patachitra and what goes as the tradition of patachitra. Tradition is defined by Edward Shils as an objective state where memory has kept a lasting imprint. "Memory leaves an objective deposit in tradition ... the deposit is carried forward by a continuing chain of transmissions and receptions. But to become a tradition ... a pattern of assertion or action must have entered into memory" (Shils 167). A way of asserting the feelings of a poet is to write a poem. In the same way, the pattern of asserting the patua memory is by painting and presenting a patachitra. The textuality of patachitra relies on the embodiment of memory, more specifically the memory of the culture. Jan Assmann and Aleida Assmann propose the concept of "communicative memory" which describes the social aspect of the individual memory (Assmann 3). In the case of the patuas, the social/traditional (circulator of Hindu gods) and the individual (Islam) are at odds. In the present study, the widely used concept of communicative memory is not intrinsically adhered to in order to arrive at what may be called "dynamic memory" which is open to receive foreign elements and maintain the state of continuity.

The paradox of Muslim painters painting Hindu gods is more than a case of cultural assimilation. The art form is open to include within itself further demands of the culture in future, but it will not let the memories of an authentic Bengali culture of olden days slip into oblivion. The themes and painting style of patachitra, which are exclusively traditional, take the effort to remember the gods and goddesses of the land, the nuances of the culture in the course of history, myths and fables of eld, and stories of a mythic past.

Works Cited

Assmann, Jan. *Religion and Cultural Memory: Ten Studies*. Translated by Rodney Livingstone, Stanford University Press, 2006, pp. 1–17.

Bhattacharya, Binoy. "The Patuas - a Study on Islamization." *The Pats and Patuas of Bengal*, edited by Sankar Sen Gupta, Indian Publications, 1973, pp. 95–100.

Bhowmick, Atul Chandra. "Bengal Pat and Patuas - a Case Study." *Indian Anthropologist*, vol. 25, no. 1, June 1995, pp. 39–46, www.jstor.org/stable/41919763. JSTOR. Accessed 24 Jan. 2024.

Chaturvedi, Acharya Ramesh. *Brahmavaivarta Purāṇa. Vol. 1*. Translated by Shanti Lal Nagar, Parimal Publications.

Eaton, Richard M. "Mass Conversion to Islam: Theories and Protagonists." *The Rise of Islam and the Bengal Frontier, 1204-1760*, University of California Press, 1993, ark.cdlib.org/ark:/13030/ft067n99v9/. Accessed 26 Jan. 2024.

Halbwachs, Maurice. "The Collective Memory." *The Collective Memory Reader*, edited by Jeffrey K Olick et al., Oxford University Press, 2011, pp. 139–46.

Hervieu-LégerDanièle. *Religion as a Chain of Memory*. Translated by Simon Lee, Rutgers University Press, 2000, pp. 83–111.

Mookerjee, Ajit. *Ritual Art of India*. Thames and Hudson, 1985, pp. 9–22.

Ricoeur, Paul. *Memory, History, Forgetting*. Translated by Kathleen Blamey and David Pellauer, University of Chicago Press, 2009.

Ruin, Hans. "The Claim of the Past – Historical Consciousness as Memory, Haunting, and Responsibility in Nietzsche and Beyond." *Journal of Curriculum Studies*, vol. 51, no. 6, Oct. 2019, pp. 798–813, https://doi.org/10.1080/00220272.2019.1652936. Accessed 26 Jan. 2024.

Sakaranaho, Tuula. "Religion and the Study of Social Memory." *Temenos - Nordic Journal of Comparative Religion*, vol. 47, no. 2, Sept. 2011, https://doi.org/10.33356/temenos.5151. Accessed 15 Nov. 2021.

Sen, Sukumar. *History of Bengali Literature*. Sahitya Akademi, 1960, p. 39.

Shils, Edward. *Tradition*. The University of Chicago Press, 1981, p. 167.

19 Memories of Her-stories as Feminist Praxis in K. R. Meera's *Hangwoman*

Puja Ghosh and Averi Mukhopadhyay

Introduction

The relation between history and memory is highly complex and contested in the social as well as the literary canon of analysis. In memory studies, "the idea of contest in the literal sense is apparently a straight forward one", as it "evokes a struggle in the terrain of truth" claimed by the recorded history (Hodgkin and Radstone 1). The purpose of recorded history is "to justify the status quo, to illustrate so, or contrariwise, to provide a basis for revolution" (Baum 19). Even if history means "the study of or a record of past events considered together, especially events of a particular period, country, or subject" ("History"), in a historically patriarchal society, history scripts the interest of powerful patriarchal ideologues, by neglecting and minimizing the reversal dynamics of women's history. The feminist historians have seen 'history' as male-centred interpretations of past events with a "focus on a predominantly male-history, thereby marginalizing gender as a category as well as women as actors in history" (Linder 310-311). In this context, memory becomes the feminist discourse in remembering the dynamic possibilities of women in the past, as memory means "the ability to remember information, experiences and people" ("Memory"). The complex relation of memory with history helps in the emergence of oral history, as Hodgkin and Radstone argue,

> one major exception to the relative reserve of history confronted with memory, of course, is the field of oral history, in which the concept of memory – the idea of memory as concept, rather than as given phenomenon – has been increasingly significant.
>
> (2003, 4)

The feminist scholars have embraced oral history as "a means of subverting the dominant historical narrative" by women to "make visible those groups, who traditionally had been silenced in historical narratives" (Abrams 155; 153). The feminist historiographers have advocated a form of oppositional historical practice through the oral history "to create work that is inclusive and further an understanding of a world, that honors the lives of women"

DOI: 10.4324/9781003508564-25

(Rotramel, 302). As Joan Sangster had pointed out, "as feminists, we hoped to use oral history to empower women by creating a revised history 'for women', emerging from the actual lived experiences of women" (92).

The word 'her-story' is actually a critical coinage by feminist historians. With reference to this, Scott veritably comments, "as the play on the word 'history' implied, the point was to give value to an experience that had been ignored (hence devalued) and to insist on female agency in the making of history" (18). The key strategy to form the feminist counter-culture to history is the oral stories of women intertwined with memory. The 'herstory' is defined as "history considered or presented from a feminist viewpoint or with special attention to the experience of women" ("Herstory"). The 'her-story' or 'her-stories' of the feminists form rooted connection with memory, as "feminist scholarship is itself a work of memory that has retrieved many women from oblivion as historical actors" (Chedgzoy 216). In this process, "memory is not a passive depository of facts, but an active process of creation of meanings" (Portelli 52), and at the same time, the memory of women resists the concept of non-existence of women in the dominant phallocentric temporal politics of history. The connection of memory is strongly associated with women's history or her-story, which is "a form of memorialisation of women's pasts" and thereby, "for feminists the retrieval of the personal meant that they could write women's history and restore women to history" (Peto and Waaldijk 79). Memory is not the stoic remembrance of past events, but its narration in the present adds dimension to the spatiotemporal politics with some effective repercussions to the dominant history, and "memory work may therefore assume a political role" (Tota and Hagen 3).

Storytelling is the most benign form of memorizing the meaningful past, as it confronts the male-dominated history with the facade of innocence in its spiralling narration. Portelli critically sketches out the purpose of storytelling, "to tell a story is to take arms against the threat of time, to resist time, or to harness time" and "the telling of a story preserves the teller from oblivion, the story builds the identity of the teller and the legacy which she or he leaves for the future" (59). Storytelling, as the narrative tool of memory in oral history, has elements of resistance against the prevalent narrative power of history to make the invisibility of women visible in the spatiotemporal junctures of history. Oral history has the "dual goal" in "women's history" or her-story "to restore women to history and to restore our history to women" (Kelly 1). It challenges the articulation of history with androcentric drift of political analysis, in which women's experiences have been relegated to the sphere of invisible darkness behind the halo of phallocentric power of men. Oral history creates the new possibility for the re-creation of women's history as well as for the re-articulation of history, where the paradigmatic shift of analysis is more visible than ever before. Reading argues,

> for feminist theory, the oral history movement also offered an important critical intervention into the long-established dichotomy between

> what was conceptualized as 'history' and what as 'memory', in which history was seen to be more legitimate, serving then to exclude women's voices from historical accounts.
>
> (2014, 206)

Memory, which works at the core of oral history, resists the misogynist assumption of male historians, who naturalize the argument that women are "incapable of a historical memory" (Melman 11). Foucault's concept of possible resistance in the place, where power is exercised, is relevant on the ground of resisting memory in opposing the prevalent power dynamics of history, as Foucault points out:

> There are no relations of power without resistances; the latter are all the more real and effective because they are formed right at the point where relations of power are exercised; resistance to power does not have to come from elsewhere to be real, nor is it inexorably frustrated through being the compatriot of power. It exists all the more by being in the same place as power; hence, like power, resistance is multiple and can be integrated in global strategies.
>
> (1980, 142)

Her-stories and Storytelling in *Hangwoman*

Working as the fictional feminist historian with "a feminist sensibility to develop what we have since defined as women's oral history" (Gluck 1), K. R. Meera evokes the sense that the masculinist narrative of history has distorted the existence of *woman qua woman*, who demands the equal status quo in history. The novel *Hangwoman* (2014) archives the her-stories of women, who lived in the past as a threat to masculine physique and intellect "to contradict the recurring notion that women were confined to the home and had thus no place in world history" (Linder 311). The novelist, Meera magnificently draws on the Indian archetypical image of grandmother as the storyteller, and reverses her role in delineating the lived experiences of the past "sheroes". The character of Thakuma[1] is curved with dexterity as the storyteller, whose storytelling is not simple in nuance, but rather has political goal in its inner and outer context. Her stories, which are in memoriam of the historically marginalized and silenced entities, suggest the drift of power in history towards the powerful and the negligence of dominant history in situating the powerless in spatiotemporal politics. Her oral memorial narratives incite the new critical dimension in proving that "masculinity is terrifyingly fragile because it does not really exist in the sense we are led to think it exists" (Kaufman 13). Although the popular idea, that "contested history can lead to silences of memory" (Bosworth 27), exists in the power politics of history, her memorial reservoir of stories impregnates the multiple voices of *women qua women*, who are keen on violating the hegemonic status quo.

Thakuma, as the old lady, possesses a vital memory of past events and narrates the history in a storytelling manner to her grandchild, Chetna. She helps her grandchild to attain the historical consciousness as an epistemic privilege. The grandmother's memorized past stories of women make her conscious about the scripted conspiracy of history, which denies the access of visibility in temporal politics to women. Chetna realizes that past history is a social patriarchal projection of masculine vivacity, as she recognizes "only rarely did the history of the women in our family get recorded" (Meera 109). Past women's stories become the epicentre in her life and consequently lead her to assert her agency by subverting the celebrated notion, which claims "history remains very much his-story" (Johansson 427). Chetna declares with firm conviction:

> It is not women who fear history; it is history that fears women. That's why there are so few of them in it. My place in it was assured only if I managed to put the noose around Jatindranath Banerjee's neck and he died in a flawlessly executed hanging.
>
> (Meera 189).

Her-stories as the lived experiences of women in the sociotemporal politics inspire her to make the fabricated patriarchal ideologies threadbare. Therefore, she denies to be "indoctrinated in a male defined value system", and unlearns the patriarchal epistemology that "women are part of the anonymous in history" (Lerner 357; 360).

The Memorial Her-story of Pingalakeshini

The historical assumption of patriarchy erases the inspirational memory of female executioner, and insists that the tradition of execution is *de facto* an androcentric occupation with the presumption that the most capable executioner is to be a man aptly, as the qualification of the executioner mandates, "only males need apply" (Meera 57; Nanjappa). Therefore, the postcolonial patriarchal society negates the possible existence of official hangwoman not only in history, but also in cultural memory, as it would be a threat to the phallocentric power in the tradition of hanging. Chetna protests repeatedly against this kind of false presumption in the news show of *Hangwoman's Diary*, when she is repeatedly hailed as the first hangwoman in India. She has already learned from her grandmother's memorized stories that one of the foremothers in her family, Tripurasundari,[2] who had taken the name Pingalakeshini, was conferred the job of execution during the time of Balban. She is not the one and only hangwoman in politicized history, as the memory of Tripurasundari confronts such false conclusion. In this advent, "the memorial" of Pingalakeshini through the oral narrative of Thakuma "may represent a political achievement" (Bosworth 28), as it politicizes the historicity of herstory. Though Tomkins has argued that "memorability grows through magnification" (1093), the most appropriate analysis here would evoke that the magnificence of women's history grows through the vital memorability of the grandmother's past herstories. If "prototypical plots" of stories "involve a person and a goal" and the "goal is anything an agent might strive to achieve" (Hogan 204; 221), Thakuma's stories always involve the historical person and the desired achievement is sometimes to establish the other side of violent history through memorized storytelling.

The memorial herstory of Pingalakeshini proves masculine power to be fragile in front of the femininity of *woman qua woman*. Thakuma narrated to Chetna that Pingalakeshini was forsaken in the company of the barbaric Tughan Khan by her husband, who "surrendered her to the Khan, hoping to save his own life" and "had taken the bag of money the Khan had thrown at him" (Meera 174; 175). Although Thakuma is the narrator of this feminist story to her potent listener, Chetna, she is not a feminist herself, rather a barrier of cultural ethos of patriarchy. Therefore, she senses foreboding in Chetna's laughter, as she is indoctrinated by the patriarchal ideologues to believe that the laughter of a woman has ominous consequences. But in reality laughter has the element of unsettling the phallic power of men. When Pingalakeshini had helped Balban, the ruler of Delhi, to overthrow the ruler of Bengal, Tughan Khan, she had asked for the death of Khan as the favour in return. When she had hanged Khan as the hangwoman, she let out the laughter, which "sounded like the pealing of bells" (176). Balban had offered her the job of hangwoman, and she had hanged thousand people during that time. The reason behind her demand for the hangwoman's job is simple in that she had analyzed the historical power to be erroneously phallic and, hence, internalized vengeance to resist the historical wrongs. Chetna has beautifully summarized Pingalakeshini's justified demand, when she replies to Sanjeev's query in the *Hangwoman's Diary* show, "women's anger is such that it cannot be satiated with the death of just one man" (177). Therefore, it is appropriately argued that "like minority groups, women cannot afford to lack a consciousness of collective identity, one which necessarily involves a shared awareness of the past" (Johansson 426), and such collective identity of past can be established in the present time through memory. As the herstory of Pingalakeshini confronts the argument, "as long as historians held to traditional view that only the transmission and exercise of power were worthy of their interest, women were of necessity ignored" (Lerner 349), and points to the fact that historians' prejudiced drift was not towards power, but towards the phallic power of men.

The job of the execution provides a tool of resistance to women against the power exercised on them violently. Inspired by the memory of Pingalakeshini, Chetna realizes that men control women first through ideology. When ideology fails, they exercise violence on their bodies to threaten the sense of equality in women, as "it is one of the mechanisms used to control and subjugate women" (Gangoli 99). When Sanjeev practises the same mechanisms on Chetna as a way of exercising power on a woman, she reverts back Sanjeev's violence in the same manner of her foremother, Pingalakeshini. She hangs Sanjeev in a theatrical manner in the news show to prove that she is capable enough to threaten him on his own ground, just as he does to Chetna in her own private home. At the end, she declares, "what the world gave me, I returned to it" (Meera 431). Although Joan Scott argues, "history's representations of the past help construct gender for the present" (2), Thakuma's memory of Pingalakeshini's story helps Chetna to reconstruct the gender dynamics for the present. Therefore, Sangster justifiably points out, "listening to women's words, in turn, will help us to see how women understood, negotiated and sometimes challenged these dominant ideals" of the past as well as of the present (91). The memorial herstory of the foremothers through the narratives of Chetna's grandmother is intertwined with the politics of past and present, as the "projects that record the life histories of the oppressed and undocumented have also had explicit political aims and outcomes" (Thomson 584).

The Memory of Annapurna

Women are indoctrinated to lead subservient roles to men in the domestic space, as the dominant belief is that the spiritual and moral growth of women are attainable only through her husband or her father's achievement of those codes. In this context, Gisela Bock's argument is apt, "men and their activities had been seen as culture and of cultural value, whereas women and their activities had been seen as natural, outside of history and society" (2). Annapurna had wanted to pursue spirituality following the cult of Buddha, was not allowed to give up home, and was advised to find contentment and satisfaction within the confines of home, as "women had been taught to aspire to the role of housewife: compliance with the role of housewife was to bring them ultimate contentment and fulfillment" (Brooks 61). "For women", the abandonment of family is considered as sin, and "to neglect her duty meant social chaos" (Kessler-Harris 332). It is the popular belief in patriarchy that "a woman's nirvana lies in her service to the husband and children" (Meera 270). Annapurna continued to practice her meditation of "the Buddha, the Dhamma and the Sangha" amidst her domestic chores, though "no one could believe that a woman could attain bliss by means other than her husband, children, clothes and jewels" (Meera 273; 272). Therefore, this commemoration, which "in contrast to history and collective memory, distinguishes events and persons believed to be deserving from those deserving of being merely remembered", proves that the constructed "women's images are only the inference and do not exist in a concretized conscious form" (Schwartz 11; Kalpagam 1687).

The earlier practitioners of Buddhism had succeeded in making the false belief in people that Buddha did not advise women to practise spirituality. The memorized herstory of Annapurna suggests the sexist misinterpretation of the real teachings of Buddha, as "Dharma is neither male nor female" (Paul 236). Rita M. Gross argues,

> a feminist interpreter of Buddhism can make a strong case that the core of the tradition is without gender bias, whatever the practical record may reveal and that sexist practices are in actual contradiction with the essential core teachings of the tradition.
>
> (210)

The core of this problem lies in the fact that Buddha preached orally and never had written any book dictating his own ideals of leading life. This gives lots of opportunity to the religious ideologues of sermons to script their patriarchal views in the name of Buddha. Therefore, the commemoration of the lived experience of Annapurna through Thakuma's memorial storytelling strongly points out that religious history is not spared from the appropriation and alternation to erase any possibility of women's saintliness. Although the androcentric historicity of ideal womanhood ascribes women to be submissive to the wills of husbands and fathers, the politicized memory of Thakuma indicates that the herstory of Annapurna fractures the historicity of submissive women. Here, "memory becomes not simply a source for the investigation of the past" (Dodd 47), rather it holds enormous capacity to subvert the social dynamics in the present time, as Chetna gains new knowledge from the story of Annapurna through Thakuma's memory and changes the present gendered politics by using the powerful invisible women's her-story.

Memory of Khona

Memory distorts the process of erasure of women as eminent astrologers and poets in the past, and opposes the scripted history, which inscribes men in such positions. At this juncture, Thakuma's reminiscence of the herstory of Khona indicates towards the disagreement with the past historians' historicity. Thakuma's commemoration in the manner of a storytelling historicizes Khona as the great astrologer and poet *on par with* the other scholarly eight gems in the court of King Vikramaditya. Khona is said to be the wife of Mihira as well as the daughter-in-law of Varaha. Varaha was the famous astronomer in the kingdom of Ujjain. Her accurate astrological predictions had come to be more profound than those of her husband and father-in-law. This led to an inferiority complex within her patriarchal guardians. They thought that they were emasculated in front of her scholarly activity in the traditional patriarchal society. It points to the fact that "men are everywhere unsure of their own masculinity and maleness" (Kaufman 14), especially when women are more capable in their professional field. The memory of Khona refutes "the claims of those who insist that women had no history, no significant place in stories of the past" (Scott 20). Therefore, the construction of woman as the "trans-historical creature" (Gordon et. al. 76) in history is totally a historical conspiracy of the patriarchal ideologues to suppress women's mobility in the present politics of power, and memory plays as the counter-discourse in reversal to posit women in history.

Historical institution makes domestication the feminine virtue, which is idealized as goodness only to devalue the women in patriarchal society. The idea of the public sphere is closely associated with men, as they are considered to be the breadwinner of the family. Therefore, naturally "a financially dependent wife" is essentially "central to the discourse of masculinity" in historical patriarchy (Walby 105). When Khona entered the public realm in the king's court as the ninth gem, she got the patronage of the king's scholarship and thereby the ability to earn name, fame and money. This ability can be considered as the acquisition of power in an otherwise male-dominated profession and in the domain of the masculine history, the idea of a working wife "meant that the husband had failed" (Kessler-Harris 335). In Khona's herstory, the earning ability threatened the masculinity of two men – at first, her father-in-law's masculinity and then, that of her husband's. Chetna learns the lesson of empowerment from the lived experience of Khona and knows how history killed the voices of empowered women, as they proved to be a threat to its veritable discourse. Learning from this particular past real story through the memorial cord of Thakuma, Chetna denies her father's control over her profession by strongly asserting in expressing her desire of hangman's prestige and power.

Memorial Consciousness in Chetna

The narration and re-narration become the most effective resisting practices in the canon of memory studies to challenge the writing of past history through the oral storytelling to establish the significance of the herstories magnificently in the past sociotemporal politics. Thakuma's oral storytelling, generated through impregnated memory, vitalizes Chetna's consciousness of the women's past which in turn helps her to assert agency in the present politics of power, as "oral history is based on a long tradition of the oral transmission of knowledge and relies on deep communication and storytelling" (Leavy 153). Thakuma's memorial vitality in remembering women's stories empowers her grandchild in expanding "a listener's sense of a vanished past" (Hershatter 372). The television interview with Sanjeev Kumar Mitra provides her opportunities to bring focus on the unequal gender politics of history and on the suppressed feminine voices of historical women. Although "television is the probably the most influential medium for presentation of oral history at the present time" (Thomson 593), the television interview of Chetna is not so simple in its dynamic dimension as the power politics between the male interviewer and female interviewee is in its veins. Sanjeev has made a contract with Chetna with the aim of gaining a lot of professional benefits through the interview in *Hangwoman's Diary* and recording the stories of past women was not in his mind though Chetna cleverly holds on to this opportunity. This indicates "a political relationship between the interviewer and respondent" that "creates an imbalance of benefits" (Scanlon 643).

Chetna, as the woman of new age, disintegrates the idea of inequality of power in the interview, when she resists the phallocentric assumption of Sanjeev about feminine power and creates new history for women through re-narration of her grandmother's memory by establishing the fact that "women's perspectives were not absent simply as a result of oversight but had been suppressed, trivialized, ignored or reduced to the status of gossip and folk wisdom", thwarting the revolutionary process of narrating memory (Anderson et. al. 106). Chetna has used this television interview in her favour by providing her "own interpretation of her experience, of her own perspective" (Anderson et. al. 19) to silence the wrong androcentric assumption of Sanjeev, whose interpretation represents the phallocentric point of view of men. As women's "relationship to past is ultimately a lived one", Chetna deliberately tries her best to use appropriate techniques of storytelling to convey power of past memories in the interview which presents her "ample opportunity to explain and clarify what they mean" (*"Understanding Feminist Historiography"* 1736; Anderson 17). In the interview in *Hangwoman's Diary*, Chetna does not only provide justice to her lived experience of the temporal politics, but also to the herstories of the women in her family and outside her family circle throughout the course of history. Chetna resists the historical phallic power at each step of her life by interrupting the phallocentric belief that male power cannot be resisted. Memory is crucial to her re-narration, as she as a feminist "cares about change", and her memory is "a creative writer, Mother of the Muses (Mnemoyne in Greek mythology), maker of stories" by which the feminists assure that "time past is not time lost" (Greene 291; 294).

Conclusion

K. R. Meera, as the novelist of *Hangwoman*, efficiently takes the role of a memory scholar, who is determined to show the sight of the silenced memory of history by constructing "women as historical subjects", as only "the historian can interpret the world while trying to change it" (Scott 17; 6). The complex weaving of memory and history in this fiction points to the fact that "a new novelistic memory is born" at this juncture of politics (Goff 94). The novelist unravels the politicized her-stories of women in the temporal history, as she was completely taken aback by the sheer invisibility of half of the human race. This is evident in her words in the *Acknowledgements* of the novel:

> What left me astounded, however, was the presence of women – rendered completely invisible throughout history. Within decaying tombs in the ancient cemetery of History were the women who had revolted inside and outside their homes, the women who had dreamed of new worlds, the women whose tresses continued to grow long and longer when their skulls had crumbled to dust. Those who did not seek them out would never know that they had indeed lived.
>
> (Meera 434)

Therefore, with the aim of writing "Indian woman's her-story" (Meera 434), Meera names her protagonist as Chetna, which is a Bangla word meaning 'consciousness'. She moulds her character with the strong consciousness of past women's memories and of the future possibilities of women to create history by remaining visible in "*Bhavishyath*" (Meera 435), which means 'future' in Bangla.[3] In this context of the novel, the dimensions of feminist studies and memory studies are strongly connected through the dynamics of past and present, as "memory is firmly situated in the present yet looks toward the future" and for feminists,

> what our know about the past, and thus our understanding of the present, is shaped by the voices that speak to us out of history; relative degrees of power and powerlessness, privilege and disenfranchisement, determine the spaces where witnesses and testimony may be heard or ignored.
>
> (Hirsch and Smith 2; 12)

K. R. Meera has situated Thakuma's memorial storytelling as the powerful resistance of memory against the practised phallic power politics in history. Here, the brilliant dexterity of Meera makes her proficient master to maintain the tonality of Thakuma and Chetna in her textual narrative, while giving it historical immutability, which cannot be erased easily by patriarchal ideologues. The oral storytelling of the grandmother in this novel is about "empowerment" particularly "to encourage 'victims' to see themselves as 'survivors'" (Abrams 154). Therefore, Thakuma's telling and Chetna's retelling of memorial her-stories reconstruct "women's history", which "critically confronts the politics of existing histories and inevitably begins the rewriting of history" (Scott 27). In spite of the tremendous power of each epoch of 'his-tory', women can always tread a new path by politicizing experience of 'her-stories' through feminist telling and memorial re-telling of such past stories of different historical women. Thus, for the feminists, memory creates the possibility of "historical visibility" of women through the criteria of "speaking out" the past (Passerini 684).

Notes

1 The grandmother is called *Thakuma* in Bangla. The contextual background in *Hangwoman* is West Bengal, and the protagonist is a Bengali young woman, who has called her grandmother *Thakuma*.
2 Tripurasundari and Pingalakeshini indicate the same person. Tripurasundari took the job of executioner and discarded her earlier name after adopting a new name, Pingalakeshini.
3 "*Bhavishyath*" is a Bangla word which means future.

Works Cited

Abrams, Lynn. *Oral History Theory*. Routledge, 2010.

Anderson, Kathryn. "Learning to Listen: Interview Techniques and Analyses." *Women's Word:The Feminist Practice of Oral History,* edited by Sherna Berger Gluck and Daphne Patai, Routledge, 1991, pp. 11–26.

Anderson, Kathryn et. al. "Beginning Where We Are: Feminist Methodology in Oral History." *The Oral History Review,* vol. 15, no. 1, Spring 1987, pp. 103–127.

Baum, Willia. "The Other Uses of Oral History." *The Oral History Review,* vol. 34, no. 1, Winter–Spring 2007, pp. 13–24.

Bock, Giesla. "Challenging Dichotomies: Perspectives on Women's History." *Writing Women's History: International Perspectives,* edited by Karen Offen, Ruth Roach Pierson and Jane Rendall, Macmillan Press Ltd., 1991, pp.

Bosworth, Michal. "'Let Me Tell You...,': Memory and the Practice of Oral History." *Memory and History: Understanding Memory as Source and Subject*, edited by Joan Tumblety, Routledge, 2013, pp. 19–33.

Brooks, Abigail. "Feminist Standpoint Epistemology: Building Knowledge and Empowerment Through Women's Lived Experience." *Feminist Research Practice: A Primer,* edited by Sharlene Nagy, Hesse-Biber and Patricia Lina Leavy, Sage Publications, 2007, pp. 53–82.

Chedgzoy, Kate. "Introduction." *Theories of Memory: A Reader,* edited by Kate Chedgzoy et al., Edinburgh University Press, 2007, pp. 216–18, http://www.jstor.org/stable/10.3366/j.ctvxcrvk7.36. Accessed 4 June, 2024.

Foucault, Michael. *Power/Knowledge: Selected Interviews and Other Writings 1972–77*. Edited by Colin Gordon and translated by Colin Gordon, Leo Marshall, John Mepham, and Kate Soper, New York, Pantheon Books, 1980.

Gangoli, Geetanjali. *Indian Feminisms: Law, Patriarchies and Violence in India.* MPG Books Ltd, 2007.

Gluck, Sherna Berger. "Women's Oral History, the Second Decade." *Frontiers: A Journal of Women Studies*, vol. 7, no. 1, 1983, pp. 1–2.

Goff, Jacques Le. *History and Memory*. Columbia University Press, 1992.

Gordon et. al. "The Problem of Women's History." *Liberating Women's History: Theoretical and Critical Essays,* edited by Berenice A. Carroll, University of Illinois Press, 1976, pp. 75–92.

Greene, Gayle. "Feminist Fiction and the Uses of Memory." *Signs*, vol. 16, no. 2, 1991, pp. 290–321, http://www.jstor.org/stable/3174512. Accessed 4 June, 2024.

Gross, Rita M. *Buddhism After Patriarch: A Feminist History, Analysis and Reconstruction of Buddhism*. State University of New York Press, 1993.

Hershatter, Gail. *The Gender of Memory: Rural Women and China's Collective Past*. University of California Press, 2011.

"Herstory". Merriam Webster Dictionary. http://www.merriam-webster.com/dictionary/herstory. Accessed 4 June 2024.

Hirsch, Marianne, and Smith, Valerie. "Feminism and Cultural Memory: An Introduction." *Signs,* vol. 28, no. 1, 2002, pp. 1–19, https://doi.org/10.1086/340890. Accessed 4 June, 2024.

"History". Cambridge Dictionary, https://dictionary.cambridge.org/dictionary/english/history. Accessed 4 June 2024.

Hodgkin, Katherine, and Radstone, Susannah. "Introduction: Transforming Memory." *Contested Pasts: The Politics of Memory,* edited by Katherine Hodgkin and Susannah Radstone, Routledge, 2003.

Hogan, Patrick Colm. *Mind and its Stories: Narrative Universals and Human Emotion*. Cambridge University Press, 2003.

Johansson, Sheila Ryan. "'Herstory' as History: A New Field or Another Fad." *Liberating Women's History: Theoretical and Critical Essays,* edited by Berenice A. Carroll, University of Illinois Press, 1976, pp. 400–430.
Kalpagam, U. "Oral History: Reconstructing Women's Role." *Economic and Political Weekly,* vol. 21, no. 38/39, 1986, pp. 1683–1687.
Kelly, Joan. *Women, History & Theory: The Essays of Joan Kelly.* University of Chicago Press, 1984.
Kessler-Harris, Alice. "Women, Work, and the Social Order." *Liberating Women's History:Theoretical and Critical Essays,* edited by Berenice A. Carroll, University of Illinois Press, 1976, pp. 330–344.
Leavy, Patricia Lina. "The Practice of Feminist Oral History and Focus Group Interviews". *Feminist Research Practice: A Primer,* edited by Sharlene Nagy Hesse Biber and Patricia Lina, Leavy, Sage Publications, 2007, pp. 149–186.
Lerner, Gerda. "New Approaches to the Study of Women in American History." *Liberating Women's History: Theoretical and Critical Essays,* edited by Berenice A. Carroll, University of Illinois Press, 1976, pp. 349–356.
Lerner, Gerda. "Placing Women in History: A 1975 Perspective." *Liberating Women's History: Theoretical and Critical Essays,* edited by Berenice A. Carroll, University of Illinois Press, 1976, pp. 357–368.
Linder, Ulrike. "Gendering Historiography." *History Workshop Journal,* vol. 7–9, no. 68, Autumn 2009, pp. 310–314.
Lindsey, Dodd. "Small Fish, Big Pond: Using a Single Oral Narrative to Reveal Broader Social Change." *Memory and History: Understanding Memory as Source and Subject*, edited by Joan Tumblety, Routledge, 2013, pp. 34–49.
Meera, K. R. *Hangwoman.* Translated by J. Devika. Penguin Books, 2014.
Melman, Billie. "Gender, History and Memory: The Invention of Women's Past in the Nineteenth and Early Twentieth Centuries." *History and Memory,* vol. 5, no. 1, 1993, pp. 5–41, http://www.jstor.org/stable/25618641. Accessed 4 June, 2024.
"Memory." Cambridge Dictionary, https://dictionary.cambridge.org/dictionary/english/memory. Accessed 4 June 2024.
Michael, Kaufman. "The Construction of Masculinity and the Triad of Men's Violence." *Beyond Patriarchy: Essays by Men on Pleasure, Power and Change.* New York, Oxford University Press, 1987.
Nanjappa, Vicky. "What a Hangman Must Know and What It Takes to Be One." https://www.oneindia.com, 10 December 2019, https://www.oneindia.com/india/what-a-hangman-must-know-and-what-it-takes-to-be-one-299364.html. Accessed 5 March 2024.
Passerini, Luisa. "A Memory for Women's History: Problems of Method and Interpretation." *Social Science History,* vol. 16, no. 4, 1992, pp. 669–92, https://doi.org/10.2307/1171316. Accessed 4 June, 2024.
Paul, Diana. *Women in Buddhism: Images of the Feminine in Mahayana Buddhism.* Asian Humanities Press, 1979.
Peto, Andrea, and Waalkijk, Berteke. "Histories and Memories in Feminist Research." *Theories and Methodologies in Postgraduate Feminist Research: Researching Differently,* edited by Rosemarie Buikema et al., Routledge, 2011, pp. 74–87.
Portelli, Alessandro. *The Death of Luigi Trastulli, and Other Stories: Form and Meaning in Oral History Suny Series in Oral and Public History.* State University of New York Press, 1990.
Reading, Anna. "Making Memory Work for Feminist Theory." *The Sage Handbook of Feminist Theory,* edited by Mary Evans et al., Sage, 2014, pp. 196–214.
Rotramel, Ariella. "Feminist Historiography." *Companion to Feminist Studies,* edited by Nancy A. Naples, John Wiley & Sons Ltd, 2021, pp. 301–320.

Sangster, Joan. "Telling Our Stories: Feminist Debates and the Use of Oral History." *The Oral History Reader,* edited by Robert Parks and Alistair Thomson, Routledge, 1998, pp. 87–100.

Scanlon, Jennifer. "Challenging the Imbalances of Power in Feminist Oral History." *Women's Studies Intnational Forum,* vol. 16, no. 6, 1993, pp. 639–645.

Schwartz, Barry. "Rethinking the Concept of Collective Memory." *Routledge International Handbook of Memory Studies,* edited by Anna Lisa Tota and Trever Hagen, Routledge, 2016.

Scott, Joan. *Gender and the Politics of History.* Columbia University Press, 1988.

Thomson, Alistair. "Fifty Years On: An International Perspective on Oral History." *The Journal of American History,* vol. 85, no. 2, September 1998, pp. 581–595.

Tomkins, Silvan S. *Affect Imagery Consciousness: The Complete Edition.* Springer, 2008.

Tota, Anna Lisa, and Hagen, Trever, "Introduction: Memory Work – Naming Pasts, Transforming Futures." *Routledge International Handbook of Memory Studies,* edited by Anna Lisa Tota and Trever Hagen, Routledge, 2016.

"Understanding Feminist Historiography." *Economic and Political Weekly,* vol. 25, no. 31, 1990, pp. 1735–36, http://jstor.org/stable/4396591. Accessed 14 October 2023.

Walby, Sylvia. *Theorizing Patriarchy.* Basil Blackwell Ltd, 1990.

Part VI

Perspectives of Memory from World Literature

20 Memory in Oonya Kempadoo's *All Decent Animals* and *Buxton Spice*

Isha Banerjee

Introduction

From its origins in oral retellings, literature has long been intertwined with memory for its transmission and preservation. As populations grew and diverse cultural and religious groups emerged, the oral tradition evolved, shaped by the collective or individual memories of speakers who drew inspiration from their myths, legends, languages, and beliefs. It will not be wrong to say that life and literature often were invigorated by each other. Over time, literature transitioned into a form of metadata, serving as a repository for authors' memories and offering a means for these memories to endure. Without the conduit of literary expression, these memories might have faded into obscurity. In a compelling essay addressing the intersection of literature with the past and the role of nostalgia in connecting present and past, Eric Sandberg aptly designates literature as the "most explicit repository of cultural memory" (Sandberg 27).

Thinking of literature as a quasi-cultural document potentiates it beyond being just a preserver of personal recollections of the past. Speaking particularly in the context of Caribbean literature, memory, as it has been employed, encompasses narratives of colonialism, slave trade, partition, social unrest, war, reconfiguration, identity, and more. Jeffrey K. Olick and others, in the introductory chapter of the book *The Collective Memory Reader*, tell of the omnipresence of memory since times immemorial. Olick and others identify a phenomenon called "memory boom" (4), occurring just prior to the turn of the 21st century that resulted from an exponential increase in the preoccupation with memory. The authors contest the idea that memory studies, being a part of the memory boom, is destined to suffer a decline in its magnitude. Instead, they assert that the field of memory studies is a promising one, listing a number of fields like neuroscience, trauma studies, psychology, inquiry of past oppression, cultural theory, social and political science, etc., that share overlapping interests with memory studies. Speaking of this interconnectedness, they highlight the relevance of memory studies in "social frameworks," "media technologies," "cultural institutions," and "political circumstances" (Olick et al. 37).

DOI: 10.4324/9781003508564-27

Defining the field of memory studies is challenging and elusive due to the diverse elements it encompasses. Yet, what adds a firm sense of weight to the role of memory studies in the realm of Caribbean literature is the resounding truth that all the aforementioned fields of studies foray into the intricate history of the Caribbean. The profound roots of trauma, epistemological violence, and sociopolitical turmoil in Caribbean history give rise to a reservoir of memories spanning individual, cultural, historical, and material dimensions. Authors from the region, including diasporic writers, draw upon this collective memory in their literary creations, anchoring the significance of memory studies within the realm of Caribbean literature.

French philosopher and sociologist Maurice Halbwachs made significant contributions to the field of memory studies, particularly in collective memory studies. Halbwachs highlighted the embeddedness of individual memories within the social frameworks by explicating the correlation that runs between them. He states that memory is not a secluded process that an individual undertakes in isolation from the world around them; instead, he says, "memory comes back to us when our parents, our friends, or other persons recall them to us" (Halbwachs 38). Halbwachs' concept, as highlighted in this chapter, becomes evident in instances where one character's personal memory inexplicably intertwines with the memories of other characters of the respective novels.

Interestingly, beyond the human dynamics at play in this collective recollection, objects and materials emerge as significant elements that elicit memory, so to say. The characters' interactions with certain objects and materials triggers memory which is not always necessarily individual to them. By looking into examples from the novels, this discussion explores the role of material items in acquiring meaning and preserving memories through their tangible existence, often transcending the constraints of time and space. An overlapping revisit to Jeffrey Olick's "memory boom" and the consideration of objects as elicitors of memories can be found in Astrid Erll's consideration of how "[p]ainting, sculpture, architecture, Internet art, movies and novels all address themes such as the fragility of memory and the ideological implications of public commemoration" (Erll, *Memory in Culture* 66). Examples such as a woman's black eyeglasses becoming a reminder of xenophobic violence and an everyday fruit transforming into a conduit to a character's childhood recollections prove valuable in highlighting Erll's assertion within this discourse.

The history of the Caribbean region makes memory an indispensable aspect of its literary output. The experiences from pre-colonial, colonial, and postcolonial periods, respectively, created sediments of memories for the people, which, reminiscent of Halbwachs' idea of collective memory, remained ingrained in their common consciousness. Caribbean novelists like George Lamming, Jamaica Kincaid, Jean Rhys, Samuel Selvon, and V. S. Naipaul, among several others, have harnessed the collective memories in their works by the virtue of relevant themes, identifiable characters, and realistic stories. Their works are a testament to the fact that memory acts as a reservoir for drawing inspiration for such retellings, and the narratives and characters end up becoming vessels through which the memories are recreated for the readers to connect with. In the thick of the cultural, social, and racial diversities in the Caribbean, "memory" becomes the linchpin that holds together the past and present and often renders a peephole into the prospective events. Looking at the present study from this lens explains the engagement that the characters display with the lived individual past, the shared collective past, and the tangible materials as potential artifacts that elicit memory.

Author of three novels, a children's book, and a latest novella, Oonya Kempadoo is the winner of the 2002 Casa de las Americas Literary Prize. Kempadoo's novels lend a new perspective to the Caribbean literary canon as she utilizes the power of memory by weaving together the common experiences of the people from dynamic island countries with her own lived experiences. As a person of a rich and diverse cultural heritage, mixed with the fact of having lived part of her life in various Caribbean countries, Kempadoo allowed the experiences to be absorbed by her consciousness, and when the artistry of writing occurred to her, it was only natural that she produced works that mirrored the various aspects of social, cultural, professional, and personal incidents that were lived by the people.

Discussion

In an introductory article on the aim and scope of "Memory Studies" as a discipline, Henry Roediger and James Wertsch state that the emergence of "Memory Studies" in the 20th century as an overarching field of inquiry pulled under its ambit the subjects of sociology, history, philosophy, literature, psychology, and anthropology (Roediger and Wertsch). In the field of literature, particularly mentioning the genre of novels, Roediger and Wertsch identify the dual role that memory plays—the novelists make the characters within their novels utilize memory for guiding their actions and the plots, and simultaneously, the novelists utilize their own memories by diving deeper into the lived experiences to give shape to their works. While generally regarded as an intrinsic and private experience for a person, memory, in literature, does more than just hearken to the past. It helps build the emotive and psychological aspects of the story, often allowing the readers to make sense of the breadth of it. Eminent scholars like Astrid Erll, Aleida and Jan Assmann, Jeffrey K. Olick, Maurice Halbwachs, and others have made pioneering contributions in the field of memory studies, and their findings prove valuable in the analysis of the relation between memory and literature. Particularly in the case of Caribbean literature, it may be said that the history of colonization, immigration, and diasporic population have contributed to the creation of a common consciousness that makes the narratives of Caribbean literature a storehouse for memory studies. Being full of such incidents that emerge out of the vivid sociocultural forces in Caribbean islands, *All Decent Animals* (2013) and *Buxton Spice* (1998) prove to be suitable works for exploring the different facets of memory.

Set in Trinidad, *All Decent Animals* unwraps the complexities of the relationships and societal expectations surrounding the central characters. The novel primarily looks into the lives of Atalanta, a returnee in the island country of Trinidad; Pierre, the French man working in the United Nations; and Fraser, the now bed-ridden architect whose characterization presents him in the liminal space between European aesthetic and Trinidadian traditionality. Kempadoo's creation of Ata seems to be based greatly on memory—she models Ata after her own lived experiences, and fictionally, Ata creates an image of herself based on her childhood recollections and how she thinks the people around her see her. All these instances create a complex of memories in Ata's mind which guide her thoughts and actions within the novel. *Buxton Spice* tells the coming-of-age story of Lula as she explores the world around her with her sister Sammy, and friends Rachel and Judy. It is interesting to note that the story ties more than just personal memory to the narrative. Much of the progression in the novel, including that of Lula's character and the action, is informed by the collective, historical, and material memory tied to Guyanese culture. The story draws as much from the historical facts of the communal unrest in Guyana as from the personal memories of Lula as she joins the dots of lived experiences and the retellings that she receives from her parents and the neighbors.

Atalanta, the protagonist of *All Decent Animals*, who is better known as Ata, is a returnee in Trinidad. After having spent a good part of her life in Europe living the diasporic identity, Ata feels overwhelmed by the feeling of rootlessness which makes her feel like she does not belong to any true nation; rather, she is left stranded by the generalized label of "Caribbean." Stripped of her unique identity, Ata feels like "[a] nonbelonger. Unrooted in place and race and in herself" (Kempadoo, *All Decent Animals* 6). Thus, it may be said that the rootlessness in one's identity may occur as a result of the lack of affirmative cultural memories or the individual's non-identification with the cultural representations. That memory is not just a function of recollection is exemplified by Ata's case—disconnectedness from cultural memory is something that makes her feels disconnected with her personhood. What Sylvia Wynter writes in her essay on the Caribbean diaspora's collective memory of deracination mirrors the non-belongingness that Ata feels. Wynter describes the feeling as "one of uprootedness" (247), which stems from the fact that the geographical displacement of the Caribbean people from their homeland is also reflected in an emotional detachment or "exile" (247) from their cultural or historical foundations. The constant catapulting of the people between contrastive sociocultural settings may aggravate the feeling of detachment, explaining why the common collective memory of the Caribbeans had been, for a long time, painted by a sense of estrangement from their roots.

Carl Becker's essay on the relationship between history and memory becomes relevant here. Becker refers to each person as a historian and identifies history as an "artificial extension of the social memory" (122). Several instances from the novels illustrate the intricate relationship between history and collective memory. A prominent example of this is seen when Trinidad's economic conditions during the colonial period is referred to by Marriette's brother. He criticizes the contemporary mercantile conditions and compares them to the economic arrest that the Trinidadians were subjected to during colonial rule as the colonizer stakeholders controlled and manipulated the business such that the Trinidadians ultimately owed their savings and assets to their employers. While scrutinizing the persistence of "neocolonialism," Angelique V. Nixon, a Caribbean and Postcolonial studies scholar, attributes its endurance more to the lasting impact of enslavement and colonization on the "minds, bodies, and spirits of Caribbean people" (Nixon) than the external forces of enforcement. The pernicious aftermath of the colonial oppression is reflected in the Trinidadian people's internalized basement of themselves, which is what Marriette's brother criticizes when he mentions how the people were selling themselves short by surrendering their historical assets to the economic stakeholders. It is the history of colonial Trinidad that Marriette's brother invokes by comparing the contemporary times with the times gone by.

Common memory also shares ties with culture since practices within a culture often engender common practices which solidify in the mannerisms of the people from that culture. Something as commonplace as food, then, becomes an important marker of the common cultural memory. The bond that Ata and Fraser share becomes the perfect example of this—their shared Caribbean ancestry is what forges a link of common memory resulting from the common food practices that they both observed during their younger years. The taste and texture of sugar apples takes Fraser back to his childhood days, just like the thought of the sharp flavor of the chenet fruit elicits a drooling anticipation in Ata.

Ata's strong memories surrounding the ritual of fruit-eating presents an interesting revisit to Maurice Halbwachs' idea of memory being "recalled to [us] externally" (38). Ata's encounter with the unidentified man during her solo stay in Blanchisseuse shows how their shared memory of Caribbean culture is triggered by references to edible items. The man, in an intimate moment, associates Ata's scent with "bitter cocoa, boiling with bay leaves, cinnamon, and nutmeg," reminiscent of his childhood (Kempadoo, *All Decent Animals* 224). A similar effect is seen on Ata who, too, is reminded of the carefree times that she spent as a child in the island country. Ata's interaction with this person and the subsequent recollection of passionate engagement with the culinary and cultural experiences of the Caribbean as a child occurs at a time when she struggles with her self-identity owing to her swerving relationship with Pierre. Examining this episode through Halbwachs' idea reveals that Ata's recollection and reconnection with her Caribbean culture occur after encountering the unidentified man, which becomes the external force that helps Ata in her recollection.

Halbwachs' idea of the external recollection of memory further proves useful in understanding the role of materials and objects in this process. Quite reminiscent to this, Jan Assmann, in his 1988 essay, characterizes "cultural memory" as a repository encompassing "repeatedly used texts, images, and rituals" (qtd. in Grabes 35). These form the basis for establishing a continuity of cultural practices, actively influencing behaviors and, not unexpectedly, dictating the culturally "correct" way of observing certain practices. Ata, presumably drawing from past experiences, highlights the proper way to eat sugar apples: sitting outdoors, using hands without involving any plates, cutlery, or napkins. It can be said that it is, in part, a result of the common memory that strengthens Ata's conviction in declaring the proper way of eating sugar apples: sitting outdoors, using hands without the use of plates, cutlery, or napkins.

Examples from *All Decent Animals* challenge the traditional role of memory as a recollection tool. Henry Otgaar and others, in a study on repressed memories, affirm the presence of such memories arising from past traumatic experiences which remain repressed in the recesses of mind and are brought back to the cognitive surface when triggered by related stimuli. Unlike the instances so far that show the omnipresent interconnectedness of memory, Fraser Goodman's character in the novel reveals signs of memory repression. Fraser, a closeted homosexual man, vividly recalls the distressing moments when his mother, Mrs. Dorothy Goodman, mistreated him in an attempt to "straighten" (Kempadoo, *All Decent Animals* 100) him during his childhood. Dorothy's oppressive actions, including confining him to a secluded room, contribute to Fraser's suppressed memory, triggering what appears to be anxiety.

During a lunch invitation to Dorothy's house with Pierre and Ata, Fraser reverts to being the "overly sensitive, tremulously unhappy small boy" (Kempadoo, *All Decent Animals* 64) he used to be as a kid. This anxiety is noticed by his friend Alan, who attributes Fraser's vexation to either his "childhood nightmares or the lack of his mother's real connection to him" (Kempadoo, *All Decent Animals* 220). The common factor in all the times when Fraser's anxiety is triggered is his mother, with whom his strained relationship is not mended until the end of his life. Thus, recollection of his childhood memories with his mother in this case becomes an unwelcome episode for Fraser. One could argue that such recollections may be erroneous and lead to "false memory" (Otgaar) due to factors like time lapse, psychopathological conditions, etc., that intervene in the recollection process, however the possibility of inaccurate recollection is dismissed in Fraser's case. Fraser's horrifying memories remain repressed throughout his adult life till the time when he battles his impending fatality, but the accuracy of these repressed memories is testified to by Mr. Goodman's guilt-ridden nonverbal reaction when Fraser finally confronts his father for never consoling him in childhood for Dorothy's harsh treatment.

Through Fraser's character, Kempadoo approaches memory from various different angles. Ranging from the cultural memory retained from the experience of eating fruits as a child to the repressed memories from his traumatic childhood, Fraser's character proves pivotal in understanding the relevance of memory in everyday life. As much as Fraser dreads death and the episodes of his seizures, the news of his illness and impending fatality makes him more aware of the power of memory. This explains why he often consoles Ata and other friends to cheer up and use the time at hand to make beautiful memories to rejoice after his death. In his pursuit of creating fond memories for his friends, Fraser urges Terence not to visit him in his final days. Fraser does not wish for his affectionate bond with Terence to be marred by the parting memory of the former's frail body as he progressively slips towards his death.

Set in 20th-century Trinidad during a period of emerging independence, the pursuit of financial autonomy in *All Decent Animals* reflects the societal context. This also explains the remark by Marriette's brother on the neocolonial economic oppression and the need for the Trinidadians to break free of it. The novel further zooms into the aspect of women's financial independence, thereby invoking collective memory in its readers, particularly Trinidadian and diasporic readers. Ata's admiration for Angelica Diaz's prosperity highlights the scarcity of financially successful women in a community still grappling with establishing financial freedom. Independent women like Diaz serve as idols for young girls, representing a rarity in the novel's contemporary setting. When Ata sees young girls heading to school, she fondly imagines them growing up to become successful and independent women, which again shows that the financial independence that Diaz materialized for herself was still a dream for many young women in the contemporary times. The individual memory of Sammy's mother sheds light on her own past struggles and perseverance, illustrating the collective memory of numerous women of color silently fighting against adversity to forge their identities. Not once is Sammy's father mentioned in the novel, which hints that Sammy was raised solely by his mother. In retrospect, Sammy's mother recalls how her cooking not only provided for Sammy but also enabled her to clothe him and build their home. This recollection underscores the challenging financial conditions faced by women at the time, with Sammy's mother courageously overcoming obstacles to achieve self-dependence and freedom.

Kempadoo's treatment of memory follows through the material objects in *Buxton Spice*. Material memory, within literature, refers to the exploration of memory through physical objects and tangible elements that elicit memory across the spatial and temporal boundaries. Exploration of material memory, in *Buxton Spice*, is first found in the remnants of an ancient mosque that serves as a symbol of the passage of time while also retaining the memories related with the historical incidents of communal unrests in Guyana. What Astrid Erll says of memory being "inherently shaped by collective contexts" (Erll, *Cultural Memory Studies* 5) holds true in this example as the sight of the old mosque triggers a cascade of interconnected individual, material, and collective memories in Lula. The dilapidated mosque fills Lula's inquisitive mind with a range of memories—she thinks of the time when she visited a mosque with her father and Mr. Mohammed to pray but is also troubled by the thoughts of the communal unrests that she heard of from her mother.

The plight of Mr. Mohammed's family exemplifies the xenophobia that the South Asian communities faced in Guyana. The fortified windows and Mrs. Mohammed's black eyeglasses are a tell-tale sign of their suffering after incendiary glass bottles were hurled at them, resulting in Mrs. Mohammed's eye injury. Lula, though not a witness of this violence, senses the distress through their fortified windows, mimicking the horror of the tragedy faced by the family. Collectively, the deteriorated mosque, Mrs. Mohammed's eyeglasses, past incidents of social unrest, and the occurrence of hate crimes in the neighborhood collectively shape Lula's memories regarding the various cultural groups and their interactions in Tamarind Grove. The DeAbro household's "prized possession" (Kempadoo, *Buxton Spice* 67), the gramophone, is yet another object that serves as a link between the cultural and material aspects of memory. Mrs. DeAbro's son, Felix, who lives in Canada, helps the family get the gramophone that becomes a material equivalent of the elitism and refinement that the DeAbro and Rodriguez ladies associate with "Away"—the term they use for referring to Canada—which alienates them from their native identities. These examples show the ability of material objects to retain and elicit memories that are of significance either individually or collectively. Andrew Jones explains that recollection is not an isolated process, similar to the views expressed by Halbwachs. The stimuli for recollection that Jones identifies are objects or artifacts and he explains the process of remembrance as a "dialogic encounter" (Jones 25) occurring between the object that elicits the memory and the person who is remembering. The examples discussed above follow this explanation as the objects become essential components in the respective characters' recollection process.

To discuss Kempadoo's use of memory in the novels without acknowledging the use of autobiographical elements would overlook the subtle yet significant way memories transcend temporal boundaries. These autobiographical elements serve as a literary representation of past experiences, acting as an extension of life itself. In an interview with Harald Leusmann, Oonya Kempadoo discusses how her memories of early childhood and professional career helped shape her characters and their actions. Kempadoo's early years in "Golden Grove" were the inspiration for "Tamarind Grove" in *Buxton Spice* and her childhood memories of leisurely activities with friends strongly parallel Lula's life in the novel. Relayed from Lula's perspective, the narrative captures the collective memory of political atrocities in Guyana, revealing her innocent yet perceptive observation of racial and communal unrest. Lula's mother, Rose, appears partially modeled after Kempadoo's own mother, who, Kempadoo recollects, was faced with the "drastically wrong" (Leusmann 111) contemporary sociopolitical conditions in Guyana.

All Decent Animals too shows reflections from Kempadoo's life. Kempadoo created the character of Atalanta with inspiration from her memories of her graphic design work followed by participation in Carnival with Peter Minshall, mirroring Atalanta's comparable career in the novel—employed by Angelica Diaz's graphic design company and collaborating with Carnival designer Slinger. Kempadoo consciously incorporates aspects of her own life, youth, and career into her characters, preserving these memories for readers to resonate with, based on their own experiences. Her reliance on autobiographical memories makes several cases for memory as a tool for preservation and restoration of human experiences. She does not just rely on her individual memory in crafting the characters of her novel for the purpose of re-living and re-presenting her own experiences, but she creates a portal, so to say, through her works, which let the readers choose and identify with parts of the narrative, allowing them to take the works, either in part or whole, to facilitate their respective recollection processes.

All these examples of the multifarious utilization of memory in the novels illustrate how the nature and significance of memories can transform, shifting from individual to collective value. By relying on the robust custodianship of memory, Kempadoo enables the recollection of such experiences, emphasizing the pivotal role memory plays in bringing forth these vivid recollections she shares. This idea seems to align with what Tanja E. Bosch writes about memory studies. Bosch identifies the interdisciplinary applicability of the field of study by acknowledging the expansion that individual memories undergo and reach out for "broader dimensions of social memory" (2) which reinforce the links between each individual recollective process to lead to a meticulous social framework. The chapter completes a thematic circle by hearkening back to Erll's view of memories as constructs shaped by collective forces. The interconnectedness of the memories, as exemplified by the characters of Kempadoo's novels, is what imparts meaning and order to the vastness of memories, where the distinctions between individual, collective, and material memories blur, promoting the recollection as a shared experience occurring in the liminal spaces.

Conclusion

Memories often revolve around objects or events connected to cultural history, seamlessly blending individual recollections into the collective consciousness. Through her novels, Oonya Kempadoo illustrates the expansive role of memory in literature. Often confined to the realm of recollection in cognitive studies, Kempadoo utilizes memory to show the common experiences of Caribbean life, while retaining the specificity of her own relation to the memories. The novels under consideration demonstrate the unique role that memory plays in literature—by providing meaning to past events by connecting them with individuals experiences, and elaborating how the individual lives respectively get affected by those events to create a collective experience. Such a reconnection with the past also provides explanations for current conditions both at the individual and social levels. Through the novels *All Decent Animals* and *Buxton Spice,* Kempadoo delves into how memory operates as an integral part of life itself.

It can be said that the presence of multiculturalism in Caribbean nations is intricately linked with their colonial past, and all of it appears to play a pivotal role in shaping the collective cultural memory of its people. A common denominator that can be deduced from the views expressed by Andrew Jones, Maurice Halbwachs, and Astrid Erll is that recollection is not an isolated process and is often triggered or facilitated by external stimuli. As is seen in the examples from the novels, even the individual memories of the characters seem to be linked with either another character, an object, or an event. The interconnectedness of memory allows readers to trace an explanation for the thoughts and actions of the characters and also explains their recollection process. The cohesive factor driving all cognitive preservation is the recognition of the past. As is evident from the instances discussed in this chapter, there operates an interconnectedness between the characters and their surroundings which proves crucial in the recollection process, and to detach the individual character's recollection from its collective, cultural ties would erode the endurance of the collective Caribbean experience. Kempadoo proves successful in her deployment of memory as a tool for highlighting this interconnected collectiveness of the Caribbean consciousness, whose very ethos lies in its history of emerging as a bricolage of memories emerging from the experiences shared by different sociocultural groups.

Works Cited

Becker, Carl. "Everyman His Own Historian." *The Collective Memory Reader*, Edited by Jeffrey K. Olick et al., Oxford University Press, 2011, p. 122.

Bosch, Tanja E. *Memory Studies: A Brief Concept Paper*. University of Leeds, 2016.

Erll, Astrid. *Cultural Memory Studies: An International and Interdisciplinary Handbook*. Edited by Astrid Erll and Ansgar Nünning, Walter de Gruyter, 2008, p. 5.

Erll, Astrid. "Material Memory: Art and Literature." *Memory in Culture*, translated by Sara B. Young, Palgrave Macmillan, 2011, p. 66.

Grabes, Herbert. "The Value of Literature from Cultural Memory." *Literature and Cultural Memory*, Edited by Mihaela Irimia, et al, Brill Rodopi, 2017, p. 35.

Halbwachs, Maurice. "Preface." *On Collective Memory*, edited and translated by Lewis A. Coser, The University of Chicago Press, 1992, p. 38.

Jones, Andrew. "Memory and Material Culture?" *Memory and Material Culture,* Cambridge University Press, 2007.

Kempadoo, Oonya. *All Decent Animals*. Farrar, Straus and Giroux, 2013.

Kempadoo, Oonya. *Buxton Spice*. Phoenix House, 1998.

Leusmann, Harald. "An Interview with Oonya Kempadoo." *World Literature Written in English*, vol 39, no. 1, 2001, pp. 107–115. Taylor and Francis Online, https://doi.org/10.1080/17449850108589349. Accessed 23 December 2023.

Nixon, Angelique V. "Rethinking Sites of Caribbean Rebellion and Freedom." *Resisting Paradise: Tourism, Diaspora, and Sexuality in Caribbean Culture*, University Press of Mississippi/Jackson, 2015, Ch. 7.

Olick, Jeffrey K., et al. "Introduction." *The Collective Memory Reader*, Edited by Jeffrey K. Olick, Vered Vinitzky-Seroussi and Daniel Levy, Oxford University Press, 2011.

Otgaar, Henry, et al. "The Return of the Repressed: The Persistent and Problematic Claims of Long-Forgotten Trauma." *Perspectives on Psychological Science,* vol 14, no. 6, 2019, pp. 1072–1095. *Sage Journals,* https://doi.org/10.1177/1745691619862306. Accessed 5 January 2024.

Roediger, Henry L., and James V. Wertsch. "Creating a New Discipline of Memory Studies." *Memory Studies*, vol 1, no. 1, 2008, pp. 9–22. *Sage Journals*, https://doi.org/10.1177/1750698007083884. Accessed 30 December 2023.

Sandberg, Eric. "'The Past Is A Foreign Country': On the Nostalgia of Literature." *History, Memory and Nostalgia in Literature and Culture*, Edited by Regina Rudaitytė, Cambridge Scholars Publishing, 2018, pp. 25–37.

Wynter, Sylvia. "We Must Learn to Sit Down Together and Discuss a Little Culture: Reflections on West Indian Writing and Criticism." *The Routledge Reader in Caribbean Literature*, Edited by Alison Donnell and Sarah Lawson Welsh, Routledge, 1996, pp. 247–253.

21 Memory, Expectation and Failure in the Theatre and Film Productions of Tennessee Williams' *The Glass Menagerie*

A Case Study

Hindol Chakraborty

Memory, as we know, synthesizes and transports. Tennessee Williams, in his path-breaking play, *The Glass Menagerie* (Bottoms), has shown how memory becomes the most important tool in presenting 'the blurred' as the reality, or rather, the reality as 'the blurred'. Human beings, precisely, depend on memory. While creating a discourse, and understanding and maintaining the same by fusing different layers of memory, we establish our reality. Thus, blurriness remains dominant in creating our reality as a solid ground of experience and behavior. This very blurriness is the premise of the 'postmodern man' who finds himself confined inside a coffin, a chain that he wants to break but finally fails to do so. E. Ann Kaplan, while looking at Polanski's and Bertolucci's films as a tool of transportation in postmodern cinema, states,

> One of the inaugural films in this new "genre" (if that's what it is) was Lucas's *American Graffiti*, which in 1973 set out to recapture all the atmosphere and stylistic peculiarities of the 1950s United States, the United States of the Eisenhower era. Polanski's great film *Chinatown* does something similar for the 1930s, as does Bertolucci's *The Conformist* for the Italian and European context of the same period, the fascist era in Italy; and so forth.
>
> (Kaplan, 1988)

In *The Glass Menagerie* we find Amanda continuously looking back at her past to live in her present and to make her present better on the basis of her experience, namely, memory. This work will peep into the tendency of Williams's use of memory in creating a 'real' discourse and will investigate how memory, despite having its blurriness, is becoming the most essential glue to (re)create a premise of understanding, known as 'reality', both in the play and in Paul Newman's 1987 film adaptation of *The Glass Menagerie*. On the other hand, I shall also try to investigate Paul Newman's cinematic adaptation of Williams's phenomenal play to re-understand whether Newman succeeded in transporting his viewers to the original essence the theatrical production had. Tennessee Williams, in *The Glass Menagerie*, has shown

DOI: 10.4324/9781003508564-28

how memory, as the most important tool, becomes a means for both creating and demolishing the wall between reality and illusion. We must note that the play was premiered in the post-World War II era when the prevalent conceptions of human conditions and existence were changing. Universal holocaust threw the human race into a meaningless world. A strange crisis came, priorities changed. Human beings were waiting for a new hope that was not at all visible. Since reality was failing to provide any meaning, a tendency of escaping the same was being noticed in every form of art and expression. Tennessee Williams in *The Glass Menagerie* presents Tom Wingfield as the central character who is delivering the opening address to the audience from the fire escape and states that he is not a magician but he has tricks that may present the reality in the disguise of illusion or the illusion in the disguise of reality. This very illusion, as the main tool for escaping the unhappy reality or the present, becomes prominent in every character of the play. We see the characters crazily trying to escape and failing. In all cases, memory plays the most important role for establishing their real existence in a 'coffined' universe. Memory, in *The Glass Menagerie*, establishes itself as the most concrete foreground in evaluating and comprehending the real existences of the characters.

Memory, Memory Studies, and the Art of Expression

As far as art, more specifically painting, is concerned, "Abstract Expressionism" was applied to American art for the first time by art critic Robert Coates in 1946 (Coates, 1946), and it became an inseparable method of the works of several notable artists like Jackson Pollock, Willem de Kooning, and Mark Rothko. They, along with their contemporaries, focused on breaking the norms of conventional artistic modesty and delved into a language, primarily visual, that went beyond cultural and geographical boundaries, resulting in a highly innovative, vibrant, and influential work of art that significantly changed the whole journey of modern art (Anfam, 2016). I shall specifically discuss two of de Kooning's works, "Woman I" (1950–52) and "Excavation" (1950), that firmly create a bridge between memory, art, and expression so that we can investigate *The Glass Menagerie* from a stand-point built on memory studies.

De Kooning's paintings show a peculiar ability to convey emotional intensity and psychological depth through the use of expressive brushworks, strong color, and dynamics of compositions. Both "Woman I" (1950–52) and "Excavation" (1950) highlight the importance of memory and emotion in the artistic practice of de Kooning. "Woman I" is widely considered one of de Kooning's most important works where we trace a highly abstracted female figure that is powerful and provocative (Elderfield, 2011). The painting is thought to be influenced by the artist's memories of his mother and other female figures from his childhood in the Netherlands (Stevens & Swan, 2005). The composition has aggressive brushwork, intense color, and distorted forms that, together, convey a sense of turmoil and complexity which is both emotional and psychological, reflecting de Kooning's phenomenological experiences and feelings. In "Excavation," de Kooning creates a densely layered, intricate composition that has been interpreted as an exploration of his own memories and unconscious mind (Elderfield, 2011). The dynamic interplay of shapes, lines, and colors in the painting evoke a sense of movement and energy, suggesting a constant process of excavation and discovery within the artist's psyche (Stevens & Swan, 2005). The painting's intensity and quality, in both emotional and expressive levels, further stress the role of memory and emotion in de Kooning's work.

The above-mentioned examples illustrate the significance of memory and emotion in de Kooning's artistic understanding and the development of his unique approach to abstraction. By working on his own experiences and feelings, de Kooning was able to create powerful, emotionally charged paintings that continue to evoke the intensity and passion for these feelings in viewers.

Memory operates in *The Glass Menagerie* as both the clarifying and the distorting lens in understanding the reality of the actions. Memory, as a tool of artistic expressions, has always been present in formation of art, both in visual and performativity. I, from this premise, shall now look at *The Glass Menagerie* and re-examine how memory plays a pivotal role in creating the 'presents' of the characters found in the play.

The Glass Menagerie at a Glance

As the play unfolds, we see that Amanda Wingfield, abandoned many years ago by her husband, lives in an apartment with her two grown-up children, Laura, a shy and slightly crippled daughter, and Tom, a frustrated young man who works in a shoe factory and dreams of adventure all the time. Amanda is a strong woman who would triumph all odds to get the best for her children. She keeps bothering Tom beyond the limits of his endurance, with matters ranging from table manners to finding a gentleman suitor for Laura. At the same time, she tries to impose her shattered dreams on the life of her reclusive daughter Laura. Due to her physical infirmity, Laura has developed a strong inferiority complex and proved herself to be a failure at every level. Amanda is aware of the gloomy future and the faint marriage prospects of her daughter. So Amanda pesters Tom to bring home for dinner a suitable young man for Laura to get familiar to, and eventually get married to. Finally, Tom brings home Jim O'Connor, one of Tom's friends working with him in the shoe factory. Amanda has made detailed preparations at home to receive Jim, the gentleman suitor. She has not only dressed Laura up for the occasion, but also presented herself in her best attire, and given the Wingfield apartment a makeover. Everything goes well until Jim comes to know the Wingfields' intention behind the dinner organized in his honor. To his great surprise, Jim realizes that he is regarded as a gentleman caller by the Wingfields. Jim tells them that he has been going steady with a girl and will be married to her soon. The Wingfields' sandcastle crumbles. The equations of their relationships are badly affected. The balance they have been maintaining for so long is upset, and nothing will ever be the same again. Amanda cannot believe her own ears when Tom tells her that he had no clue that Jim was engaged to be married. A desperate and furious Amanda shouts at Tom in accusation.

AMANDA: That's right, now that you've had us make such fools of ourselves. The effort, the preparations, all the expense! The new floor lamp, the rug, the clothes for Laura! All for what? To entertain some other girl's fiancé! Go to the movies, go! Don't think about us, a mother dressed, an unmarried sister who's crippled and has no job! Don't let anything interfere with your selfish pleasure! Just go, go, go – to the movies.
TOM: All right, I will! The more you shout about my selfishness to me the quicker I'll go, and I won't go to the movies!
AMANDA: Go, then! Go to the moon – you selfish dreamer!
(Williams 85)

With his patience exhausted, he would take no more of his mother's stifling demands on him. Nothing can keep him any more at home, not even the feeling of sympathy he has for Laura. He leaves home, as his father did years ago, in pursuit of a more adventurous life. Laura withdraws into the world of her glass figurines.

As Tom tells us right at the beginning, *The Glass Menagerie* is a memory play; and it is both sentimental and non-realistic. The dramatic action is the sentimental recollections of Tom as he returns to visit the lower-middle-class apartment house in St. Louis, where he lived with his mother and sister before he, like his father, deserted them, following the fiasco of the gentleman caller arranged for Laura. As he reaches what was once his home, but which is now completely deserted, reminiscences of the past begin to fill his mind. He recalls the time he spent there, and his mother and sister; he also recalls his father, the mysterious man in the portrait hanging on the wall, who fell in love with long distances and deserted the family. More importantly, he recalls the events leading to his own departure from home, leaving his mother and sister behind. Tom's nostalgic recollections constitute the non-realistic action of the play. It is non-realistic because it is Tom's memory after all. Before our very eyes, Tom turns time back "to that quaint period, the thirties, when the huge middle class of America was matriculating in a school for the blind" (Williams 4), and to the time of the Great Depression, the Spanish Civil War, and the political and labor unrest of the 1930s. C. R. Deepa Ratna writes:

> As the great depression has left many men unemployed, they began finding solace in alcohol, left their families and never returned.
> (Deepa Ratna 1009)

The social background of the play, by creating a sense of urgency, intensifies the personal conflicts, which heightens the drama. Then in Scene 1, Tom puts us in touch with the poignant story of his ill-fated family, "in the pleasant disguise of illusion" (Williams 4). Soon we find ourselves in the world of his memory.

Non-realism in *The Glass Menagerie*, the Film

The Glass Menagerie was first made into a film by Irving Rapper in 1950. Williams called the adaptation the most awful travesty of a play he had ever seen. In the opinion of Maurice Yacowar, the film serves as a textbook demonstration of how insensitive compromises can ruin a film adaptation. Adapting *The Glass Menagerie* was not an easy task. Another adaptation scripted by Tennessee Williams himself and directed by Anthony Harvey came in 1973. Harvey's film is considered much better than that of Rapper. The film, like the play, opens with Tom (John Malkovich) returning to his abandoned apartment house in St. Louis. Except for the opening shot, the entire film is shot in the apartment itself, making the audience feel extremely claustrophobic, and, as a result, at the end of the film, all that one wants to do is to leave the apartment, and perhaps never return. Climbing up the fire escape, Tom finds the apartment abandoned, the windows broken, and the floor of the house cluttered with debris. As he looks about the house, his recollections of the past begin to emerge from the layers of his memory like silent phantoms. He lights a cigarette and begins his long introduction to this memory play. As he finishes the introduction, we find ourselves in the midst of the dramatic action, which will take us to Tom's second departure from the apartment at the end of his nostalgic reminiscences, this time never to return.

The special characteristics of the play, namely, its filmic, poetic, and non-realistic aspects along with its theatricality, cause various problems in the process of adaptation:

> Williams conceived *The Glass Menagerie* in a nonrealistic mode, with expressionistic lighting and music and with a filmic flaw of short scenes. But the filmic elements in a theatrical production may not work the same way when used in a film.... Williams seems to forestall any filming of the play, when he cited in his production notes the "unimportance of the photographic in art." Reality is "an organic thing which the poetic imagination can represent, or suggest, in essence, only through transformation.
>
> (Yocwar 9)

Newman decided to make the film with absolute fidelity to the stage play, perhaps because of the filmic nature of the play. What he overlooked was the fact that just as the poetic dimensions in each genre of literature work quite differently from the other, the poetic dimension of a play is bound to be different from that of a film adaptation of the play. The element of poetry is not an easy thing to capture on screen through photographic realism. Still, any adaptation of a stage play is bound to be quite theatrical while the basic requirement of screen adaptation is to make a film, at least as cinematic as theatrical, if not more. The dramatic action in the film is advanced and the tension sustained purely through the means of spoken words. This is more the technique of the theatre and less of the screen. Newman does not give visual representation to most of what is brought on stage primarily through spoken words; what is worse is that he does not succeeded in striking the fine balance between visual and verbal representations in the film. As the film begins, we see Tom walking towards a huge rundown building. As the camera follows Tom, or rather, as we follow Tom, he suddenly turns and looks at us for a while, as if he wants to tell us something to our face, or is annoyed at being followed. He goes up to the closed door of the building and tries it. Unable to open the door, he walks towards the fire escape of the building. He stops abruptly again, looks at us for a while and moves ahead and climbs the fire escape. The camera pans up the stairs that lead to his apartment, leaving Tom behind. Soon we find ourselves in the apartment waiting for Tom. The opening shots are built on suspense. Our anxiety and impatience are heightened. The camera pans across the broken windows, dilapidated walls, and the scattered debris of the deserted flat. Tom lights a cigarette and begins his introduction. Roberta Costa mentions: "The camera plays an important role in the film; it can be defined the fifth character on scene. It is not just a device; it is a curious and even voyeuristic observer that works in order to surprise the audience" (Costa 110).

Amanda Plays Her Memory, or the Memory Plays Amanda?

Amanda Wingfield is probably the most crucial character in *The Glass Menagerie*. Through her, Williams portrays the confusion between reality and illusion. We see her recalling her youth when she used to be charming and attend gentleman callers. Astrid Erll, in her discussion on commemorative memory, states,

> Among the "usual suspects" of interdisciplinary memory studies are forms of explicit, identity-creating, and often official commemoration – acts of memory in any case, which actors are aware of. Such conscious acts of memory are an important, visible and much discussed part of memory culture.
>
> (Erll, 2022).

Amanda thus lives (in reality) in an illusion that she is still such a desirable woman. Throughout the play Amanda tries to carry her memory and its experience onto her daughter Laura, and by doing so, she attempts to bring her memory back to her real life afresh. Tom actually commemorates the tragic existence of his family and as he declares it as a memory play, we understand that the narrative will operate in the flashback mode. Amanda remains in her illusion in order to find perfection in her reality and creates a make-believe world. Memory here as a tool creates passage between illusion and reality and transports the characters from one to the other. It leaves Amanda in a world that fluctuates between these two premises. She uses her memory as the escape mechanism to endure her present position in life. The story of her attending seventeen gentleman callers in a single evening has been told so many times that it finally becomes her reality. The tragedy of Amanda is that despite all her attempts she fails to escape her reality.

Tom and the 'Memory' Play

Tom Wingfield is the protagonist of *The Glass Menagerie* and he is seen to address the audience from the fire escape of their apartment. The fire escape signifies his attempt to escape the fire of his reality. Whatever happens on stage is based on Tom's memories and he declares that they are sometimes clear and sometimes blurred. If we depend on our memory that was once our present, a blurriness remains in between clarity and non-clarity. Memory is identified with the illusions of the characters throughout the play. Tom, whenever he addresses us, is in the uniform of a navy officer. This states that Tom is in his reality now which is different than the play, and that the reality is changed from the memory he is talking about. We notice that the stage is dimly lighted and the play is enormously sentimental, and thus, it is not realistic. Tom's father, Mr. Wingfield, who is only present in the photograph, signifies the bridge between the past (memory) and the present (reality). The portrait rather evokes the memory in a memory. We, as audience, get involved with the on-stage actions as if it is the reality, despite knowing that they are coming out of Tom's memory and ultimately confuse the non-reality with reality.

Laura, Her Illusion, and the 'Memory'

Laura has been presented as the most fragile character in the play. She, although Amanda tries her best to project her as Amanda's youthful counterpart, is a character truly out of the realistic world. Amanda admitted Laura in a business school and painfully discovers that she was not attending the classes. Laura never enables herself to cope with the 'real' universe. Here, too, memory plays an important role as we learn that Laura had a high school crush, Jim O'Connor. She and Jim attended the music sessions and he asked her nickname. Laura misunderstood the question and thought that Jim was asking about her disease. She replied that she had Pleurisies and Jim thought it was 'blue roses'. This memory remains as a wound in Laura's existence and has been instrumental in her gradual withdrawal from reality. Bert Cardullo examines: "She is too good for this world, the Romantics might say, and for this reason she could be said to be sadly beautiful or bluely roseate" (Cardullo 85). As her escape mechanism, she chooses to live in her own world of illusion crowded by the glass miniature models of animals, the glass menagerie. Here Laura's memory operates as a tool to transport her from reality to illusion. Laura has crippled legs and Amanda never allows Tom to call her 'crippled' or abnormal as she believes that Laura has possessed enough charm to seduce the gentleman callers. Amanda lives in her own past old days through Laura. In a particular situation, it is disclosed that Tom's colleague Jim is coming to meet Laura as her suitor. This very Jim was Laura's high school infatuation and when they meet Laura collapses. Her memory collapses her in her present.

Memory on the Front Seat

In the opening scene of *The Glass Menagerie*, the stage direction states:

> The scene is memory, and is therefore nonrealistic. Memory takes a lot of poetic license. It omits some details; others are exaggerated.
>
> (Williams 4)

The shades of the play are created by the points of view of Tom who is acting both as the character and the narrator. He, like the other characters, is surrounded by illusion. Music and symbolism also play significant roles throughout. Tom declares that the play's lack of realism along with its high drama, too perfect symbolism, and frequent use of music are because of its origin in memory. We know that fictional works are derived from imagination and they must convince their audience that they are something else by being realistic. A play that is drawn from memory is thus a product of reality and it apparently has no need to drape itself over the conventional mode of realism in order to seem real. The creator of such a work can cloak the true story in fathomless layers of melodrama and metaphors and still remain firm in its substance and reality. This privilege is fully used by both Tennessee Williams and Tom Wingfield. We have noted that Tom is not the only character haunted by memory. Amanda, too, lives in a continuous pursuit of her past, of her bygone youth. She clings to the old records of her childhood exactly as Laura binds herself with her glass animals. For all of them, memory is the only crippling force that prevents them from discovering solace in the present reality of the offerings of the future. Still, in the case of Tom, memory is the vital force that enables him to act the course of the play in the path of achieving artistic creation. Thus, in *The Glass Menagerie*, memory 'is' the play. It evokes the illusions of the characters. In the case of Laura, memory transforms her reality and then becomes the memory again when Jim tells her that he is not yet married, but is engaged. Memory, both as the theme and the technique in this play, becomes one.

Film and Theatre: The Cosplay

To adapt a work of art has an aim to transport it from one medium to another, retaining or recreating the basic features and significance of the original one into the new medium. The challenge in adapting a literary or theatrical work into a film lies in transposing the true essence of the work from its literary or theatrical matrix to that of film. In translating a novel, a short story, or a play, one must translate ideas as well as descriptive events into appropriate visual analogues pregnant with meaning; an act of transcreation actually. The film-maker should not only arrest the story of the literary original in visual images on the screen, but also translate the narrative and the dramatic dynamics of the work onto the screen. The formal and rhetorical narrative devices of the text must be realized through the techniques of film. Bernard Shaw's remark on adaptation is very expressive in this case. He phenomenally comments, "Do not treat my printed text with blindly superstitious reverence. It must always be adapted intelligently to the studio, the screen, the stage, or whatever the physical conditions of performance may be" (Dukore 166).

Conventional notions of the superiority of literature to film often dominate the adaptation discourse. Robert Stam, in his Introduction to *Literature and Film*, says, "First it derives from the a priori valorization of historical anteriority and seniority: the assumption, that is, that older arts are necessarily better arts" (4). Literature thus automatically assumes superiority over the filmic adaptation of it, firstly by virtue of its being the older art between the two, and secondly by being the source of the adaptation. If we try to look at the process of adaptation with our preconceived ideas of the superiority of the literary work, concepts such as fidelity or infidelity, preservation or deformation become the tools or premises for our evaluation of the merits or the demerits of a work of adaptation. In such a case, the film-maker primarily has three significant alternatives: (1) to remain truthful to the literary work following its chain of events in a systematic way while translating them into images so that the work remains intact; (2) to use the original merely as a background or an inspiration; and (3) to radically re-interpret the text while remaining faithful to the spirit of the literary one.

Tennessee Williams and Paul Newman: The Lack(s)

Paul Newman's adaptation of Williams's *The Glass Menagerie* is a typical example of the actual translation of a play into a film. As he was obsessed with fidelity to the original, Newman wanted to make his film as close to Williams's classic play as possible, forgetting the fact that "the success of movie versions of plays is measured by the extent to which the script rearranges and displaces the action and deals less than respectfully with the spoken text" (Sontag 28). Newman's version of the play was not conceived in authentically cinematic terms, and as a consequence, we got rather a poor adaptation. In order to reach the expectations of the audience, screen adaptations of classics often try to remain true to the original through an almost literal translation of the text into the film. The question of faithfulness, however, is a controversial and liquid issue. The very idea of a ditto extractable meaning or nectar in a text has been severely challenged by the Poststructuralist critics, for whom any text is an assortment of images and symbols. Since a literary work is no exception, it erupts at various angles in place of a single extractable meaning, and hence, has possibilities of multiple interpretations. "In fact, when critics refer to the 'spirit' or 'essence' of a literary text what they usually mean is the critical consensus within an 'interpretative community' (Stanley Fish) about the meaning of the work" (Stam 15). In the background of the complex modern hermeneutics, the question of fidelity to the original in film adaptation becomes much more problematic. It actually produces an inferior clone in its attempt to reach public expectations. In *Novels into Film*, George Bluestone talks about Lester Asheim's findings in this regard:

> Lester Asheim in his sample of twenty-four film adaptations, found that seventeen increased the love emphasis; that sixty-three per cent of all the films in the sample had a romantic happy ending, but forty per cent (one fourth of the entire sample) required an alteration of the story to accomplish it; and that in no case was a negative ending retained.
>
> (42)

Conclusion

Memory, thus, as a tool, plays vibrantly both in the theatrical production and film adaptation of *The Glass Menagerie* to create the foreground of 'real' understandings of the characters. Memory has always been considered to be a major topic in creating and comprehending modern literature, art, and films. Marcel Proust's seven-volume *A la recherché du temps perdu* (Proust) started this trend. The text deals with smell and taste that erupt from deep memory, a potential that science subsequently has proved as possible. Like Tennessee Williams, in writings of towering figures of modern literature such as James Joyce, Virginia Woolf, or William Faulkner, memory has played an important role in pursuing the issue of how we know what we know. Scientists continue to study the operational methods of memory. Recent researches and understandings look at memory as a shift from the brain's hippocampus to the cortex, or as storing either elaborated (episodic) or factual (semantic) data. Hence, parts of the information remain and parts slip away and indeed the parts are capable to shape the fictional past as the actual past. We notice quite a similar function of memory in *The Glass Menagerie,* both in the stage production and the filmic treatment on screen; in creating a passage between illusion and reality of the characters because perhaps remembering itself can affect the nature of the memory. At the same time, the film adaptations have attempted a realistic presentation of the play but failed due to lack of usage of the language that film itself has.

Works Cited

Anfam, D. *Abstract Expressionism* (2nd ed.). Thames & Hudson, 2016.

Bluestone, George. *Novels into Films*. Johns Hopkins University Press, 1957.

Bottoms, Stephen (ed.). *The Glass Menagerie*. Bloomsbury India, 2014.

Cardullo, Bert. "The Blue Rose of St. Louis: Laura, Romanticism, and *The Glass Menagerie*." *The Tennessee Williams Annual Review*, vol. 1, 2001, p. 85.

Coates, R. M. "The Art Galleries: A Great Painter." *The New Yorker*, April 1946, pp. 34–37.

Costa, Roberta. "Tennessee Williams's The Glass Menagerie: Three Movies for One Play. 2015–2016." Universita Ca'Foscari Venezia, Master's Degree Programme Thesis. http://dspace.univ.it. Accessed 18 June 2023.

Deepa Ratna, C. R. "Great Depression in Tennessee Williams's *The Glass Menagerie.*". *Journal of Emerging Technologies and Innovative Research*, vol. 6, no. 3, 2019, p. 1009.

Dukore, Bernard F. "Bernard Shaw: The Director as Dramatist." *JSTOR Collection*. Penn State University Press, vol. 35, no. 2, 2015, pp. 136–167.

Elderfield, J. *De Kooning: A Retrospective*. Museum of Modern Art, 2011.

Erll, Astrid. *The Hidden Power of Implicit Collective Memory*. Memory, Mind & Media, 2022, pp. 1-17.

Kaplan, E. Ann (ed.). *Postmodernism and its Discontents*. Verso, 1988.

Proust, Marcel. *A la recherché du temps perdu, Volume 1-2*. Gallimard, 1919. https://googlebooks.com. Accessed 6 July 2023.

Sontag, Susan. *Sontag on Film*. Hamish Hamilton, 2017.

Stam, Robert. *Literature and Film: A Guide to the Theory and Practice of Film Adaptation*. Willey-Blackwell, 2004

Stevens, M., & Swan, A. *De Kooning: An American Master*. Alfred A. Knopf, 2005.

Williams, Tennessee. *The Glass Menagerie*. Penguin Books, 2009.

Yocwar, Maurice. *Tennessee Williams and Film*. F. Ungar Publishing Company, 1977.

22 Voices of Resonance

Cultural Decolonization through Collective Memory within Indigenous Literatures of Canada

Urmi Sengupta

Memory Studies, in keeping with its revolutionary approach towards the 'truth claim' of subjective memory, invites an interrogation of the coercive invalidation of the memory of the marginalized as orchestrated by the power-centre of any nation. With a firm determination to explore the intriguing yet hardly explored relationship between memory and history, the discipline often strives to look into the distortion, misrepresentation and repression of the memory of the disempowered that overshadows the construction of the official discourse of history of a settler colony. The power politics underlining the settler colonization of Canada emerges to be a fertile ground for such critical engagements. The basic difference in the historical consciousness of the Native-Canadian populace and their English/French colonizers constructs a well-structured rationale for the so-called European 'civilizing mission' that the colonized have been subjected to, for over five hundred years. Being members of an oral culture, the Aboriginal people of Canada have encapsulated their traditional knowledge of survival within a rich repertoire of oral narratives and disseminated it through inter-generational storytelling sessions, since pre-colonial times. However, the hierarchical oral/written binary deeply rooted within the Western worldview induces the colonizer to dismiss the indigenous culture and civilization, as 'primitive' as opposed to the more 'modern' one of their own. Such an attitude helps justify colonization through the problematic discourse of the 'White-Man's burden' of 'civilizing' the 'savage Indians', who do not have chronologically documented (written) linear progressive understanding of history, within their traditional oeuvre of knowledge.

It is only because of such an overbearing grand narrative encompassing colonialization that the Native-Canadians have long been (mis)represented in mainstream media and academia through the colonizer's gaze and the Euro-Canadian version of history has been established as the unquestionable monolithic 'Truth' within and beyond the borders of Canada. When historian Pattrick Hutton acknowledges that "the meaning of history is dependent upon the structures to which facts are fitted" (Hutton 535), it is such 'structures' of oppression that he hints at – ones that expose the cracks and fissures within the so-called 'multicultural mosaic' of the nation that claims to provide equal rights and privileges to its racially diverse population. The act of

DOI: 10.4324/9781003508564-29

positing the indigenous historical consciousness as an equally viable way of understanding and interpreting the past has the potential to subvert the colonial discourse of history. But it was not before the latter half of the twentieth century that this much-needed intervention into the colonial machinations of history-writing gained momentum, through a deliberately orchestrated process of blurring the hitherto sharp edges of the oral/written binary in the literary works of the pioneering indigenous writers of Canada.

As two of the first-generation indigenous literary artists credited to have used the colonizers' language (English) and their medium of expression, i.e. writing, as effective weapons against colonial atrocities, the Okanagan writer, educator, visual artist and publisher Jeannette Armstrong (b. 1948) and the Salish-Cree performing artist, storyteller and activist Lee Maracle (1950–2021) have been instrumental in mapping the subversive potential of orality in questioning the power structures that have repressed the marginal voices of the disempowered for ages. Their illustrious literary careers bear testimony to a conscious yet organically spontaneous attempt to inscribe the traditional 'oral' within the folds of the contemporary 'written' in such a way as to highlight the importance of collective memory, communal remembrance and the intuitive art of listening in forging an alternative 'history' for their respective communities. This 'history' is not only a repository of their pre-colonial ancestral knowledge and culture but also encapsulates those narratives of racial discrimination, encroachment of aboriginal rights and a dismissive denial of the indigenous value systems that hardly receive the attention they deserve at a national and an international level. In the light of Maracle's *Ravensong* (1993) and Armstrong's *Whispering in Shadows* (2000), two seminal novels that highlight the coming-of-age experiences of indigenous youths in relentless negotiation with colonial forces of cultural assimilation, this chapter aspires to explore the significance of this collective communal memory in building an active resistance against colonial oppression, subvert the systemic and systematic erosion of cultural autonomy and overhaul the forces of political disempowerment that have overshadowed the lived experiences of the indigenous people of Canada for centuries.

Lee Maracle, a member of the Stó-lo (Coast Salish) First Nation from British Columbia, was one of the earliest to bring about a momentous shift in the popular perception of the indigenous population from being meek and submissive victims of racism to being active warriors who registered their decisive protest against colonial oppression through the power of the pen, through her autobiographical work *Bobbi Lee: An Indian Rebel* (1975). It hardly comes as a surprise therefore that Armstrong, who began her literary career a decade after, lauded her for the very fact that "This book [*Bobbi Lee: An Indian Rebel*] was spoken at a time when writing was not considered to be a 'useful' endeavour in the ongoing struggle of our people" (Armstrong, "Foreword" 15). This self-proclaimed "recently decolonized woman" (Maracle, *Bobbi Lee* 1) then went on to pen her first novel *Ravensong*, in which she moved another step towards decolonizing of the indigenous mind by exemplifying her firm opinion that instead of being in opposition to each other, 'oratory' and 'writing' should go hand in hand in a way that the very process of artistic creation emerges to be one of 'healing' the scars inflicted upon her community by the years of displacement from the traditional lands, the encroachment upon the hunting, gathering and fishing rights, a systematic imposition of the language of the oppressor through the Euro-Canadian education system and formal restriction on certain cultural practices that had been integral to the Salish identity even in the early colonial times.

The ethical and psycho-social turmoil that the seventeen-year-old exuberant protagonist Stacey is subjected to, bears testimony to this unconventional yet poignant attempt at locating the oral and written at the crossroads of the contemporary colonized existence of Canadian aboriginality. She is faced with a perpetual tussle between an organic urge to adhere to her Salish heritage and a desire to be accepted and welcomed into the Euro-Canadian social circles that have opened up to her, courtesy of her Western schooling experience. Her conscious attempt at unlearning the oral/written binary rooted within her Euro-Canadian education by engaging with the ancestral tales, dream visions of the community Elders' ceremonial speeches, trickster myths, grief songs and the creation stories, as postulated in her essay 'Preface: You Become the Trickster', highlights the urgent need "to integrate two mediums: oratory and European story" (Maracle, *Sojourner's Truth* 11) within the indigenous storytelling practice. Though the outcome of such an integrated approach often boasts of a rising action–climax–falling action structure, typical to Western storytelling, the unfolding of events often tends to defy the boundaries' linear progressive chronological time. Situating the events within the circular value-loaded time of indigenous consciousness emerges to be a more viable practice. An open-ended multi-perspective suggestiveness that leaves room for pluralistic interpretations replaces the traditional Western structure of conflict resolution. This stance foregrounds the legacy of indigenous oral storytelling which would grant as much autonomy of expression and interpretation to the audience as to the oral narrator. Inscribing the 'oral' within the 'written', thus, culminates in a Native-Canadian culture-specific intervention within the generic framework of a novel – one that harps upon the need to re-evaluate an oral tradition mostly dismissed as 'imaginary', 'pre-modern', 'unscientific' and therefore, an 'inauthentic' resource for delving into the past of the settler colony and its plethora of indigenous population. The Anishinaubae storyteller Kateri Akiwenzie-Damm's call for refraining to implement what she refers to as "the cookie cutter approach" (Dattaray, "Images" 91) highlights the need to stop using Western parameters to interpret and evaluate indigenous literature, and the pioneering step towards that end would be an acceptance of the validity of a consciousness of time and history starkly different from one's own.

As a writer keen on formal experiments, Maracle aspires "to make new memories for her people as a backward and forward visionary that is as someone who connects the generations" (Fee et al. 206) by resorting to this special historical consciousness in the most pivotal narratorial junctures of the novel. The catastrophe about to strike Stacey's rural community finds a singular but befitting premonition in her young sister Celia's poignant narrative filled with a strange expectant silence which is permeated by visions from a past, safely encapsulated within her collective communal memory which has impacted the worldview of her grandmother, mother and, in turn, her as an individual. The evocation of the traumatic memory of mass genocide following the arrival of the early European settlers in 'tall ships' emerges to be in complete contradiction to the official history of Canada which has been constructed to justify the colonial agenda of these 'pioneer' settlers. Sharply skewed towards the colonizers' standpoint, the latter highlights how the indigenous populace were almost begging to be 'discovered', 'saved' and 'civilized' by the gallant 'white' settlers. Native-Canadian scholar Renate Eigenbrod interrogates the sinister politics underlying the oral/written dichotomy perpetuated by the colonizer in "The Oral in the Written: A Literature between Two Cultures":

> Those who know how to write are in control and use their power to appropriate land that is not theirs. Oral communication on the other hand includes the ability to remember "it" (the injustice) and therefore function as a weapon, as a means of defense.
>
> (Eigenbrod 90)

No wonder these 'injustices' are often pushed under the carpet to make way for dominant narrative of the 'brave' and 'masculine' European pioneer-settlers 'conquering' the harsh landscape, bitterly cold climate and the 'savage tribes' to establish control over the land and name it 'Canada'. The etymological roots of this name lies in the Spanish word 'Acanada' or 'nothing here', making the nomenclature of the country itself an act of colonial politics. Thus indigenous 'remembrance' proves to be intrinsic to an effective decolonizing of the official history of Canada. The Hong Kong flu epidemic of 1954 that wreaks havoc within Stacey's village is juxtaposed with her vision of a yesteryear epidemic that ravaged the community during her grandmother's childhood. Both the catastrophes bring to light the complete apathy of colonizers in the face of such exponential loss of indigenous lives. While the community Elder Ella, who was a witness to the older epidemic, survives to relive the trauma of ailing Salish men dying without medical attention on the streets of the 'white town', the current epidemic, too, reduces the community to a hapless victim of 'a hierarchy of care': "Under the shabby arguments about hospitals being full and doctors already overworked lay an unspoken assumption: White folks were more deserving of medical care than us" (Maracle, *Ravensong* 69). This attitude serves to uncover the Euro-Canadians' lack of concern for the wellbeing of people they have historically professed to 'protect' and take complete responsibility of. It hardly comes as a surprise, therefore, that they fail to understand or respect the ecological ethics of the indigenous population, and consequently realize the seriousness of the adversities caused by the steady destruction of their ancestral territories through the industrial and urbanizing endeavours of the colonizer.

The Aboriginal people of Canada are deeply connected to their land – it is, in fact, a microcosm of their entire cultural repertoire. Furthermore, man and nature do exist in a mutually exclusive and dichotomous relationship within the indigenous worldview – the entire 'living world' for them is a beautifully codependent interacting universe. Every animate or inanimate facet of nature consists of what the Cherokee storyteller Thomas King considers to be "All my Relations" (King ix) – a part of a Native-Canadian family, connected to its human members by carefully nurtured bonds of respect and responsibility. Being an attentive listener and an empathic receiver of the messages sent out by the land and nature, thus, emerges to be imperative to the community's survival. Celia acts as a safety net to the antics of her sister Stacy who is ready to compromise with her larger responsibilities to fulfil her dreams of studying at the University of British Columbia and curving her niche within the 'white' society. Her years-long engagement with the indigenous ethics helps her grasp the implications of the interactions between Cedar and the trickster Raven. The message encoded within these conversations, however, keeps eluding Stacey till she learns to accept her indigenous identity with pride and conviction, as a part and parcel of her post-epidemic self-realization. As Maracle postulates in *Oratory: Coming to Theory* (1990), it is the flagbearers of the oral legacy who can truly fathom the significance of the Native-Canadian worldview, because "an orator is simply someone who has comes to grips with the human condition, humanity's relationship to creation, and the need for a human direction that will guarantee the peaceful coexistence of human beings with all things under creation" (11). An effective revival of the subversive zeal inherent within the collective communal memory within the rich gamut of written cultural creations thus functions as the most productive method to ensure remembrance, retention, revival and intergenerational perpetuation of such collective morality that reflects the 'mentality' (*mentalites*) (Le Goff 166) of the Aboriginal people of Canada – ones that highlights the "comingled beliefs, practices…images, myths, values recognized and tolerated by a society" (Confino 1389). A detailed analysis of the communal memory emerges to be largely synonymous to the in-depth critical engagement with the collective mentality of these communities.

The Native-Canadian cultural consciousness has, therefore, held the key to the collective mentality of the community since eons. Whether it is Stacey, come to care for her 'sister Cedar' with as much tenderness as her human sister Celia, or whether it is Will, the teenager protagonist of *Will's Garden* (2010) who respects "Ol' Gramma moon" (Maracle, *Will's Garden* 1) with as much fervour as his own ailing grandmother – every young-adult character of Maracle's literary universe seem to re-emphasize them, through their decisive actions. Their feeling and realizations find a resounding cross-community validation in the coming-of-age novels of Armstrong.

Whispering in Shadows, her second novel, completed fifteen years after *Slash* (1985) and widely hailed as the first novel ever written by an indigenous woman in Canada, is one of the foremost of such works. Driven by the all-encompassing zeal to establish herself as a painter within the Euro-Canadian intellectual circle, Penny Jackson is all set to leave the comfortable nook of her Okanagan home-village. Yet she cannot disregard the warmth that spreads across her heart and soul as she feels the resonances of the ancestral songs once sung by her long deceased 'Tupa' (great-grandmother) within the rhythmic humming of the bluejays who could fly uninhibitedly from the blue skies of her Reserve to the murky ones of the present urban accommodation. Just like her younger literary contemporary, Armstrong too thus harps upon a process of cultural 'reclamation' – one that calls for a resurfacing of oral voices thwarted by the social, cultural and linguistic marginalization brought about by the infiltration of Western academic and religious institutions, across centuries. *Whispering in Shadows* undoubtedly provides one of the most sensitive insights into this process of 'reclamation'.

Being hailed as "a rich tapestry of poetry, description, letters and journal entries" that "explore the intricate relationship between land, language and community, in the Okanagan" (Dattaray, "Soft Power" 76), the novel incorporates both the 'oral' and the 'performative' as a repository of the 'collective mentality' of a community, in the face of rapid erosion of Okanagan traditions. As the aspiring painter is reduced to working as an apple picker in the city, the memory of her Tupa Susapeen's words keep her afloat. The hopping bluejays resurrect those memories. "Wake up, the huckleberries are watching the trails, waiting. We can pick again today. The mountain is good to us. We are lucky. We will have plenty this winter" (Armstrong, *Whispering* 19–20), they chirp. It is as if nature encapsulates within its folds the wisdom of her grandmother. She lives on through her words. These words harp upon the ritualistic knowledge of berry picking, which has been steadily losing its relevance in the light of the erasure of the berry-picking trails by the coercive machinery of urbanization. This episode appears to be one of Armstrong's preferred areas of thematic engagement – recurring almost like a refrain across her literary oeuvre. One of its most heart-warming expressions may be found in her iconic poem "Wind Woman" (1978), where an adult woman revisits the childhood memory of Maggie, her village Elder, enriching her with community wisdom in the garb of berry-picking lessons. Her passion for this motif might be attributed to her heritage of empowered female ancestors, most notably her grand-aunt Hum-Ishu Ma (Mourning Dove) (1884–1936) who is the first female novelist of Native-American literature. Her novel *Cogewea* (1937) and her rich gamut of oral narratives undoubtedly laid the cornerstones of the creative endeavours of her deserving successor.

The recurrent tendency of re-narrativizing this specific memory exemplifies beautifully the Native-Canadian theory of 'Land Speaking' that resonates with the understanding of the special bond between the land and the community which informs the worldview of Maracle. "Voices that move within as my experience of existence do not awaken as words. Instead, they move within as the colours, patterns, and movements of a beautiful, kind Okanagan landscape" (Armstrong, 'Land Speaking' 176), says Armstrong. Each of these facets come together in Penny's paintings, making them a part of a fascinating continuum of the indigenous Canadian, particularly Okanagan, creative process. Penny's artistic integrity comes under the radar too, when she is stereotyped for adhering to the "Native-American format" (Armstrong, *Whispering* 127) by the mainstream 'connoisseurs' of artwork. Faced with the herculean task of not succumbing to the pressure of the neo-liberal Canadian economy that strives to promote cultural tourism through the buying and selling of 'exotic' indigenous art, helps her discover her inner strength anew. It is such moments of epiphany in her own artistic career that induced Armstrong to establish the En'owkin Centre in Penticton Reserve in British Columbia in 1980. Described in its official webpage as a "dynamic institution which puts into practice the principles of self-determination and the validation of cultural aspirations and identity" ("En'owkin Centre") this institution takes active initiative in curating the threatened indigenous artistic expressions by designing courses on Aboriginal oral traditions offering workshops on visual and performative artistry. Each of these projects emphasize the ecofeminist indigenous notion of 'Soft Power' that encapsulates to "the feminine process that has the power to heal the world and the individuals in it" (Armstrong, *Looking at the Words* 8). This collective ideology, that imbues the women of the matrilineal and matrifocal communities with the prestigious responsibility of nurturing and preserving the ecological balance of their traditional lands, reverberates through the pages of both the novels in question.

The mnemonic glimpse into their grandmothers' lives resurrect this hitherto dormant 'Soft Power' within Stacey and Penny, prompting them to display a sense of 'response-ability' and responsibility towards their ancestral ecology. The former refers to the ability to take cognition of the messages nature strives to communicate to the Indigenous Self, the latter highlights the moral standpoint of never exploiting nature to satiate human greed. Nature has its own unique way of expressing the trauma of exploitation – she is also equipped with the ability to send out foreboding premonitions about the detrimental consequences of this exploitation on the future survival of humanity. As the legacy bearers of a formidable line of female Elders, who have breathed life into such ethics, both the protagonists display an empathy towards nature that would largely evade any non-indigenous individual. No wonder Penny is extremely disturbed by the hurtful stance towards nature adopted by her 'white' partner Francis in his bid to satisfy the demands of the capitalist economy. Her heart breaks at "the snap of apples being broken off their limbs" (Armstrong, *Whispering* 20). It makes her "gently put them into the bag" (21), in an act of kindness, swinging the bag to stop them from hurting themselves by bumping against the ladder as she climbs down. Stacey, too, looks for elements of social regeneration within the ecological ethics of her communal 'grandmothers', in order to safeguard her diseased and ravaged community from the onslaught of any future calamity.

Collective memory not only plays a pivotal role in imparting such powerful ecological ethics but also induces the two literary stalwarts to look for lessons of cultural revival within the layers of their oral history. This initiates a systematic process of inscribing them within the European narrative framework of a novel. Colourful storytelling sessions light up the important junctures of the narrative landscape. *Ravensong* as a novel is in fact predicated upon a story-within-a-story structure where the story of the epidemic is narrated in retrospect to a young Salish boy by his mother, aunt and grandmothers. The story of *Ravensong* begins as an answer to a query made by Stacy's son Jacob, twenty-five years after the epidemic of 1954, about the specific cause of his cousin Jimmy's suicide. He wants to know why his cousin Jimmy had killed himself. In keeping with the techniques of Salish storytelling he is 'given' a non-didactic multi-perspective by each of Stacey, Momma, Rena and Celia from their own standpoints. Such open-endedness leaves him free to seek his own answers, make his own judgements and form his own opinion about the incident. Maracle condemns the colonizers for their inability to tell multidimensional stories – "from four different directions at the same time" (Maracle, *Ravensong* 86). Such disdain towards accommodating plural perspectives is indicative of their closed-minded attitude and basic intolerance towards worldviews different from their own.

Maracle also chooses to incorporate elects of the 'performative' within the 'written' identifying it as the most poignant yet hard-hitting avenue of expressing the otherwise inexplicable pain of the epidemic-ravaged community. It is a grief song, retrieved from the depths of the rich treasure of collective memory, which helps the women negotiate with the death of dear ones. Actions indeed speak louder than words! The nerve-wracking cadence of the wailing song, the drum beats and the rhythmic body movements of the women has a cathartic effect upon the lamenters. They continue to expunge their trauma till "relieved of their grief, the women laughed" ((Maracle, *Ravensong* 198). Laughter and humour are used as a defensive mechanism, often to overhaul power equations. Laughter has the subversive quality of transforming a song that laments death into one that celebrates the will to live, thereby undercutting the attempts of the 'white' man to shatter their confidence through their disgraceful apathy, shameful discrimination and withdrawal of access to advanced healthcare in times of such all-encompassing crisis. As Maracle points out in her interview "From Discomfort to Enlightenment": "We have our storytelling rules. Humour opens people up to the subject of change, the possibility of change. (Fee et al. 212). This 'change' embodies the desired communal transformations that would empower them to bridge the interracial gulf between them and their colonizers, paving the path towards an irradiation of their mutual negativity and suspicion towards each other in the distant future. Such an optimistic approach towards the colonial crisis, therefore, throws light upon one of most pertinent life lessons that emerges out of Maracle's and Armstrong's preoccupation with their oral traditions.

Other relevant learnings also find their way into the hearts of the Western-educated indigenous youth, who can identify with the dilemmas of protagonists of the two novels in question. The family storytelling sessions teach Penny and Stacey the importance of patience and anticipation. Instead of badgering their mother, sister or aunts with probing questions, they would rather stick to "the Indian thing of waiting for the story to unfold" (Maracle, *Will's Garden* 8). They further learn to take cognition of the indigenous storytelling ethic which postulates that just as an hesitant narrator should be pestered to narrate her story, no reluctant or disinterested individual should be forced to engage with the story as audience/reader. The novels further provide a fertile ground to exemplify a literary as well as extra-literary syncretism between pre-colonial indigenous traditions and colonial cultural productions mediated by colonization. Armstrong embarks upon the fascinating journey of restructuring the Western genre of novel to accommodate indigenous concerns, by seeking the blessings of the ancestors through the Okanagan ritual of fasting prior to commencement of any important project. The conscious evocation of the soft responsive voices of the sister-spirits for protecting an uninitiated Penny in the beginning of the novel through the traditional song of the 'Wailing Night Bird' and her organic identification with the Copper Woman, the original mother-spirit of the Okanagan community, at its very end brings Penny's life to a complete circle, in keeping with a quintessentially Native-Canadian understanding of the 'circularity' of life. The Okanagan worldview of life being "a circle that has to happen in people" (Lutz, Contemporary Challenges 20) is exemplified through the journey of Penny, from naivety to wisdom, from self-doubt to self-determination, from ignorance to enlightenment till she can situate herself within the legacy of her female ancestors. Thus, 'night bird' or The Owl who facilitates this reclamation of Penny's identity plays the vital role of a trickster that keeps the 'modern' Indigenous Self rooted to its oral traditions.

The trickster figures, resplendent in their antics of humour, wit and sarcasm, emerge to be unique in their role of preservation of Native-Canadian traditional beliefs. They are shapeshifting anthropomorphic animal spirits with gender variability who had been an intrinsic component of indigenous orature since the pre-colonial times are often seen to permeate their contemporary literary universe as indomitable interrogators of the colonial power equations. Armstrong posits the Okanagan trickster Coyote (Spirit of the Prairie Wolf) as the representee of the cloistered and lonely existence of the aboriginal youth within the urban centres of Euro-Canadian civilizational 'glory'. Alienated from their roots by the mainstream forces of cultural coercion, mainly the Indian Residential School System, they belong nowhere, gradually losing their way in the quagmire of prostitution, theft, fraudulence, violence and substance abuse. No wonder the sense of being a failure and resultant frustration finally culminates in suicide: "She [Penny] thinks of that one Coyote in the papers, in some city – how someone had opened the door of an elevator, how it had ridden to the top of an apartment building and ran around crazily and jumped to its death" (Armstrong, *Whispering* 253). The Coyote trickster, once emblematic of the pre-colonial free-spirited Okanagan people, here embodies the destitute and urbanized Indigenous Self – trying to survive the wounds of racism, unemployment, displacement and abuse within a 'whitewashed' society that fails to accommodate them within its restrictive folds.

In keeping with the fiery spirit of her literary contemporary, Maracle, too, never limits the role of the trickster Raven (Spirit of the Common Raven) within the Salish creation story in which he snatched water and fire from the clutches of the villainous Gray Eagle, thereby saving the lives of the water- and light-deprived humanity. Raven permeates the firmament of Maracle's novel as the omnipotent, omnipresent, omniscient identity that holds the complex strands of the narrative together. The recurrent humour-laced interactions between Raven and Cedar in *Ravensong* helps the readers, both within and outside the community, to navigate through the complex maze of non-negotiation that the Salish people have adopted as a defence mechanism against the all-encompassing waves of Euro-Canadian cultural assimilation. With every act of injustice, "the silence grew fat, obese. It had taken Raven almost a century to drive the people from the village; still the villagers would not communicate with the others" (Maracle, *Ravensong* 23). Thus, while Cedar represents the unchanging and the traditional, the trickster Raven personifies the spirit of change and transformation. He plunges them into the throes of the epidemic in order to force them out of self-orchestrated segregation. As Maracle herself explains to Jennifer Kelly in "Coming Out of the House: A Conversation with Lee Maracle": "Our culture is one that looks at life as a process of constant spiritual growth and social transformation. A culture that does not have Raven is stagnant, it is incapable of transformation" (Kelly, "Coming out" 76). Till the time Stacy is not completely invested in her community, she is unable to understand the message underlying the Raven's song and its futuristic role in the growth, transformation and evolution of the Salish people.

Both the writers display tremendous craftsmanship in using language – both the ancestral and the imposed ones – as a major tool for forging an alternative oral 'history' for their people. Language is not merely a tool of basic communication for its speakers – it encapsulates within it the culture, customs and belief system of the entire community. The deliberate erasure of the native languages from the collective consciousness of the indigenous children by the Residential School System, leads to language-politics that the two writers address deftly through their works. In the Introduction to their interview with Maracle, "From Discomfort to Enlightenment", Margery Fee and Sneja Gunew discuss how she "reworks language from a non-Western perspective to suite the Salish sensibility" (207). Examples of such 'reworkings' are liberally strewn in every corner of their novels. They come as a not-so-gentle reminder of the fact that the language in which they write has been forced upon them by the colonizer and simply cannot express their emotions as poignantly as their own native tongues. Elders, their worldviews still not percolated by colonial impositions, often tend to revert to their native language during ceremonial offerings, speeches and formal declarations. Many of these linguistic cross-overs bear testimony to the inability of English as a language to capture the culture-specific nuances of the Salish language. The powerful words of the Elder Ella are articulated during the funeral of the warrior-woman Nora in *Ravensong*: "For us, the word rain images woman-earth, the tears of birth and endless care-giving. In English, rain is just water collected on dust balls too heavy to remain floating in the atmosphere" (21). More 'untranslatable' a concept, greater is the need to convey its significance to the English-educated younger generation of the Salish community. Subversive interventions into the English language through a deliberate distortion of the grammar, spellings and syntax of the same emerges to be a major tool of cultural protest too. Such linguistic rebellion is dealt out beautifully by Maracle in her poem "Performing" (1998) where the narrator not only chooses to convey her pain at being forced to speak in 'Ink-lish' (and not English) to her Ta'ah (the Salish word for Grandmother) (Maracle, 'Performing' 184). Strongly laced with sarcasm, this English poem not only retains some Salish words, it also highlights how a half-hearted and inadequate proficiency in the colonizers' language can never compensate for the loss of her ancestral tongue. It ultimately serves to render her 'speechless'. The linguistic politics that underlies the Euro-Canadian colonial project is thus interrogated through multifarious narrative techniques by the indigenous literary artists. While Maracle masquerades her discontent in the garb of humour, Armstrong takes a more serious metaphorical approach to it. The gender neutrality of the Okanagan language embodies the notion of gender equality in a way which is difficult to articulate in the colonizer's language. The latter, after all, has emerged out of a patriarchal society. The gender hierarchy that contaminates its intellectual firmament fills Penny with a sense of foreboding, as she continues to be humiliated by her 'white' partner Francis. Her former partner, who was a community 'insider', would never treat her in this manner. She is further convinced that English can never communicate the deep philosophies encapsulated within a language where the same word denotes both 'Sky' and 'breath'. Her fatal lung cancer propelled by an over-exposure to pesticides, thus, almost comes as a poetic (in)justice to the Indigenous Self, deeply affected by the colonial destruction of nature. Armstrong's implementation of courses on 'Applied Ecology and Conservation' in the En'owkin Centre comes as a constructive response to this crisis. A certificate course on 'Aboriginal Language Revitalization' equips the students with the strength to combat the psychological repercussions of a coercive 'language shift' mechanism.

An effective interrogation of the oral/written binary of the Western worldview from within the framework of Memory Studies thus opens up some pathbreaking avenues of academic and cultural criticism of the Euro-Canadian colonial enterprise. As the repository of the communal wisdom, moralities and lessons of survival, indigenous orature deserves a validation as a reliable source of colonial history – different from and often contradictory to the mainstream narrative of history but no less authentic than the same. Mapping the colourful contours of collective memory through a conscious, systematic yet organic process of inscribing the 'oral', the 'performative' and linguistic nuances within the written cultural production thus emerges to be a tool of cultural decolonization no less effective than any political activism that clamours for indigenous sovereignty in the face of colonial deprivations. Having the potential to reclaim their rapidly eroding social, cultural and political autonomy, it holds the promise for a better, brighter, decolonized and oppression-free existence for the indigenous communities of Canada.

Works Cited

Armstrong, Jeannette. "Foreword." *Bobbi Lee: An Indian Rebel, edited* by Lee Maracle, Women's Press, 1990, pp. 15–16.

Armstrong, Jeannette. "Land Speaking." *Speaking for the Generations,* edited by Simon Ortiz, University of Arizona Press, 1998, pp. 174–195.

Armstrong, Jeannette. *Looking at the Words of our People: First Nations Analysis of Literature.* Theytus Books Ltd, 1993.

Armstrong, Jeannette. *Slash.* Theytus Books Ltd, 1985/2000.

Armstrong, Jeannette. *Whispering in Shadows.* Theytus Books Ltd, 2000.

Armstrong, Jeannette. "Wind Woman." *An Anthology of Canadian Native Fiction in English,* edited by Armstrong Jeannette and Lally Grauer, Oxford University Press, 2001, p. 109.

Confino, Alan. "Collective Memory and Cultural History: Problems of Method." *The American Historical Review,* vol. 102, no. 5, December. 1997, pp. 1386–1403, https://doi.org/10.1086/ahr/102.5.1386. Accessed 23 March, 2022.

Dattaray, Debashree. "Images from the Spoken Word: A Contemporary Study of Kateri Akiwenzie-Damm's *My Heart as a Stray Bullet* and *Standing Ground.*" 2019, https://www.se.edu/international-student/wp-content/uploads/sites/85/2019/09/NAS-2009-Proceedings-Dattaray.pdf. Accessed 5 September 2022.

Dattaray, Debashree. "'Soft Power': Marginalized Aesthetics in Jeannette Armstrong's Fiction." *At the Crossroads of Culture and Literature*, edited by Suchorita Chattopadhyay and Debashree Dattaray, Primus, 2016, pp. 73–84.

Eigenbrod, Renate. "The Oral in the Written: A Literature between two cultures." *The Canadian Journal of Native Studies,* vol. 15, no. 1, 1995, pp. 89–102.

"En'owkin Centre." *En'owkin Main Webpage.* En'owkin Centre, https://www.enowkincentre.ca. Accessed 5 December. 2016.

Fee, Margery, Sneja Gunew, and Lee Maracle. "From Discomfort to Enlightenment: An Interview with Lee Maracle." *Essays on Canadian Writing,* vol. 83, no. Fall 2004, pp. 206–221.

Hutton, Patrick. "Recent Scholarship on Memory and History." *The History Teacher,* vol. 3, no: 4, 2000, pp. 533–548, https://doi.org/10.2307/494950. Accessed 24 March, 2022.

Kelly, J. "Coming Out of the House: A Conversation with Lee Maracle." *Ariel: A Review of International English Literature,* vol. 25, no. 1, 1994, pp. 73–88.

King, T. "Introduction." *All My Relations: An Anthology of Contemporary Canadian Native Fiction,* edited by Thomas King, McClelland and Stewart Ltd, 1990, pp. ix–xvi.
Le Goff, Jacques. *Constructing the Past: Essays in Historical Methodology*. Edited by Le Goff and Nora Pierre, Columbia University Press, 1985.
Lutz, H. *Contemporary Challenges Conversation with Canadian Native Authors*. Fifth House Publishers, 1991. Print.
Maracle, Lee. *Bobbi Lee: An Indian Rebel*. Women's Press, 1990.
Maracle, Lee. "Performing." *An Anthology of Canadian Native Fiction in English,* edited by Armstrong Jeannette and Lally Grauer, Oxford University Press, 2001, p. 184.
Maracle, Lee. *Sojourner's Truth and Other Storie,* Press Gang Publishers, 1990. Print.
Maracle, Lee. *Oratory: Coming to Theory*. Gallerie Publications, 1990.
Maracle, Lee. *Ravensong*. Press Gang Publishers, 1993. Print.
Maracle, Lee. *Will's Garden*. Theytus Books Ltd, 2002.

23 Revisiting African Origins through Memory Codes

A Study of Alex Haley's *Roots*

Rachel Irdaya Raj

Introduction

Humanity recognized the value of transferring information and experiences to future generations long before written history was recorded. This is demonstrated by the drawings and pictures made by prehistoric cavemen during the Stone Age. This practice has been the norm across civilizations around the world. The four originating civilizations of the Old World – Egypt, Levant/Mesopotamia, India and China (Maisels 3) – have a similar kind of narrative. Archaeological evidence unearthed much later provides testament of the same. Ancient Celtic bards were renowned for their memorizing skills that included songs, stories and poems. Long before the prehistoric Celts, Aboriginal Australians were known to record vast amounts of knowledge in their memory and transfer it to future generations (Hamacher, 2019). American sociologist Carl Couch asserts that "all preliterate ancient societies with a complex social structure made extensive use of orality to preserve information" (Couch 29). The key component or the driving force behind this knowledge transfer is memory. "The methods by which information is accumulated, preserved and shared within purely oral cultures rely solely on memory" (Kelly 36). Without memory it is highly impossible to share and transfer knowledge specially in an era where written documentation is unheard of.

Author Lynne Kelly in her book *The Memory Code: Unlocking the Secrets of the Lives of the Ancients and the Power of the Human Mind* (2017) defines orality as:

> making knowledge memorable. It was about using song, story, dance and mythology to help retain vast stores of factual information when the culture had no recourse to writing. It was first step to understanding how they could remember so much stuff. The definition of stuff was growing rapidly to include… laws and ethics, geology and astronomy; genealogies, navigation… ideas about where they had come from, and, of course, what they believed. Indigenous cultures memorised everything on which their survival – physically and culturally – depended.
>
> (1)

DOI: 10.4324/9781003508564-30

Multitudes of tribal people living in Africa practised this tradition of orality. The people who specialize in maintaining this knowledge base are called by different names. "In Africa there are the *n/om k" ausi* of the !Kung San and the *!gi:ten* of the /Xam, the *Xhosa imbongi*, the *bulaam* of the Kuba, the Haya *embandwa*, the Yoruba *bablawo* and the *griot* of West Africa" (Kelly, 2017). In fact, the profession of griots was considered a sacred responsibility by the tribals in West Africa. According to Duane Hamacher, "In oral cultures, knowledge is power. It is imperative that the most important knowledge be maintained and preserved by a few select custodians who have proven their worth" (3). 'Primary orality' is an information technology, a tool that increases the ability of humans to process information and so increase the amount and complexity of information preserved in cultures with no access to writing (Kelly xvii). Without a proper structure and a methodology as to how this knowledge is retained in memory, the essence of orality is lost. Thus, memory became an essential medium for knowledge transfer from one generation to the next.

Memory and Culture

The Merriam-Webster dictionary defines memory as "the power or process of reproducing or recalling what has been learned and retained especially through associative mechanisms". The *Oxford Dictionary of Psychology* defines memory as "the psychological function of preserving information, involving the processes of encoding, storage, and retrieval". Memory can also be viewed as a transient product of the activities of remembering and reminiscing, which occurs in the context of social interactions between people and their environments (Jones and Russell 269). Memory as a concept is embedded in most living organisms including the human species. With the progress in science and technology, research in the domain of memory is no longer restricted to the field of psychology but has also percolated to the other fields including history, sociology, archaeology, neurosciences and literature. "As an all-encompassing sociocultural phenomenon, memory plays an important role in various areas of social practice... memory as an interdisciplinary phenomenon has become a key concept of academic discourse across established fields" (Erll 1). The concept of memory as field of study emerged in the 1920s with French sociologist Maurice Halbwachs' text *La mémoire collective*. Though he is considered to be the founding father of memory studies, the discipline of memory studies has always been transdisciplinary with scholars from various disciplines and across nations studying memory and culture. Sigmund Freud, Henri Bergson, Emile Durkheim, Maurice Halbwachs, Aby Warburg, Arnold Zweig, Karl Mannheim, Frederick Bartlett and Walter Benjamin are a few notable scholars.

Anthropological and semiotic theories suggest that culture can be viewed as a three-dimensional structure, consisting of social elements (people, social connections, institutions), material elements (artefacts, media) and mental elements (ways of thinking, mentalities) that are culturally determined (Posner 1989). Thus, the corpus of reusable texts, pictures and rituals that are unique to every culture in every era and whose "cultivation" helps to maintain and transmit that society's self-image is referred to as cultural memory (Assmann 132). Elaborating about cultural memory, Astrid Erll and Ansgar Nunning in their book *Cultural Memory Studies* opine that,

> "cultural memory" can serve as an umbrella term which comprises "social memory" (the starting point for memory research in the social sciences), "material or medial memory" (the focus of interest in literary and media studies), and "mental or cognitive memory" (the field of expertise in psychology and the neurosciences). This neat distinction is of course merely a heuristic tool. In reality, all three dimensions are involved in the making of cultural memories. Cultural memory studies is therefore characterized by the transcending of boundaries.
>
> (4)

Cultural memory encompasses the collective memory of several individuals living in a particular community within a stipulated period of time. "While the collective memory endures and draws strength from its base in a coherent body of people, it is individuals as group members who remember" (Coser 22). The Great Depression, the Jewish Holocaust, the 9/11 attack and several other such events are all examples of collective memory. The testimonies of the survivors of these tragedies act as memory for the future generations. The term "collective memory" was initially used by Maurice Halbwachs in his seminal work *Social Frameworks of Memory* (*Le cadres sociaux de la mémoire*), originally published in 1925. The book was later edited and translated into English with the title *Maurice Halbwachs' On Collective Memory* by Lewis A. Coser in 1992. In his book, Halbwachs discusses how individual memories are influenced and structured by the social context, emphasizing that our recollections are shaped by the groups we belong to and the societal frameworks within which we live. These frameworks include our families, classes and nations. According to him, "it is in society that people normally acquire their memories. It is also in a society that they recall, recognize, and localize their memories" (Coser 1992, p. 38). For every individual, the process of remembering is governed by the social contexts and social cues. This process when done in isolation also draws upon our social identities and employing languages and symbols that we are familiar with (Olick et al. 19). According to Halbwachs, every collective memory requires support from a group that is constrained in both time and space (Coser 22). Therefore, we find that memory and culture co-exist and make it possible for civilizations to learn from each passing generation.

Cultural Memory and Literature

Literature is a culture's memory, a collection of commemorative acts that encompass the knowledge that a culture has stored, almost all of the texts that a culture has generated and the means by which a culture is constituted. Each new text is carved into memory space through the process of writing, which is both an act of remembrance and a fresh interpretation (Lachmann 2008). "Works of literature help produce collective memories by recollecting the past in the form of narratives" (Erll and Rigney 112). Poetry, fiction, biographies, movies, documentaries, digital stories, and so on are a perfect medium to store cultural memory.

Astrid Erll in her book *Memory in Culture* states that "literature manifested in all genres and media technologies, both popular and 'trivial' literature as well as canonized and 'high' literature have served – and continue to serve – as media of memory" (144). The African American literature is one such genre that exemplifies how literature functions as a mimesis of cultural memory. It talks about the Africans wanting to retain their ethnicity and cultural heritage. Given their generational trauma of being taken away from their homeland, they have strived to be a part of the American nation, while retaining their own identity. From the first poems of Phillis Wheatley to Langston Hughes' poems during the Harlem Renaissance; from Zora Neale Hurston's *Their Eyes Were Watching God* (1937) to Lorraine Hansberry's *A Raisin in the Sun* (1959); from Alice Walker's *The Color Purple* (1982) to Toni Morrison's *Beloved* (1987) – their literature is filled with poignant tales of subjugation and their fight for redemption. This practice of retaining and passing on their culture to the next generation has always been the norm of the Africans much before they were captured and enslaved in America. As Kansteiner rightly says, "memories are at their most collective when they transcend the time and space of the events' original occurrence. As such, they take on a powerful life of their own... and become the basis of all collective remembering as disembodied, omnipresent" (189).

Alex Haley's novel *Roots* substantiates this in a wonderfully woven story. A Pulitzer winner, *Roots* chronicles the journey of Kunta Kinte and his descendants, portraying how the memory of their African roots and the trauma of slavery are collectively preserved and transferred to the next generation. Away from their native place, the Africans had no choice but to create their own world in this new nation. Their world was a mirror image of the Americans; still they forged their unique identity within the constraints. They valued their relationships a lot and the family was of vital importance to them. Also, their faith in God and comfort in one another kept them united. Their journey is filled with many nameless individuals preserving their history through their oral narratives even in a land alien to them. Alex Haley rightly acknowledges his "immense debt to the griots of Africa – where today it is rightly said that when a groit dies, it is as if a library has burned to the ground". A result of a twelve-year-long research, *Roots* is a drop in that mighty ocean telling us how they used memory and orality to preserve their cultural heritage.

Analysis

The novel begins in the year 1750, in a small village called Juffure in Gambia, West Africa, where our protagonist, Kunta Kinte, is born. As we follow his life for the next sixteen years, we are introduced to their lifestyle, their customs and traditions in elaborate detail. Life for these Africans – the Mandinka tribe – is so organized, their roles chalked out with such clarity, that we can only marvel at it. They were bound to one another by their common traditions and values, by their folklore and music. Their family structure and social practices kept their community together. As the novel unfolds and is narrated by Kunta, we soon become a part of his journey. In Juffure, children up to five years known as the 'first kafo' were in the care of the grandmothers, when all the men and the women in the village left for their work in the fields. According to Halbwachs,

> in primitive tribes, the old are the guardians of traditions... because they are the only ones to enjoy the necessary leisure to determine the details of these traditions in their exchanges with other old people and to teach them to the young during initiation.
>
> (Coser 48)

Kunta and his friends are taken care of by his grandmother Yaisa and another old lady, Nyo Boto. Storytelling was a favourite part of the entire day for here the children not only enjoyed the stories but also learnt many moral values. The children also learnt a lot about their forefathers, the history of their tribe, their culture, etc., in these sessions.

When Kunta was about eleven years old, he and his fellow mates were taken to a far-off place in the jungle where they were trained to be men. For the next several months, Kunta and his friends learnt to master the art of survival. The first lesson that Kunta learnt was to follow the stars to guide him to his destination. One of the most important lessons that the boys were taught was to be united. For a mistake committed by any one of them earned them all a sound whipping. Thus, the boys "began to understand that the welfare of the group depended on each of them – just as the welfare of the *tribe* would depend on them one day" (Haley 97). The boys were also taught to converse in 'sira kango' – a method in which the phonetic sounds of the Mandinka language were interchanged and spoken in a way that only the men could understand. It was their secret language that could not be understood by their women or by people of another tribe. As part of their training, a renowned griot came to their camp. The griot narrated about the great deeds of the ancient kings, holy men and warriors who lived a century ago. The griot exclaimed, "the history of our people is carried to the future in here", and he tapped his grey head (Haley 102). At sixteen, Kunta began to feel lonely and restless with his life. He wanted to go on adventurous trips, to explore the world outside. All his dreams come crashing down one morning when he is captured by the white men whom they called 'toubob'. That morning, Kunta had just got off his sentry duty and went into the bushes to chop wood for a drum he intended to make for himself. They clubbed him hard till he fell unconscious. When he wakes up, he finds himself naked and chained inside a ship. The hardships that he endured for the next four months were terrible. Throughout this agony, he keeps beseeching his Allah to save him. For the rest of his life, Kunta regrets not being alert that morning.

Four months later, he lands in America and is sold in the slave market. Kunta never gave up hope and tried all kinds of superstitions to harm the white Americans. He tries to escape and on his fourth attempt his master, John Waller, got so angry that he chopped off a part of his foot. He was then bought by his master's brother – William Waller, the doctor who treated him. On his plantation in Virginia, Kunta learns to be a gardener and later on a driver. As he grew accustomed to the environment there, Kunta observed that the blacks in America were identical in many aspects to his people back in Africa. Their body language, facial expressions, their articulation and the women's hair styles – these were very much similar to that of his native place. And above all, Kunta had to admit that the "blacks' great love of singing and dancing was unmistakably African" (Haley 225). Memory plays a vital role in helping Kunta remember his own experiences and to establish a connection with the Africans over here. What saddened him was the fact that "these black ones in this place had no knowledge whatsoever of who they were and where they'd come from" (Haley 225). While the other blacks gave up their identity, Kunta vowed never to do the same. And so, he passes on his African legacy to his daughter in the future. Kunta did not give up on any of the practices that he learnt at his home. He made it a point to say his evening prayers. He continued to practice his studies by drawing Arabic characters on the floor of his small hut. The Mandinka tribe had a method of counting the years by rains and the months with each new moon. Kunta continued to do this to calculate his age. He regularly dropped coloured pebbles in a gourd to keep track of his age. "Lieux de memoire originate with the sense that there is no spontaneous memory, that we must deliberately create archives, maintain anniversaries, organize celebrations, pronounce eulogies, and notarize bills because such activities no longer occur naturally" (Nora 12). Some years later, Kunta comes across a fellow slave who was a moslem. They embraced and greeted each other saying "Ah-salakium-salam! Malakium-salaam! The words came as if neither of them had ever left Africa" (Haley 299). It is evident from this incident that memory helps in retaining their cultural practices. As Pierre Nora aptly says "Memory is life, borne by living societies founded in its name. It remains in permanent evolution, open to the dialectic of remembering and forgetting… susceptible to being long dormant and periodically revived" (8).

Kunta had been in America for twenty years when he realizes that he has to get married if he ever wants to continue his family lineage. After many compromises, he finally gets married to Bell, who works as a cook on the same plantation. Kunta is overjoyed when he is blessed with a baby girl and he names her Kizzy. Soon Kizzy becomes a playmate to Anne, the daughter of his master's brother, and Kunta has to drive his daughter over to the other plantation every weekend. Though he hated the idea of his daughter being treated like a doll, he still looked forward to taking his daughter out as this was the only time he was alone with his daughter. It was on these long buggy rides that Kunta taught her Mandinka words, their African culture and how he was captured. "Pointing at a tree, he'd say 'yiro', then downward at the road, 'silo'. As they passed a grazing cow, he'd say 'ninsemuso', and went over a small bridge, 'salo'... pointing to a small sluggish river... Dat a bolongo" (Haley 375). Kunta told his daughter that back in his homeland he had lived near a big river called Kamby Bolongo. For the people in Africa, the river is a sacred site where they hold rituals, cleanse themselves of impurities and establish spiritual connections with their ancestors. Thus, Kunta is determined to transfer his memories to his daughter so as to preserve their cultural heritage. And orality played a significant role in this whole process of transmission. Six generations later, a few Mandinka words still retained in the memory of Kizzy's great grandchildren helps in tracing the tribe back to the village of Juffure. These words become memory codes that helped in discovering the genealogy of one African family.

When Kizzy is sixteen, she forges a travel pass for a fellow black, Noah, who she was in love with. Noah is caught and Kizzy is sold in the slave market to a man named Tom Lea from North Carolina. From here the story shifts its focus to Kizzy. The man brutally rapes her and she gives birth to her son, George Lea. A heartbroken Kizzy vows to keep her father's African memories alive and tells her son all about it. George grows up to be an expert in training cocks for fights and wins a lot of money for his master. In time, George gets married to a slave from another plantation called Matilada. Together they have eight children, and every time a child was born the tradition about narrating the African's ancestry was carried out. Years later, their master Tom Lea goes bankrupt and is forced to sell his slaves to another owner. By now, all of Kizzy's grandchildren are grown up with families of their own. Just before they leave she tells them "any y'all gits mo' chillums fo' I sees you ag'in, don't forgit to tell 'em 'bout my folks, my mammy Bell, an' my African pappy name Kunta Kinte, what be yo' chillun's great-great gran'pappy!" (Haley 583). George's fourth son, Tom, gets married to Irene and they have seven children. And very religiously the story of the great African is narrated with every child's birth. By this time, the Civil War ends and the blacks are free from slavery. Tom's daughter, Cynthia, gets married to Will Palmer and they have a daughter named Bertha. Cynthia insisted on gathering the whole family where she narrated her family's history all the way to Kunta Kinte. Bertha gets married to Alexander Haley and they have a son whom they name Alex Haley. Alex grows up listening to his ancestors' stories and is intrigued by the consistency in the story for over six generations. "The quest for memory is the search for one's history" (Nora 13) and thus, we find Alex Haley doing extensive research over the subject which finally takes him back to the village of Juffure in Africa. Over there, he listens to the African griot's narration and is overwhelmed with emotion when the griot narrates about Kunta Kinte's disappearance exactly the way he has heard it from his parents. The villagers gather around the ancestral tree and perform a dancing ritual. This ancestral tree holds a significant place for the community as they gather over there for all their events and rituals.

Conclusion

Alex Haley's journey is an eye-opener; he realizes how every black in America must be somehow linked to Africa and it only takes a few clues and a griot to trace back their ancestral roots. Haley's *Roots* fundamentally altered how the blacks thought about their history. Kunta Kinte's experiences reflect how they struggled to preserve their ethnicity and their cultural heritage. Throughout he resists assimilation but eventually gives in after realizing the fact that survival is more important. A part of his soul dies when he makes this decision. But his spirit is rekindled with the birth of his daughter Kizzy. It is with her that he goes down the memory lane, reliving his past life. "The task of remembering makes everyone his own historian" (Nora 15) and Kunta Kinte becomes the custodian of preserving the history of his familial roots. The mantle of African heritage that Kunta passes on to his daughter is thus faithfully carried forward to the next seven generations.

Though *Roots* is a work of historical fiction, it is deeply embedded in memory studies, as it explores the transmission of memories through several generations. It illustrates the idea of collective memory shared within a community. The novel chronicles the journey of Kunta Kinte and his descendants, portraying how the memory of their African roots and the trauma of slavery are collectively preserved and transmitted through generations. The family's identity and sense of belonging are shaped by their common experiences of servitude, hardship and perseverance. There are moments of remembering and forgetting throughout the novel, where characters fight to remember their origins, especially in the face of repressive circumstances or efforts to obliterate their cultural identities. The mnemonic objects like Kunta's pebbles collected in a gourd, the river, etc., evoke memories and act as tangible reminders of the home that they have left behind. Thus, memory and storytelling became an integral part of the African Americans to pass on their cultural heritage to the next generation.

Works Cited

Assmann, Jan, and John Czaplicka. "Collective memory and cultural identity." *New German Critique* 65 (1995): 125–133.

Colman, Andrew M. "*Memory.*" *A dictionary of psychology*. Oxford University Press, 2015. Oxford Reference. Date Accessed 24 Apr. 2024 <https://www.oxfordreference.com/view/10.1093/acref/9780199657681.001.0001/acref-9780199657681-e-4951>.

Coser, Lewis A., editor. *Maurice Halbwachs: On collective memory*. Translated by Lewis A. Coser. University of Chicago Press, 1992.

Couch, Carl J., Mark D. Johns, and Shing-Ling S. Chen. *Information technologies and social orders*. Transaction Publishers, 1996.

Erll, Astrid. *Memory in culture*. Palgrave Macmillan UK, 2011

Erll, Astrid, and Ann Rigney. "Literature and the production of cultural memory: Introduction." *European Journal of English Studies* 10.2 (2006): 111–115.

Erll, Astrid, et al., eds. *Cultural memory studies: An international and interdisciplinary handbook*. Walter de Gruyter, 2008.

Haley, Alex. *Roots*. Vintage, 1991.

Hamacher, Duane W. "The Memory Code: how oral cultures memorise so much information." *The Conversation* (2019).

Jones, Siân, and Lynette Russell. "Archaeology, memory and oral tradition: An introduction." *International Journal of Historical Archaeology* 16 (2012): 267–283.

Kansteiner, Wulf. "Finding meaning in memory: A methodological critique of collective memory studies." *History and Theory* 41.2 (2002): 179–197.

Kelly, Lynne. *Knowledge and power in prehistoric societies: Orality, memory, and the transmission of culture*. Cambridge University Press, 2015.

Kelly, Lynne. *The memory code: Unlocking the secrets of the lives of the ancients and the power of the human mind*. Atlantic Books, 2017.

Lachmann, Renate. "Mnemonic and intertextual aspects of literature." *Cultural memory studies: An international and interdisciplinary handbook*, edited by Astrid Erll and Ansgar Nunning. PDF, 2008, 301–310.

Maisels, Charles Keith. *Early civilizations of the old world: The formative histories of Egypt, the Levant, Mesopotamia, India and China*. Routledge, 2003.

"Memory Definition & Meaning." *Merriam-Webster*. Merriam-Webster. Date Accessed 24 Apr. 2024 <www.merriam-webster.com/dictionary/memory>.

Nora, Pierre. "Between memory and history: Les lieux de mémoire." *Representations* 26.1 (1989): 7–24.

Olick, Jeffrey K., Vered Vinitzky-Seroussi, and Daniel Levy, eds. *The collective memory reader*. Oxford University Press, 2011.

Posner, Roland. "What is culture? Toward a semiotic explication of anthropological concepts." *The nature of culture*, edited by W. A. Koch. Brockmeyer, 1989, 240–295.